Delivering on Promises

Chicago Series on International and Domestic Institutions
Edited by William G. Howell and Jon Pevehouse

Other Books in the Series

Delivering on Promises

*The Domestic Politics of Compliance
in International Courts*

LAUREN J. PERITZ

THE UNIVERSITY OF CHICAGO PRESS   CHICAGO AND LONDON

The University of Chicago Press, Chicago 60637
The University of Chicago Press, Ltd., London
© 2022 by Lauren J. Peritz
Published 2022
Printed in the United States of America

31 30 29 28 27 26 25 24 23 22   1 2 3 4 5

ISBN-13: 978-0-226-82213-6 (cloth)
ISBN-13: 978-0-226-82215-0 (paper)
ISBN-13: 978-0-226-82214-3 (e-book)
DOI: https://doi.org/10.7208/chicago/9780226822143.001.0001

Library of Congress Cataloging-in-Publication Data

Names: Peritz, Lauren J., author.
Title: Delivering on promises : the domestic politics of compliance in international courts / Lauren J. Peritz.
Other titles: Domestic politics of compliance in international courts | Chicago series on international and domestic institutions.
Description: Chicago ; London : The University of Chicago Press, 2022. |
Series: Chicago series on international and domestic institutions | Includes bibliographical references and index.
Identifiers: LCCN 2022016001 | ISBN 9780226822136 (cloth) | ISBN 9780226822150 (paperback) | ISBN 9780226822143 (e-book)
Subjects: LCSH: World Trade Organization. | Court of Justice of the European Union. | International courts. | International courts—Political aspects. | International courts—Case studies. | International economic relations—Political aspects. | International cooperation.
Classification: LCC KZ6250.P469 2022 | DDC 341.5/5—dc23/eng/20220504
LC record available at https://lccn.loc.gov/2022016001

Contents

CHAPTER ONE

International Adjudication, Stakeholders, and Domestic Divisions

1.1 Introduction

In June 2018, the Trump administration raised tariffs on steel and aluminum imports from Canada, Mexico, the European Union, and other trading partners, citing national-security concerns.[1] In November, affected countries initiated a lawsuit in the World Trade Organization (WTO). As the dispute began winding its way through the WTO adjudication process, the European Union (EU) pressured the United States (US) to lower its trade barriers.[2] Stepping outside WTO legal channels, the EU imposed retaliatory tariffs on politically sensitive industries, including American-made motorcycles and whiskey.

Within the US, this trade dispute fueled divisions among stakeholders. Some steel and aluminum producers benefited from the protection, while industries relying on these materials as inputs, as well as those targeted by the retaliation, suffered. When the Biden administration assumed office in 2021, the controversy intensified. Interest groups such as the American Iron and Steel Institute and the United Steelworkers applauded the tariffs and demanded their preservation, crediting them for a long-overdue boost in capacity investments.[3] On the other side, steel-consuming industry groups argued that their removal would offset soaring material prices. Producers suffering from EU retaliation pressed for a truce.

The domestic stakes of this trade dispute are significant, as both sides enjoy influence in the United States' most consequential political battleground regions.[4] As of this writing, the Biden administration, torn between competing priorities, has not altered the tariffs.[5] If the US loses the WTO dispute, as it has in many similar previous cases, it will have to decide whether to comply with the international legal ruling or defy it. Either decision will activate resistance from domestic groups. Hence, with such steep political consequences, the deadlock is likely to persist, making compliance more difficult.

This WTO dispute also carries serious and broad-reaching implications for the global trading system. Should the US defy the ruling, other nations may decide to disregard their WTO obligations as well.[6] A pattern of mutual defection could lead to escalating trade wars, as the EU's preemptive retaliation foreshadowed, and a weakening of the decades-old global trading system. This example illustrates why one cannot assume that governments will readily comply with rulings from international courts, especially when domestic political divisions are acute. Yet such compliance is fundamental to the institutions these courts serve. If members of an international organization (IO) flout court rulings with impunity, then other states have little reason to follow the IO's rules either. Compliance with international courts is essential if IOs are to survive and fulfill their promise of fostering cooperation among states.

Given such challenges, it is important to understand when and how IOs effectively promote international cooperation. The difference between cooperation and conflict is highly consequential. Trade wars among countries can escalate into economic crisis, possibly destabilizing diplomatic relations. Smoldering tensions over regulations can lead countries to abandon their treaties, leaving global markets reeling. Political science has long held that international relations is "anarchic" and cooperation is tenuous. While governments may agree to rules of behavior, there is no central authority to ensure that states follow through. Nevertheless, governments routinely rely on international courts—including the WTO Dispute Settlement Mechanism and the Court of Justice of the European Union—to settle their disputes. If courts fulfill their mandate, their legal decisions should induce policy change and reform relations between disputing governments. For instance, a country found to be in violation of its free trade obligations should rescind the offending policies and restore trade flows with partner countries. In this book, I demonstrate that while international economic courts do indeed deliver results, they are only effective at restoring interstate cooperation under certain conditions.

Scholarship has long held that domestic political constraints within governments—that is, institutional and partisan divisions of authority—facilitate cooperation between states and that they lock in governments' promises to one another, making those commitments more credible. I show that in the context of international courts, the same domestic political factors can actually undermine interstate cooperation. States routinely break their treaties when political circumstances make cooperation too burdensome. These problems are especially common in international trade, where countries face domestic pressure to "cheat"—for example, by doling out subsidies or imposing tariffs that help politically influential interest groups. International courts are designed to provide enforcement. And yet governments would often rather ignore or evade adverse rulings. The reason for this goes beyond the particular preferences of any political leaders or ideological sentiments. This book demonstrates that governments with many internal political checks or entrenched partisan opposition are less likely to abide by court verdicts. Domestic constraints lock in violations of international law. Governments then hide behind such hand-tying factors as justification for ignoring unfavorable legal rulings, undercutting international cooperation.

This book makes two key contributions to the study of international organization. First, it demonstrates that IOs can, in fact, elicit cooperation from reluctant governments. Scholars have long puzzled over these institutions' effectiveness: Do they actually advance cooperation among governments? Or are they simply expressions of states' underlying preferences for international cooperation? I untangle this puzzle by focusing on international courts. Reluctant governments are often dragged before a court, found guilty of breaking their international commitments, and ordered to modify their policies. When states do bow to international pressure and comply with these legal orders, their actions reveal the impact of the court. By inducing compliance from reluctant litigants, international courts provide a crucial illustration of institutional effectiveness. Thus the performance of courts sheds light on the fundamental balancing act between a state's desire for international cooperation and its need to preserve sovereignty.

Leveraging novel and extensive data, I demonstrate that the World Trade Organiation Dispute Settlement Mechanism (WTO DSM) and the Court of Justice of the European Union (ECJ) have advanced international economic cooperation in concrete ways. For the WTO, this book provides two empirical tests. With unprecedented scope and precision, I assess the trade policy reforms governments make to comply. My data draw on government documents, parliamentary debates, industry publications, and newspaper articles in multiple languages. They show that governments do adjust policy and abide by WTO judgments. Buttressing these findings, I also assess the economic impact of legal rulings. I measure the effect of rulings on product-level trade flows between disputing countries by employing statistical methods for causal inference. This entails estimating what trade would have been without WTO intervention and comparing it to actual trade flows. My precise analysis of trade patterns reveals that WTO rulings not only induce formal compliance but also boost trade between disputing countries. Thus international adjudication can indeed restore trade cooperation.

For the ECJ,[7] I examine hundreds of "infringement" disputes in which the European Commission, a central executive body, sues member states for breaking EU law. I focus on disputes about the EU's internal market. ECJ judges routinely find that states have violated their free trade commitments and order them to remove barriers to European commerce. Examining trade flows within the EU, I find that these rulings have led governments to expand trade within the community and deepen their reliance on the internal market.

The performance of these two international economic courts is telling. First of all, their impacts can be measured more directly than those of international courts that preside over human rights, security, and territorial conflict. By identifying an effect these highly active courts have on state behavior, one can establish the possibility that less developed institutions—those with fewer resources or weaker enforcement mechanisms—can be refined to improve their performance.

The second key contribution this book makes is to advance our understanding of how domestic politics affect international cooperation. Many studies have shown that domestic political constraints foster interstate cooperation and that veto players improve the credibility of commitments governments make to their foreign partners by locking in compliant policies. Extending this literature, I demonstrate that both formal and informal veto players in government can undercut international cooperation. Governments are more likely to flout the rulings of international courts when they are beholden to dueling domestic demands. Political constraints do not simply obstruct compliance but also incentivize government leaders to exploit flexibility in international institutions and evade enforcement. These patterns of noncompliance are consequential. When powerful states defy courts to curry favor from influential domestic constituents, they undermine their commitments to international cooperation. Political constraints *within* governments can ultimately undercut the ability of international courts to induce cooperation *between* governments.

The chapters that follow demonstrate how veto players can undercut compliance with rulings from both the WTO and the ECJ. I trace the veto players mechanism through case studies and statistical analyses. Neither all governments nor all policy issues face the same domestic political constraints. In some, institutionalized divisions of power, such as a bicameral legislature or federalism, impose crucial obstacles. In others, polarized party politics can thwart legislative action and leave executives wary of alienating their opposition. By locking in trade barriers, domestic veto players undercut the WTO's ability to induce compliance and restore trade between litigants. Likewise, in ECJ disputes, defendants with more internal political constraints are less responsive to judgments. They show a smaller boost in intra-EU trade from pro-liberalizing rulings.

While my theory is tested in the context of two high-profile international economic courts, it is not limited to this setting. The arguments are potentially relevant to other international courts that adjudicate disputes that carry domestic distributive implications. To the extent that other courts' rulings benefit some domestic groups while harming others, they also confront similar compliance problems tied to domestic veto players. My predictions may bear out in non-economic domains, forcing scholars to rethink conventional wisdom on domestic politics and international cooperation.

These findings have important implications. The first concerns policymaking. When can governments rely on international courts for satisfactory dispute resolution? Research demonstrates that plaintiff governments initiate WTO disputes both to curry favor from certain domestic groups and during times of political turnover. By understanding a defendant government's calculations, potential plaintiffs can discern whether lawsuits will deliver the results they seek. Plaintiffs can deploy their legal resources with finer-tuned aims and may expect greater rewards for their litigation expenditures if they target more unified governments.

The second implication concerns the design of international economic courts. Flexible courts—that is, those allowing temporary defections—are predicted to be more stable over time. I demonstrate that governments are keen to exploit this flexibility. Under pressure from domestic constituents, governments prolong lawsuits and evade judgments. Consequent trade losses are hard to recover as markets and firms adjust. Courts that offer more targeted flexibility to address evolving domestic circumstances may achieve greater effectiveness without sacrificing stability.

More broadly, the findings speak to the growing backlash against international legalization and economic globalization. Commentators have questioned the continued relevance of the WTO DSM. These critiques struck a chord when the US blocked the appointment of new WTO Appellate Body judges, crippling WTO DSM operations, and when the EU flagrantly rejected certain rulings. Likewise, the United Kingdom's exit from the EU has prompted widespread pessimism about the durability of the ECJ. The countries that pioneered the post-Cold War enthusiasm for international legalization now display some of the most pronounced resistance to these courts' authority. This book makes clear that, far from an idiosyncratic historical moment, this tension is a fundamental one in international affairs. International courts can only fulfill their mandates—to resolve disputes and promote lasting cooperation—when there is sufficient political will and domestic institutions to support them. If courts overreach with significant incursions on state sovereignty, they may be met with resistance—not necessarily from national leadership, but rather from a constellation of domestic stakeholders.

International courts are vulnerable to failure if obligations are onerous and staunch penalties for noncompliance are imposed. These problems are most pronounced for democratic states (Rodrik 2011). In the WTO, countries confront complex and restrictive rules, and there is good reason to think democratic countries' resistance to court judgments is due to legitimate grievances. A key remedy would be to expand the flexibility of these courts to accommodate entrenched domestic interests. Broadening the range of circumstances in which noncompliance is permitted is a first step. As the global economic environment shifts, international courts, too, must adapt.

1.2 Argument in brief

When are international organizations effective in promoting cooperation among states? Since the 1950s, the international political landscape
has grown increasingly legalized (Abbott et al. 2000; Goldstein and
Martin 2000).[8] The number of international agreements has exploded,
and these legal instruments regulate nearly all domains of international
relations, including economic matters such as trade and finance, technical standards, security concerns such as nuclear nonproliferation, human
rights issues such as child labor, and environmental standards such as
greenhouse gas emissions. States have constructed new and increasingly
precise rules to guide their interactions.

More precise rules can impose more stringent constraints on the policies and practices of signatory states. When states find international
obligations too onerous, they stray from the treaty terms, inciting conflict. States embroiled in disputes routinely seek assistance from international courts (ICs). They delegate authority to international judges,
trusting them to interpret and apply the law to the controversy at hand.
Yet it is not obvious why governments should acquiesce to courts'
decisions.

Scholars have long highlighted the anarchic nature of international
politics (Art and Jervis 1985; Gilpin 1981; Milner 1991; Oye 1985; Waltz
1979). There is no centralized source of authority that presides over sovereign states. States voluntarily bind their hands through international
agreements, contracts they can break at will (Mearsheimer 1994). States
are reluctant to delegate too much authority. The international institutions countries create, including ICs, are limited in their ability to induce
state cooperation. Despite their legal procedures and appearance, ICs
are fundamentally different from domestic courts. ICs cannot force their
judgments on states; they rely on voluntary acquiescence. Enforcement
also hinges on state support. The community of states has to decide to
impose penalties on errant governments (Kono 2007). Poor information
and well-known collective action problems make decentralized enforcement unreliable (Thompson 2009).

In this context, it would seem that states should be reluctant litigants.
If defendant governments are rarely held accountable to the judgments
of ICs, then perhaps those legal decisions carry little value. Judgments

that are seen as mere suggestions would be expected to deliver little benefit to plaintiffs, and so countries might hesitate to bring forward their grievances.[9] And yet, as the trend toward greater legalization suggests, nations do frequently pursue international adjudication, especially to address economic disputes. States spend millions of dollars from their treasuries pursuing lawsuits and defending against foreign accusations. What do these efforts buy them? It remains unclear whether and when ICs successfully resolve treaty violations and promote cooperation.

This book demonstrates how the effectiveness of international courts is a function of the domestic politics of litigant governments. My argument begins with the foundational veto players theory, which holds that institutional and partisan constraints on decision-making power shape a government's ability to form and reform policy (Tsebelis 1995, 2000, 2002). This parsimonious theory lends durable insight into why governments cooperate in international affairs. A broad literature demonstrates that political constraints within government often *facilitate* international cooperation, especially in the domain of trade (e.g., Dai 2006; Leeds 1999; Mansfield, Milner, and Rosendorff 2002; Milner and Rosendorff 1996, 1997). Governments vary in their domestic political structure, some having far more institutional checks and balances or partisan divisions than others (Lohmann and O'Hallorn 1994; Milner 1997; Keefer and Stasavage 2003). Governments with internal divisions in authority—that is, more veto players—are thought to be better at upholding their international commitments. Domestic veto players raise the barriers to joining international agreements, since any single pivotal player can obstruct accession or ratification (Mansfield and Milner 2012; Mansfield, Milner, and Pevehouse 2007). They ensure that governments do not enter treaties that garner only lukewarm support. As a result, states with more constraints enter only those treaties they truly intend to follow. The treaties represent a credible commitment: a serious promise about future behavior (Martin 2000).

However, these constraints are an imperfect safeguard. States routinely break their international promises when political and economic circumstances make cooperation too burdensome. An impending election might prompt a leader to disregard international commitments. A sharp economic downturn may prompt a government to levy excess tariffs, default on debt, or otherwise defect on its treaty terms. In response to these violations, plaintiff states sometimes bring their grievances to an IC. Adjudication can help to enforce the commitments. ICs often rule that the defendant government has violated its treaty obligations and orders reform.

While veto players theory has illuminated why governments abide by international treaties, it also has implications that have not been previously examined in the context of international courts. Compliance with adverse rulings is rarely a simple process. Because of their distributive implications within states, rulings on economic matters are especially sensitive to domestic politics. Consider international trade. Exporters and importers tend to have conflicting preferences over trade policy. Suppose a government reduces barriers to trade in line with the requirements of a treaty. Import-competing industries may experience increasing economic pressure due to trade liberalization and oppose the policy shift. Conversely, export-oriented industries prefer the increased access to foreign markets that trade agreements promise. Consumers may enjoy lower prices at home thanks to import competition. So those groups are likely to favor the policy shift. Within a given country, international economic cooperation is a curse for some and a boon for others. The distributive implications make international economic disputes domestically divisive (Goldstein and Martin 2000; Milner 1997). In such conflicts where tensions run high, domestic political constraints tend to lock in violations of international law and actually *undercut* international cooperation.

I present two complementary explanations for how domestic constraints affect compliance with the rulings from ICs. For one, veto players simply obstruct the adoption of new policies. Opponents mobilize and urge political representatives to block the policy. Even holding international factors fixed, some legal decisions are more difficult to implement than others. Some rulings can be implemented by executive action (administrative rules) whereas other times, new domestic legislation must be enacted (laws). When an adverse ruling can be implemented by administrative rules alone, domestic leaders are less constrained by other political actors. When legislation is required to implement a ruling, domestic leaders' hands are tied. The consequence is that domestic political factors, along with the characteristics of the international legal ruling, jointly dictate compliance. Gridlock is not the full story. Second, savvy governments also use international courts opportunistically (Brewster 2011). By exploiting loopholes, governments can assuage domestic groups that oppose compliance while staving off international retaliation. In this respect, governments can use features of ICs to balance competing pressures from domestic and international sources.

Together, my account of gridlock and opportunism extends veto players theory and explains the cross-national variation in compliance with international rulings that previous research has left unexplored. My theory sheds light on why some governments comply readily while others refuse to do so, ultimately contributing to the successes and failures of an IC to fulfill its mandate.

1.3 Broader context

1.3.1 Landscape of legalization

By addressing the broader question of IC effectiveness, this book speaks to the trend toward legalization in international affairs. States generally behave as if they believe international courts are useful. One telling indicator is that governments go to great lengths to construct these institutions. ICs have proliferated in recent decades (Romano 1999). At present count, twenty permanent international courts and formal dispute settlement systems are actively used with more than a dozen others that were operational in prior decades.[10] These courts have jurisdiction to hear disputes over a range of matters, from territorial to economic to humanitarian affairs, and they are designed to serve a range of functions, including the enforcement of treaty law.[11] If one expands the definition of international courts to include other institutional variants—arbitration panels, monitoring bodies, and ad hoc tribunals—the number grows to eighty that have been or continue to be in use.[12] Many of these courts have been created since the 1990s, in the wake of the Cold War, as shown in figure 1.1.

A second telling indicator is that governments delegate the authority to adjudicate disputes on a wide range of issues. Rather than merely assigning ICs symbolic roles—legal veneers—governments entrust them with meting out legal judgments and coordinating enforcement (Carrubba and Gabel 2015). The WTO DSM and the ECJ have received some of the most widespread scholarly attention and scrutiny. These two courts are parts of deep international agreements—regimes that impose significant obligations on their members. Both are highly legalized. They have formal procedures that countries are obliged to follow, their rulings draw on a precise body of law on a wide range of issues, and countries

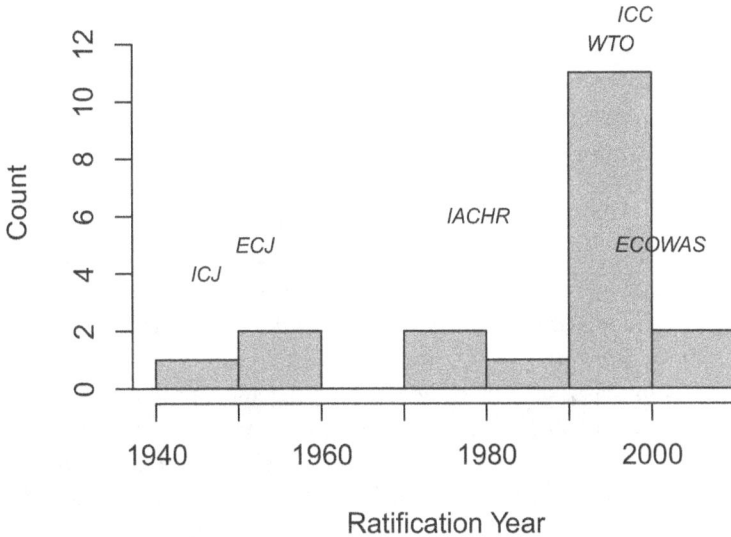

FIGURE 1.1. Count of International Courts by Ratification Year
Note: ICJ = International Court of Justice, ECJ = Court of Justice of the European Union,
IACHR = Inter-American Court of Human Rights, WTO = World Trade Organization
Dispute Settlement System, ICC = International Criminal Court, ECOWAS = Court of Justice
of the Economic Community of West African States.

delegate authority to them apply the law to substantial conflicts (Goldstein and Martin 2000).

The WTO DSM aims to resolve interstate trade disputes. WTO treaties cover trade and trade-related issues ranging from intellectual property and services to potentially competing goals like environmental protection, cultural preservation, and public health. But countries do not
always adopt WTO-consistent policies. When countries are in conflict
over alleged breaches of treaty obligations, they may sue one another
and obtain a binding verdict from a panel of experts. The losing government then bears the responsibility of implementing the judgment. The
WTO emphasizes that the first priority is for defendants to withdraw
contested measures rather than provide compensation or accept retaliation.[13] A fundamental goal of WTO dispute settlement is to advance
multilateral trade liberalization.

Likewise, the EU is widely understood to be the most significant IO
to date in terms of economic integration (Alter 2001). Although the EU
regulates a broad range of issues, economic matters remain central to its
mission. The free movement of goods, labor, and capital within EU ter-

ritory; common external trade policy; and, for many members, a single monetary policy fall under the organization's purview. The ECJ is a supranational legal system that employs standing judges who issue legally binding rulings. States that fall short of their obligations are held accountable before the court.[14]

There is a third indicator that governments regard these two prominent courts as useful: they frequently adjudicate disputes. The WTO DSM and ECJ are highly active in their respective domains. Since its establishment in 1995, the WTO DSM has presided over 584 complaints, averaging around 24 cases per year. Formed in 1952, the ECJ has overseen more than twenty thousand cases at a rate of several hundred per year.[15] Many cases fall under the EU's infringement procedure, the main avenue used to enforce treaty obligations. Some EU members are sued several times each year through the infringement procedure. The number of cases on the WTO DSM and ECJ dockets far exceed those of any others. By contrast, the International Court of Justice ruled on its first case in 1948 and has adjudicated only 156 lawsuits since then, at a rate of just over two per year.

Finally, the price tag of litigation suggests that states value international adjudication. Looking at the WTO, the most litigious members are the US and the EU. The US files on average five WTO lawsuits per year, and some estimates suggest the legal fees alone exceed one million dollars per lawsuit (Bown and Hoekman 2005). Likewise, the EU files an average of four WTO complaints per year at similar expense. Insofar as states behave in generally rational ways, they should only wage international lawsuits when they expect doing so delivers rewards, domestic or international. By a similar logic, states ought only to defend themselves against accusations if those adverse judgments carry some negative consequence. If the IC rulings carried no consequences whatsoever—domestic or international—rational state leaders would likely ignore lawsuits altogether.

1.3.2 Overcoming inferential challenges

Whether or not IOs promote cooperation remains a central puzzle because of two inferential obstacles. The first is whether countries formally comply with their international commitments; it is often difficult to detect noncompliance or distinguish it from compliant policies, especially when those policies are subtle and the international obligations are intricate. The second is whether compliance means that governments adopt substantially different behaviors. In most international contexts, state compliance does not equate to the effectiveness of an IO (Downs and Rocke 1995; Downs, Rocke, and Barsoom 1996; von Stein 2005).

Compliance is endogenous to institutions. States tend to craft treaties that reflect their preexisting preferences. That a state abides by the terms of its international agreements does not mean that those treaties can be credited with inducing the state's cooperative behavior. Perhaps governments would have cooperated anyway. Perhaps a treaty was merely aspirational. As a result, observing compliance ordinarily tells us little about the effect of international treaties and institutions on state behavior.

International courts help researchers to untangle this puzzle. A state that is brought before an IC and found to be in violation of its commitments evidently does not want to comply. Litigation is costly for defendant states. Countries that break international promises and hold fast throughout litigation reveal their preferences for noncompliance. Therefore, when a government does ultimately abide by an adverse ruling, despite its preferences, we can infer that court had an impact. By intervening, the IC has shifted the defendant government's calculus, making noncompliance less enticing. By examining a government's behavior in response to adverse court rulings, researchers can overcome the usual endogeneity problem. Courts thus supply a rare window into the broader question of whether IOs advance state cooperation.

Understanding an IC's effect requires a closer look at the structure of the disputes they adjudicate. Many interstate economic conflicts— most pointedly, international trade—resemble the canonical "prisoner's dilemma" (Snidal 1985). Countries share an incentive to cooperate by jointly liberalizing their trade policy. Lower trade barriers, economists generally agree, are efficient. By efficiently using limited productive resources, countries can enjoy mutual gains. At the same time, each country has a unilateral incentive to defect—that is, to erect trade barriers while its trading partner maintains open borders. This benefits the cheater and leaves the cooperator worse off. Disputes arise precisely because governments "cheat" on their previous promises. A cheating country breaks its commitments to keep trade barriers low, thereby exploiting another country's good-faith effort to cooperate.

Through the lens of the cooperation problem, scholars have offered game-theoretic accounts of WTO dispute settlement (e.g., Bagwell and Staiger 1999; Maggi 1999; Rosendorff 2005; Sattler and Bernauer 2014).

Governments interact repeatedly over time, and at each point of inter-action they can cooperate or defect. If a state defects now, does it re-turn to cooperation later? The WTO DSM provides a way for countries to compensate one another for these short-term violations. Plaintiffs can sue defendants for missteps. They can obtain a legal ruling and get the defendants to reform, perhaps with a small penalty. In this view, the WTO aims to restore a cooperative equilibrium where countries each maintain low trade barriers. The punishment for cheating has to be large enough to be a deterrent yet small enough so that a government does not abandon the trade regime altogether (Milgrom, North, and Wein-gast 1990). By striking the right balance, the WTO DSM helps to stabi-lize the multilateral trade regime and ensure cooperation in the long run (Trebilcock and Howse 1999).

Trade is not the only international economic issue with which states struggle to cooperate. The EU aims to create a labor market in which workers can move with ease. At least in theory, states collectively gain from an efficient labor market that allows workers to relocate and fill jobs. Much like with trade, states have a mutual incentive to reduce ob-stacles and allow workforce mobility. But states also have incentives to place limitations on foreign workers. For instance, they might want to make it easier for their own nationals to enjoy secure employment by protecting them from competing with a larger EU workforce. Countries may be tempted to "cheat" and ignore the EU's free movement of labor principle.

Reflecting this international cooperation problem, the ECJ adju-dicates disputes over labor market restrictions. Many states have been sued for restrictive policies. In these instances, ECJ judgments aim to re-store cooperation. In nearly any aspect of the international economy by which countries seek mutual gains from cooperation, and face individ-ual incentives to cheat, conflicts arise. ICs are routinely called on to sup-ply legal decisions to induce a return to cooperation. Thus the question of when ICs succeed or fail is not a narrow inquiry into trade politics; it is a broader concern about how institutions can pave the way for inter-national economic cooperation.

Whether governments do comply with the decisions of international courts remains an open empirical question. Although legal rulings from both the WTO DSM and the ECJ are ostensibly binding, governments are reluctant to acquiesce. Some ICs have centralized mechanisms for inducing compliance. For instance, the ECJ can authorize fines on recalcitrant states, although for reasons elucidated by Carrubba and Gabel (2015), this is rare. Other courts rely on decentralized enforcement, where states must pursue rule violators until they obtain a satisfactory outcome. As Johns (2012) and Johns and Pelc (2018) highlight, the WTO membership pressures defendants to comply with rulings. This approach is feasible when the conflict resembles the prisoner's dilemma. One country's defection is another country's cost; therefore the latter has an incentive to punish the former to induce compliance. Many studies chart out mechanisms for enforcement in international dispute settlement. Few reveal whether and when governments that lose international legal disputes bow to these enforcement efforts.

This book offers two complementary assessments of international courts. The first considers policy reforms governments make when they lose lawsuits. I determine whether states implement new compliant policies mandated by adverse rulings and revoke preexisting policies struck down by the court. It is often difficult to discern whether a country has complied with its legal obligations; the law can be ambiguous and it may be unclear whether policies are consistent with the law (Goldsmith and Posner 2005; Reus-smit 2004). IC rulings clarify what count as compliant policies, resolving ambiguity and clarifying where breaches occurred (Kucik 2019; Lauterpacht 1982; Tallberg 2002a). These rulings supply information needed to evaluate compliance. And compliance is telling because states "jealously guard" their sovereignty (Jackson 2006; Voeten 2007).

At the same time, formal compliance is of less interest if it fails to bring about deeper cooperation. Some governments comply without undertaking meaningful measures that reflect the spirit of the law.[16] Reluctant states skirt unfavorable legal rulings by removing one offending policy only to replace it with another that accomplishes similar effects. Thus the second way I scrutinize IC performance is by focusing on behavioral outcomes. I assess whether the policy reforms governments make in response to rulings substantially deepen interstate economic cooperation.

It is no easy task to determine whether IOs are effective in promoting cooperation. But the chapters that follow make significant strides toward this goal. I argue that international courts help to cut through the selection problem that plagues many studies of IOs. Through their adverse rulings, courts identify cases in which defendant governments prefer not to abide by their international commitments and delineate the scope of their breaches. When governments do comply, despite their revealed preferences, this highlights the court's influence. And I show what, precisely, is achieved by compliance. Formal policy reforms routinely carry behavioral consequences—e.g., restored trade flows between litigant states or shifting markets. This book unlocks the compliance and effectiveness puzzle for two landmark international courts and offers ideas that may reach more broadly to other domains of international relations.

1.4 Contributions and implications

This book offers several insights into the role of international courts in global economic affairs. First, I show that ICs do accomplish a vital function. Their intervention in economic disputes can help to contain conflicts so countries can reestablish stable cooperative relations rather than letting disputes escalate. Some international legal scholars see ICs as powerful instruments for promoting cooperation; these scholars emphasize that rulings are binding on governments and chart out the extent of legal obligations, clarifying which policies or actions are consistent with those obligations. To explain why states vary in their responses to international rulings, research tends to emphasize legal capacity— countries vary in their ability to comply. Complementing this scholarship, I turn my attention toward the inner workings of defendant governments. Domestic politics within litigant states determine when ICs succeed or fail.

My findings also offer guidance to governments using ICs to advance their national objectives. Satisfactory dispute resolution is not always attainable. Prospective plaintiffs can deploy their legal resources with finer-tuned aims and may expect greater rewards for their litigation expenditures if they target consolidated governments; this may result in governments timing lawsuits to coincide with waning political divisions in defendant governments. Research shows that plaintiffs initiate WTO disputes to buy support from certain domestic groups or appeal to foreign audiences, including during times of political turnover (Bobick and A. Smith 2016; Chaudoin 2014; Davis 2012; Gray and Kucik 2017). Far less is known about how shifts in the constellation of power within defendant governments affect compliance with court rulings. By turning their attention to a defendant's calculations, potential plaintiffs can better discern whether their lawsuits will serve only as public demonstrations of solidarity or may feasibly achieve policy results.

Second, there are implications for the design of international courts. A rich literature examines how courts are designed—e.g., the extent of legalization, whether judges exercise discretion, or the strength of enforcement (Carrubba 2005; Gilligan, Johns, and Rosendorff 2010; Johns 2012, 2015; Koremenos, Lipson, and Snidal 2001). Design choices are thought to reflect rational decisions by diplomats and government officials seeking to promote interstate cooperation while guarding against overly burdensome obligations. How does this architecture bear out in reality, once court operations are underway? Whether highly legalized ICs help to settle disputes and restore cooperation remains an open question.

Linking the institutional design literature to an account of performance, I highlight how governments are keen to exploit flexibility in ICs. Flexibility mechanisms—opportunities for temporary tolerated defection from international obligations—are supposed to make an institution more stable over time (Gilligan, Johns, and Rosendorff 2010; Rosendorff 2005). Flexible courts may retain broader participation, particularly from the most powerful countries that can credibly threaten to exit. But this can go too far. If countries abuse this flexibility at will—for example, by dragging out legal proceedings and evading punishment—they undercut a court's effectiveness. While the literature has posited this balancing act in theory, I offer empirical evidence showing how it works in practice.

Flexibility mechanisms are ostensibly there to be used very sparingly. In theory, governments temporarily default on their free trade obligations only when they encounter unusual political or economic events that make these requirements onerous. For example, in the WTO, countries are permitted to enact trade barriers through the safeguards criteria during times of crisis, such as in the wake of a natural disaster. Once the event passes, the country should return to compliance. However, in the WTO, states seem to take advantage of flexibility mechanisms in systematically different ways. Domestic political structures prompt governments to use institutional flexibility to their advantage with some frequency, not as chance, one-off events. Governments with many domestic political constraints are most likely to exploit this wiggle room (Pelc 2013)—for example, by dragging out international legal proceedings and evading punishment. Yet these are precisely the same WTO members whose cooperation is needed to ensure the long-term stability of the international regime. As a result, flexibility may fail to bring about long-term cooperation from the most sophisticated litigants. Procedures that provide excessive leeway for tolerated noncompliance undercut cooperative aims.

Diplomats or politicians seeking to strengthen international economic courts might be able to craft revisions to address this imbalance. Increasing the precision of rules and establishing monitoring mechanisms to see whether IC judgments are correctly implemented could avert some misuse. At the same time, ICs might be modified to offer greater leniency when domestic institutional veto players block compliance. To some extent, the WTO makes a nod in this direction. When governments face legislative gridlock and fail to implement legal rulings, the WTO may extend deadlines for compliance. The US and EU stand out as the most savvy users of the WTO. Many other states with fewer resources struggle to use adjudication to achieve their political aims. It might be beneficial to expand the WTO DSM's formal flexiblity mechanisms while increasing institutional verification that the mechanisms are appropriately applied; this would level the playing field between states. Ultimately, these revisions could preserve broad participation in the regime and increase long-term compliance, furthering the multilateral goals of the organization. More generally, ICs might improve their effectiveness by accounting for the diverse domestic political obstacles that governments face in complying.

Finally, this book lends insight into a fundamental question in the study of international politics: how healthy is the marriage between international and domestic institutions? ICs impose their judgments of what is legal or illegal on sovereign states, while those states are beholden to their own competing domestic interests. Government leaders walk a fine line between acquiescing (or not) to international rule of law while their decisions are subject to domestic institutional constraints and domestic stakeholders. Tensions at the national level may generate demands for divorce.

The WTO provides a compelling illustration of why domestic dynamics matter. WTO rulings require states to reform their trade policies, a process that is challenging precisely because it makes markets more vulnerable to the competitive forces of economic globalization. When domestic groups obstruct the reforms prescribed by the WTO, we see the erosion of what has long been the legal cornerstone of global trade. Recent challenges to the WTO have been structural rather than due to the idiosyncrasies of individual political leaders. For instance, under the Trump administration, the US thwarted legalized dispute settlement by blocking the appointment of new Appellate Body judges. This decision can be traced back to the domestic tension between those who support or oppose the multilateral trade regime—the winners of economic globalization and those who have fallen behind. At the same time that the US and EU have been backpedaling, other states have been actively seeking WTO adjudication. These other countries represent a broader geography and range of economic development than the litigants of the organization's early years. Where international dispute settlement delivers benefits to key domestic stakeholders, and where opposition groups do not have out-sized influence, we can continue to expect countries to rely on ICs. The evidence in chapters that follow suggests that international legalization is not likely to fade away anytime soon.

1.5 Case selection, methodology, and organization

I test my arguments through an extensive empirical analysis of the aforementioned international economic courts. I focus on *economic* courts because their impact can be assessed through a wealth of economic data. International trade records are available for the majority of countries and products, going back decades. I examine trade flows over time for states that were prosecuted for violations and compare them to corresponding trade patterns for states that were not subjects of legal action. Analyzed with appropriate statistical methods, these data allow me to draw valid comparisons and discern the effects of legal rulings on interstate cooperation. In the language of causal inference, I observe suitable control units, compare them to the treated units, and draw inferences about causal effects. Leveraging these economic data yields insights into the performance of the ICs.

Data availability sets international economic courts apart from institutions that adjudicate other aspects of interstate cooperation. It is far more difficult to assess the impact of rulings on human rights, security, or territorial disputes. The Inter-American Court of Human Rights has jurisdiction over serious human rights violations, including disappearances, torture, and detention of political dissidents.[17] Systematically measuring this court's impact is a nearly impossible task. Is restitution made to all victims of past crimes? Are political leaders deterred from committing further violations? Outcomes are rarely reported—at least not in a standard way across member states. And outcomes go unreported for states that have *not* been prosecuted. It is infeasible to compare states that violated international law to those that have not, since only infractions are tracked. That means we cannot draw conclusions about the impact of international legal rulings on human rights practices. Restated in the language of causal inference, because we observe only treated units and do not observe suitable control units, we cannot draw conclusions about causal effects.

By focusing on the adjudication of economic disputes between states, this book provides an empirically rigorous assessment of one category of ICs. My arguments may apply to the broader range of courts. Any time there are domestic political constraints and divergent domestic preferences at work, we should expect similar patterns for (non)compliance.[18] In particular, my arguments might be fruitfully applied to the adjudication of international territorial conflicts, as such conflicts also activate domestic political divisions.

There are two other reasons I investigate the WTO DSM and ECJ. These institutions are the most active and, ostensibly, most influential (Brutger and Morse 2015). Many countries seek legal remedy or are held accountable for previous missteps at these courts, so the volume of disputes and their perceived importance make them amenable to empirical study. And, importantly, these courts enable me to test different parts of my theoretical argument. The WTO allows me to evaluate the impact of judicial rulings on both trade policy and trade flows. This yields a nuanced account of compliance and cooperation. Because the vast majority of states in the international system are WTO members, I can test the domestic politics portion of my argument with the broadest possible scope. This includes comparing democracies to nondemocratic countries. I probe whether the institutional checks and balances and partisan competition that are so fundamental to democracy may stand in the way of compliance.

In any empirical study, the challenge is to control for all relevant factors that could confound the mechanism of interest. This study is no exception. WTO disputes involve different plaintiff governments with varying capabilities to sway the defendants they sue. To complement my WTO analysis and control for many such factors, I turn to the second institution, the ECJ. The ECJ adjudicates thousands of infringement disputes in which the European Commission sues states for breaking EU law. All these lawsuits have the same plaintiff. Likewise, EU members agree to common regulations on numerous other aspects of the economy. In methodological terms, the ECJ disputes provide statistical control for numerous potential confounding variables. At the same time, these cases have variations on the key explanatory variable: while all member states are democracies, they vary in their domestic constraints. By analyzing ECJ rulings, I can unpack the domestic political constraints mechanism and differentiate among different forms of constraints within democracies. By looking at both the WTO and ECJ, my book offers a more thorough test than could be obtained by examining a single institution.

This project draws on multiple methodologies. A rational choice approach guides the theory. My argument takes seriously the idea that states and the political groups within them act strategically. These actors choose among potential courses of action based on their desire to maximize their short- or long-term gains. However, political groups within states face problems of incomplete information. They may have an imperfect grasp of what the future holds, what roads other political actors have gone down, or the legal decisions an international court will reach. I do not treat a state as a unitary actor but rather recognize the conflicting preferences among core domestic actors, including executives, legislators, and the interest groups they may represent. I also allow for the possibility that strategic political actors make mistakes. They may incorrectly assess the consequences of joining an international regime and miscalculate the concrete costs and benefits of participating in legal disputes years after acceding. The preferences of different political actors may shift at different stages of international cooperation as they learn about consequent costs and benefits. In short, my argument adopts a rational choice perspective and highlights that international politics is often a stochastic and messy enterprise.

I test my theory with a combination of large-N data, statistical methods, and case studies. The empirical analysis is based on three original datasets that demonstrate (1) policy reforms that governments make to comply with WTO rulings; (2) the impact of WTO rulings on trade flows between disputing governments; and (3) the impact of ECJ rulings on member states' trade with the rest of the European community. The statistical results highlight broad patterns in the data. I buttress these findings with case studies to trace the mechanisms.

The remainder of the book proceeds as follows: Chapter 2 presents my theory and positions it within the IO literature. I argue that government compliance with international rulings yields insight into institutional effectiveness. I make the case that domestic veto players can hinder compliance with rulings from ICs. This chapter offers insights into the distributive politics of trade cooperation and the distinctive obstacles governments face when confronting international rulings.

Chapter 3 supplies a brief overview of the WTO and EU courts, explaining their approaches to enforcement. I discuss governments' opportunistic use of these courts. The remainder of the chapter delineates my assumptions about the key actors, actions, and preferences that give rise to my theoretical predictions.

Chapters 4, 5, and 6 contain the empirical tests of my theory. Chapter 4 tests my hypotheses at the WTO, which adjudicates disputes among democracies and nondemocratic governments alike. I assess the policy impact of WTO rulings by evaluating trade policy reforms governments make to comply. My novel dataset on policy compliance with rulings is a core empirical contribution. Governments are less likely to comply when they face constraints at home. The timing of litigation and the duration of (non)compliance indicate that states sometimes evade rulings to assuage domestic constituents.

Chapter 5 examines the impact of WTO rulings on markets. I measure the effect of rulings on product-level trade flows between disputing countries. My approach goes beyond previous research that evaluates the trade value of WTO disputes (T. Hofmann and Soo Yeon Kim 2017; Bown and Reynolds 2015; Chaudoin, Kucik, and Pelc 2016; Bechtel and Sattler 2015). The evidence shows that by locking in trade barriers, domestic veto players can undercut the WTO's ability to restore economic cooperation between disputing governments.

Chapter 6 tests my argument with trade-related disputes at the ECJ. Judges routinely find that defendant states have violated their EU commitments and order them to remove barriers to commerce. Analyzing these disputes, I show that defendants with more internal divisions of power, both institutional and partisan, report a smaller boost in intra-EU trade. This chapter buttresses my core findings regarding the WTO, suggesting that variation among robust democracies also matters.

The concluding chapter summarizes the book's contributions and highlights its policy implications. I offer an appraisal of ICs in a time of backlash against global economic institutions. International dispute settlement is an inherently political process; as these courts reconcile governments, it is vital that they also deliver recovery to firms, interest groups, and key sectors of the economy in order to remain a salient force.

CHAPTER TWO

A Theory of International Courts, Compliance, and Domestic Veto Players

International courts (ICs) occupy an unusual position in the landscape of international relations. They supply authoritative interpretations of the formal rules governing state behavior while also depending precariously on the consent of states to do their bidding. This tension—between the ostensible authority of law and state sovereignty[1]—is complicated by domestic politics within countries. The legal decisions ICs render affect the political balancing act within national borders. Rulings tend to generate domestic winners and losers. For international economic affairs, the distributive consequences are pronounced. States that embrace international legal decisions must compel dissatisfied domestic stakeholders to come around. Or they must find a way to advance the agenda of groups that support the court while sidestepping domestic opposition. The tension between courts' formal authority and practical dependence on key domestic stakeholders raises this question: when, if ever, do ICs encourage states to comply with their treaty obligations?

Legal scholars argue that states overwhelmingly comply with international law. Louis Henkin famously stated that "almost all nations observe almost all principles of international law almost all of the time" (Henkin 1979, 47). According to this sanguine view, states recognize the formal treaties they sign and the customary law they inherit as being in their interest. Violations are usually inadvertent missteps and conflicts arise primarily because states disagree about the interpretation of their obligations (Chayes and Chayes 1993). An IC's main task, then, is to re-solve ambiguity in the interpretation and application of the law. Its le-gal judgments inform states and cultivate greater adherence to interna-tional law.

Many political scientists, by contrast, cast doubt on this perspective and ask whether ICs actually advance compliance with international law. Suppose that states and the political actors within them operate ra-tionally according to self-interest (Fearon 1998; Jervis 1976; Lake and Powell 1999; Stein 1990). In that case, international laws are mere guide-lines that a state chooses to follow or not as it sees fit (Abbott and Sni-dal 1998; Axelrod and Keohane 1985). A state violates international law when its leadership prefers different policies from what the law requires (Grieco, Gelpi, and Warren 2009). International obligations are merely inconvenient constraints that a state does not always want to follow. The function of ICs, in this view, is to shift a state's cost-benefit calculation. Adjudication prompts enforcement from the international community and incentivizes litigant states to reform.

Thus there is little consensus on how well, and under what conditions, international courts promote compliance with international law. As Al-ter pointedly noted, "what factors influence whether or not international courts enhance compliance with international law? In truth, we know surprisingly little about the relationship between international courts and state compliance" (Alter 2003, 51). The increased activity of ICs in-vites a critical assessment of their performance (Shany 2012). Whether and when courts encourage countries to abide by their international ob-ligations remains a crucial empirical question.

Furthermore, even if ICs do encourage formal compliance with trea-ties, it is unclear whether such compliance advances international co-operation in meaningful ways (Downs, Rocke, and Barsoom 1996). For instance, IC rulings may succeed or fail to promote economic integra-tion between countries. Perhaps adjudication reduces the risk of armed conflict over territorial disputes by offering an authoritative decision on land borders; or perhaps a decision is promptly ignored. International rulings might help to mitigate human rights abuses by evaluating and publicizing past violations, or they may do little to curb the most egre-gious crimes. A central puzzle is whether the formal institutions states create, and the international laws they are built upon, are actually effec-tive in facilitating interstate cooperation. ICs present, as I will argue, a revealing manifestation of this puzzle.

This chapter provides a framework for understanding the ICs that address interstate economic affairs. I offer a theory of when ICs promote compliance with law and how this translates into cooperative outcomes. Domestic political factors shape how courts perform. Divisions of authority within governments—veto players—have cross-cutting effects in the international arena. While scholarship has long emphasized that domestic veto players can promote adherence to international law, here I show how they systematically obstruct compliance with court rulings and thus lock in violations. Yet my argument goes beyond traditional veto players theory. Governments are not only unable to comply but use that seeming inability as cover for defying court rulings. Tolerated noncompliance has been built into international courts. When domestic constraints are substantial, institutional flexibility in an IC can stabilize the organization in the long run. Thus my theory sets out conditions for when we should expect better compliance to translate into more effective international institutions.

2.1 Cooperation, compliance, and international courts

2.1.1 International cooperation

States face fundamental cooperation challenges in international affairs. To overcome barriers inherent to their collective endeavors, states construct international institutions (see, e.g., Keohane 1982; Snidal 1985; Morrow 1994). Appraising these institutions' performance prompts a closer look at the challenges they are designed to solve (Koremenos 2016). Here, the focus is on how multiple sovereign nations can *collaborate* on matters that extend beyond national borders when they have reasons to break their promises (Stein 1982).[2]

International economic courts preside over areas of law where cooperation challenges abound. Beyond merely coordinating countries around uncontroversial standards, many international economic organizations aim to help governments collaborate when they are strained by competing incentives (Keohane 1984; Stein 1990). On the one hand, governments have an incentive to contribute to collective endeavors—by abiding by shared rules of conduct—and then reap the benefits of cooperation. On the other hand, each government is interested in pursuing its own individual agenda. Sometimes this means breaking the rules and free riding on the actions of others. Although collective action problems

take different forms, international economic cooperation is often modeled as the familiar "prisoner's dilemma" where each country chooses
between cooperating or defecting without knowing what choice the
other is making (Martin 1999).

International trade poses a quandary. Countries have a mutual interest in exchanging goods and services freely. But under certain conditions, they may also have unilateral incentives to impose trade barriers (Conybeare 1984; Krugman 1991; Gowa and Mansfield 1993). For
instance, a government might use trade barriers in response to short-
term crises, interest group pressures, or times marked by institutional
constraints, such as a divided government. When a country opens its
borders to imports from foreign markets, it prioritizes the benefits of
global commerce, reaping efficiency gains of specialization. Doing so
exposes the country to the risk that its trading partners apply tariffs on
its exports, hurting its own domestic industry. Alternately, the country, guarding against this costly scenario, might prefer to restrict imports of foreign goods. Trade policies aimed at protecting domestic
firms are often referred to as "beggar-thy-neighbor" policies because
they raise revenue at the expense of other countries. A government
that uses such policies may provoke retaliation, prompting a spiral of
protectionism (H. Johnson 1953). A breakdown in trade cooperation
is generally inefficient because countries are foregoing the benefits of
specialization.

How do countries overcome this type of cooperation problem? Decades ago, Keohane (1986) theorized that international institutions can
help governments escape from a prisoner's dilemma cooperation problem by formalizing mechanisms of reciprocity. Governments interact repeatedly over time and can condition future treatment of one another on
their past interactions. Treatment is both contingent on other states' past
actions and equivalent (or balanced) in rewards or punishment (Axelrod 1984; Axelrod and Keohane 1985). International institutions provide a platform for this kind of reciprocity. They delineate terms of cooperation and establish proportionate, targeted punishments when those
terms are breached, breaking a chain of sequential retaliation.

This account lends insight into how international trade agreements
work. Bagwell and Staiger (1993, 1) highlighted precisely how multilateral trade cooperation involves "a constant balance between . . . the
gains from deviating unilaterally from an agreed-upon trade policy . . .
[and] . . . the expected future benefits of maintaining multilateral coop-

eration with the understanding that the latter would be forfeited in the trade war which followed a unilateral defection" (see also Bagwell and Staiger 1999). Trade agreements are self-enforcing rules of the game: contracts between states that declare a shared intention to maintain low trade barriers with reciprocal consequences for those that renege. They offer assurance that countries will keep trade barriers low, facilitating free exchange and the efficiency gains that come with specialization. By formalizing the standards for reciprocity and specifying consequences for breach, trade agreements are thought to move states from an inefficient arrangement of high trade barriers to a more efficient one of low barriers. The courts examined in the chapters that follow—primarily the World Trade Organization's Dispute Settlement Mechanism and secondarily the Court of Justice of the European Union, insofar as it addresses economic integration—are in place to support trade cooperation.

International trade is not the only domain in which these collaboration problems arise (Lipson 1984). From nuclear proliferation to coordination on monetary policy, states often face similar challenges. International cooperation on environmental protection follows a logic parallel to that on trade (Hardin and Baden 1977; Hahn and Richards 1989; Soroos 1994). For instance, around the globe, countries are facing the ill effects of human-induced global warming. Governments have a collective interest in cooperating to mitigate further environmental degradation. Yet environmental protection measures can be costly. Reducing consumption or substituting clean energy can generate additional short-term costs to industries and consumers, potentially undercutting business interests. Thus each country might prefer that others reduce greenhouse gas emissions while their own businesses and consumers enjoy unmitigated energy consumption and pollute. States strategically choose between coordinating environmental policy and shirking collective aims (Wood 2011). As with international trade, environmental treaties are intended to move from a suboptimal outcome—for example, of unrestrained pollution—to a preferable one—for example, where each government upholds environmental protection measures and deliver collective benefits (Barrett 1997). By delineating the terms of cooperation and reciprocity, these treaties offer governments some assurance that all members will abide by established environmental standards.

Thus states attempt to solve collaboration problems in many different domains by crafting international institutions.[3] International trade is not exceptional in terms of the tension between collective aims and incentives for opportunistic behavior, nor is it uniquely fraught with disputes. While the empirical chapters that follow probe the performance of international courts in the domain of trade, some of the insights may be applied to other areas of international relations that reflect the same type of collective action problems.

Because many international institutions are designed to solve difficult collaboration problems, they are not a fail-safe solution (Martin 1992). For instance, if a government breaks its free trade commitments, it often enjoys impunity until another country challenges its breach. Even the highly institutionalized WTO cannot reliably monitor the compliance of its members. Likewise, in preferential trade agreements, it is up to member states to track whether trade partners follow treaty terms (e.g., the United States-Mexico-Canada Agreement, the successor to the North American Free Trade Agreement). In the EU, the European Commission is tasked with enforcing EU legislation, but its monitoring capabilities are limited and it largely relies on voluntary reporting from states. These institutions face a common challenge: how to induce compliance. Violations often go unnoticed and enforcement is unreliable. Compliance problems have broad effects. For example, when governments violate trade agreements, they undermine the collaborative equilibrium—other states might then prefer to impose trade protection to counter the harm done. Noncompliance by a few leads to a worse outcome for many. This has the overall impact of discrediting of the institution and weakening of its future influence.

Alleviating compliance problems is a central goal of many, if not most, international courts. ICs perform a range of functions that serve states and, in some instances, non-state actors.[4] Some provide administrative or constitutional review functions. Others, including the WTO DSM and the ECJ, focus on dispute settlement and enforcement. In this capacity, ICs aim to resolve conflict, sometimes facilitating out-of-court settlements in the shadow of the law. In their enforcement capacity, ICs adjudicate state compliance with international law and pull levers of politics to compel defendants to adjust their behavior. As Alter (2014) emphasizes, among judicial roles, enforcement activity may be the most challenging. That is because in this capacity, foreign judges evaluate whether government policies and practices are consistent with international law, strike down violations, and order reform. Enforcement activities are significant incursions on the authority of states. Lacking coercive powers, ICs enjoy only a limited ability to induce cooperation.

It is widely thought that international courts operate by distributing information to states and non-state actors, but to what end—and how this actually matters for state compliance—remains a point of debate. Scholars disagree about what causes states to break their international commitments in the first place. Some view noncompliance as largely inadvertent (Chayes and Chayes 1993). Compliance problems arise when legal obligations are ambiguous or governments lack the capacity to correctly implement the law. Governments may be unclear about their international commitments. Treaty violations are simply missteps because countries largely see the law to be consistent with their interests—or they understand their legal obligations and lack the capability or resources to fully perform those duties. This "managerial" perspective suggests that if international organizations (IOs) are to improve compliance, they should provide states with better information, clarify legal obligations, and provide bureaucratic resources to alleviate domestic capacity problems.

According to the "managerial" view, ICs supply information in several ways: Their legal rulings provide an expert assessment of an alleged violation, making a defendant government aware of why it should reform its policy or practice. By interpreting and clarifying legal obligations, these rulings help governments to more accurately embrace international law. When states suffer from bureaucratic limitations, courts offer expertise that facilitates compliance.[5] These mechanisms may best explain IC activity when they serve an administrative review role or help countries coordinate around uncontroversial standards.

Yet this perspective is unsatisfying when applied to the international economic courts examined here because of the underlying cooperation problem. While there are collective benefits in cooperation, states often have unilateral incentives to break their international commitments. There will be some occasions in which states prefer to act opportunistically. According to a rational choice framework, governments are well aware of international obligations, and noncompliance is the result of a calculated decision (Downs and Rocke 1995; Staiger 1995). Governments break their commitments whenever the benefits of doing so outweigh the expected penalties. These situations should be rare. Because governments voluntarily join international institutions, they generally only enter those prescribing actions they intend to adopt anyway (Downs,

Rocke, and Barsoom 1996). Nonetheless, when (perhaps unforeseen) circumstances favor it, states do break their international commitments. It is incumbent upon ICs to shift these cost-benefit calculations.

ICs shift countries' cost-benefit calculations in several ways. For one, they can vet instances of potential treaty violations, deliver verdicts, and publicize their judgments, setting off "fire alarms" (McCubbins and Schwartz 1984). As Milgrom, North, and Weingast (1990) theorized, a minimal legal body that lacks coercive authority can still orchestrate community enforcement to support a cooperative regime. It does so by tracking the reputation of each actor—that is, past choices to cooperate or defect—and whether actors that had defected had paid compensation to make amends. By then distributing this information to interested parties, the legal body can help members of the community penalize and reward past behavior accordingly. In this manner, it can leverage decentralized enforcement to promote a collaborative equilibrium. Milgrom, North, and Weingast's model thus explains how an international court can coordinate enforcement. ICs share information that shifts the behavior of bystander states in the international community, which in turn alters litigant states' cost-benefit calculations (Gilligan 2006).

These insights are resonant in the context of the multilateral trade regime where decentralized enforcement is key (Maggi 1999). Dispute settlement mechanisms like the WTO's advance trade cooperation by verifying violations of trade agreements and informing bystander countries, thus facilitating the biting effect of a tarnished reputation. This activity complements existing enforcement mechanisms, "making anarchy work" better (Kono 2007). The public condemnation of an adverse IC ruling sullies a country's reputation, potentially creating long-term costs. Aggrieved states can collect penalties or compensation sanctioned by the court. Thus in numerous ways, ICs can make community enforcement work more consistently and efficiently (Johns 2012; Johns and Pelc 2018). This perspective suggests that if international courts help states more effectively penalize noncompliance and reward law-abiding behavior, they can improve compliance rates.

While these accounts focus on how ICs coordinate international enforcement, other scholarship has highlighted domestic sources of compliance with the law. It is well established that domestic audiences can incentivize countries to escalate enforcement efforts and bring their trade grievances to international courts (Davis 2012; Chaudoin 2014). Choices

by governments to litigate, and to avail themselves of these legal avenues, hinge on domestic political institutions. ICs can likewise harness
the influence of domestic political networks. For instance, in the EU's
legal system, subnational actors such as private litigants, lawyers, and
judges in national courts have been instrumental in expanding the au-
tonomy and supranational authority of the ECJ (Burley and Mattli 1993;
Mattli and Slaughter 1998). With the support of key domestic actors, the
ECJ has generated judicial doctrine embraced by national courts and
the support emboldened the ECJ to issue legal rulings that sometimes
run against the interests of certain member states (Alter 1998). ICs provide information on the domestic interests of stakeholders and, in the
case of the WTO system, shape plaintiff states' efforts to enforce international law (Davis 2012). Certainly, not all ICs achieve this degree of
integration into national systems. Nonetheless, this scholarship makes
clear that domestic institutions and political partners abet international
legal rulings and usher along compliance from reluctant states.

The aforementioned research on compliance does not adequately
evaluate domestic political factors that *hinder*—as opposed to promote—
the enforcement activity of ICs. When court rulings condemn breaches
of international law, domestic politics in the targeted country becomes
pivotal. These kinds of rulings often require governments to take positive action, such as amending or revoking a law or replacing an administrative measure. In these instances, "even if a government wants to . . .
change problematic legislation or encourage national judges to heed an
international judicial ruling, a government may lack the ability to influence key substate actors to follow their will" (Alter 2014, 281). To give
effect to international legal rulings, governments must rely on the support of pro-compliance domestic actors; they must also overcome opposition from anti-compliance ones. Both flavors of domestic actors must
work through their home political institutions to influence compliance
activity (Dai 2006). In the latter part of this chapter, I chart out how ICs
encounter domestic political obstacles to their enforcement efforts and
when we can expect the activity of these domestic groups to alter international economic cooperation.

2.1.2 Distinguishing between compliance and cooperation

Compliance with international law means that countries adopt policy
and practices that conform to the specific obligations delineated in the

law (Raustiala 2000; Simmons 2000; Guzman 2002). International legal scholarship tends to emphasize the idea that domestic policy, rules, and procedures are consistent with the "letter of the law."[6] For instance, has a government passed legislation that protects political liberties, bans child labor, or prohibits torture? If its domestic policy correctly reflects these political rights, workplace restrictions, and prohibitions in accordance with its international legal obligations, it has complied.

Formal compliance does not always mean that a state has embraced the substantive goals of the law (Downs, Rocke, and Barsoom 1996). While a country might comply with an international treaty, that compliance can bring about little cooperation if the rules simply lay out what the state would otherwise do in the absence of the treaty. Conversely, state conduct can go against rules but reflect the cooperative aims of the law (Ruggie 1982). Following the previous examples, the parallel questions are: Does a government now refrain from imprisoning political dissidents? Has a government that ratified the 1999 Child Labor Convention actually eliminated child labor within its borders? Has a government that ratified the 1985 Convention Against Torture now ensured no one is tortured within its territory? If a government has behaved in accordance with its substantive international commitments, the cooperative aims of those treaties have been satisfied.

Compliance and cooperation, while distinct from each other, are routinely conflated. As Martin (2013) warns, when trying to determine the impact of international organizations on state behavior, scholars have incorrectly relied on assessing whether governments comply. This can spell confusion when evaluating domains of international cooperation as diverse as trade and humanitarian law. Sometimes, states devise policies that are consistent with the letter of the law—that is, they are compliant— but that nonetheless undercut the cooperative aims of the relevant international agreement. This could be due to willful distortions in which governments cleverly skirt their substantive obligations. Other times, behaviors fall into a gray zone not covered by the law making it difficult to discern whether the cooperative aims are being met. This latter scenario isn't necessarily accidental. Treaties are sometimes deliberately vague to allow for a range of interpretations (that is, an "incomplete contract"), further confounding any conclusions we might draw about the objectives of the law (Rosendorff and Milner 2001; Horn, Maggi, and Staiger 2010). In yet other instances, governments might exploit this ambiguity in trade rules by formally complying while also finding other means to deny market access to trading partners (Chaudoin, Kucik, and Pelc 2016), under-cutting the cooperative aims of the international agreement.

The mismatch between compliance and cooperation can be seen in the domain of international trade. One example comes from the fraught trade relations between the United States and Japan. In 1993, the US firm Kodak petitioned the federal government for protection, argu-ing that Japan had engaged in anticompetitive practices that assisted Fuji Corporation. This turned into a high-profile dispute in which the US Trade Representative alleged that the Japanese government had imposed unfair barriers to trade that cost Kodak $5.6 billion in sales (Schweitzer 1996). Some of the alleged practices included "a system of exclusive distribution relationships, artificially high prices that subsi-dized Fuji's research," cash payments to wholesalers and retailers, and "interlocking trade associations committed to price stability and avoid-ance of competition" (Hershey 1995). Driven at least in part by politi-cal optics, the US brought its grievances to the WTO for adjudication in June 1996 (Durling 2000, 343). As Davis (2012) explains, "the Kodak-Fuji film dispute provides an example of how strong political pressure can lead to a WTO dispute on an issue that would not otherwise appear to have been a likely case for adjudication" (118). Two years later, the WTO rejected the United States' claims and concluded that Japan's poli-cies were consistent with WTO rules—Japan had complied with its inter-national obligations. This is because the trade obstacles in question were not in the competence of the WTO. Yet the ruling highlighted a gap in the treaties: the absence of regulations on competition.

Despite this legal determination, stakeholders in the US complained that the Japanese policies impeded US market access and undercut the cooperative aims of the multilateral trade regime. Japan had engaged in "highly managed trade that [ran] counter to the spirit of the WTO" (Garten 1995, 50). As Durling (2000) explains, the US eventually ob-tained an important policy initiative from Japan in the dispute's after-math. Japan agreed to a bilateral cooperation agreement on competition law.[7] This helped to close the gap in WTO rules and to set standards for deeper cooperation between the two nations. Whether governments are savvy at using trade policy to their political advantage while skirting their legal obligations[8] or they simply stumble into a gray zone in the law, the result is that compliance need not generate substantive cooperation.

Trade is not the only domain in which this inconsistency arises; sim-ilar difficulties appear in international human rights and humanitarian

law. An example concerns the United States' treatment of suspected terrorists. The US is a long-standing proponent of the United Nations Convention Against Torture (CAT) and has long advocated for the principles represented in this treaty. But when US compliance with the CAT
was challenged over the treatment of prisoners at the Guantanamo Bay
military base, a legal debate ensued. Government lawyers went to great
lengths to distinguish "enhanced interrogation techniques" from torture to show that they were indeed in compliance with the letter of the
law. The US government drafted a series of memoranda justifying Bush-
era interrogation techniques (Bybee 2002; Yoo 2002). Detractors argued
that the memoranda, which aimed to justify the legality of US military
conduct, were poorly reasoned and unconvincing (Goldsmith 2007). For
instance, legal scholar and Bush administration official Jack Goldsmith
criticized the documents for being "riddled with error."[9] According to
this critique, "enhanced interrogation" was merely a euphemism for torture, and the US military had failed to embrace this fundamental tenet
of international human rights law.[10] In short, while the US offered extensive legal arguments to defend its compliance, many called into question whether its practices upheld the humanitarian principles in the treaties. Whether driven by lawyerly maneuvering or ambiguity in the law,
this incident helps demonstrate that compliance without cooperation is a
problem that extends beyond the international trade regime.

   This type of mismatch calls for a careful look at both formal compliance and cooperative outcomes. A contribution of this book is to tease
apart compliance and cooperation in the context of the multilateral trade
regime. In the chapters that follow, my empirical investigation of the
WTO is structured accordingly. Chapter 4 examines state efforts to comply with WTO rulings by looking at how states adjust their trade policies to conform to their formal obligations. Chapter 5 is concerned with
whether state behavior is consistent with trade liberalization principles. It
examines the economic consequences of WTO rulings—whether they restore disputed trade—and uses these as a basis for assessing cooperative
outcomes. But rather than taking on these two concepts as wholly separate, I argue that they intersect in an important way in certain contexts.

2.1.3 International courts as a window into effectiveness

The difficulty in separating compliance from cooperation is rooted in a
fundamental selection bias problem in empirical research. Governments

voluntarily enter international agreements. As Downs, Rocke, and Barsoom (1996) observed, "we do not know what a high compliance rate really implies. Does it mean that even in the absence of enforcement states will comply with any agreement . . . or does it mean that states only make agreements that do not require much enforcement?" (383). States will only ratify trade agreements with concessions they are willing and able to implement. Governments are more eager to join human rights agreements when they already abide by the standards contained therein. Just because a government's policies and practices conform with its international legal obligations does not mean the obligations have *caused* those behaviors. Ordinarily, it is problematic to infer that an institution has promoted cooperation simply because states comply with their formal obligations.

Besides the challenge highlighted by Downs, Rocke, and Barsoom, there is another obstacle to evaluating the effectiveness of IOs: it is nearly impossible to monitor the full range of opportunities for compliance. How often does the trade ministry of a government contemplate raising tariffs on a trading partner only to conclude that it prefers to maintain its free trade commitments? Do governments often consider imprisoning political dissidents but then determine it is better to abide by international treaties on civil and political liberties? Typically, empirical research only observes missteps—instances in which governments broke the rules. Only a few studies convincingly measure compliance opportunities (e.g., Davis and Shirato 2007; Davis 2012). Even then, not all breaches of international agreements are observed as often only those breaches that trigger a dispute can be easily identified.[11] Because it is nearly impossible to obtain a representative sample of events that have led to compliance or noncompliance, it is difficult to evaluate effectiveness.

ICs offer researchers a window into understanding the performance of IOs.[12] By adjudicating disputes, interpreting the law, and broadcasting decisions, ICs reveal crucial information about state preferences. To see how this works, one must differentiate between different stages of compliance.

Scholars distinguish between two stages of compliance in international relations (Fisher 1981; Simmons 1998). First-order compliance is when a state abides by standing, substantive rules, often embodied in a treaty (Simmons 1998, 78). In the WTO, a government complies in this first sense if its trade policy and practice reflect its commitment to low trade barriers. In the domain of international investment, a government first-order complies if it upholds its commitments to refrain from expropriating foreign assets. And with respect to the inter-American human rights system, a state complies when it prohibits torture and forced disappearances in its territory.

When a state fails to comply with treaty terms, disputes commonly arise. International organizations often contain formal mechanisms for dealing with these disputes. The WTO Dispute Settlement Mechanism handles interstate conflicts over trade barriers and related breaches of the multilateral trade regime. The International Centre for the Settlement of Investment Disputes (ICSID), likewise, helps to resolve conflicts between states and firms over issues like expropriation, contract enforcement, and other investment concerns. And the Inter-American Court of Human Rights (IACHR) evaluates alleged cases of torture, disappearances, political imprisonment, and other breaches in its member states. When these courts determine a state has broken its international obligations—first-order noncompliance—it typically issues an adverse legal ruling. Adverse rulings require the state to correct the violation.

Second-order compliance is when a state adjusts its policy and practice after an initial violation, often in response to the authoritative decision of a third party (Simmons 1998, 78). In the WTO, a government complies in this second sense if, upon losing a legal dispute, it removes the illegal trade barrier. With respect to investment treaties, a government may have expropriated foreign assets and may subsequently lose an ICSID ruling. It second-order complies when it makes appropriate restitutions through compensation and damages. For the IACHR, second-order compliance may mean making restitutions to families, revising policies, and penalizing officials responsible for human rights violations. In short, first-order compliance refers to how a governments' policies and behavior conform with their primary legal obligations. But they sometimes break these commitments. This is where an international court, arbitration body or dispute settlement panel may step in and instruct them to correct violations. If a government abides by the IC's ruling, it is second-order complying.

Distinguishing the different stages of compliance helps disentangle the selection problem. As noted above, it is ordinarily problematic to infer that an IO is effective by observing that governments first-order comply with their treaty terms. By contrast, second-order compliance lends special insight into institutional effectiveness. By focusing on situations where a state violates its substantive obligations and then adjusts its policy or practice to correct the violation—second-order compliance—we *can* draw inferences about effectiveness. This is what makes international legal disputes so revealing.[13]

Governments are faced with second-order compliance decisions only in special circumstances. For one, they must be sued and found guilty of treaty violations. Only when it is clear—by legal verdict or otherwise—that a government has broken its original treaty commitments does that government make a decision on whether or not to second-order comply. A government's history of such decisions reveals its preferences. The adverse ruling provides a reasonable basis for assuming that a respondent government prefers not to abide by its treaty obligations. In other words, the circumstances that led to a second-order compliance decision demonstrate the government's underlying reluctance to follow international obligations.

Lawsuits at the ECJ, for instance, often result from a multistage procedure in which governments defend against allegations that they have violated EU law. The procedure resolves violations that have arisen from simple reporting failures (König and Mäder 2013) well before they are considered by judges. Only the most intractable cases persist to an adverse ruling. At this point, a losing respondent government has a choice. On the one hand, it can correct the violation in response to the ruling, against its original preferences, assuming those preferences are steady over time. On the other, it can maintain the treaty-violating policy or practice according to its original preferences, ignoring the legal ruling. When a government corrects a breach in spite of its preference, this points to the influence of the institution. ICs therefore reveal information that cuts through the selection problem.

There is another way in which ICs lend insight into effectiveness, which concerns their role as information providers. The judicial process helps with the detection problem discussed above. This service may be particularly crucial in enforcing trade commitments among democracies, since countries tend to obfuscate their trade barriers (Kono 2006). Once a government is found guilty of violating its treaty obligations—that is, first-order noncompliance—the legal process systematically distinguishes second-order compliance from noncompliance. Not only do courts convey information to the community of states about the legality of one government's policy but litigation also publicizes respondent government interests that produced the initial violation. For instance,

Davis (2012) demonstrates that litigation also conveys the plaintiff government's resolve to enforce the law and take a hard-line stance to protect the interests of domestic stakeholders. Rulings highlight infractions and explicitly differentiate legal from illegal policies. Courts broadcast information that governments and private actors—both domestic and foreign—can leverage.

In international trade, these functions are apparent. For example, in the infamous Boeing-Airbus WTO disputes over airplane manufacturing subsidies, the Dispute Settlement Body found both the United States and European Union to be in violation of their obligations. Litigation revealed the extent to which industry stakeholders influenced US and EU trade policy. And the WTO rulings offered a public legal interpretation of the nuanced Agreement on Subsidies and Countervailing Measures. Similarly, in the dispute between the US and Canada over the latter's magazine tax, the WTO panel clarified the boundary between an illegal trade barrier and an acceptable cultural exemption. Until that point, the line between trade protection and cultural preservation had gone undefined.

Moreover, adverse legal rulings force a losing defendant government to respond. Some governments adjust their policies and behavior to implement a ruling; others do not. By specifying the requirements for implementation, ICs provide criteria against which one can evaluate second-order compliance and define a success rate. Second-order compliance and defiance are both observable. By contrast, with first-order compliance, we rarely know how to measure "compliance opportunities" and therefore cannot know the success rate for an international treaty. In summary, by revealing government preferences and by defining a subset of cases in which second-order compliance and noncompliance are both clearly observable, international courts do offer insight into institutional effects.

2.1.4 Selection forces

While court rulings and second-order compliance lend insight into the force of international institutions, this logic has limits. Several potential sources of selection bias may complicate inference. The first of these concerns initial violations of international law. First-order noncompliance—that is, breaking treaty commitments—reflects the influence of domestic stakeholders. For example, many WTO disputes arise because a defendant created trade barriers to help politically influential industries (e.g., US steel tariffs to protect domestic steel producers). Those same domestic groups are likely to oppose downstream compliance when the WTO rules against the trade barrier. If a stakeholder has enough clout to induce initial violations, it might also be expected to block compliance with legal rulings that censure the violation. As a result, adjudication tends to isolate "hard" cases where it will be most difficult for the IC to encourage compliance. This research design may tend to underestimate IC effectiveness.

Second, only some suspected violations of international law provoke lawsuits. Plaintiff countries decide whether or not to challenge a potential defendant's violation, and because litigation is costly, they choose carefully. One possibility is that complainants prefer to sue in cases when their probability of obtaining compliance is high and they avoid suing when the probability is low. When compliance is unlikely, lawsuits are merely a waste of resources and a prospective complainant will prefer to avoid the cost. In this telling, lawsuits—and thus adverse rulings—are more common in the conflicts where there is a high probability that the defendant complies. This form of selection bias would cut in the opposite direction from the one discussed above—adjudication isolates the "easy" cases where the court is more likely to induce compliance.

This second potential form of selection bias is not likely to be a serious concern. Davis (2012) shows that in the WTO, the decision to litigate is systematically driven by the plaintiff's domestic politics; lawsuits are not aimed merely at recovering trade with foreign markets. Delivering a "win" is not the principle goal, and plaintiff governments may sue even when they have little hope of obtaining full compliance from obstinate defendants. Rather, complainant governments sometimes choose litigation at the WTO as a costly signal to key domestic constituencies. Domestic groups view these trade disputes as evidence the government is taking a hard-line stance to protect their interests. In short, the selection of lawsuits may be driven by different factors than the defendant's probability of compliance. Evidence from Davis (2012) dispels the suspicion that complainant decisions to litigate at the WTO select for the "easy" cases.

A third potential source of selection bias concerns judicial discretion. One prominent idea in the literature on IOs is that delegation to courts should create a space where regular politics and power disparities do not shape how the law is interpreted and applied. Despite these aspirations, some international judges or panelists may selectively exercise their authority. In the ECJ, judges are particularly wary of backlash from member states (Carrubba and Gabel 2015). Resistance could take the form of recontracting (Alter 2008) or member states reining in the court's authority (Garrett, Kelemen, and Schulz 1998). In order to promote the *apparent* effectiveness of the institution, judges might choose to rule against defendant states only when the chances for subsequent compliance are high. Not all defendants are equally amenable to adverse legal rulings. Some may be more defiant, particularly when the issue being adjudicated is politically sensitive. If international judges rule against compliance-prone defendant governments and in favor of obstinate ones, then they could boost second-order compliance rates.

There are observable implications for this third possible form of selection. Adverse rulings should be more common for minor or politically tepid issues. By contrast, on major, politically controversial issues, judges should tend, instead, to rule in favor of defendant governments. Similarly, judicial discretion might lead to fewer adverse rulings against the most obstinate or powerful countries. These potential tendencies highlight the need to account for *cross-national* differences in adverse rulings and whether any such differences explain compliance rates. The following section examines domestic political sources of compliance and noncompliance, offering a way to tease apart these cross-national differences.

2.2 Domestic politics of compliance

2.2.1 Defining domestic constraints

Governments have incentives both to uphold and to violate their international commitments. Abroad, there is pressure from other governments to cooperate on economic issues. For example, governments pressure their trading partners to maintain liberal trade policies such as low tariffs on imported goods. Reciprocal rewards and punishments encourage states to maintain cooperative policies in international affairs. But at home, state leaders experience divergent pressures from domestic constituencies. Especially with economic issues, some domestic actors support deeper international cooperation (Dai 2007) while other constituencies press leadership to enact policies that undercut these aims—for example, trade barriers to protect an industry. The way these divergent domestic pressures shape international affairs depends on the preferences of key domestic actors, the power they exert in government, and the political institutions they navigate. This section will unpack the domestic political factors that shape compliance and international cooperation.

Within a country, political actors have divergent preferences over international cooperation. In the domain of international security, there are "hawks" and "doves" whose opposing preferences are driven by different strategic calculations, ideological orientations, or historical allegiances. Similarly, international human rights are often the subject of contrasting domestic positions (Simmons 2009). For example, some domestic groups advocate a zero-tolerance stance, bringing cooperation on human rights to the forefront of their states' foreign policy agendas. They may press leadership to support active missions in regions where violations occur. Others prefer less enforcement. When human rights treaties run counter to local morals, domestic groups may actively undermine their implementation (Vilán 2018). Nevertheless, on few issues are domestic groups more acutely in opposition with one another than they are over a country's engagement with the global economy.

International economic issues generate deeply divided preferences precisely because of their distributive implications. These cleavages are apparent in international trade. As the Heckscher-Ohlin framework makes evident, an individual's position in the domestic economy should shape his or her experience with increasing exposure to trade. Some will be made relatively worse off and others better off. This, in turn, drives preferences, with some people wanting trade protection and others wanting trade liberalization. Many interest groups represent import-competing industries and prefer policies that secure targeted protection. Trade liberalization can pose a threat to these groups by expanding imports, increasing competition, and driving down prices of the goods they produce. Exporter industries, by contrast, tend to support reciprocal trade liberalization. Far from a threat, liberalization brings efficiency gains, and when foreign governments reciprocate, exporters enjoy sales to wider markets.

Both importer- and exporter-focused interest groups have strong incentives to politically mobilize. Mobilization takes the form of pressuring representatives to adjust trade policy according to their interests (Grossman and Helpman 1992), which have traditionally been understood to fall along factor or industry lines. Firms, in particular, lobby their governments to defend policies that benefit them.

Lobbying activity need not fall neatly along factor or industry lines. There are also intra-industry divisions over trade, in which some firms will support a trade-liberalizing measure that others in the same industry oppose (I. Kim 2017; Osgood 2016). Intra-industry divisions tend to be pronounced where there is more product differentiation, pointing to a far greater divergence in demands over trade policy than traditional factor-based models might indicate (Osgood 2017). Regardless of the cleavages along which protectionist and liberalizing demands align, these lobbying efforts have been a key driver of US and European trade enforcement. As Shaffer (2003) has highlighted, the private-public partnership between firms and the US Trade Representative (USTR) helps to explain the targets and priorities of US trade enforcement efforts. More recent research demonstrates that patterns of expenditures by firms on lobbying shape US monitoring and enforcement of WTO agreement terms (Brutger 2017; Ryu and Stone 2018). Whether firms' advocacy efforts "pay off" and are converted into trade policy depends on how responsive policy-makers are and the ensuing political process.

Voters too have preferences over trade policy, but compared to interest groups or firms, their positions are not well formed or informed (Hiscox 2006). Trade policy can be technocratic and inaccessible to voters. Savvy politicians may even exploit these characteristics to avoid electoral repercussions (Kono 2006). As consumers, voters might prefer the availability of lower-cost goods that trade liberalization brings, but they face well-known problems in mobilizing. Ideological considerations further blur public perceptions and trade preferences (Guisinger 2017). Compared to industry and sector-specific interests, voters-as-consumers are largely thought to be less successful in shaping trade policy (Kono 2009).

Politicians vary in their own inherent preferences, as well as in the electoral pressure to which they are exposed (Carey and Shugart 1995). Politicians in different branches of government experience domestic pressure in various ways, depending on the composition of their constituencies. Scholars have long argued that legislators prefer more protectionist trade policies than prime ministers or presidents do (Lohmann and O'Halloran 1994; Mansfield and Busch 1995). Legislators respond to local, narrow constituencies who often benefit from targeted protection.[14] By contrast, executives, with their broad constituencies, are thought to be more sensitive to the aggregate benefits of international trade cooperation. Subsequent work has cast doubt on the relative preferences of presidents, senators, and representatives in the context of US trade politics (Ehrlich 2009; Karol 2007). Yet the durable insight of this literature is that across different offices, politicians experience divergent pressures on trade policy that vary with the composition of their constituencies.

Exogenous economic and political shocks can change the relative power of different interest groups and voters. An economic downturn that acutely harms an industry may lead groups to pressure their politicians for policies that benefit them. Typically, these groups are highly informed about whether current trade policy is helping or hurting their business. WTO disputes make abundantly clear how shifts in economic conditions can spur trade protection. For example, when the Canadian magazine industry suffered unprecedented decline, industry officials urged parliament to impose a controversial tax to stave off foreign competition.[15] Subjected to increased pressure from mobilized industry groups, politicians often shift their preferences. Similarly, political shocks can shift different groups' relative power. An upcoming election can make politicians sensitive to preferences in a key electoral district. Due to shifting incentives, leadership turnover can raise the risk of treaty violations (Gray and Kucik 2017). Under these conditions, politicians are more likely to implement trade protection policies that provoke international disputes.

Countries vary in the degree to which political authority is concentrated within government. Autocratic governments are characterized by their highly concentrated nexuses of political power—there are minimal or no constraints on executive authority (e.g., China). In (quasi- or fully) democratic regimes, constraints on political power vary widely. Such variation depends on institutional checks on executive power, such as the presence of a unicameral or bicameral legislature and the fractionalization among political parties in the legislature (reflecting presumed preference heterogeneity). Another contributing factor is whether the party that controls the executive enjoys a majority in the legislature and the extent of that majority. When an executive faces an opposition legislature, the level of constraint varies with the fractionalization of the opposition. Taken together, domestic institutional and partisan divisions form *veto points* in government (Tsebelis 1995).

Democratic institutions and veto points capture different concepts. A country's level of democracy depends on voter access, civil liberties, political competition, and numerous other factors. Variation in veto points more narrowly reflects the constellation of constraints on power that political leadership faces. Nonetheless, for practical purposes, there is substantial overlap.

To see how veto players compare between regime types, consider a couple of examples: Viet Nam, in recent decades, has been considered an anocracy or autocratic regime (depending on the year). There are only modest constraints on executive power in Viet Nam; legislatures may be overwhelmingly dominated by members of the executive's party and exert little real force. In 2012, the country had a very low veto points score, reflecting the fact that, despite a constitution establishing legislative institutions, it remains for all practical purposes a one-party communist dictatorship, according to the widely-used Polity index and country reports (Marshall and Jaggers 2012). By contrast, take the United States, which is ranked as a robust democracy on the Polity index. As in other full democracies, there are significant constraints on executive power that come from legislative bodies and variations in partisan alignment. In the US, veto points are higher in the years that different parties hold the presidency and one or both legislative bodies than when the branches of government are held by the same party.

The degree to which political authority is divided matters for policy formation and reform. As Tsebelis (2000) explains, "every new policy outcome is a departure from a previous policy outcome . . . For the status quo to change, a certain number of individual or collective decision-makers have to agree to this change" (441). Where divisions in authority are substantial, it is harder to change existing policies because more political actors can block change. Institutional constraints on power—formal checks and balances—limit policy-making. For instance, in the US, treaties negotiated under executive authority must be ratified by Congress. Likewise, veto points arise from the partisan composition of the government. When the legislature features a relatively strong opposition party or many opposition parties, there are also significant obstacles to policy change. In parliamentary settings, policy proposals typically have to be approved by the relevant actors within each party of the government coalition. When coalitions are tenuous, there is a higher risk that MPs defect on parliamentary votes. This absence of internal cohesion generates more veto points. As veto points increase, political authority becomes more fragmented and policy more difficult to change

(Henisz 2000; Tsebelis 2002). Thus veto players theory expects policy stability—no significant change in comparison to the status quo—to be caused by many veto players, by incongruence in the policy preferences among them, or by the absence of internal cohesion in any collective veto player (reflecting the decision rules governing them).

Veto points determine how responsive governments are to shifts in preferences and power. When a government has low veto points, only a few political actors must coordinate, and it is easy to change policies in response to shifting preferences or exogenous conditions. Autocratic regimes are relatively agile, as a change in circumstances can lead to even dramatic policy reversals. Conversely, when a government has many veto points, policy change is difficult because it requires coordination among many political actors. Democratic governments with the most institutional checks and partisan divisions rarely pivot as circumstances shift. Only major changes in industry preferences or political power can alter policy. It is well established that domestic veto players and political divisions often impede the adoption of international treaties, particularly trade-liberalizing agreements (Milner and Rosendorff 1997; Martin 2000; Mansfield, Milner, and Pevehouse 2007). As the following section details, these same factors have downstream implications for international cooperation.

2.2.2 How domestic constraints impact international cooperation

A government's domestic politics drives its international economic behavior (see, e.g., Keohane and Milner 1996; Martin 2000). The domestic divisions of authority that are pivotal to democracy affect international cooperation in several ways: First, domestic veto players constrain governments when they join international agreements. Milner (1997) shows that formal international cooperation hinges on the consent of disparate actors within a country: the executive, the legislature, and domestic interest groups must come together to support an international agreement. If one or more of these do not endorse a treaty, the treaty is apt to fail and the country reverts to the status quo. When there are more checks and balances between multiple branches of government, treaties are less likely to be ratified because there is a greater risk that some domestic actors are willing to block the agreement. So "[m]ultiple veto players . . . narrow the set of [treaty] proposals that can be domestically ratified" (Simmons 2009, 69). Similarly, legislatures with many political parties, or parties whose preferences differ substantially, are less likely to clear the hurdle to ratification. For instance, as the European states negotiated the terms of regional economic integration, governments with many domestic constraints faced difficulty in securing consent from their national parliaments (Benz 2004). Whether domestic constraints are partisan, institutional, or both, they make it more challenging for governments to adopt new international agreements.

Domestic veto players can limit the expansion of international obligations whenever there are significant divergences in preferences and avenues for groups to exert political influence in service of these preferences. International trade is particularly susceptible, as discussed above. This goes back to the fundamental structure of the cooperation problem: when international cooperation resembles a prisoner's dilemma and different domestic groups hold preferences antithetical to one another, domestic veto points can matter a great deal.

This bears out in trade politics. In a given country, different domestic groups tend to hold conflicting preferences over trade policy.[16] Opposing preferences translate into disagreements about trade policy. Starting from a status quo of unilateral protectionism, as has characterized the trade politics of many countries in the years preceding the Generalized Agreement on Tariffs and Trade (GATT), veto players have had a chilling effect. Divisions in power have significantly constrained trade liberalization (Milner and Rosendorff 1997; Mansfield, Milner, and Pevehouse 2007). The more veto points, the greater the risk that one domestic group thwarts efforts to form international agreements. When governments do succeed in signing treaties, domestic constraints make it more difficult for them to implement their obligations—for example, to correctly adopt laws and regulations (Mansfield and Milner 2012). This same logic carries over to the revision of trade agreements. For instance, WTO obligations have expanded over multiple negotiation rounds. Domestic veto players should likewise make it more difficult for countries to reach an agreement and to implement new requirements.

Once a country has joined a trade agreement, its multiple veto points tend to support compliance with that treaty (Milner and Rosendorff 1997). Interest groups often pressure politicians for trade protections that benefit their targeted industry, sector, or region. Sometimes the protection they demand violates trade agreement terms. Governments with substantial divisions in authority are thought to be less responsive to industry demands for new trade protections. Interest groups (or firms) will have to persuade many political actors to support a new policy. Veto players make it more difficult for a government to reverse status quo trade policies. Trade agreements formed by states with more political constraints are thought to represent more credible commitments about future policy than those by governments with few (Mansfield, Milner, and Rosendorff 2002). By locking cooperative arrangements in place, veto players should improve a government's first-order compliance.

Treaty violations can come about through multiple avenues. And accordingly, the status quo tendency can be stronger or weaker depending on the form of policy in question (Bowen 2015). Administrative and legislative measures differ, with the former activating fewer domestic veto players than the latter. Each country follows its own trade policy process with corresponding variation in domestic constraints. For instance, in the US, firms that stand to benefit from a new policy (e.g., antidumping duty) often lobby the USTR, who works in cooperation with legislative and executive branches to provide protection. Industry groups or other interests may directly lobby members of Congress to pass beneficial legislation (e.g., subsidies or technical barriers to trade) or the president to impose tariffs (e.g., safeguards). In the EU, the European Commission takes a leading role in initiating external trade policy in consultation with private stakeholders and member states (Shaffer 2003). Regulatory measures that deliver targeted protection—like safeguards or antidumping duties—must be passed by the European Council and the European Parliament. Not all trade disputes concern new trade policies that deviate from a cooperative status quo. Some disputes question the legality of long-standing policies that predate the trade agreement. In these instances, domestic veto players may not promote international cooperation at all.

Beyond locking in compliance with international agreements, domestic political divisions affect enforcement. Governments do occasionally violate treaty terms, and aggrieved countries may choose to pursue legal action. In the context of the WTO, Davis (2012) demonstrates that a plaintiff government's decision to litigate, rather than pursue trade grievances through informal bilateral means, serves as a signal of support to domestic stakeholders. Executives that face significant domestic constraints—and thus less capacity to reach informal compromises with foreign states—are more likely to use international litigation as a political tool. Litigation is a visible demonstration that foreign treaty violations, and the costs they incur, will not be tolerated. Domestic institutions on the plaintiff's side shape international law enforcement.

On the other side, defendant governments are likewise constrained by domestic political institutions. While divisions of power in plaintiff governments favor increasing the use of international legal remedies, those same factors tend to impose limits on the effectiveness of international legal disputes. Defendant governments must contend with the constraining effect of domestic veto players as they respond to these enforcement efforts.[17] While veto players decrease the risk that a government will violate its trade agreements, they form an imperfect safeguard. Shifting political or economic conditions can lead to breaches. And not all trade violations are easily detected. Democratic governments are known to use more discrete and technocratic forms of trade protection that deliver economic benefits to targeted groups while evading public attention (Kono 2006). Domestic constraints in defendant states can blunt the impact of legal enforcement.

When a government violates its substantive international commitments, political divisions make it more difficult for a country to restore international cooperation. Sometimes reversing the violation may require nullifying an old law or passing a new one. In international trade, political actors who benefit from a trade barrier have a strong incentive to obstruct reform. For instance, legislators might block a law that implements a WTO ruling. This can be seen in the abovementioned WTO dispute between the US and Canada over trade barriers on periodicals, known as the "magazine dispute." Partisan fighting between Canada's Tory and Liberal parties and between Canada's upper and lower houses of Parliament obstructed compliance with the ruling.[18] When a state has many divisions, special interest groups are more likely to find a sympathetic ear in government (Ehrlich 2011). Second-order compliance becomes less likely as formal domestic veto points increase.

Governments that lose international legal disputes face especially pronounced obstacles to second-order compliance. Two mechanisms contribute. First, international adjudication increases the publicity of the defendant's violation, raising the stakes of the dispute. Rulings supply information to potential domestic stakeholders. By disentangling the law on a particular violation, rulings clarify how the treaty terms should be interpreted. It may be more difficult for the government to grant similar trade protections to that industry in the future. No longer can that state plead ignorance or point to ambiguity in the treaties. Where perhaps some policies might have been thought to evade enforcement, legal rulings publicly declare what constitutes a violation. This can expand the defendant government's stakes in the dispute due to the downstream consequences.

Second, the heightened scrutiny of an international legal dispute and the public rulings they produce may entrench divergent domestic preferences. The process to withdraw a trade policy found to be in violation of international law can differ from the process by which the initial policy came about. Despite fixed political institutions, different veto players are activated at each step. At the policy adoption stage, interests may be fairly narrow. Other stakeholders might not pay attention to the matter, and few veto players would be activated. Once an international dispute unfolds and foreign judges order a government to withdraw a policy, more veto players are activated. Rulings exacerbate controversy because they have distributive implications, producing divergent domestic consequences for different groups (Rogowski 1989; Hiscox 2002). By benefiting one segment of a population while hurting another, these rulings fuel disagreement over compliance (Garrett, Kelemen, and Schulz 1998). Domestic groups who were not affected by the initial policy may be drawn into the dispute. Adjudication draws the attention of numerous pro- and anti-compliance constituencies who then have a compelling incentive to work through political institutions. Groups that might otherwise have paid little heed to the original policy develop preferences over it by virtue of the international dispute.

This can be seen with enforcement efforts at the WTO DSM. Consider a ruling that dismantles a barrier to trade. The ruling demands that the defendant government revoke protections that an influential import-competing industry group previously enjoyed, creating a loss (at least in the short run). Second-order compliance is seen as a harm—one that the domestic group is remiss to accept. The group then has a strong incentive to take a hard-line stance in opposing compliance. When defendant states do not comply with legal rulings, the WTO can authorize cross-industry retaliation (e.g., if the import-competing US steel industry retains trade protections, foreign retaliation is targeted at US agricultural exporters). Cross-industry penalties makes previously disinterested domestic groups into stakeholders.

A long-running WTO dispute between Brazil and the US illustrates this dynamic. Brazil, a major cotton exporter, initiated the dispute (DS267) in 2002 against specific provisions of the US cotton program. In September 2004, a WTO dispute settlement panel found that certain US agricultural support payments and guarantees—including (1) payments to cotton producers under the marketing loan and countercyclical programs and (2) export credit guarantees—were inconsistent with WTO commitments. The programs in question were initially put in place through legislation.[19] Despite the many formal veto players that could have blocked their initial passage, they garnered little attention. After a lengthy litigation process, the panel judges sided with Brazil: the US cotton program constituted a violation of its WTO obligations. When the US attempts to reform the program were found to be insufficient, a compliance panel authorized Brazil to retaliate. The dispute drew the attention of many other domestic stakeholders, including industries that enjoyed similar subsidies (anti-compliance, including other US program crops) and those that might be targeted by Brazil's retaliation (pro-compliance, including holders of US patents and copyrights). Those groups applied pressure on legislators to preserve or withdraw the subsidies. More formal veto players were therefore activated at the compliance stage. There was little legislative progress, and the US eventually negotiated a controversial bilateral settlement with Brazil.

In summary, the same mechanisms that make international courts useful also entrench anti-compliance domestic groups. Rulings incentivize these groups to use all political levers at their disposal to obstruct second-order compliance. This may entail urging legislators to veto legislative amendments or petitioning administrative agencies for continued protection.

Faced with an adverse ruling, leaders decide whether and when to second-order comply. This decision is shaped by short-term economic conditions and long-term institutional constraints. Leaders who face acute exogenous shocks have little short-term *incentive* to comply with rulings. Leaders who face more domestic veto points experience greater institutional and partisan political *obstacles* to complying. Conditional on going to trial and losing the case, a leader who faces more veto points at home has an incentive to wait for the exogenous shock to pass. Rather than complying immediately, a leader who faces more veto points, and thus high obstacles to compliance, is more likely to violate the international agreement until political or economic conditions change.

Hypothesis 1: Conditional on a government violating a treaty, domestic political divisions should be associated with less compliance.

This leads to an additional implication. International legal disputes address a range of policies. Some address whether a defendant's legislation is consistent with international obligations. When international judges find a violation, this usually means that legislation must be revised within the defendant's legislative body. Such revisions require consent from many legislators—compliance is subject to multiple veto points. In these instances, domestic groups may be able to lobby successfully against compliance. By contrast, other international disputes concern policies that can be modified through unilateral acts (e.g., an executive order or an administrative measure) alone. For example, a government's ministry of trade or department of commerce can adjust tariffs, quotas, etc. under the direction of state leadership in order to bring that government's trade policy into compliance. These types of measures are subject to fewer *formal* veto points, yielding a simpler compliance process. Court rulings that demand new legislation (or amendments) generate a more complicated compliance process that opens more avenues for domestic political obstruction than do rulings that require administrative measures or executive acts alone. This leads to the next hypothesis:

Hypothesis 2: Governments are more likely to comply with adverse international rulings when administrative measures are required than when legislative measures are required.

A related implication is that we should see domestic political constraints having a stronger negative impact on the compliance process when legislative measures are required than when only administrative measures are needed. In other words, the risk that one key player thwarts compliance is higher when participation from a larger set of political actors is required.

Formal institutional veto players are not the only constraints shaping compliance. Even when a disputed policy can be modified through unilateral acts (e.g., an executive order or an administrative measure), domestic divisions matter. Executive decisions are influenced by political considerations. To see why domestic divisions also impose *informal* constraints, consider the political context. Executives are reluctant to provoke resistance from other political actors. Those other actors might later exercise veto power regarding the same policy issue or other issues where an executive needs support. In other words, where veto players can promise to reciprocate by imposing future constraints, political leaders account for the long game.[20]

Many studies of veto players focus on single-shot decisions: they account for which actors can obstruct a given policy proposal at a specific time. I extend the fundamental insight of veto players theory to over-time decisions. In political systems with many veto players, there is a greater long-run threat of obstruction. Even if a given policy proposal is not strictly vulnerable, political actors sometime behave as if the decision is subject to many veto players. In these long-term calculations, veto players can still cast a shadow, as illustrated by US institutions.

One important trade policy procedure in the United States demonstrates this dynamic. The US Trade Act of 1974 grants the president authority to impose and remove trade barriers. Section 201 of the act (19 U.S.C. § 2251) allows for temporary "safeguard" measures to be imposed in order to help a suffering domestic industry adjust to import competition. Ordinarily, trade associations or firms initiate an investigation in order to obtain temporary trade protection. The US International Trade Commission (ITC) assesses the claim and determines whether there is a compelling justification. If the ITC makes an affirmative injury determination, then it may recommend an increase in import duties, a quota on the products at issue, or a modification to or imposition of any other restriction on imports. Those recommendations are submitted to the president for approval. The president can decide whether to enact the recommended trade protections or not. In other words, based on the report and recommendations of the ITC, the executive has formal unilateral authority to enact a safeguard.

But that is not the end of the process. The president is required to submit a report to Congress, describing the action he or she selected and the reasons for it. If the president's choice differs from ITC recommendations, Congress may enact a resolution of disapproval. A formal statement of legislative disapproval carries important consequences. In such a case, the ITC's recommendation becomes the trade remedy, and the president must officially implement it within the month. This means that Congress weighs in as a post hoc veto player. Congress can use its authority to overturn presidential decisions on safeguards. Knowing this threat exists, a president may anticipate congressional preferences and choose a safeguard action that elicits legislative support. Veto players need not act immediately to impose political constraints.

Another way to see how divisions in political authority generate indirect constraints is by considering reciprocity. The US president enjoys the authority to introduce and remove trade barriers such as import tariffs through executive order without consent from Congress under section 122 of the Trade Act of 1974. However, this formal authority is not without qualification. Using executive power absent the support of party leadership in the legislature could undermine future party support. In divided governments, the executive and the legislature interact strategically. Most executives cannot afford to ignore the preferences of legislators, even when those legislators do not wield a formal veto *over that particular issue*. Rather, they can exercise veto power on other related policy issues. For example, suppose an executive complies with an adverse WTO ruling by removing a safeguard against the party's prevailing preferences. If that executive then attempts to enact a new international trade agreement, the legislators may be less willing to ratify it to give the treaty effect. In other words, the leader who ignores legislators on one trade policy may have difficulty obtaining support on another issue where legislators do enjoy formal veto power. Strategic interaction and reciprocity may mean that actors in a government who cannot directly block compliance with international legal rulings may nonetheless systematically cast a shadow of power that cosntrains a leader's decisions.

This highlights another implication of my theory: *delayed compliance*. Executives who face more domestic veto points cannot easily obtain changes in trade policies from legislatures. Rather than comply promptly with international rulings, executives may be expected to work to obtain support from co-partisans or legislative leadership. Executives should be more likely to prolong the use of trade barriers that can be formally changed unilaterally, even when doing so constitutes a violation, until they garner sufficient support. In some international disputes, leaders may also postpone compliance until they face fewer veto players and the political process is easier. This leads to the following hypothesis:

Hypothesis 3: Conditional on a government violating a treaty, domestic political divisions should be associated with delayed compliance or prolonged periods of noncompliance.

The first and third hypotheses lay out distinct predictions that help to unpack the mechanisms linking domestic political constraints to compliance. Although we cannot ultimately identify the set of preferences held by the different domestic actors in each international dispute, as those preferences filter through political systems, they create observable results.

The first considers whether governments ultimately comply or not, during the years under study, without regard to the timeline explicitly set by an IC. A finding in support of only H1 would suggest the logistical hurdles of divided government create insurmountable obstacles to compliance in some countries, locking in violations of international law. This is largely consistent with bureaucratic capacity explanations of compliance (Chayes and Chayes 1993; Börzel et al. 2010). According to a capacity explanation, governments fail to comply because they cannot garner resources or coordinate agencies to implement international rulings. Noncompliance is viewed as inadvertent rather than an intentional decision to violate international commitments.

The third hypothesis, by contrast, considers whether governments adopt compliance measures by the deadline set by an IC. For example, many WTO rulings set an eighteen-month window; after that deadline elapses, any compliance activity is considered delayed. A finding in support of only H3 would suggest that opportunistic behavior is more common; it would suggest that there are some domestic actors with varying degrees of influence that seek to block compliance. Delayed compliance is a deliberate move by certain key players within a domestic government to "buy time." It is the constellation of political conditions, institutional or partisan, that determines whether they succeed in doing so. Thus governments use the timing of compliance activity opportunistically: they can benefit by retaining a policy violation longer while forestalling international enforcement.

Evidence in support of both the first and third hypotheses would point to a mixture of inadvertent and deliberate compliance problems. Some governments drag out disputes to navigate a challenging domestic political pathway. Delays occur because government leadership must work to obtain consent from key stakeholders in order to implement an IC ruling.

These hypotheses use veto players theory to give a parsimonious account for why some governments readily comply with the rulings of ICs while others refuse. They capture the fundamental balancing act that

governments face when applying international law. International rulings impose foreign decisions on sovereign states. Political competition
among diverse domestic interests drive a state's willingness to acquiesce.
Stakeholders in trade disputes such as unions, firms, and industry groups
cannot directly change trade policy themselves; they must lobby officials
and obtain the support of political actors who then work through domestic institutions. For instance, suppose an IC strikes down an industry subsidy as a violation of a trade agreement. The industry might want
to preserve this helpful but illegal subsidy and thus opposes compliance.
But in order to convert that preference into policy, the group must con-
vince a legislator that its preference is more important than countervailing considerations, and that legislator must vote on the group's behalf to
block a policy reform. When domestic stakeholders lobby against compliance, their preferences are converted into policy only when political
institutions allow. Veto players are thus pivotal for blocking or enabling
the policy reforms that drive a state's compliance.

2.2.3 Domestic constraints and institutional design

The preceding section asked whether international courts are effective
in shaping government policy and practice and argued that their impact
hinges on the domestic politics in litigant states. It left unexplored how
the design of the IC affects performance. Different institutional designs
may lend themselves to higher compliance rates and potentially greater
impacts on state behavior. Likewise, some designs may open up greater
opportunity for domestic veto players to obstruct their operation. This
section will address this concern.

States often design international institutions with flexibility mechanisms in order to mitigate compliance problems (Abbott and Snidal 1998;
Koremenos, Lipson, and Snidal 2001; Carrubba 2005). Political and economic conditions shift in unforeseen ways, sometimes forcing government leaders to face an unsavory decision. States can break their international commitments and accept penalties from foreign governments.
Foreign penalties may take the form of proportionate retaliation or a
sullied reputation. Or they abide by international commitments and accept domestic fallout. Domestic penalties might take the form of economic repercussions—for example, weaker performance in an import-
competing sector—or political repercussions, such as the loss of electoral
support from key constituencies. Flexibility mechanisms permit gov-

ernments to sometimes violate treaty obligations, giving them the wiggle room to avoid such a dilemma. By permitting short-term violations under certain circumstances, flexibility mechanisms can enhance long-term cooperation if they prevent countries from abandoning their international agreements (see, e.g., Bagwell and Staiger 1999; Bown 2002; Kucik and Reinhardt 2008). The architects of trade agreements face a delicate balancing act (see, e.g., Pelc 2009, 2013; Johns 2014; Johns and Peritz 2015). Too much flexibility and the regime becomes useless; too little and governments may abandon the international regime altogether. In general, flexibility mechanisms are successful if they restore long-term compliance.

Flexibility mechanisms take many forms. Commonly, treaties include escape clauses and exceptions. This is particularly common in trade agreements (Kucik 2012; Pelc 2016). Governments activate these legal mechanisms in order to relax or temporarily abrogate their primary international obligations. But specific exceptions written into a treaty are not the only way states exercise flexibility. Dispute settlement mechanisms are institutional features that some scholars believe increase flexibility and thereby improve the stability of an institution (see, e.g., Rosendorff 2005). Formal dispute settlement can provide flexibility to states. These mechanisms enable governments to break their commitments, engage in lawsuits, and pay compensation before returning to compliance.

Like international agreements, courts vary in their design. Some ICs are designed to be relatively strong. Countries delegate significant authority to these institutions, and their rulings demand meaningful concessions from respondent states. As Johns (2015) demonstrates, these highly legalized international courts are most successful in promoting interstate cooperation when they rule on a precise body of law where states' obligations are clear.

Other courts are weaker. Governments entrust them with less authority to make decisions, and such ICs allow states more leeway when enforcing international law. They may be less legalized and demand only modest concessions from respondent states. The degree to which courts grant flexibility to disputing governments varies. States accused of breaking their international commitments may have more opportunity to seek negotiated settlement before resorting to litigation. Once they enter the litigation process, those same governments may also enjoy more control over the dispute timeline and the legal stages undertaken. Flexibility in the design of the ICs themselves can give governments much-needed leeway. Such designs can enable countries to address the domestic political or economic conditions that produced an interstate dispute in the first place.

The WTO DSM is designed with a variety of flexibility features. It allows respondents to significantly prolong the legal process and delay compliance without penalty: there are no retroactive damages owed to a complainant for the time that an illegal trade barrier remained in place (Brewster 2011). These flexibility features have significant implications for the domestic politics of compliance. On the one hand, they serve to accommodate the domestic obstacles a defendant faces when attempting to bring its policy into compliance. On the other hand, this also means that a defendant has an incentive to draw out legal proceedings deliberately—they file appeals, negotiate extensions to the compliance deadline, enter into noncompliance proceedings, and fight retaliation requests by the complainant. Delay strategies may be particularly advantageous when a respondent state faces domestic pressure to defy the court. Governments can delay through these legal means to pacify anti-compliance groups.

This points back to the underlying debate about the drivers of noncompliance. The relationship between domestic veto players and noncompliance could be explained in two ways. On the one hand, compliance problems might be due to capacity limitations. Governments fail to comply with legal rulings because they lack the ability or resources to do so. Previous literature has examined the role of legal capacity in WTO disputes. Guzman and Simmons (2004) argue that developing countries face resource limitations that render them less able to launch effective legal cases against potential trade law violators.[21] Likewise, developing countries in particular may lack the legal or bureaucratic capacity to effectively *defend* against lawsuits. If governments fail to comply simply because they do not have the domestic resources to implement a ruling, then domestic veto players just happen to correlate with inertia in the policy process. On the other hand, compliance problems may have political origins. Governments fail to comply with legal rulings because crucial political actors seek to block policy reform. Veto players are instrumental in the process. Noncompliance is then the result of a deliberate effort by some domestic actors.

To further differentiate these explanations, I look at how *flexibility* in the dispute settlement process is used. Governments with capacity problems cannot easily take advantage of complicated flexibility mechanisms. Such a government will have difficulty navigating an appeals process, requesting formal extensions of an implementation deadline, fighting noncompliance accusations, etc. Delays in compliance will reflect inaction rather than active legal maneuvering. If capacity problems were the main driver of noncompliance, then veto points would not be correlated with the number of legal stages.

By contrast, if noncompliance is the result of veto players seeking to obstruct policy reforms, then governments will actively use flexibility mechanisms. In the WTO DSM, this means prolonging the period of noncompliance by undertaking additional legal stages (appeals, extensions, etc.). Delays in compliance will reflect active legal maneuvering rather than inaction. So if noncompliance is chiefly driven by politically motivated actors, then domestic veto points should be correlated with more legal stages. This leads to the following hypothesis:

Hypothesis 4: Conditional on an adverse legal ruling, the more domestic constraints in the respondent government, the more legal stages are undertaken.

The decision to appeal an adverse ruling or extend an implementation deadline is rarely political in the same way that flagrantly disregarding the ruling would be. Those steps are legal under the WTO system and carry almost no penalty to the defendant. By contrast, flouting a ruling incurs reputation costs for the defendant government and invites retaliation. Governments that want to resist the WTO ruling should use legal routes to avoid policy reform.

If we simultaneously observe that governments with more veto players delay compliance and also pursue more legal stages, then we can conclude that leaders are constrained by veto players who actively thwart compliance. Simultaneously finding support for hypothesis 3 and hypothesis 4 suggests that governments use flexibility in ICs opportunistically. Once international institutions become involved in a dispute and policy change is mandated from outside the domestic system, a government can then hide behind the veto players logic to defy those international demands.

2.2.4 Alternative explanations

There are alternative explanations that deserve careful attention. The first is that compliance with international legal rulings depends on the political sensitivity of the dispute at hand. Some disputes concern particularly inflammatory issues. For example, several high-profile lawsuits at the WTO have challenged the EU prohibition on hormone-treated meat. In 1996, the US and Canada brought a legal complaint, arguing that the prohibition was a breach of its obligations under a number of WTO agreements on agriculture, sanitary and phytosanitary measures, and technical barriers to trade.[22] The WTO panel favored the complainants and upheld the ruling against the EU on appeal. The regulation of health and safety standards in the food supply remains a politically charged topic. As the science on the issue evolves, the European public remains leery of hormone-treated meat (Poletti and DeBievre 2014). The EU has largely disregarded the WTO's ruling. By this telling, noncompliance may have little to do with the many veto points in the EU or the access farmers have to influence the legislative process. Rather, noncompliance may have resulted because there is a widespread perception across the EU that the WTO decision is the wrong one—that it prioritizes free market principles over the health interests of Europeans.

Likewise, political sensitivity could drive compliance with rulings from the ECJ. States might flagrantly disregard judicial decisions that counter their interests (Caldeira and Gibson 1995; Garrett, Kelemen, and Schulz 1998). For example, the United Kingdom (while it was an EU member) opposed a series of ECJ rulings on labor laws. Some seemed to be political lightning rods, since social policy activates significant sovereignty concerns. Falkner, Hartlapp, and Treib (2007) explain that the 1996 Tory government openly refused to accept the court ruling[23] and did not take any decisive steps to comply before it was replaced by the incoming Labour government. Because EU rules had the potential to significantly alter the labor market and provoked widespread condemnation, the UK purposefully resisted ECJ authority until the domestic political environment shifted. The political sensitivity of a dispute may be an important factor in determining whether or not a government complies with international court rulings.

A second alternative hypothesis is that second-order compliance is simply about international power politics. The countries most equipped to resist unfavorable international rulings are those holding the most power, economically or otherwise. Less powerful countries, by contrast, are more likely to abide by rulings. In trade disputes, their economies are more vulnerable to retaliation should they defy an adverse ruling. There is no doubt that the economic clout of countries is a factor in international trade disputes. The question is whether the domestic veto players in a defendant government are highly correlative with that government's power. If so, then the apparent effect of veto players in obstructing second-compliance may actually be due to that government's relative immunity to retaliation. The following chapters address this alternative argument with a series of empirical tests. For instance, if IOs are constructed by powerful states to institutionalize their interests, then we should worry that the "deck is stacked" against low-power states. They might run afoul of international law more often, get sued with higher frequency, or suffer more adverse judgments than their high-power counterparts. My empirical analysis dispels several of these possibilities in the context of the WTO. Throughout, I make every attempt to empirically distinguish between alternative explanations and show how international power politics alone cannot explain the compliance patterns we observe.

2.3 Status quo bias and international rulings

Before turning to the empirical tests of my theory, another question must be addressed: how is it that governments can overcome the status quo bias that veto players generate in order to join an international agreement in the first place, only to break those promises and encounter insurmountable hurdles to second-order compliance later? The answer lies in how domestic veto players exert their influence at different stages of international cooperation.

Thus far, I have identified several points at which domestic politics influence international cooperation. To summarize: Governments negotiate treaties that are satisfactory not only to foreign governments but also domestic constituencies. With a signed treaty in hand, leaders go home to legislators and the public they represent to request ratification. The more domestic veto players, the more likely it is that groups that oppose the international agreement will find a sympathetic ear in government and block ratification (Ehrlich 2011). Thus policy reforms are impeded when there are domestic groups with different preferences and multiple political constraints in government. Anticipating this roadblock, leaders negotiate treaties that satisfy domestic veto players, which in turn narrows the scope of feasible commitments.

Domestic politics affect how well governments abide by the treaties they do ratify. The literature predicts that treaty violations are rare when there are many domestic constraints because (1) only those treaties that received broad domestic support would ever be ratified and (2) violations likewise occur only when there is consent from multiple veto players. Finally, when violations do occur, governments with many veto players are less likely to correct those missteps (that is, second-order comply). At this stage, political constraints lock in violations, undercutting the effectiveness of international courts. Across all three steps, we see a bias toward maintaining the status quo.

Yet at each stage of international cooperation, political actors have access to different information and encounter different incentives. This can be seen with trade agreements and their enforcement. First, joining trade agreements and reversing violations involve different calculations. During negotiation, states speculate about their future impact. Scholars have long regarded international agreements as incomplete contracts; governments cannot foresee or regulate all possible challenges that arise, nor can they reach consensus on each and every contingency (see, e.g., Bagwell and Staiger 2001, 2005; Copeland 1990; Horn, Maggi, and Staiger 2010). Some governments deliberately negotiate ambiguous treaties in order to ensure future flexibility of interpretation. Within states, domestic actors are also under-informed. Interest groups may be uncertain a priori about how proposed international obligations impact them because this entails long-run projections. During the negotiation stage, stakeholders such as industry groups or firms may anticipate that the agreements will benefit them. They may not have a clear idea about how those same obligations can become detrimental years later, and they may not anticipate their implications for future disputes. With little incentive to oppose the treaty during the negotiation stage, veto players may be less salient.

For example, when the United States negotiated the core agreements of the WTO during the Uruguay Round, high-tech firms saw multilateral liberalization as a net benefit. The WTO opened foreign markets for US high-tech sales and included crucial intellectual property protections. At the time, these export-oriented firms had relatively few foreign competitors. Firms that have since become dominant in mobile phone technology (e.g., Motorola and Apple) could not have foreseen that those same liberalization policies, in the wake of China's admission to the WTO, would pose direct threats to their economic welfare. Perhaps they could not have anticipated that rare earth minerals, which are crucial to this technology, would be a point of trade contention. And yet, in 2015, the United States sued China at the WTO over the latter's export restrictions on minerals needed for mobile battery technology at the behest of several high-tech firms. Had US stakeholders anticipated the downstream consequences, they might have pressed the US government to demand different protections in WTO agreements. Or they might have ensured accession terms for China that reduced the risk that country would employ export restraints. In short, interest groups that consent to one set of treaty terms may find those same obligations come back to haunt them many years later in the wake of unforeseen technological, economic, or political developments.

That calculation changes once the operations of an international agreement are underway. Domestic groups confront new ways in which their nation's trade commitments affect welfare, and they have reason to take hard-line positions. Exporter-oriented industries might witness a boost in foreign sales that follows multilateral liberalization, and consumers can benefit from lower prices that are thought to result from lower trade barriers. Import-competing industries might see the protections they previously enjoyed dismantled over time. Some scholarship has shown that among democracies, different electoral systems grant greater political leverage to interest groups rather than voters (Rogowski and Kayser 2002). Governments with single-member districts may be more sensitive to the protectionist demands of organized special interest groups than those with proportional representation, which tend to be more responsive to the diffused interests of voters as consumers.

In line with this argument, institutional discrepancies can explain first-order compliance with WTO agreements. Governments with single-member districts are known to more frequently break their WTO obligations than those with proportionate representation (Rickard 2010). Once special interest groups see concrete loses from trade liberalization, they tend to press their representatives for targeted trade protection. Influential industries can demand violations of trade agreements. Electoral institutions that give them a more direct pathway to influence policy generate more missteps. This might occur even when the same groups have (knowingly or unwittingly) allowed their government to accede to the multilateral trade regime. In summary, once an international agreement is in place, the specific benefits or losses become apparent to different domestic groups, potentially fueling controversy.

When governments break their international commitments and are

subjected to adverse legal rulings, the stakes are heightened. A growing literature on precedent in ICs highlights how legal obligations evolve
over time (Pelc 2014; Kucik 2019; Verdier and Voeten 2014). Although
the WTO does not officially allow precedent to be incorporated into
panel decisions, judges interpret the treaties with an eye toward consistency, and governments behave as if previous rulings constrain future
ones. In this sense, rulings at the WTO are applicable beyond the con-
fines of any particular dispute. This has consequences for the domestic groups that stand to gain or lose from rulings. Legal obligations are
clarified and made concrete through rulings; it is only after these rulings
have delineated the full implications of treaty terms that a treaty's impact is known and stakeholders are activated. Moreover, the precedent-
setting nature of rulings raises the stakes of the dispute (Kucik, Peritz,
and Puig, forthcoming). Industry groups and firms that anticipate losing
protective trade barriers due to an adverse ruling see less opportunity
for future protections. At this point, domestic stakeholders press political representatives to impede second-order compliance.

For example, take the 2001 US steel tariffs. When the US government imposed the tariffs to protect domestic steel manufacturers, those
safeguards were promptly and resoundingly struck down by the WTO.
All eyes were on the United States to see whether it would abide by its
free trade commitments. The domestic steel industry fought to retain the
protections once the public WTO ruling had highlighted the violation.

Likewise, in the European Union, when economic integration is under dispute, the calculus changes. Compliance is nearly always controversial in lawsuits brought before the ECJ. These are cases in which
member states are sued for allegedly failing to comply with their obligations to advance the European single market. Adverse trade rulings
identify cases in which a member state—or politically influential constituencies within its borders—has a clear preference to violate EU law. The
rulings isolate cases in which (1) important constituencies within states
do not want to comply and (2) domestic controversy is particularly acute.
IC judgments fuel hard-line domestic groups in defendant governments
by targeting beneficiaries from existing trade barriers and raising the domestic stakes of the dispute.

There is another reason governments manage to overcome the status
quo bias in the initial stages of international cooperation: joining treaties and responding to international litigation involve different collective
action problems. The formation and ratification processes generate dif-

fused interests. Because industries and sectors are likely unaware of the direct impact treaty terms have on them, they have have fewer incentives to mobilize and petition politicians for support. By contrast, when defendant states are found to be in breach of their international obligations, the dispute typically focuses on one industry, sector, or domestic group. These distinctions are exacerbated by the distributive conflict that is inherent in trade politics. Rarely are general trade barriers challenged in WTO disputes. More commonly, particular sectors or industries are the subject of complaint. Among the first 450 lawsuits filed at the WTO, approximately 15% concerned broad trade legislation while the remainder targeted specific industries (e.g., steel manufacturing, cotton farming, apple growers, and gambling).

By contrast, the distinctive penalties associated with compliance—that is, losing illegal trade protections—are borne primarily by the target groups; thus they represent more concentrated interests. They have the *incentive* and the *ability* to mobilize and lobby for support (Grossman and Helpman 2001). The anti-compliance constituencies are expected to exploit institutional checks and balances or leverage partisan divisions to block compliance. On the pro-compliance side, there are few groups with the incentive to mobilize.[24] Unless there is an industry singled out for retaliation, pro-compliance constituencies are not directly affected or those effects are diffuse (e.g., consumers). Faced with well-established barriers to mobilization and having fewer incentives, domestic groups that might otherwise benefit from compliance with adverse trade rulings may do little to sway outcomes.

In short, international legal disputes tend to activate domestic distributive conflict. Rulings entrench and mobilize anti-compliance groups. These groups seek political support from veto players in government and subsequently attempt to block second-order compliance. Second-order compliance is especially vulnerable to veto players when previous stages of international cooperation—treaty formation and first-order noncompliance—were not.

2.4 Conclusion

Across many issues, from trade and investment to human rights, governments use international courts to address their grievances. This chapter has laid out a theoretical framework for understanding when ICs succeed or fail to promote cooperation. Domestic political incentives and institutions within defendant governments explain whether and when international rulings elicit compliance. Compliance with these legal interventions helps to illuminate the effectiveness of ICs.

It is well established that, at least with respect to international trade, governments are likely to litigate their disputes when there are clear domestic political benefits (Goldstein and Steinberg 2008). Some plaintiffs choose litigation as a costly signal of support to crucial domestic groups. With respect to the WTO, domestic politics incentivize governments to proactively enforce the multilateral trade regime. Davis (2012) demonstrates that "on the complainant side, governments file a formal legal complaint for WTO adjudication as a costly signal to domestic and foreign audiences of the government's support for exporter interests" (20). Other governments rely on international legal rulings as political cover for unpopular policies (Allee and Huth 2006). Domestic politics factors into a government's decision to *initiate* litigation.

By contrast, I argue that these domestic incentives not only drive plaintiffs to litigate but also shape the decisions of defendant states. Political divisions affect a government's *response* when it is convicted of violating international commitments and held accountable before a legal body. They explain why some evade enforcement.

My argument prompts us to rethink the relationship between democratic accountability and international courts. While governments on both sides of a lawsuit are beholden to their own domestic constraints, they react in vastly different ways. Davis (2012) shows that the checks and balances of democratic political institutions push in favor of international legalization. By contrast, my argument indicates that those same institutions impose limits on the effectiveness of legalization; they restrict an IC's ability to induce meaningful cooperation between governments once disputing states have chosen to hash out their grievances in a legal forum.

A rich literature has also examined the tendency of governments to follow or violate their primary trade obligations, especially under the multilateral trade regime (Milner 1997; Martin 2000; Mansfield, Milner, and Rosendorff 2002). Notably, Rickard (2010) shows that democracies display different rates of first-order compliance with WTO agreements (e.g., whether they violate rules on tariffs, antidumping, or subsidies) depending on their electoral system. By contrast, my theory traces out when one should expect governments to *reverse* treaty violations in response to IC rulings. Second-order compliance depends on domestic political constraints within those states. Few studies consider compliance with WTO rulings. The research that does largely ignores domestic politics, instead emphasizing important features of the international system (e.g., Bown 2004b; Davey 2009).

This chapter has articulated how domestic veto players can hinder state compliance with international rulings. Compliance problems have implications for international cooperation. ICs are hampered by politics within the governments they aim to reconcile. This suggests they are failing to offer defendant states the tools they need to manage internal domestic distributive problems and still follow through on international obligations. By focusing on the very situations where international legal bodies come into direct conflict with sovereign states, the empirical chapters that follow unpack this important stress test for international cooperation.

In the next chapter, I extend my argument by delineating the domestic and international political players in my theory and elaborating on their choices. I provide background information on the two international courts that are the focus of the book: the WTO Dispute Settlement Mechanism and the Court of Justice of the European Union.

CHAPTER THREE

The Design and Operation of Two International Courts

The previous chapter introduced this book's motivating puzzle: when are international organizations effective in promoting cooperation between countries? I argue that international courts (ICs) lend special insight into this puzzle. Governments accused of breaking their commitments are reluctant to answer to an IC. If they do agree to participate in legal proceedings and the court rules that a violation occurred, those governments are disinclined to concede. This pathway of resistance illuminates government preferences. And so when a state complies with an adverse ruling, despite its apparent preference to evade its international obligations, it is likely the IC encouraged that behavior. By examining international rulings and then tracking compliance, I focus on the most intractable disputes—a hard test of an international court's influence on state behavior. Not all countries are equally responsive to adverse international rulings. Some governments readily comply with these judgments; others resist. I argue that a major driver of cross-national variation is the domestic political constraints within states. Governments with many formal and informal veto players tend to be less responsive to international rulings, thereby undercutting an IC's effectiveness.

Before turning to empirical tests of my theory, I clarify the tests' institutional context and background. This chapter accomplishes three tasks: First, I justify my case selection. The World Trade Organization's Dispute Settlement Mechanism is the primary institution I examine, and the Court of Justice of the European Union (ECJ) is the secondary institution. These ICs are exemplary tests for my argument because they are among the most highly legalized and widely used. Second, this chapter supplies background information for each institution. I explain how interstate disputes progress to adjudication and how rulings are enforced in each. This discussion lays out the context for interpreting the empirical tests conducted in later chapters. Third, I explain my assumptions about the domestic political actors who drive compliance decisions. I chart out their preferences and the sequence of actions. This provides additional justification for my hypotheses.

3.1 Landscape of legalization

The international political landscape has grown increasingly legalized (Abbott et al. 2000). A vast array of international treaties regulate global affairs on issues ranging from foreign investment, trade, and monetary issues to nuclear nonproliferation, climate change abatement, and human rights standards. International legalization is characterized by three key attributes: First, governments are increasingly obligated to follow formal international legal commitments; they are beholden to international rules. Second, many of these rules are increasingly precise, clearly delineating permissible and impermissible behavior; states find less gray areas open to interpretation. Third, governments increasingly delegate authority to international institutions to apply rules and, importantly, settle their disputes. As governments craft international agreements with greater degrees of obligation, precision, and delegation, so too must they establish common standards for dealing with alleged violations (Goldstein and Martin 2000).

One striking development in this vein is the proliferation of ICs. At present count, thirty-eight formal ICs with permanent or indefinite jurisdiction have been in operation. If one expands the definition of international courts to include dispute settlement mechanisms, arbitration bodies, and ad hoc tribunals, the count grows to eighty-three. These latter institutions have varying degrees of legalization, but each uses third-party judges or arbiters to apply international law and settle disputes. Many address international or transborder economic issues, most commonly trade and investment disputes.

Table 3.1 summarizes the array of international legal bodies that have

TABLE 3.1 **International Judicial Bodies Currently in Force**

		Substantive scope		
	Membership	Broad	Limited	Total
	Universal	4	32	36
	Constrained	6	41	47
Number of courts		10	73	83

Note: Calculations by author with updates to data from Project on International Courts and Tribunals.

or continue to be in use, based on updated data from Romano (1998).[1] These bodies can be differentiated in two dimensions: First is membership. For many international legal bodies, membership is constrained regionally, as seen in the East African Court of Justice, the North American Free Trade Agreement (NAFTA) Dispute Settlement Panel—while NAFTA was superseded by the United States-Mexico-Canada Agreement (USMCA) in July 2020, its dispute settlement mechanism remained largely intact—and many others. In some such bodies, membership is open to all states. Examples include the International Criminal Court, the International Court of Justice, and the International Labor Organization's Commission of Inquiry. The second dimension concerns legal competencies and substantive scope—that is, whether the institution addresses a broad range of issues or a specific issue area. Ten international courts have broad mandates; thirteen international courts and dispute settlement bodies focus specifically on economic issues; and several others focus exclusively on human rights or humanitarian law.

Among this array of ICs, the two that have received the most widespread attention and scrutiny are the WTO DSM and the ECJ. Both are highly active, adjudicating many disputes each year.[2] They are often touted as successful instruments of enforcement for the international organizations they serve. This makes them ripe for study by political scientists who are often skeptical about their performance. As the international legal landscape becomes more complex, there are growing calls to identify conditions under which these two courts advance interstate cooperation.

The main purpose of the WTO DSM is to settle disputes among member states over alleged barriers to trade. The WTO's membership is broad. With 164 member countries from around the globe, it reaches the vast majority of the international community. At the same time, its substantive reach is limited in that the DSM deals specifically with trade disputes. Despite these limits, an increasing number of its cases navigate the lines between trade liberalization and competing values such as environmental protection and cultural preservation.

There is a high demand for WTO dispute settlement services. The US government files an average of five lawsuits per year. This pace of use remains steady despite the costs. Some estimates place the legal fees for an initial dispute at about a million dollars (Bown and Hoekman 2005; Finger 2010), and expenses grow rapidly if a case proceeds to panel and Appellate Body rulings. Likewise, the European Union, which participates in the WTO as a single entity, files an average of four lawsuits per year at similar expense. The frequency of litigation and nontrivial expenses speak to the—at least perceived—value of the WTO. Governments behave as if the dispute settlement system is useful.

The ECJ is the main judicial apparatus for enforcing EU law. The EU, as a regional organization, is more limited in its membership than the WTO. At present count, there are twenty-seven member states (with the United Kingdom having recently exited). At the same time, as the central judicial body, the ECJ has a far broader substantive mandate than the WTO DSM. The ECJ has authority to address all aspects of European integration, especially the enforcement of the single market, including the free movement of goods, capital, services, and labor.

The ECJ has adjudicated thousands of cases about alleged breaches of EU law. Its cases cover everything from working conditions to environmental standards to investment practices. One of the most contentious topics is trade integration: a large share of rulings strike down barriers to the free movement of goods. Member states are accused of breaking their free trade obligations, and these failures risk undermining the single European market. Many states seem to take ECJ rulings seriously. Rather than ignoring the court, states challenge rulings they disagree with and abide by others. Governments behave as if the court wields authority and serves a useful function in promoting European integration.

Although these two ICs differ in their breadth of membership and substantive scope, they are similar in that they are both highly legalized. They adjudicate many seemingly intractable disputes with plenty of apparent success (Phelan 2015). They outpace other ICs in their activity; countries far more frequently resort to the services of the WTO and ECJ than other international tribunals. It helps to put their activity in context. Consider the International Court of Justice, the United

Nation's landmark judicial body, which has adjudicated 158 disputes in its seventy-three years of operation. Or consider NAFTA's dispute settlement system, which has seen 119 disputes. Both WTO and ECJ case loads are many times larger. Consequently, researchers can be justified in examining their performance using statistical methods and drawing conclusions about their successes and failures.

3.2 Case selection

I examine the WTO DSM and the ECJ for three reasons. First, as noted above, these courts are the most widely used and highly legalized in history. This book aims to uncover whether and when ICs promote economic cooperation between countries. By focusing on active institutions that are heavily used and perceived to be important—not sitting idly on the sidelines of international affairs—I can directly address the question of effectiveness. The WTO is the cornerstone of the multilateral trade regime (Rose 2004; Gowa and Soo Yeon Kim 2005; Subramanian and Wei 2007). Its court is seen as the exemplar for international dispute resolution (Hudec 1999), and there is widespread agreement that its verdicts matter. Likewise, the ECJ has "developed a supranational legal order," wielding a degree of influence "remarkable for an international tribunal or court" (Carruba, Gabel, and Hankla 2008, 436). As evidenced by the heightened scrutiny these two courts have received from political scientists, economists, and policy-makers alike, their performance is widely thought to matter.

Due to their use, these highly legalized courts lend particular insight into the broader trend of legalization in international affairs. Countries delegate significant decision-making authority to these courts and are obligated to follow their rulings, which rely on an increasingly precise body of law. Both encourage the early settlement of disputes prior to a formal legal judgment. About 60% of complaints brought to the WTO are settled before a panel ruling. Likewise, about two-thirds of the European Commission's infringement investigations are resolved before the ECJ renders a ruling. Some scholars credit the high early-settlement rates to the shadow of enforcement the ICs cast and the precision of the law on which they rule (Goldstein and Steinberg 2008; Johns 2015; Busch and Reinhardt 2000a; Gilligan, Johns, and Rosendorff 2010). Once called upon to render a verdict, both courts overwhelmingly find the defendant government has broken at least some of its international commitments (94% at the WTO; 85% of trade-related cases at the ECJ). Neither is shy about admonishing states.

By showing the varied performance of these two highly legalized ICs, this research reveals when their efforts to enforce international law work and when they fall short. If even the most allegedly successful ICs founder, then what hope is there for weaker and less legalized regimes to elicit compliance from recalcitrant states? A finding that the WTO DSM and ECJ have no detectable influence on state behavior would suggest that lower-profile courts are unlikely to be justifiable by many states' calculations.

The second reason I examine the WTO and ECJ concerns research design. They offer variation needed to test my core hypothesis that domestic political constraints hinder compliance with international rulings. Both courts have presided over many disputes affecting numerous countries. WTO litigants hail from around the globe; ECJ litigants span Europe and exhibit different domestic political circumstances. In statistical terms, both courts feature variation in the explanatory variable: the number of domestic political constraints. Moreover, both courts seem to have variation in compliance outcomes. Neither has a perfect track record of compliance, nor does either abjectly fail in regard to countries disregarding its rulings. They display variation in my dependent variable.

By pairing and jointly examining these two courts, I am able to test different parts of my theory about domestic political constraints. At the WTO, defendant governments include democratic and nondemocratic regimes and high-income industrialized and low- or middle-income economies from across the globe. This variation allows me to test my hypotheses about how formal and informal veto players in defendant governments shape compliance with international legal rulings. I am able to draw comparisons between democratic and autocratic regimes. Democracies have many more veto players than do autocracies, and the WTO's broad scope of membership allows me to test the effects of these fundamental political constraints on compliance.

Yet the hypotheses presented in chapter 2 are not merely about different regime types; I am interested in variation within democratic governments. This is where the ECJ is illuminating. The defendants, while all democratic European states, vary in their domestic political constraints. Some have more institutional checks and balances or partisan divisions than others, and many of these features can be systematically distinguished. By examining ECJ rulings, I am able to focus on variation among democratic governments. The EU's extensive requirements ensure many other factors are held fixed. Global political and economic events often touch the entire region similarly. EU members are constrained by the same external policies to govern their relationship with non-EU markets; most are subject to the same European monetary policy,[3] and all are vulnerable to prosecution from the same body, the European Commission. By looking at cross-national variation across EU members, I can more accurately isolate the effect of formal and informal domestic veto players on compliance with international rulings.

To summarize, the WTO and ECJ each provide variation in the explanatory variable of interest. The WTO enables coarser comparisons between democratic and nondemocratic governments. The ECJ allows for more fine-grained comparisons among democratic governments. By looking at both international courts, I am able to investigate different aspects of the domestic politics mechanism.

The third basis for case selection concerns measurement. Because these ICs have the richest track records of successes and failures, they are more amenable to analysis than rarely used courts. If countries very rarely use a court, there is far less one can learn, empirically, about that court's performance. To study the effectiveness of rarely used courts, one would have to focus on assumption-laden arguments about deterrence. Empirical tests would rely on perhaps a handful of idiosyncratic case studies and could be driven by unobservable selection mechanisms.

These two courts are ripe for systematic empirical analysis because they both adjudicate international economic disputes. As such, their performance can be assessed in similar ways. For the WTO, I examine both the policy reforms governments implement to comply with adverse rulings and the impact of rulings on interstate commerce—specifically trade between disputing governments. This involves measuring the impact of rulings on trade flows for exactly those products under dispute. In the ECJ, numerous disputes are aimed at enforcing the single market, and I focus on these trade-related cases. Trade flows between defendant governments and the remainder of the European community are a useful metric for the court's success in promoting economic integration. Increases in imports in the wake of pro-integration rulings are suggestive of trade cooperation; a lack of discernible increases suggests a defendant government has largely ignored the court's pro-integration rulings. These trade fluctuations are observable and measurable outcomes. International *economic* courts offer a clear window into the effectiveness puzzle.

By contrast, it is more difficult to evaluate the performance of ICs that adjudicate non-economic issues. Consider international human rights and humanitarian law. Courts might be deemed effective when they deter war crimes, encourage restitutions to victims of torture, compel governments to reform prisons, or induce other measures. Many of these goals evade systematic measurement.[4] Some egregious human rights violations such as genocide are mercifully rare events, making a statistical analysis impractical. Others leave unspecified what baseline state behavior would be without the intervention of the court. For instance, take political imprisonment: we don't know what the rate of imprisonment would have been if a country had not been condemned by an IC; without that information, it is nearly impossible to discern the effect of a legal ruling. The important activities of many non-economic international courts resist systematic analysis.

In the sections that follow, I introduce the main mechanics of these international courts. This supplies the background for chapters 4, 5, and 6, in which the theoretical claims are tested.

3.3 Dispute settlement at the WTO

The WTO DSM provides a venue for governments to adjudicate trade disputes, enforces the terms of liberalization, and stabilizes the multilateral trade regime. According to the organization's self-characterization, "the dispute settlement system provides a mechanism through which WTO Members can ensure that their rights . . . [are] enforced. This system is equally important from the perspective of the defendant whose measure is under challenge, since it provides a forum for the accused government to defend itself if it disagrees with the claims raised by the complainant" (World Trade Organization 2021b). The system is supposed to rectify violations that hurt plaintiffs while providing due process for defendant governments that believe their policies are consistent with WTO obligations. According to WTO parlance, the system includes the Dispute Settlement Body, the tribunal-like entity that assembles panels of experts to adjudicate trade disputes, reevaluates the

findings in the case of an appeal, makes recommendations for implementation, and authorizes retaliation where applicable. With nearly
all countries counted among its membership, and broad coverage over
trade-related issues, the WTO DSM enjoys jurisdiction over a large portion of the global economy.

3.3.1 Which countries use the system?

3.3.1.1 MEMBERS, DISPUTANTS, AND RESPONDENTS   The majority of
states in the international system are WTO members and are thereby
covered by its treaties. However, not all states are equally likely to participate in disputes. In the first couple decades of the WTO's operation,
slightly less than half of the membership engaged in formal legal disputes
over violations of their trade obligations. Countries can enter disputes
as plaintiffs or defendants; in the parlance of the WTO, they are "complainant" or "respondent" states, respectively. This does not mean that
other members had no missteps or grievances with one another's trade
practices. Rather, in each case, litigant governments had sufficiently intractable conflicts backed by persuasive enough domestic interests and
adequate legal resources to turn to the DSM. Innumerable conflicts are
settled outside the WTO's purview through diplomatic means. These
conflicts never appear on the court's docket.

Table 3.2 provides a brief overview of the characteristics of WTO
member states ($n=164$), WTO disputants ($n=75$), and the respondent
governments subjected to adverse WTO rulings ($n=26$) between 1995
and 2018. Disputes can take several years to weave their way through the

TABLE 3.2 **Countries in World Trade Organization (1995–2018)**

	Sample average[†], $\mu(sd)$		
	Members	Disputants	Respondents, adverse ruling[‡]
Trade (%GDP)	83.1 (45.3)	72.3 (48.9)	57.6 (24.5)
Democracy	4.0 (5.8)	5.7 (5.7)	6.2 (5.4)
Veto points	0.3 (0.2)	0.4 (0.2)	0.4 (0.2)
Number of countries	164	75	26

Note: [†]Each country is counted once, even when a country has participated in multiple disputes. [‡]Covers only respondents with adverse rulings between 1995 and 2015, due to case duration. The EU is counted as a single entity. Democracy is measured with Polity score [1,10] and veto points are measured with political constraints index [0,1]. Sample means are not statistically different at conventional significance level.

system; many in this sample had not reached a legal ruling by 2018. Thus the sample of respondents with adverse rulings covers only disputes filed through 2015; subsequent years will expand the number of different countries in this group. For each set of countries, the sample average and standard deviation are calculated for several variables. Countries' trade is measured as a portion of their gross domestic product (GDP) as of 2018, their levels of democracy are measured by Polity scores (rescaled to range from 1 to 10) as of 2016, and their domestic veto points (0 to 1 scale) are measured as of 2016, the most recent year for which comprehensive data are available (World Bank 2013; Kaufmann and Kraay 2015; Henisz 2000).

Disputant countries tend to differ somewhat from the membership at large. Disputants have larger economies and, as shown in table 3.2, are slightly less trade reliant than the average WTO member.[5] They possess somewhat stronger democratic institutions and feature slightly more domestic political constraints, although these differences fall far short of statistical significance.

Only some WTO disputes ultimately produce rulings. The states that are subjected to censure through adverse rulings—that is, as respondents held accountable for trade violations—can be compared to the broader group of disputant states. Losing respondents tend to be somewhat less trade dependent and possess slightly more robust democratic institutions than the broader sample, although these differences are again not statistically significant. The respondent sample is indistinguishable from the disputant sample in terms of domestic veto points.

These patterns dispel concerns about serious selection effects in WTO dispute settlement on the basis of a state's political attributes. It is well established that states with the largest markets are the most frequent users of WTO adjudication (Bown and Hoekman 2005). But that does not mean that litigant states are exceptionally reliant on trade: disputes are motivated by far more complicated factors than economic need. Some states settle their grievances early or acquiesce to adversaries with retaliatory capacity before escalating to involve a panel of international judges. Democratic states and those with more political constraints than the average WTO member are slightly more apt to pursue formal dispute settlement, as a broad body of research on international courts has shown (Allee and Huth 2006; Davis 2012; Bobick and A. Smith 2016; Busch 2000). At the same time, losing respondents are

not drastically different from the set of states that resolve their grievances without a formal judgment. Domestic political institutions do not
appear to be a key factor in driving this attrition.

3.3.1.2 LITIGATION FOR HIGH INCOME COUNTRIES Delving deeper into
the record of WTO disputes, a few patterns emerge. First, the most active litigants are the United States and the European Union—recall that
the EU participates as a single member. Between 1995 and 2018, the
WTO oversaw 573 disputes. In this time period, the United States filed
123 complaints and defended against 151 accusations of trade violations
in formal legal disputes. These numbers suggest that the US government
has, at least over the past two decades, maintained an active interest in
using legalized means for addressing its trade disputes. For the European Union, the corresponding counts are 99 and 85, respectively. Other
active disputants include Canada, Japan, and South Korea. Canada has
filed 39 complaints and responded to 23. In examining the WTO system,
we stand to learn the most about how democratic states with large economies resolve their disputes.

However, the WTO is not solely the purview of the rich. Middle-
income countries increasingly use the DSM. For example, Mexico, Thailand, India, and China were somewhat reluctant to file lawsuits in the
early years of their membership—China joined the WTO in 2001—but
since 2005, these countries have waged nearly one-third of complaints.
Lower-income countries do use the WTO to settle disputes—albeit
infrequently—both as complainants and respondents (Bown 2004a). The
least developed countries (LDC) almost never use the system. As the
middle- and low-income countries have grown more willing to use legalized dispute settlement, we can learn more about how partial and nondemocratic states, and countries with smaller economies, resolve trade
quarrels.

The inclusion of middle- and lower-income countries is important
to the WTO's agenda (Bown 2010). The WTO officially asserts that its
DSM is constructed to serve as an equalizing force. It aims to "level the
playing field" by using rules and procedures to give lower-income countries greater leverage against larger economies; the "system, to which all
Members have equal access and in which decisions are made on the basis of rules rather than on the basis of economic power, empowers developing countries and smaller economies by placing 'the weak' on a more
equal footing with 'the strong'. In this sense, any judicial law enforce-

ment system benefits the weak more than the strong because the strong would always have other means to defend and impose their interests in the absence of a law enforcement system" (World Trade Organization 2021a). In theory, the system is supposed to counteract power politics.

But official WTO materials also concede that these aims may not always bear out in reality. WTO disputes can be prohibitively costly for low-income countries, even when legal resources are allocated to assist this group (James Smith 2004). Countries with low incomes face bureaucratic and budget constraints that limit their ability to pursue lengthy lawsuits against larger economic powers. Relatedly, powerful complainants may be able to extract concessions from low-income countries without relying on the WTO. LDCs experience these limitations most acutely; they typically lack the ability to retaliate effectively and are vulnerable to other points of leverage like foreign aid. In the rare instances they are able to bear the costs of litigation, low-income countries may become willing to use adjudication to address their trade disputes (Davis and Bermeo 2009).

One reason that disputes are so costly is the duration of the process. Disputes typically last several years before they reach resolution. The initial stage is called "consultations," bilateral negotiations behind closed doors. Many conflicts are settled early at this stage. But consultations can take months and lawsuits often linger on the WTO's docket far longer. Should negotiations fail and states resort to litigation, they embark on a multiyear process. At this stage, there are often delays before a panel is formed and litigation commences, particularly as states clash on procedural matters.

Due to the lengthy process, it is sensible to examine WTO disputes that have had ample time to progress through litigation. Any empirical analysis that involves a comparison across disputes should allow for several years to have elapsed after a dispute has been initiated. For this reason, I truncate the sample of disputes in the analysis that follows. I restrict my focus to the 450 complaints initiated between 1995 and 2012, allowing them six years to develop before assessing outcomes. It is for this sample of disputes that I evaluate participation patterns.

Table 3.3 provides an overview of disputes initiated at the WTO between 1995 and 2012. They are categorized according to complainant and respondent roles. The first column shows dispute counts for complaints that were settled early through negotiations or dropped by complainants. The second column shows counts for disputes that went for-

TABLE 3.3 **Summary of First 450 WTO Disputes by State Characteristics**

		Settled early	Reached ruling	Rate
Complainant	**High-Income**	**164**	**137**	**46%**
	United States	56	43	43%
	European Union	49	36	42%
	Low/Middle-Income	**87**	**62**	**42%**
Respondent	**High-Income**	**151**	**150**	**50%**
	United States	56	43	43%
	European Union	49	36	42%
	Low/Middle-Income	**101**	**49**	**33%**
Complainant v.	High v. Low/Middle	60	36	38%
Respondent	Low/Middle v. High	48	49	51%

Note: Data cover 450 disputes initiated from 1995 to 2012. Calculations based on World Bank classifications. When a dispute has multiple complainants, the country with largest economy is counted.

ward in the legal process to the litigation stage. The third column shows the rate of litigation for disputes filed between 1995 and 2012 for complainant and respondent types.

High-income countries are not only the most frequent users of the WTO DSM but also push for litigation as complainints more often than low- or middle-income countries do. The US is especially litigious as a plaintiff (Davis 2012). On the respondent side, it is clear that the US is also most likely to fight against allegations by resorting to litigation. Low- and middle-income respondents are least likely to hold out through litigation. They are more willing to strike a deal with a complainant—a presumed compromise, although the explicit terms of early settlement are rarely publicly disclosed. The EU sits somewhere in the middle. As a target of many complaints, the EU is slightly more likely to settle early than to litigate.

The power dynamics vary widely. In the context of trade politics, economic clout is generally the best indicator of power. High-income countries often have large consumer markets for imported goods, potentially diverse production, and the capacity to retaliate against others when trade grievances arise. Thus it is informative to compare high-income countries to middle- and low-income countries. Approximately two-thirds of disputes to date have involved pairs of high-income countries. The remaining third reflects significant economic imbalance between disputants. When the complainant has a significantly larger economy than the respondent, the dispute is about twice as likely to be settled early than to be litigated. In table 3.3, I classify cases as imbalanced whenever the country with the larger economy has about twice the GDP of the country with the smaller economy, calculated for the year the dispute started.

These patterns are important for assessing WTO performance. If most disputes featured powerful complainants suing weaker respondents, evidence showing that respondents comply would be uninformative. It would be difficult to untangle institutional effects from those of the traditional power dynamics that international relations theory has long emphasized. Powerful plaintiffs, rather than the institution, could be inducing compliance. Conversely, suppose most disputes involved low- or middle-income countries suing high-income respondents and this rarely produced compliance. It could mean that the WTO is ineffective, but it could alternatively mean that power politics overwhelms whatever effect rulings have. We would not want to condemn the WTO on this basis. Fortunately, neither extreme appears to be the case. Instead, the data demonstrate a range of complainant-respondent pairs represented in the disputes. And those power dynamics, as will be shown in subsequent chapters, are not correlated with compliance. There is variation in dispute outcomes that cannot be explained by a conventional power politics story.

3.3.2 WTO procedures

A WTO dispute has several stages. It begins with the two-month bilateral consultation period in which the disputing countries conduct formal negotiations behind closed doors. The consultation stage allows the plaintiff to present its legal claims. The plaintiff sets out its allegations, specifying which WTO treaty terms the respondent allegedly violated. The respondent provides its rebuttal. It aims to persuade the complainant why the policies or practices in question are consistent with WTO terms. Both parties can submit reports to establish market impact.

Bilateral consultations are often a successful way to resolve the dispute. The negotiations lead to a settlement about 60% of the time. Governments that reach a settlement at this stage tend to divulge little public information about the terms. Shielded from public view, these settlements represent compromises that governments reach with an eye toward assuaging key domestic actors. At this stage, domestic audiences are narrow—sometimes consisting of just the interest group or sector

with immediate stakes in the dispute. Nonetheless, this bargaining process occurs in the shadow of the law, since failed negotiations lead to litigation and a formal ruling (Busch and Reinhardt 2000a). Rulings cast a
shadow because they are supposedly binding and shape subsequent outcomes for governments.

Early settlements are compromises that both governments can use to
satisfy their domestic constituents. One illustration can be found in Brazil's 2002 complaint against the US over taxes on imported citrus products.[6] Brazil alleged that since the 1970s, Florida had applied an excise
tax that treated domestic and foreign producers unequally, a barrier to
trade that violated key terms of the GATT. Brazil argued that the tax
protected domestic citrus producers and limited the importation of processed citrus products—like frozen concentrated orange juice—that represented Brazil's most significant exports to the US. Bilateral talks between officials and industry representatives stretched out for two years.
Under the shadow of litigation and potential retaliation, the disputants
reached a settlement: the Florida legislature voted to reduce its orange
juice tax; Brazilian importers would be required to pay only one-third
as much, and that tax revenue would go to the Florida Department of
Citrus to fund research projects instead of advertising campaigns.[7] This
compromise satisfied Floridian and Brazilian producers and sweetened
ongoing trade talks between the two governments.

When bilateral consultations fail, complainants can move into the litigation phase.[8] Litigation begins with the formation of a panel of WTO
experts—international judges—from the Dispute Settlement Body.
These panelists evaluate the substantive claims. Governments present
their legal positions, information on the market impact of the alleged
trade barriers, and other submissions to support their claims. Sometimes
this process pushes disputants into a settlement before the panel renders its verdict and litigation is ended. Take, for example, Mexico's 2003
complaint against the US regarding antidumping duties on cement.[9] Although the governments initiated litigation, they stalled and resumed bilateral talks. No ruling was needed because the US and Mexico reached
a mutually agreed solution and withdrew their complaints. As part of
the settlement, the US drastically reduced its duties for three years and
eliminated duties thereafter while Mexico opened its cement markets to
US competition. The US cement industry weighed in on these negotiations. A representative from the Southern Tier Cement Committee said
that the agreement was one in which all sides could claim victory.[10] This

settlement highlighted an apparently efficient outcome in which neither party bore the costs of litigation and trade barriers were lowered, a welcome adjustment from the perspective of the broader WTO membership.

More often, litigation moves forward and the panel of WTO jurists reaches a ruling on the merits. The ruling is called a "panel report," which consists of a detailed assessment of factual and legal aspects of the case. In almost all rulings (94%), the panel finds that the respondent has breached WTO obligations with respect to at least one legal claim. This means the judgment usually requires the respondent to change some aspect of its trade policy. Some scholarship has highlighted the importance of judicial restraint in WTO disputes (Creamer 2017; Busch and Pelc 2010). Panel reports are thought to reflect an effort by judges to balance political incentives against strict legal interpretation. While panelists might temper their rulings to avoid backlash, this cannot be the entire story. Because almost every ruling finds some respondent violations and demands substantial policy reform, it is clear that judges have not shied away from their legal duties. As a result, litigation produces rulings that almost always require action from the respondent government. Rulings are not merely superficial; they request substantive compliance from states.

Governments can accept a panel ruling or appeal it. Approximately 65% of rulings are appealed, most often by the respondent. This frequency is revealing. It suggests that WTO judges do not explicitly craft their decisions to maximize compliance. If panel rulings simply formalized the policy preferences of respondents, there would be little reason to appeal. Rather, the panel report includes recommendations that one or both disputants consider significant enough to challenge. Appeals take many months. In some of the most complex cases, they have spanned a decade, a prolonged process that can drive up legal costs and lost revenue while trade barriers remain in place. At this point, the Appellate Body (AB), which has seven standing judges,[11] reassess the panel decision.

The AB considers the disputants' submissions and can uphold, modify, or reverse the panel judgment. Most of the time, they modify the panel report. Few rulings are completely preserved in every respect; even when upheld, the AB tends to modify the reasoning. And only very rarely are panel reports completely reversed so that the respondent is absolved. Some of these rare instances have occurred when the AB has found that the complainant did not have standing or did not abide by

proper dispute settlement procedures. For example, in DS60, Mexico
had sued Guatemala and prevailed. Then the AB reversed the panel ruling to favor Guatemala (respondent) due to the fact that Mexico (complainant) did not adequately identify the trade barriers it took issue
with.[12]

Other times, the AB has a substantial reason for overturning a panel
ruling. For example, in three disputes over EU tariffs on computer
equipment, the appeals judges determined that the panel had misinter-
preted a key part of the GATT treaty.[13] Among the first 450 WTO disputes, there were more than 160 rulings against the respondent and only
8 substantive reversals[14]—meaning that in the vast majority of cases, the
respondent is still facing an adverse ruling that requires it to remove or
reform its trade barriers.

3.3.3 Compliance and avoidance

Following litigation, disputes progress to the compliance stage. If the
ruling uncovered a violation of WTO obligations, the respondent is required to comply. Governments may have to implement new policies or
correct the problematic ones. Discriminatory tariffs may need to be adjusted, subsidies revoked, tax codes revised, or other trade policies modified. Recognizing that these policy reforms can be difficult to implement, the dispute settlement procedure allots a grace period, called a
"reasonable period of time" (RPT). The RPT is determined on a case by
case basis. Disputant governments can negotiate that time frame or, failing agreement, rely on arbitration. The WTO guidelines suggest a deadline of fifteen months after the ruling, although the disputants and arbitrator have flexibility to set a shorter or longer RPT. Arbitrators take
into account the complexity of the implementation measures, often allowing a longer grace period for the most complex cases. The expiration
of the RPT is the compliance deadline. If a respondent fails to make required policy changes by the deadline, it has not complied. Figure 3.1
summarizes the typical timeline of a dispute that goes through the appeal process.

Compliance is not a uniform process. Because governments enact
trade policy through different instruments, sometimes regulatory and
other times statutory, there is important variation. Regulatory compliance, where an administrative measure or an executive act is needed to
enact a compliant trade policy, may be relatively uncomplicated. Ad-

Consultations	Panel Convened	Panel Report	Appeal	(non) Compliance

```
|            |              |              |
|            |              |              |
|            |              |              |  - - - - - -
|___ 60 days ___|___ Usually 1 to 2 yrs ___|___ RPT usually 1.5yrs - - - - - - -
|_____|_____|_____|_____|
         EARLY SETTLEMENT              RULING(s)          IMPLEMENTATION
```

EARLY SETTLEMENT	RULING(s)	IMPLEMENTATION
(PRIVATE – Litigants Only)	(PUBLIC – Foreign and Domestic)	(PUBLIC – Foreign and Domestic)

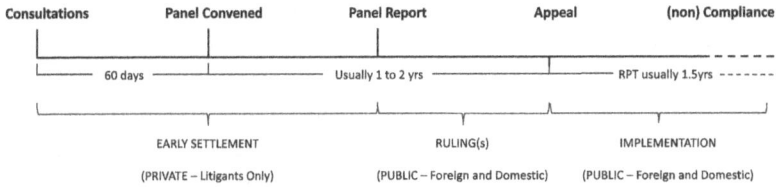

FIGURE 3.1. Stages of Typical WTO Dispute with Corresponding Audience
Note: In the years studied, 94% of panel rulings found the respondent violated at least some WTO obligations.

ministrative agencies like a government's department of commerce or ministry of trade can, sometimes acting under the direction of the executive branch, adjust regulations to bring the government into compliance with a WTO ruling. Despite this seemingly straightforward process, policy reforms are subject to the influence of political actors who can act as informal veto players. For example, the United States establishes a procedure to determine its response to an adverse WTO ruling and although controlled by an administrative body, it incorporates guidance from legislators: "The decision to implement an adverse finding by a WTO panel or an Appellate Body report is a political one. The USTR first consults with the Department [of Commerce] before deciding on how to respond . . . the USTR may hold consultations with appropriate congressional committees," and only then does the USTR decide whether and how to comply.[15] As Davis (2012) notes, the USTR acts not as an autonomous agency but rather experiences "intrusive supervision from Congress" (186).

In other instances, compliance cannot be achieved with administrative measures alone. Instead, governments have to pass new legislation to implement a ruling. This requires coordination among members of Parliament or Congress, and more politicians can block the adoption of legislation, raising the risk that the government fails to comply. Divisions among political parties often complicate legislative reforms. Thus the obstacles a government faces in complying with adverse WTO rulings varies with the form of its trade policy and its internal political processes.

While the WTO's dispute settlement procedure may seem highly regimented, it actually gives disputants room to maneuver. Governments can sidestep adverse rulings in several ways (Reinhardt 2001): First, when complainant or respondent governments appeal panel rulings, they set in motion a process in which an appellate panel is formed and reevaluates the ruling in light of new arguments presented by the disputants. This can add a year or more to a dispute. Throughout appeals, the respondent retains the WTO-inconsistent policies without penalty.

Second, the respondent can demand an extension of the compliance deadline. In several disputes, the RPT has been extended multiple times over the course of several years. For example, in DS184, Japan and the United States agreed to extend the compliance deadline three times. Initially, in December 2003, the US secured an extension to July 2005.[16] The US justified its extension by asserting it was still looking to reach a mutually agreed solution. No settlement was ever secured, but the extension process did buy the respondent valuable time. Japan agreed not to pursue retaliation so long as the US continued to work on domestic legislation necessary to comply. From the perspective of the respondent, not only do such WTO-sanctioned delays stave off retaliation but they also deliver trade benefits. While the trade barrier remains in place, the respondent holds onto market protections that its domestic industry can enjoy—for example, WTO-inconsistent import tariffs on steel preserve market share for domestic steel producers.

Third, if the deadline passes and the respondent has not demonstrated compliance, the complainant will need to initiate another legal stage, compliance proceedings. This sets into motion an extended legal process. Another panel of judges is composed. This time, disputant governments submit their claims about whether the respondent's new policies and practices (if any were adopted) satisfy the original ruling. The compliance panel evaluates these claims and issues another verdict. In most of these compliance proceedings, the judges find that the respondent has not fully complied and that it continues to be in breach of WTO rules. Further legal proceedings are required if the complainant seeks compensation.

Only after these avenues are exhausted can the complainant seek remedies: compensation or temporary countermeasures. Brewster (2011) has noted that this process leaves a "remedy gap" in the WTO system. Any penalties that the WTO authorizes cannot be applied retroactively. Respondents can maintain trade barriers that benefit their own domestic industry at the expense of foreign competitors throughout this lengthy legal process with minimal consequences. In effect, obstinate respondents enjoy a period of protectionism without negative repercussions. Many governments want to take advantage of this "wiggle room"

(Pelc 2013). And, it might be particularly valuable to respondents that face a complicated domestic process that makes it onerous to implement WTO-compliant policies. With these procedures and opportunities for respondents to avoid repercussions, it would seem enforcement through the WTO is incomplete.

3.3.4 Selection pressures in the WTO dispute process

International courts supply institutional tools that states can use or not use and a series of legal stages that alter states' strategic interactions. Not all prospective plaintiffs are equally likely to pursue legalized dispute settlement. Countries sometimes resolve their grievances bilaterally before escalating to adjudication (Huth, Croco, and Appel 2011).

Motivations for pursuing negotiations versus litigation are often political. At the WTO, litigation can be a performance targeted at certain domestic audiences (Allee and Huth 2006; Chaudoin 2014; Davis and Shirato 2007). Davis (2012) demonstrates that prospective plaintiff governments use litigation as a costly signal to politically influential stakeholders. As the most litigious member, the United States' choice whether to negotiate or adjudicate reflects clear domestic political motives. Under divided government, US executives are particularly sensitive to the political support of industry groups and are eager to curry their favor. Bringing WTO legal complaints about foreign trade barriers signals a hard-line stance on trade. The action conveys that the US is willing to stand up to foreign adversaries and promote domestic industry interests.

That adjudication is a political choice has implications for my research on respondents' compliance. Complainants do, of course, weigh economic incentives in the selection of a dispute forum. All else equal, a complainant prefers to prevail in the WTO ruling and ensure the respondent removes the trade barrier in question. But these victories are far from guaranteed and complainants still do pursue disputes that lack a clear pathway to economic gains. This means that trade grievances are not selectively litigated at the WTO in a way that would bias research conclusions about second-order compliance.

Once states initiate formal complaints, the shadow of enforceable WTO judgments also affects the dispute process. States have an incentive to settle early, prior to panel (and Appellate Body) rulings (Busch and Reinhardt 2000a, Gilligan, Johns, and Rosendorff 2010). Many countries prefer to reach these settlements without the heavy hand of

WTO judges scrutinizing their alleged treaty violations and then publicizing a verdict. Early settlements are private. Privacy shields state leaders, on both the complainant and respondent sides, from domestic scrutiny (Johns and Rosendorff 2009). Privacy also protect litigants from having to "share" the proceeds of their bargains more widely with the membership (Kucik and Pelc 2016; Johns and Pelc 2014).

It is far from clear how a respondent's domestic political constraints affect the early settlement of a dispute. On the one hand, disputes that result in judgments are among the most intractable ones: conflicts that could not be resolved during pretrial negotiations. These challenging cases may involve the most obstinate respondent governments. Unwilling to capitulate to the pressures of complainants, these same respondents may be most resistant to adverse WTO rulings. Selection bias at this stage could potentially prolong disputes in which compliance is least likely. On the other hand, respondents with many domestic constraints may be more likely to settle their disputes early during pretrial negotiations. The privacy of pretrial negotiations allows leadership to skirt domestic opposition. Domestic veto players generate higher hurdles to compliance with adverse rulings. Early settlements might allow those governments to reach a deal in which fewer domestic veto players are activated. If selection bias occurred at this stage, it could isolate disputes where government leaders face fewer domestic veto players. Ultimately, the relationship between early settlement and domestic political constraints is an empirical question, one I evaluate in chapter 4.

3.3.5 Decentralized enforcement and performance

These selection forces matter because WTO litigation is more than mere performance. As a relatively strong court (Alter 2014; Johns 2015), the WTO Dispute Settlement Mechanism's relevance hinges on its ability to supply forceful judgments that sustain a rules-based system. In turn, those judgments can be enforced through reciprocity and penalties by the community of member states.

Recent scholarship highlights that enforcement at the WTO is decentralized (Johns 2012; Phelan 2015; Johns and Pelc 2018). The DSM relies on the community of states to take initiative at every step along the way. States monitor one another's trade policy. If there is serious concern that one government has broken WTO rules, another state must step forward as plaintiff and initiate a dispute. The complainant foots the bill for conducting a lawsuit. This is thought to create a collective action problem where countries are tempted to free ride on the enforcement efforts of others (Johns and Pelc 2018). The entire WTO membership benefits from enforcement, yet no single state wants to shoulder the burden of serving as the complainant.

Once a lawsuit is underway, the same enforcement challenges arise. WTO panelists issue their judgment, typically finding that the respondent violated its trade commitments. Once a verdict is issued, the respondent is required to implement the ruling through its own domestic policy and practice. Yet there is little institutional support for monitoring whether the respondent complies. WTO procedures request the respondent provide regular status reports on its progress. But there are no clear expectations for the details of these reports, nor do any officials verify that reported policy reforms are sufficient to achieve compliance. Ordinarily, the monitoring burden falls on the plaintiff, which must check whether the respondent has made sufficient steps toward compliance and, if it has not, pursue continued legal action. This involves the compliance procedure and request for remedies discussed above. Again, the complainant must bear the enforcement burden and pursue retaliation.

Besides the disputants, other states often have a stake in a WTO dispute. The respondent's trade policy might harm them in a similar way as it does the plaintiff. Or the case may establish standards akin to legal precedent (Pelc 2014; Kucik, Peritz, and Puig, forthcoming). Since a WTO dispute has broader importance beyond its effects on the plaintiff and the respondent, the DSM allows states to enter the proceedings as "third parties." Third parties usually support the plaintiff. Their presence reflects the perceived international importance of the dispute.[17] High-profile disputes with diffuse economic effects may be most likely to attract third-party participation. These are the disputes in which defendants may be most unwilling to concede. Third parties can only contribute to enforcement in limited ways. They cannot seek remedies as the plaintiff can, and because they cannot participate in settlements with the respondent, they tend to benefit less than plaintiffs do (Bown 2005a; Kucik and Pelc 2016).

As a result of this decentralized system, disputes may be left without clear resolution. There are sometimes disparities between what the WTO reports in its legal records and what happens within respondent governments. Respondents might take a wait-and-see approach in order to try to avoid compliance. From the respondent's perspective, this

strategy is sensible. Complainants have political incentives to file WTO
disputes in order to appeal to domestic audiences (Davis 2012; Chaudoin 2014). Yet a complainant might see diminishing returns in pursuing its lawsuit and drop the complaint, deeming it futile. This enables
the respondent to escape repercussions. With little to no monitoring and
decentralized enforcement, the WTO gives governments substantial opportunity to ignore adverse rulings.

These features make it difficult for other countries in the international
community to glean information about compliance trends. Suppose that
a government has reported to the WTO that it complied with the ruling
and the report went unchallenged by the complainant. This could mean
the respondent's compliance measures were satisfactory. It could also
mean that the complainant dropped the lawsuit for strategic reasons: the
respondent was obstinate and further efforts seemed futile, or the respondent implemented partial measures and the complainant could not
justify further legal expenditures. More problematic, it is also possible
the respondent compensated the complainant, violating the core goals
of the WTO: the most-favored nation treatment and national treatment
principles (Kucik and Pelc 2016). Bystander states are left with little information about how well the DSM performed. This lack of information
makes it more difficult for the community to penalize noncompliant respondents through reputation costs or other indirect penalties.

Taking a step back, it seems that the WTO DSM has little incentive to
close these gaps. An IC's claim to legitimacy is delicate. When governments defy rulings and noncompliance is publicized, the court's authority may be undermined. Then respondents might take its rulings as mere
suggestions, leading to devolving influence. WTO panel judges face a
political balancing act (Brutger and Morse 2015). In a sense, then, the
gap between respondents' reports on compliance and the actual policy
reforms they enact—whether sufficient or insufficient—is a useful ambiguity. Likewise, decentralized enforcement means that judges do not
have to address second-order compliance problems. If the plaintiff government drops the dispute for any of the aforementioned reasons, the
WTO can publicly declare it a success.

In summary, decentralized enforcement within the WTO has two
major implications. The first is that a decentralized system of enforcement makes respondents' domestic political divisions salient. The WTO
court has ample informal opportunities for flexibility—including delays
and tolerated noncompliance—that savvy governments may want to ex-

ploit. Governments with many domestic political constraints may be especially prone to use these opportunities. The second implication concerns assessing the WTO's performance. Researchers cannot assume that WTO records identify all instances of noncompliance with rulings; rather, many go underreported. Neither a complainant's persistence nor institutional monitoring provide adequate information. To determine whether or not a respondent complied, one must look directly at the policy reforms. This makes studying compliance with WTO rulings a challenging empirical task—one I take on in chapter 4 by looking at adjustments in trade policy.

3.4 Economic integration and the ECJ

3.4.1 Constructing a single market

Like the WTO, the European Union also dismantles barriers to commerce among its member states. Free trade is fundamental to the EU goal of a single market and states aim to reap the mutual gains that arise from trade cooperation. But the EU goes much further than the WTO does. The European community has created a system of deep economic interdependence among all members. As the EU's own website materials put it, "the Community's primary mission is to create a common market" (European Union 2021). Free trade in goods is only one component of the single market. The EU also requires free movement of capital, services, and labor.

All member states are obligated to implement their EU obligations at the national level. These obligations take the form of directives and regulations issued by the European Commission and the European Council, which states incorporate through domestic law or policy. Many directives eliminate barriers to commerce in specific areas—for example, by standardizing tax rules or competition policy across members. Others create policies that reduce unfair competition within industries or sectors—for example, directives that eliminate the use of certain pesticides in agriculture or require environmental standards in waste disposal. Directives ordinarily apply to all members of the EU and must be implemented at the national level.[18] It is the responsibility of the governments to report to the Commission how they implemented the directive or how their laws already meet community requirements.

States sometimes violate important EU obligations and they can do so in different ways. They can fail to notify the Commission of their national implementation measures in due time, they can incorrectly transpose European law into domestic law, or they can implement only a portion of the required measures (Börzel et al. 2010, 1373). Member states might violate EU law by imposing de facto barriers to commerce, thereby obstructing the single market. All states have been found to have broken EU law at some point, although some have more fraught records than others. For instance, in the 2019 annual report monitoring the application of EU law, the Commission found that Luxembourg, and Lithuania had among the fewest new open cases for violations of EU law, whereas Spain, Italy, and Greece faced the highest number (European Commission 2019, 22).

Directives on the internal market, taxation, the customs union, and competition are often the sources of controversy. Occasionally, national governments staunchly resist. When influential domestic groups oppose EU law, governments can be particularly resistant. For example, the controversial 1993 Investment Services Directive brought significant new security regulations. It was intended to break down states' protectionist non-tariff barriers to domestic market entry and enhance transparency standards (Warren 1994). Many firms opposed these regulations, with the United Kingdom and Germany particularly sensitive to financial sector interests. Other times, the obstacles are institutional—countries may lack the bureaucratic capacity to make the necessary changes. So although governments are legally obligated to implement directives, they might fail to do so. The Commission can investigate and—if necessary—bring a formal lawsuit to the ECJ.[19] When a state fails to implement a directive, it risks provoking a lawsuit. In an "infringement dispute," the Commission sues a state for not (first-order) complying with its obligations.

3.4.2 Infringement procedure and the ECJ

The infringement procedure consists of three main steps: First, the Commission sends a letter of formal notice to a member state indicating that there is a suspected violation of EU law. This is the triggering event for the process. Sometimes this conflict is simply a matter of reporting problems—the state failed to notify the Commission precisely how the EU law was incorporated into its national policy. Reporting problems are easily resolved. But sometimes this step uncovers substantive disagreements between the Commission and the national government. The state has an opportunity to formally present its view, rebutting the allegations. In its rebuttal, the state explains why existing national policy is consistent with EU law and why the Commission's concerns are unfounded.

The second step is an assessment in the form of a reasoned opinion. The Commission evaluates the infringement case in view of the state's submission. If the Commission still considers the state to be in breach of EU law, it sends a reasoned opinion that details the reforms needed for the state to come into compliance, explains how the state is breaking EU law, and requests that the state report measures taken within a specified period, usually two months. If the state fails to comply with the reasoned opinion within that time period, the Commission may refer the matter to the ECJ.

The third step is a lawsuit. If the state still does not comply, the Commission brings a lawsuit to the ECJ. This procedure is established in Article 258 of the Treaty on the Functioning of the European Union (TFEU; formerly Article 169 under the prior treaty). Both the Commission and the national government submit written statements. Observations can also be submitted by other national authorities, EU institutions, and sometimes private individuals. Depending on the complexity of the case, three, five, or very rarely fifteen judges (one from each EU15 state, constituting the whole court) and an advocate general evaluate the case. Many cases then move on to an oral hearing stage, which is a public lawsuit. Lawyers from both sides present the case to the judges. The judges deliberate and deliver their verdict. As compared to the WTO dispute system, the ECJ is more active. Between 1978 and 1999, the ECJ ruled on over one thousand infringement disputes against the fifteen core member states of the EU (Börzel and Knoll 2012). Activity increased over this time period and was highly unevenly distributed among states.

Figure 3.2 shows the frequency of infringement lawsuits brought against member states by the Commission for an ECJ ruling between 1978 and 1999. Figure 3.2(a) aggregates the data by year, where the increase after 1995 in part reflects the enlargement of the EU. Figure 3.2(b) shows the lawsuits by target member state, distinguishing between cases initiated before and after the 1995 expansion.

When the verdict favors the state, it absolves that government of any further action and the case is closed. When the verdict favors the

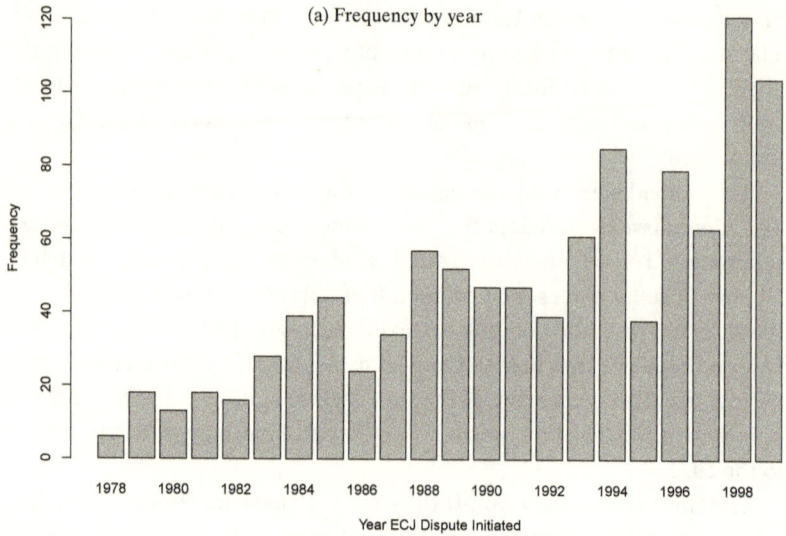

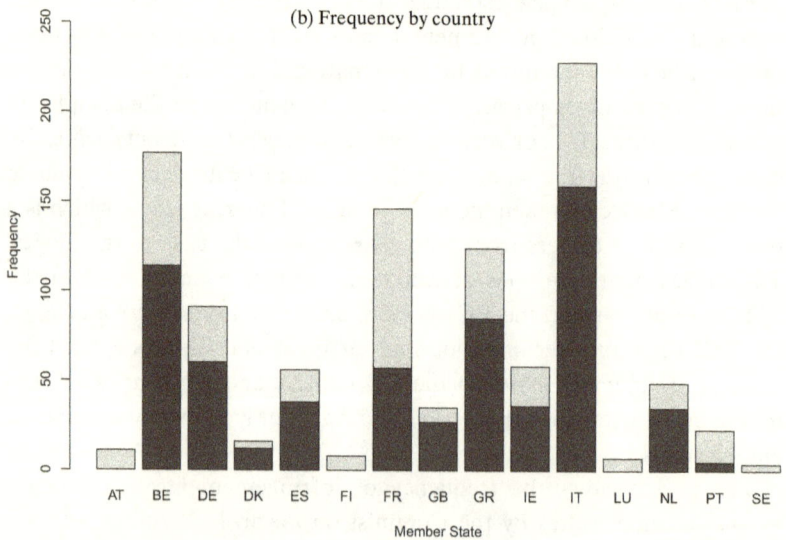

FIGURE 3.2. Frequency of Infringement Disputes Brought to the ECJ, 1978 to 1999
Note: Data are from Börzel and Knoll (2012) and cover all issue areas. In (b), the shading denotes cases before (dark gray) and after (light gray) the 1995 EU expansion.

Commission, the state is required to implement the ruling through its policy and practice. A full 95% of the infringement rulings from disputes initiated between 1978 and 1999 favored the Commission—that is, the state was found to be in violation of EU obligations (Börzel and Knoll 2012).

ECJ rulings set additional procedures in motion. The Maastricht Treaty, signed in 1992, gave the ECJ the power to impose fines on a member state that fails to take the necessary measures to comply with ECJ judgments under Article 228. However, the Commission must first undergo an additional lawsuit and obtain a judgment of continued noncompliance before any fines are approved (TFEU Article 260). This is rare. Among the ECJ infringement cases where the Court ruled against the member state (between 1978 and 1999), the Commission pursued continued investigations about one-quarter of the time through another reasoned opinion under Article 228 (Börzel and Knoll 2012). That is not to say that the remaining three-quarters of rulings prompted states to comply; there may be instances where the Commission chose to ignore continued violations. The Court does not routinely track state behavior in this respect. Many of the resolved disputes may, in fact, be instances where the Commission chose to exercise forbearance.[20]

Once a reasoned opinion on noncompliance is issued in accordance with Article 228, the vast majority of accusations are settled or withdrawn. In only 6% of those accusations (between 1978 and 1999) did the Commission go back to the ECJ for another ruling, the prerequisite for imposing fines. In the extended data I present in chapter 6, I find that just under 13% of trade-related infringement rulings between 1987 and 2012 prompted noncompliance proceedings. Regardless of what time period one looks at, the attrition pattern suggests that the Commission uses its enforcement capacity sparingly. Carrubba, Gabel, and Hankla (2008) argue there is a risk that states will reject or override an ECJ ruling that is too onerous. One interpretation of the data is that the Commission exercises discretion, perhaps sparing ECJ judges the difficult task of ruling a second time against states that are demonstrably obstinate.

In recent years, the ECJ has started to impose financial penalties on states for failing to implement EU directives. One of the first high-profile cases of the court authorizing fines was Case C-387/97, *Commission v. Greece*. In this dispute, Greece had been disposing of toxic waste in an environmentally hazardous manner. The Commission sued, secured a first ECJ ruling, and subsequently found that Greece had failed to comply with the court's judgment. The Commission brought continued non-compliance charges against Greece through the Article 228 process. The ECJ ordered Greece to pay the Commission a penalty of 20,000 euros for each day it further delayed implementing measures necessary to comply with the original judgment issued six years prior (see 2000 ECR p. I-5047). The fines ultimately totaled ten million. Nonetheless, the rarity of these cases raises the possibility that the ECJ, too, is wary of rebuking states only to be ignored.

The Commission uses the infringement procedure as a tool to promote the supremacy of European law (Chalmers, Davies, and Monti 2014, 341), address obstacles to economic integration, and pursue a pro-free trade agenda (Bednar, Ferejohn, and Farrett 1996), even if it exercises discretion in doing so. Infringement lawsuits are instrumental in the process of legal integration. A large portion of these disputes directly address barriers to intra-European trade in particular (Tallberg 2000; Panke 2007; Sverdrup 2004). Building on data compiled by Börzel and Knoll (2012), I collected data on infringement disputes brought to the ECJ from 1999 to 2012 and then determined the subject areas of these cases. Just under 40% of them concerned barriers to intra-EU trade and commerce. With these extended data, I found that between 1987 and 2012, the ECJ ruled on approximately one thousand trade-related infringement disputes against the fifteen core countries.[21] Trade-related infringement lawsuits challenge policies such as quantitative restrictions, pricing schemes, discriminatory taxes, technical standards, etc.

In the majority of lawsuits on these trade-related issues, the ECJ favored the Commission. During the period I examined, 88% of the trade-related rulings determined the state was guilty of breaching its EU obligations. Adverse trade rulings require the defendant to dismantle its illegal barriers to the EU's internal market. These judgments are pro-trade liberalizing, parallel to the WTO's adverse rulings. What these patterns suggest is that the Commission is willing to enforce EU law on the core issues of economic integration and that the court rebukes states for their failures to fulfill EU obligations. But the Commission rarely pursues second-order noncompliance concerns, and the ECJ therefore has little opportunity to assess the merits of that form of accusation. As we saw with respect to the WTO, one cannot lean on legal proceedings alone to evaluate whether defendant countries complied with adverse rulings from the ECJ.

Infringement disputes are not the only cases the ECJ takes on. The other major type of case, which accounts for a large share of the court's activity, concerns the preliminary ruling system. This is a parallel adjudicatory process by which national courts make references over questions of EU law to the ECJ. Preliminary reference cases arise when a private litigant brings a lawsuit to a national court and the national court decides that EU law is relevant to the case. The national judges ask the ECJ for an interpretation of EU law. Once the ECJ judges issue their opinion, that recommendation is passed back down to the national court. Then the national judges make a final ruling, leaning on the full weight of the domestic legal system. As many scholars have argued, this process is central to the legal integration of Europe because it allows national courts to enforce EU law and ensure its supremacy over national law. It has been instrumental to the EU's economic and political integration (Carrubba and Murrah 2005; Stone Sweet and Caporaso 1998; Stone Sweet and Brunell 1998b).

The preliminary ruling system is unique in the landscape of international courts.[22] It relies on the authority of national courts to give ECJ rulings force. As a result, it does not encounter the same kinds of compliance and enforcement problems pervasive among international courts (Gilligan 2006). Under the preliminary ruling system, a government agency or politician that disregards a national court's judgment following the ECJ recommendation is not only in breach of EU law but has also pushed back against the authority of its own *national* legal system. In this respect, the preliminary ruling system resembles a supranational or federal system more than an international one (Stone Sweet and Brunell 1998a; Alter 2001; Bednar, Ferejohn, and Farrett 1996). By contrast, under the infringement dispute system, a government agency or politician that disregards an ECJ ruling is rejecting an *international* mandate. The infringement dispute system is vulnerable to the same kind of second-order compliance problems we observe in other international courts.[23]

3.4.3 Shadow of the court and compliance

States do not always comply with ECJ rulings. While noncompliance problems are nearly universally acknowledged, there remains a long-standing debate over their root causes (Stone Sweet and Brunell 1998a; Mattli and Slaughter 1998). This debate echoes the larger puzzle of compliance in international organizations, with some scholars attributing violations to inadvertent errors and others highlighting the deliberate and opportunistic breach of international obligations.

Some instances of noncompliance are attributed to capacity limitations (Haas 1998; Linos 2007; Gray 2014). Governments may lack resources to adjust policy in response to an adverse ruling, as suggested by a "managerial" perspective of international organization (Chayes and Chayes 1993). Administrative inefficiency, limited budgets or poor bureaucratic capacity may explain persistent violations of EU law (Börzel 2001; Börzel et al. 2010). Some states that do possess adequate resources fail to efficiently allocate them in order to achieve compliance (Mbaye 2001). There may also be significant mismatch between EU obligations and national policy. If the demands from the EU deviate far from the domestic status quo, governments find implementation far more onerous (Thomson 2009). These governments continue to violate EU law, even under the heightened pressure of legal enforcement. By contrast, governments with plenty of bureaucratic resources on hand are better equipped to implement EU law. Their task is particularly manageable when EU law aligns well with their existing practices; these are "shallow" commitments in the parlance of Downs, Rocke, and Barsoom (1996). In short, some scholars interpret noncompliance as inadvertent, due to the mismatch between state ambitions and what states can realistically achieve with limited resources.

However, in many instances, states with ample bureaucratic capacity also clash with the court (Börzel et al. 2010). Recognizing this, many scholars emphasize the enforcement function of the Commission, working with the ECJ, and argue that noncompliance is caused by divergent preferences (Garrett and Weingast 1993). When a government's aims conflict with the court, that state may be reluctant to implement an ECJ ruling. These conflicts can be particularly acute when it comes to enforcing a single European market (Siegel 2011). Pro-integration rulings threaten to impose heavy costs on segments of a defendant government's economy by overturning national laws that support certain sectors (Garrett, Kelemen, and Schulz 1998). The costs may prove intolerable. Prescribed policies they are unwilling to adopt, governments directly defy the court entirely.

Chapter 6 weighs in on this debate by offering systematic evidence that supports the latter view. Some noncompliance problems can be credited to the work of influential constituencies within governments that oppose ECJ rulings. Those groups can pull the political levers in government to make the compliance process more cumbersome, eventually obstructing the court's efforts to advance economic integration.

It is certainly possible that this threat of unilateral noncompliance influences the calculations of the European Commission in choosing to initiate lawsuits and of the ECJ judges when they craft their rulings. But, given that the vast majority of infringement disputes result in findings of violations, it is clear that EU judges do not ignore the missteps of member states entirely. Whether the ECJ disproportionately shies away from enforcement in response to the domestic politics of member states is an open question. But the evidence does not seem to support this form of strategic discretion. Among the 1,033 ECJ infringement rulings issued between 1978 and 1999, Belgium and Spain, the states with the most political constraints (measured by veto points in 1999), were subjected to adverse ruling rates of 95% and 98%, respectively. Those with the fewest political constraints, Greece and Denmark, were both subjected to adverse ruling rates of 94%. The rates across these groups are statistically indistinguishable.

Noncompliance by individual states is not the only obstacle the court encounters. States also collectively resist through "override"—that is, they pass secondary legislation that constrains the court's authority (Carrubba, Gabel, and Hankla 2008). While scholars agree that collective resistance is rare, they debate how to interpret this fact (Stone Sweet and Brunell 2012; Carrubba, Gabel, and Hankla 2012). Some argue that EU institutions—including the court—have chiefly facilitated transnational exchanges that facilitate further integration in the service of states' goals (Stone Sweet and Brunell 1998a). Rulings reflect the collective preferences of states, so there is little opportunity for meaningful resistance—much less for override—to arise. On the other hand, some scholars argue that the EU legal system serves the interests of powerful states (Garrett 1992) and that judges are especially wary of issuing controversial rulings against powerful governments, lest they provoke widespread backlash (Larsson and Naurin 2016). The downstream threat of noncompliance can have a chilling effect. In an effort to avoid override, ECJ judges may only rule against a government only when it anticipates support, or at least tacit acceptance, from other powerful members (Garrett, Kelemen, and Schulz 1998).

In applying my theory to the ECJ, I leverage an important implication from the aforementioned literature: the court avoids controversial judgments that could provoke coordinated dissent. On matters of eco-

nomic integration, which can be especially fraught, the ECJ may be reluctant to issue broad adverse rulings. Instead, it tends to target specific
barriers to trade in individual states. These types of rulings, rather than
uniformly affecting the European community, narrowly impact particular sectors of defendant governments' economies. In turn, this can
fuel opposition among affected domestic groups. For instance, by striking down a national law favoring domestic pharmaceutical products over
those produced elsewhere in the EU, an adverse ruling energized opposition from the firms and the interest group representing that state's
pharmaceutical industry. When domestic groups encounter significant
costs, they are apt to pressure their governments to defy ECJ rulings.
Whether they succeed in blocking compliance depends on formal and
informal veto points in their government. Therefore, to understand the
ECJ's role in promoting the single market, it is again crucial to consider
domestic political constraints, the internal factors that drive each state's
reaction to targeted rulings.

3.4.4 Centralized enforcement and ECJ performance

Compared to the WTO, the ECJ features more centralized means for
enforcement (Phelan 2015). Whereas individual plaintiffs must shoulder
the enforcement burden in the WTO, the European Commission bears
that responsibility in the ECJ. The Commission is at a distinct advantage
in this respect. It can draw on the shared resources of the EU and overcome the collective action problem that WTO enforcement entails.

　　The Commission leads enforcement efforts in a couple ways. When a
country is judged to have violated EU law, it is obligated to report its implementation measures to the Commission. The Commission monitors
progress and publicizes its findings. Every year, the Commission draws
up an annual report on its monitoring of the application of EU law including compliance with ECJ rulings. In addition, the body can call for
fines on recalcitrant states. The ECJ routinely authorizes penalties and
the Commission can call for additional financial sanctions when original
efforts fail.[24] For example, the Commission's 2018 report summarizes its
enforcement efforts with the seeming intent to name and shame obstinate states:

> The Commission took Italy to Court for a second time, as the Italian author-
> ities did not comply with a Court earlier ruling . . . the Court confirmed that

Italy had granted illegal state aid to the hotel industry in Sardinia. The Commission ordered Italy to recover illegal aid amounting to close to €15 million. Still today, almost €13 million have not been recovered. (European Commission 2018, 12)

The penalties strike a black mark on the reputation of the noncompliant state, and failure to pay could mean the country is eventually denied aid from EU coffers. In these respects, ECJ rulings enjoy enforcement through the support of the Commission.

Centralized enforcement does not completely resolve compliance problems, however. The Commission, even with the backing of the ECJ, cannot easily compel a member state to comply (Panke 2007), and it can take a while for the Commission to obtain authorization from the ECJ to impose penalties. An example from France illustrates this point clearly. When the ECJ struck down France's ban on British beef, an effective barrier to intra-EU trade, the French government defied the ruling. One British newspaper reported, "The Commission admitted it was powerless to take swift action against France over the continued blockage of British beef . . . it would take years to go back to court to seek fines and compensation." And the French government's delay was driven by domestic political constraints. The UK minister of agriculture, Lord Whitty, said, "The French are clearly out of order. [They] may not move until after the French elections."[25] The domestic political constraints—here, an upcoming election and politicians' concerns about upsetting agriculture interests—meant that the EU's centralized enforcement process was unlikely to induce compliance.

A key enforcement challenge plagues the EU. As Carrubba and Gabel (2015) argue, the Commission, in cooperation with the ECJ, is reluctant to enforce rulings against obstinate defendant governments. Because noncompliance, especially when it is highly visible to the EU community, threatens the court's legitimacy, the Commission is wary of provoking backlash (Caldeira and Gibson 1995). So the Commission sometimes tacitly permits defiance, once the legal process fails to elicit reform (König and Mäder 2014).[26] In summary, the centralized approach to enforcement is imperfect because of the strategic interaction between EU institutions and member states.

Given the Commission's incentives, persistent second-order noncompliance is almost surely more common than official EU reports suggest. As noted above, countries are only rarely prosecuted for ignoring the court's verdict; many more instances likely go unchallenged and are thus underreported (Falkner et al. 2005). Thus we cannot trust legal steps in ECJ disputes to serve as an accurate indicator of compliance. An objective measure is needed (Börzel 2001; Hartlapp and Falkner 2009). In chapter 6, I look at the *economic impact* of infringement rulings on disputes over the EU's internal market. While I cannot systematically discern whether the state in each case complied with ECJ rulings, as I do with the WTO, I can trace whether the cases collectively appear to prompt the expected boost in intra-EU commerce. This approach side steps some potential biases that come from the Commission's selective enforcement of rulings.

Other scholars have taken a similar approach to understand the effect of ECJ rulings on member state behavior. Gabel et al. (2012) and Carrubba and Gabel (2015) also focus on intra-EU commerce as a revealing metric. They estimate the impact of rulings on intra-EU trade flows and find a significant positive effect for one category of cases, preliminary references, but not for infringement rulings (Gabel et al. 2012, 1133). The literature concludes that preliminary reference rulings attain higher compliance rates than infringement rulings and attributes the discrepancy to enforcement failures. Preliminary rulings, as noted above, are implemented directly though a nation's own legal system, bypassing domestic political impediments (Stone Sweet and Brunell 1998b; Carrubba and Murrah 2005). Infringement rulings, by contrast, must be incorporated into national policy through legislative or administrative action. Taken alone, the literature's null finding on infringements might lead one to conclude that the ECJ is largely ineffective. That is, despite the many provisions in EU law for enforcing rulings and the Commission's authority to pursue these routes, countries are not responsive to the court.

The apparent null effect, however, belies a more complicated domestic dynamic. Unlike preliminary references, infringement rulings are subjected to significant obstacles to implementation. Defendant governments must garner the consent and cooperation of multiple domestic political actors in order to comply with these rulings. Their legislatures must overcome partisan divisions to enact pro-integration bills; administrative agencies must cultivate support from industry groups to ensure new policies are correctly implemented. As I show in chapter 6, these domestic political constraints matter in a systematic way, consistent with my theory. By testing the theory presented in chapter 2 in the context of the ECJ, I am able to add crucial nuance to the literature on the ECJ's effectiveness in ushering along European economic integration.

3.5 Players, preferences, and actions

The previous sections described formal procedures and enforcement in two international courts, leaving unspecified the preferences of and actions available to the political actors involved in the legal disputes. In this section, I chart out my assumptions about the key players in my theory. I use a simple, stylized model of a trade dispute to explain the sequence of events that produces compliance and noncompliance. The goal here is not to provide a complete game theoretic model. My argument allows for the possibility that some political actors make errors in judgment or fail to exercise adequate foresight. A fully specified model of this process would need to account for stochastic behavior and might obscure rather than illuminate the dynamics. Rather, my goal is to clarify the assumptions underpinning the hypotheses described in chapter 2.

3.5.1 Sequence with unitary actor

Consider the relevant political actors. I assume that when governments participate in a multilateral trade agreement, they can follow the trade agreement or violate it. Following the treaty means abiding by the terms of trade liberalization, while violating it means imposing trade barriers.[27] The possibility exists that one government will accuse another of breaking the treaty terms: a defendant state risks being sued by a plaintiff. Either the plaintiff is another state, in the context of the WTO, or it is the Commission, in the context of ECJ infringement disputes. I assume the plaintiff wants the defendant to comply with its international commitments. In the context of international trade, the plaintiff urges the defendant to keep trade barriers low. But the plaintiff's decision-making process is not the focus of my inquiry, so I set aside the nuances particular to its calculations. For instance, I do not account for the different preferences domestic actors within the plaintiff country might hold, as other research on the WTO has emphasized (Davis 2012; Chaudoin 2014). Instead, my focus is on the domestic political actors within the *defendant* government.

Let us begin with a simple unitary actor account of compliance decisions and international economic courts. Here, the defendant government is represented simply by an Executive. The Executive decides whether to first-order comply or not with an existing international agreement. If it follows the status quo and keeps trade barriers low, this is first-order compliance. If it passes a protectionist policy, this is first-order noncompliance. First-order noncompliance prompts a lawsuit from the plaintiff. The international court rules either in favor of the plaintiff or the defendant with some probability. A ruling in favor of the defendant allows the trade protection policy to stand; because the court sides with the defendant and validates the policy, the Executive escapes any international penalties. A ruling in favor of the plaintiff, conversely, strikes down the trade policy as a violation of the international agreement. In this case, the Executive decides whether to abide by the ruling and remove the trade barrier—second-order compliance—or ignore the ruling and retain the trade barrier—second-order noncompliance. Second-order noncompliance carries an international penalty such as a damaged international reputation, loss of future cooperative opportunities, or sanctions. This leads to a simple conclusion: *first-order non-compliance* only occurs when the Executive decides it is worth the risk; *second-order compliance* only occurs if the Executive is sufficiently concerned with international penalties.

However, it is clear that an Executive's decisions about compliance with international rulings do not affect all domestic groups evenly. Adjustments to trade policy carry distributive implications; they benefit some and are detrimental to others. As the Stolper-Samuelson theorem posited, those "winners" and "losers" of trade policy reform depend on the relative abundance or scarcity of factors of production in a country (Stolper and Samuelson 1941). According to this model—which is a useful starting point even if its account is oversimplified—an expansion in trade leads to an increase in the return to a country's abundant factor (e.g., capital and skilled labor in the US) and a fall in the return to its scarce factor (e.g., unskilled labor in the US).[28] That means when the Executive favors second-order compliance—revoking the protectionist policy—those who once enjoyed shelter from import competition stand to lose (e.g., the owners of the scarce factor). At the same time, those who benefit from reciprocal liberalization and thrive in a global economy see relative gains from compliance with the court's ruling (e.g., the owners of the abundant factor). Conversely, if the Executive ignores the ruling, the groups' positions would be reversed. Constituents sheltered from trade competition would continue to enjoy their protected status, while those who could reap the benefits of an open global economy might suffer from international penalties in the form of reciprocal market closures. With these domestic distributive factors laid out, more nuance can now be added to this stylized account. Which domestic constituents does the Executive respond to, and what happens when the government is not a unitary actor on trade policy?

3.5.2 Sequence with divisions in government

Building on the unitary actor logic, we can now consider the decision tree under a government with divisions. Suppose that the defendant contains two main players: an agenda setter and a ratifier. For any policy change to take place, the agenda setter must secure consent from the ratifier. Yet these actors hold different preferences regarding international reputation. The ratifier cares more about international pressures than does the agenda setter, so they often clash on policy decisions. For ease of exposition, I assume here that the agenda setter is the Legislature and the ratifier is the Executive.[29] The argument could also be applied in parliamentary regimes—with the government and the opposition—albeit with less acute constraints on the agenda setter's power. Scholars have highlighted strong similarities between divided presidential systems and coalition governments in parliamentary systems in terms of these checks between agenda setters and ratifiers (e.g., Fiorina 1991; Laver and Shepsle 1991). Despite this broad applicability across different types of government, for simplicity of exposition, I use the language for presidential systems.

I further assume that the Legislature cares less about international reputation and the Executive cares more. In a foundational study, Milner (1997, 36) explains what drives the branches' different interests: "The national focus of the executive and the more local concerns of legislators help explain why . . . [they] have distinct policy preferences." Executives will prefer international cooperation when the political benefits from international cooperation outweigh the costs. In these instances, "the no cooperation outcome is seen as worse than the cooperative one. In the face of noncooperation the domestic economy would be worse off and hence their reelection chances would be worse" (Milner 1997,

46). National benefits from cooperation and foreign retaliation for defection often render Executives more amenable than Legislators to international cooperation.

These divisions in government map onto preferences over trade policy. Legislatures are widely thought to be more protectionist than Executives, who prefer more liberal trade policy. The constituencies to whom Legislators versus Executives are held politically accountable differ and this shapes the trade policies each political actor prefers (Weingast, Shepsle, and Johnsen 1981; Lohmann and O'Halloran 1994). Individual Legislators tend to be responsive to the geographically concentrated and often parochial interests of the stakeholders in their districts (Shugart and Carey 1992). In the case of international trade, industry groups that are disadvantaged—for example, import-competing groups—are particularly successful at politically mobilizing, especially when geographical proximity bolsters their capacity for collective action (Busch and Reinhardt 2000b).[30] Stakeholders such as firms and interest groups sometimes push their representatives to deliver targeted trade protection that helps them (Grossman and Helpman 1992; Staiger and Tabellini 1987) through extensive lobbying efforts. Conversely, constituents that stand to benefit from more liberal trade policy—for example, voters as consumers—face well-known obstacles to political mobilization. Legislators are thought to be less responsive to these dispersed interests, as shown in some recent empirical research (Betz and Pond 2019).[31]

Executives, in contrast to Legislators, have national constituencies spanning a broad range of trade interests and care about reducing the losses incurred in all districts. They are thought to be more attuned to the efficiency gains that international trade delivers to the broader national economy, including to exporter-oriented industries alongside the import-competing ones. As Lohmann and O'Halloran (1994) argue, "if given discretionary powers to set trade policy, the President would implement measures that trade off the marginal benefits derived from protecting industries in one district against the marginal costs imposed on all other districts. . . . protection levels will be lower when the President alone sets trade policy than when Congress passes trade legislation" (600). This contrast between protectionist Legislatures and pro-liberalizing Executives has been documented in a number of contexts and is often attributed to the constituency size of these respective offices (e.g., Lohmann and O'Halloran 1994; Bailey, Goldstein, and Weingast 1997; Destler 2005).[32] Thus when there are divisions between branches of government, the Legislature counters the Executive to drive trade policy in a protectionist direction. Note, however, that this assumption of trade policy direction is not critical to the argument: my conclusions remain the same if Legislators and Executives held preferences in the opposite direction.

Trade policy preferences shape the path that international litigation takes. The first step is whether or not the (prospective) defendant government follows or violates its international commitment. The Legislature decides whether or not to first-order comply with the treaty. If it complies, then the status quo is maintained—low trade barriers, liberal policy.[33] In this discussion, I assume that a first-order treaty violation involves some positive action—the government passes a policy that violates the treaty. A more general model could allow that some treaty violations are "status quo" policies. In this alternative scenario, the first-order compliance dynamics would be simplified and the second-order compliance dynamics would remain the same. If the Legislature chooses not to comply, it puts forth a policy proposal—high trade barriers, protectionist policy. But because the defendant government is divided, the Executive must consent to the Legislature's proposal to give it effect. If the Executive blocks the proposal, the status quo is still maintained— low trade barriers, liberal policy. If the Executive allows the proposal, it passes into policy—high trade barriers, protectionist policy. This outcome represents first-order noncompliance because the defendant government violates its international commitment. Recall, the sequence of decisions is not critical. It could be reversed were the Executive to move first and the Legislature second. The point is that under divided government, one branch can veto the other's policy proposal. Unless both approve the proposal, the status quo of first-order compliance is maintained.

The second step is a lawsuit. When the defendant adopts the proposed policy and (allegedly) breaks its international commitment, a plaintiff brings its lawsuit before the international court. The court can side with the plaintiff or with the defendant. The Executive and Legislature within the defendant government are uncertain about what the court will decide. Suppose the court sides with the defendant; in this scenario, it rules that the plaintiff's allegations were not well founded, or that the defendant's policy was actually first-order compliant. Or, it could be that the court does not anticipate a ruling would be effective in inducing the defendant to remove the violation. The court could aim to avoid second-order noncompliance (Carrubba, Gabel, and Hankla 2008). By siding with the defendant, the court allows the protectionist policy—high trade barriers—to remain in place. This trade protection outcome has domestic consequences. It is desirable for the Legislature because it aligns with the protectionist preferences held by this actor. The result is also satisfactory to the Executive. Because the court sided with the defendant, the protectionist policy is legitimized in the eyes of international audiences. This absolves the defendant government and spares it from incurring international repercussions. In this case, the Executive does not bear international reputation costs or experience direct retaliation. Suppose instead that the court sides with the plaintiff; it confirms the allegations and issues an adverse ruling. In other words, the court determines that the defendant's policy is a violation of its international obligation: first-order noncompliance. The court demands the defendant government reverses the policy.

The third step hinges on whether or not the defendant complies with the court's adverse ruling. Suppose the Executive ignores the ruling; it refuses to reverse the protectionist policy and is therefore second-order noncompliant. Conversely, suppose the Executive tries to comply with the adverse ruling; it proposes reversing the protectionist policy, but in order to succeed it must gain legislative support. The Legislature can reject the policy reversal: second-order noncompliance. Either way, the protectionist policy remains in place. This keeps the Legislature happy, since it holds more protectionist preferences. Moreover, trade protection may appear to the Legislature to be particularly desirable at this stage.

But second-order noncompliance is an undesirable outcome for the Executive. Its government is publicly rebuked by the court. The Executive suffers international repercussions. Its reputation might be damaged, or it could endure direct retaliation. This includes commensurate trade barriers, in the case of the WTO, and fines, in the case of the ECJ. Of course, in reality, some Legislators will also suffer from these repercussions, but on average their costs will be less severely felt than those borne by the executive branch.

The last possible outcome is that, like the Executive, the Legislature also yields to the court's adverse ruling. With both domestic actors in alignment, the protectionist policy is reversed and we have second-order compliance. The low trade barrier status quo is restored. This is a good outcome for the Executive, who prefers liberal trade policy and avoids international punishment. After losing a lawsuit, the international penalties induce the Executive to change its preference ranking so that

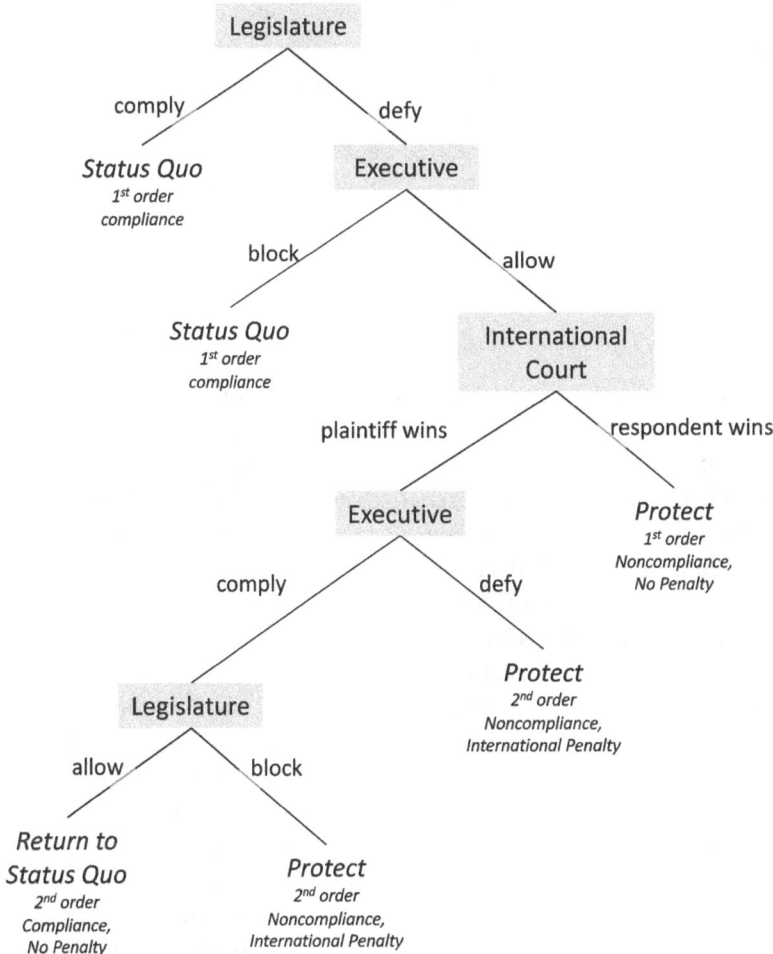

FIGURE 3.3. Decision Tree for International Lawsuit with Domestic Veto Players

second-order compliance—that is, restoring status quo liberal policy—is more desirable than protectionism. But the Legislature would find this outcome to be the worst option, since it prefers the protectionist policy. The Executive and Legislature, at this point, come into conflict.

Figure 3.3 illustrates the decision tree. This sequence of events demonstrates that the divided government model significantly complicates compliance dynamics. With two players in the defendant government, first-order noncompliance only occurs when the Executive decides it is worth the risk to choose the trade protection policy and the Legislature agrees. Holding the Executive's preferences constant, the Legislature's consent is a more demanding requirement; hence the conventional wisdom that veto points improve first-order compliance. Following an adverse ruling, second-order compliance only occurs if the Executive is sufficiently concerned with international reputation (sanctions, etc.) and the Legislature acquiesces. Again, holding the Executive's preferences constant, this is a more demanding condition. Veto points reduce the likelihood of second-order compliance.

3.5.3 Lock-in effect of domestic veto players

This stylized model clarifies the cross-cutting role of domestic veto players at different stages of international trade cooperation. Initially, first-order noncompliance (protectionist policy) would only be enacted if both the Legislature and the Executive agree. This idea is well developed in the literature (e.g., Milner 1997; Mansfield, Milner, and Rosendorff 2002; Mansfield and Milner 2012). Yet there are many circumstances where this mechanism is an imperfect safeguard against rampant protectionism. Perhaps the Executive is sensitive to a forthcoming election or an economic downturn that makes a protectionist policy more enticing in the short run. Then the Executive might allow the Legislature's protectionist proposal to pass, instigating the lawsuit. It is also possible that the Executive might expect to evade international reprimand, anticipating that the court will rule in the defendant state's favor. For instance, the Executive might think the protectionist policy occupies a legal gray area, as many WTO disputes certainly show. Or the Executive might anticipate that the court preemptively avoids incendiary rulings. The Executive might think it can assuage the Legislature and avoid downstream problems under the assumption that the court wouldn't dare challenge the country's protectionist policy. These calculations are plausible given the uncertainty in dispute settlement. And it may be that neither the Executive nor the Legislature has adequate foresight to peer down the decision tree in order to avoid undesirable outcomes.[34] Another contributing factor is term limits. Some Executives may never have to face the consequences of their noncompliance if their tenure in office is ending.

Once the court strikes down the protectionist policy, veto players in the defendant state are likely to matter a great deal. Here, I draw on the insights of prospect theory: losses are more severely felt and desperately avoided than gains are enjoyed and sought (Kahneman and

Tversky 1979). The Legislature, sensitive to pressure from stakeholders, is acutely opposed to giving up trade protection. For instance, suddenly reversing agriculture subsidies would generate a negative shock on farmers who have adjusted their business practices to the status quo. The Legislature would then be expected to hold firm on noncompliance (that is, retaining protection). The stickiness of policy is widely recognized in the US Congress. Legislators sometimes pass temporary economic measures such as benefits or transfers with the expectation that once in place, these policies will become popular and garner sufficient political will to make them permanent.[35]

Conversely, the Executive is acutely opposed to international chastisement. Defying an international legal ruling is a public event, and other states will pay careful notice. If the Executive is worried about being branded an uncooperative regime or unreliable partner in international agreements, it will suffer negative repercussions. Again this is plausible: violating an international legal ruling on trade might make it harder for the Executive to credibly commit to another treaty in another international domain (Keohane 1986; Axelrod 1984; Guzman 2002). In short, the adverse ruling generates foreign penalties for the Executive and domestic losses for the Legislature that entrench both sides. The international dispute raises the stakes. The second-order compliance decision becomes especially vulnerable to domestic veto players.

This stylized model also lends insight into the trade-offs in institutional design by showing how flexibility can sometimes backfire. Recall that flexibility mechanisms enable governments to sometimes breach their free trade commitments to alleviate domestic political pressure without being forced to abandon the international agreement. These mechanisms take various forms (Kucik and Reinhardt 2008; Pelc 2009, 2011). Under WTO rules, for instance, governments are permitted to enact safeguards, temporary trade barriers, when there is an import surge that threatens a particular industry. Other research has highlighted how international courts can provide institutional flexibility (Rosendorff 2005) by providing a route for countries to temporarily break the rules and make amends by accepting proportionate retaliation, ultimately restoring cooperation. When the dispute settlement process itself is quite flexible, defendant governments may struggle to come back into cooperation. An adverse ruling can exacerbate domestic divisions within the government. The more entrenched and oppositional the domestic veto players are, the more difficult it is to reverse treaty violations.

3.5.4 Democratic Institutions and Applicability

The international trade dispute model sketched out above highlights a contrast between democratic governments—those with meaningful divisions of authority—and autocratic governments—those that more closely resemble a unitary actor model. The model demonstrates how divisions in authority generate veto points that can lock in protectionist policies that contravene international court rulings. One caveat is that the discussion has assumed stakeholder preferences that are typical in advanced industrialized economies. In these countries, a long-standing push for trade liberalization and reciprocal market access is countered by protectionist stakeholders—for instance, through the lobbying activity of firms and interest groups. Protectionist stakeholders tend to be geographically clustered and able to sway Legislators. This generalization is reasonable, since the countries most often embroiled in WTO disputes and the EU members fit this characterization. Yet as Milner and Kubota (2005) highlight, this same story would not apply in developing countries that undergo democratization. In the latter context, Executives—representing the elite under formerly autocratic rule—make concessions to the broader public that now enjoys the franchise. Such concessions include trade liberalization, which promises economic gain for the average worker who now finds a global economy in which to sell their labor (according to the Stolper-Samuelson theorem). Thus the Legislature, representing the broader public, will tend to prefer liberalization. For developing countries, the constellation of protectionist and liberalizing preferences held by various political actors, and the political influence those actors exert, would differ. However, veto players are still expected to generate barriers to second-order compliance.

In unpacking the domestic politics mechanisms, my model speaks to a large share of international legal disputes. Regime type is widely shown to drive adherence to international trade agreements. While democracies are thought to violate trade agreements less frequently than their autocratic counterparts (Mansfield, Milner, and Rosendorff 2002), they are more apt to use complex non-tariff barriers to trade (Kono 2006). Complex trade barriers are more likely than simple tariffs to instigate formal legal disputes at the WTO. This research provides a possible explanation for why, all else equal, democracies more commonly appear as defendants in WTO disputes than autocracies. My theory aims to explain why there is variation in compliance once countries with different political structures—featuring a range of divisions between multiple domestic veto players—have been prosecuted for trade policy violations.

Moreover, among democratic governments, there is variation in the extent to which trade interests are represented. The relative push and pull between liberalizing and protectionist stakeholders reflects, among other things, the electoral system in place. Some research finds that countries with plurality electoral rules are more responsive to demands for trade protection (e.g., Persson and Tabellini 2005; Tsebelis 2002). They are also more likely to be named as defendants in international trade disputes (Rickard 2010; Davis 2012), perhaps due to their responsiveness to localized industry-specific demands. Yet the link between electoral system and international cooperation on trade is hardly a settled issue. Other important research contends that countries with proportional representation electoral rules are more responsive to narrow interests such as industry-specific demands for protection (e.g., Bueno de Mesquita et al. 2003; Rogowski and Kayser 2002). Plurality systems might inhibit second-order compliance insofar as they produce more divided governments with at least some political actors who are beholden to protectionist interests.

By emphasizing domestic divisions in authority, the international trade model described above aims to explain the wide range of outcomes among different democratic institutions. While not all countries are equally likely to engage in a trade dispute and face censure from a court, the strategic interaction that produces litigation leads to a range of defendant governments. These governments vary in executive power in relation to legislative checks. Consequently, there is variation in the extent to which entrenched domestic interests can lock in trade policy.

This chapter has provided fundamental background on the WTO DSM and the ECJ. It has justified the case selection from a research design perspective. I have also described the sequence of events and incentives of key political actors in my theoretical model. While I did not present a fully specified game theoretic account, I have provided additional justification for why domestic veto players should routinely obstruct second-order compliance. Chapter 4 tests my theory at the WTO by examining a policy-based measure of compliance. Chapter 5 examines the trade impact of these WTO rulings. Chapter 6 tests my theory at the ECJ using trade-liberalizing rulings and a trade-based measure of European commerce. Chapter 7 concludes.

Policy Compliance in WTO Disputes

The previous chapters set out a theory linking features of domestic politics to the successes and failures of international courts in promoting interstate cooperation. A government's compliance with international rulings depends on the formal and informal constraints legislatures impose on executives and the preferences of constituents—for example, interest groups that have access to policy-makers. Defendant governments resist unfavorable rulings and retain their trade barriers when institutional constraints and local pressures converge. International adjudication is more successful in delivering policy reform when defendants overcome the hurdle of divided government and the constellation of interests they represent. Domestic political systems that feature more institutional checks and balances, have more partisan conflict, and are responsive to the different preferences of their constituents generate higher hurdles. The theory also highlights different types of policy reforms governments make to address international rulings. Building on canonical veto players theory, I highlighted the formal and also informal political obstacles to policy reform in the context of IC rulings. When many governments disregard the rulings of international courts, there are broader repercussions. Rampant noncompliance risks undermining the delicate authority of an institution and its cooperative aims.

This chapter presents the first empirical test of the theory by examining dispute settlement at the World Trade Organization. I begin by tracing the domestic veto players mechanism through a series of examples. The cases show how the different domestic political factors can act as a barrier to policy reform. Not all WTO rulings or countries face the same hurdles; political constraints can take a range of forms. The examples supply a plausibility check and demonstrate how the theory plays out in different contexts.

Illustrations are suggestive, but systematic evidence is needed. To test the argument of this book, I look at all rulings where the WTO ordered policy reform, determine whether or not defendants complied, and analyze the link to the governments' domestic constraints. Unfortunately, this task is far from simple, because official WTO records are an insufficient source. As noted in chapter 3, the WTO Dispute Settlement System relies on decentralized enforcement. Complainant states must pursue their grievances until they extract compliance from respondents or obtain adequate concessions. Sometimes plaintiffs see the endeavor as futile and give up on it. The WTO itself does not monitor or verify whether respondents correctly implement its legal rulings. As a result, a systematic test of my theory requires tracing precisely how governments reform their policies, taking WTO records as a mere starting point. To remedy this gap in knowledge, I constructed a novel dataset on government (non)compliance in all adverse rulings.

Policy reform can be thought of as a "hard test" of compliance, more akin to the definition of compliance favored by political science. The data in this chapter form a complete and systematic record of states' (second-order) compliance behavior under the WTO Dispute Settlement System—to my knowledge, the most comprehensive yet. I evaluate the theory through a series of statistical tests using these data and show that domestic political constraints are strongly associated with a decreased rate of compliance with legal rulings. These results are robust to a range of empirical tests. Chapter 4 concludes by highlighting the need to examine the economic consequences of WTO rulings, alongside policy compliance, to assess whether and when international trade litigation brings about meaningful cooperation among states.

4.1 Tracing the domestic politics mechanism

4.1.1 Contrasting examples

While many WTO disputes are idiosyncratic—involving different plaintiff countries, different products, and various trade policy instruments—a few cases with very similar profiles have arisen. These rare instances of matched cases offer insight into the domestic politics of dispute resolution. By holding other factors fixed, matched cases help isolate the political conditions that encourage or inhibit compliance with adverse rulings. And fortuitously for this research, two very similar disputes arose when the European Union brought complaints to the WTO in the early years of the dispute settlement system.

For several years, the European Union objected to foreign governments' tax schemes that limited markets for European exports of alcoholic beverages such as spirits, whiskeys, and liquors. In the first formal trade dispute, which occurred under the old GATT system in 1987, the EU submitted a complaint against Japan. It alleged that Japan's liquor tax law was discriminatory, favoring domestic alcohol producers and inflating the price of comparable foreign products.[1] The panel sided with the EU. In response to the panel decision, Japan replaced the GATT-incompatible regime with a new tax system. But the new scheme's different beverage categories were again designed in such a manner that imported drinks were predominantly subject to higher tax rates than similar domestic products. Unsatisfied with the revised but differential tax treatment between EU exports and Japanese liquors, the EU considered the dispute unresolved. Thus it was only a short time after the WTO Dispute Settlement Mechanism was established in 1995 that the Europeans revived the issue and brought a subsequent complaint against the Japanese government.[2] In its submission to the WTO, the EU argued Japan's system was discriminatory because it continued to levy a substantially higher tax on equivalent foreign products than the predominantly Japanese-produced alcohol, shochu.

The EU's grievances did not end with Japan. Less than two years later, the EU brought a similar complaint against South Korea over the latter's liquor tax system.[3] European whiskey sales to South Korea had fallen sharply, and EU officials argued this was because the Korean government violated its WTO obligations by levying a 130% tax on alcohol imports but not on the local equivalent product, soju.[4] The two disputes worked their way through the legal process. In both, the panels sided with the EU, finding both tax schemes incompatible with WTO obligations. In the case of Japan, the WTO scrutinized whether the products in question were substitutes and the extent to which the favored alcohol, "shochu, is essentially a Japanese product."[5] With respect to the complaint against Korea, the WTO panel followed the same logic and determined that the tax clearly constituted a trade barrier.[6] The adverse rulings required both Japan and Korea to reform their tax schemes. The rulings against discrimination allowed for either raising taxes on domestic alcohol or lowering taxes imposed on imported alcohol. Both Japan and Korea had a range of policy options for complying with the adverse rulings.

Several factors, in addition to the plaintiff and products, made the two disputes comparable. Both disputes concerned legislative measures of similar design: differential taxes for equivalent domestic and imported alcoholic beverages. The EU cited the same legal claims (GATT art. III §2) in each complaint, and the panel applied nearly the same rationale for its adverse ruling in each case. Both disputes went through an appeals stage where Appellate Body judges upheld the adverse ruling, and both required WTO arbitration in determining the reasonable period of time—that is, the deadline for implementation. While legal proceedings take many flavors, the extent of the WTO's procedural involvement in each case was essentially the same. On the defendant countries' sides, there were also some relevant similarities. Both Japan and Korea are advanced industrialized democracies with robust engagement in international trade. Yet neither has the economic might of the European Union, creating a power imbalance in each trade dispute. The political-economic contexts had enough commonality to make the comparison across cases informative.

Despite these parallels, the disputes followed different trajectories at the compliance stage. The Korean government, with its recently consolidated political power, promptly complied by dismantling its discriminatory liquor tax law, as will be explained below. The Japanese government, with domestic partisan discord, did not, and many years elapsed before the problematic tax scheme was adequately revised. The following discussion argues that different domestic political constraints in the defendant governments helped to shape the compliance process and the ultimate resolution of each trade dispute.[7] When the European Union prevailed in its challenge to South Korea's liquor tax system, the defendant government had a reasonably smooth path to compliance. This is not to say the adverse WTO ruling was well received by domestic stakeholders. Political pressure was mounting for the government to defy the WTO. As one newspaper reported, "at stake besides soju itself are votes. . . . soju is the drink of choice for South Korea's poor, a group the government is wooing before next April's parliamentary elections."[8] At that time, Korea had relatively few veto points. The National Congress for New Politics (NCNP) party had created a parliamentary majority by incorporating as many opposition legislators from the Grand National Party (GNP) as it could. By 1999, the ruling coalition held a majority in the National Assembly, which facilitated the passage of economic reform bills (Sunhyuk Kim 2000, 176). A stable coalition government was not the only relevant political feature. Korea's unicameral legislature also helped to streamline the process of legislative reforms. Thus, for a robust democracy, Korea featured relatively few domestic political constraints.

In response to the ruling, Korea promptly considered several approaches to revising the tax law. The Ministry of Finance and Economy initially suggested an amendment with 100% tax hikes on both domestic soju and imported spirits but, due to political pressure, lowered that proposal. The major parties in the legislature agreed that some reform was necessary, although they differed on the extent. The GNP preferred a 50%–60% tax rate, whereas the NCNP supported 70%–80%. Disagreement occurred even within the NCNP, as legislators were under pressure from the industry, which openly criticized the government for "attempting to raise the price of the drink of the common people."[9] Despite these controversies, the ruling coalition reached consensus and passed two acts to apply the same rate of 72% to both whiskey and domestic soju.[10] Korea addressed the ruling by complying completely within the reasonable period of time for implementation.[11] Given the circumstances, it is likely that stakeholders who wanted to retain the differential liquor taxes could not leverage political veto players to derail the efforts at reform. Although testimonies about the firsthand experiences of legislators serving in the National Assembly would be needed to decisively identify the causal effect of domestic veto players, the evidence suggests that Korea's modest political constraints facilitated compliance.

In contrast, for Japan, divisions of partisan power appear to have complicated the compliance process. The WTO Appellate Body upheld the adverse panel ruling in late 1996. The implementation deadline was set to February 1998, allowing Japan a fifteen-month period of time to reform its Liquor Tax Law. At the time, there were divisions of political authority in Japan that generated multiple veto points. A new electoral system for the Lower House had been introduced in 1994 introducing uncertainty and fragmentation of political power (Pempel 1998). The thirty-eight-year dominance of the Liberal Democratic Party (LDP) had recently ended, leading to "rampant party realignment" and a "massive overhaul" of the Japanese party system (Pempel 1997, 333). Importantly, "enduring institutions of conservative political dominance had been reconfigured. The previously stable party system had been completely deconstructed" (Pempel 1998, 136). As LDP rule was shaken and a coalition of opposition parties came to have more voice in policy-making, these changes prompted a new approach to trade disputes (Davis 2012 194). While these were perhaps not the most acute divisions of political power Japan has experienced over the course of its WTO membership, the period following the adverse ruling was one of an increased number of domestic veto players.[12] With these political obstacles coinciding, Japan did not comply within the timeline set out by the WTO. Despite the early 1998 deadline, Japan decided to "gradually increase the tax on shochu . . . [through] October 2001"[13], prolonging the period of noncompliance by years. Industry leaders in the EU attacked the Japanese government for "dragging its feet on the implementation of [the] WTO ruling . . . over as long a period as they think they can get away with."[14] The disputants reached a compromise that included short-term compensation and long-term policy reform.[15] Long-term reform featured an amendment to Japan's Liquor Tax Law, which was eventually passed by a small margin. Within the House of Councilors, the LDP, Heisei-kai, Social Democrats, and Democrats/New Green Wind parties favored the amendment while the Communist and New Socialists/Peace Union parties opposed it. Japan ultimately made only partial and belated policy reforms.

The evidence suggests that divisions among multiple political parties paired with a bicameral legislature may have made it challenging for the Japanese government to pass legislation to comply with the ruling. Again, without a detailed first-hand account of the events that transpired, one cannot be certain that domestic veto players were the root cause of Japan's belated and partial compliance. Nonetheless, it is clear the political obstacles were higher in Japan than they were in Korea when each government confronted international censure for its respective alcohol tax schemes. This interpretation is consistent with the cross-national, time-varying measure of a country's veto points by Henisz (2000). Veto points are measured on a scale of 0 to 1 with larger values denoting more constraints. At the time of the lawsuits, Korea had 0.45 veto points and Japan had 0.60. The difference (0.15) is substantial: it exceeds one standard deviation in the sample of countries participating as defendants in WTO disputes (0.12). In summary, the two trade disputes were similar in numerous respects but differed in terms of the domestic political constraints within the defendant governments and produced different compliance outcomes, consistent with my theory.

Of course, not all WTO disputes can be paired through contrasting examples to discern the role of domestic politics. Rather, countries encounter many different types of obstacles to compliance arising from formal and informal constraints in domestic government. The following section describes these different types of obstacles and how they have altered the outcomes of WTO disputes.

4.1.2 Political constraints as obstacles to compliance in WTO disputes

How and why do some policy reforms proceed while others stall? Domestic political constraints in government can obstruct compliance with WTO rulings through a range of pathways. The architecture of a government generates the first and most important source of constraints that stymie reforms. Institutional checks and balances create formal veto points. The constraints in divided governments are greater than in unified ones; bicameral legislatures generate more constraints than unicameral systems. In WTO disputes where legislative reform is needed, institutional constraints are particularly salient.

A second source of constraints comes from federalism, because policies may be more difficult to implement at the national level when coordination with state or provincial government is required. Several WTO disputes have stagnated or led to long-standing violations of trade rules precisely because subnational governments were reluctant to implement national trade priorities.

The third source of constraints comes from political parties. Partisan divisions generate formal barriers to policy reform. If the executive and legislative branches are held by different parties or members of rival parties cast opposing votes on legislation, there are multiple formal veto points. Additionally, political actors can act through informal channels. Partisan politics is never a "single-shot" game; obstruction on one proposed policy today leads to reciprocation tomorrow.

Each of these forms of domestic constraints has affected the trajectory of WTO disputes. The examples that follow trace these domestic political constraints, as they have sometimes blocked compliance or otherwise affected dispute resolution. Beyond imposing hurdles to compliance, these political constraints may also incentivize government leadership to use WTO rules opportunistically. A further example traces how respondent governments can use flexibility in the dispute settlement mechanism, especially delays in legal proceedings, to balance these domestic constraints against complainant demands.

4.1.2.1 BICAMERALISM The structure of a government's legislative branch can affect compliance with international rulings. This source of veto players has figured prominently in some WTO disputes over technical barriers to trade.

A complicated area of WTO rules, the Technical Barriers to Trade (TBT) agreement was included in the Uruguay Round because governments recognized that technical regulations on commerce inevitably impact trade. Often complex in design, technical regulations can have dual effects. On the one hand, governments rely on these measures to achieve their public policy goals—for example, informing consumers, protecting the environment, and advancing public health. Governments have a strong interest in maintaining authority to regulate these domains free from international oversight. The same regulations can have the side effect of impeding trade, recognized by the WTO to be a "normal and legitimate consequence of such regulation."[16]

Yet on the other hand, governments sometimes use these technical regulations in opportunistic ways. They might claim a regulation is in place to inform consumers, advance public health, or achieve other legitimate goals and that trade restrictions are merely an unfortunate side effect. These claims are sometimes disingenuous: the policy may actually be in place to shield domestic producers from foreign competition. The problem is when the chief purpose of such regulations is to disrupt trade and deliver a competitive advantage to domestic producers. Because of the technical complexity of these regulations, it is often difficult to distinguish between legitimate public policy goals and disguised trade protection. This ambiguity around a government's intent and the regulation's effect has led to several high-profile TBT disputes at the WTO.

It is in this complicated regulatory space that the United States ran afoul of WTO rules. The US Farm Bill of 2008 contained a country-of-origin labeling (COOL) requirement.[17] Section 11002 set forth the COOL requirements. It required retailers, such as grocery stores and supermarkets, to notify their customers about the source of certain foods. Spanning a wide range of products from meats to vegetables, the COOL

requirements ostensibly provided consumers with useful information
about where their foods were produced, giving them the tools to make
healthful choices. In one congressional debate over the Farm Bill, Representative Bono (R-CA) argued:

> Country-of-origin labeling [is] the act of simply letting US consumers know
> where the product they're picking up in the grocery store is from. Sounds sim-
> ple, logical and straightforward; yet for too long Congress has been putting
> off the implementation of mandatory COOL.[18]

The Farm Bill was passed into public law when both the House and Senate favored it by a sizable margin, overcoming a presidential veto. It took
effect in 2008 with the COOL requirement in place. And promptly, the
labeling requirement was challenged by the United States' major trade
partners.

Canada and Mexico filed complaints at the WTO, arguing that the
COOL rules constituted a technical barrier to trade. The rules encouraged consumers to favor domestic products over comparable imported
ones.[19] Their chief concern was the COOL statute's impact on the meat
industry. Canada and Mexico claimed that this measure was disguised
protectionism that was reducing the consumers' demand for their products. With the labeling requirements, the complainants alleged, US consumers would "buy American" at the expense of their exported and
nearly identical products. Rather than provide consumers with important information for making health-conscientious choices, the COOL
rules might simply prey on consumers' unsubstantiated fears or biases
about the quality of similar imported products. The trade impact was
thought to be substantial. For the cattle industry alone, Mexico anticipated a loss in export sales of approximately $400–$600 million annually, representing a nontrivial share of Mexican agricultural and ani-
mal production value.[20] A complicated legal battle ensued (Howse and
Levy 2013).

In 2011, the WTO panel determined that the US had violated several provisions of the TBT agreement and other obligations. The US
appealed, seeking a reversal, but the Appellate Body substantially rejected that contention and upheld the panel's findings. Arbitration followed, in which the US, Canada, and Mexico negotiated a set of statutory and regulatory changes that the US would need to implement in

order to comply with the ruling. They also negotiated a timeline for compliance. Citing the complexity of the legislative process in this instance, the US requested a long grace period: "If the United States makes statutory changes to bring the COOL measure into compliance, the entire process would take substantially longer than 18 months."[21] Canada and Mexico contended that six months was sufficient. There was nothing unusually complex about the technical measures under consideration, they argued, and lost sales during that interim would be substantial. The arbitrator ultimately awarded ten months, setting the implementation deadline in May 2013.

To assuage the plaintiffs as the May 2013 deadline approached, the US Department of Agriculture (USDA) issued a modification to the COOL provision through its administrative process.[22] But there had been no progress toward statutory reform, and Mexico and Canada remained unsatisfied. They argued that the modifications were actually more restrictive, rather than less, and caused further harm to Mexican and Canadian exporters. They challenged the US again through compliance proceedings, and the WTO judges determined the COOL measures continued to violate trade obligations.

In the US, domestic groups were divided over the issue. The farm lobby had initially urged the American government to stand firm. In particular, the National Farmers Union and the US Cattlemen's Association requested the government file an appeal and maintain the COOL requirements (Chase 2014). Yet other domestic groups, wary about Mexico and Canada retaliating, pressed for compliance. In a May 2016 letter to the US Senate, the COOL Reform Coalition, which comprised over 100 firms and industry groups, demanded legislation to repeal the labeling provisions. The coalition, which included fruit and vegetable growers and numerous processed food producers, cited "serious economic harm to US firms and farmers that export to our neighbors."[23] The domestic political standoff persisted, and the complainant governments sought compensation. Mexico was authorized to retaliate over $227 million per year; Canada over one $1 billion per year. This was the second largest retaliation authorization on record, and it sparked criticism (Bown and Brewster 2017).

Under this heightened pressure, the House of Representatives Committee on Agriculture advanced a bill that would repeal the COOL requirements. This bill passed the House in June 2015 by a wide margin and with bipartisan support.[24] Partisan divisions were not the main obstacle in this instance. Rather, the legislative process thwarted compliance. Once in the Senate, the proposed legislation failed to advance.[25]

The Senate considered a separate measure to repeal COOL for selected products. This bill failed to progress beyond introduction.[26] It is not surprising that the Senate was the effective veto player in this case. The farm lobby wields considerable sway in Congress and, of course, farmers' interests are most persuasive to legislators representing rural areas. Because all states enjoy equal representation in the Senate, it is thought to be more amenable to rural preferences than the House of Representatives, with many more legislators hailing from population-dense urban areas. If this logic is correct, the implication is that the farm lobby had an easier time garnering support in the Senate than in the House.[27] Persuaded by agricultural interests, the Senate twice blocked bills that would bring the US into compliance.

This example demonstrates how bicameralism has been a key obstacle to US compliance. Because legislative reforms were required, this institutional veto point was especially troublesome. It was not until many months later that the Senate approved the repeal of COOL requirements through an omnibus spending bill and the USDA rules were finalized to bring the US into compliance.[28] The move was applauded by the complainants and US exporter groups alike and averted an estimated $1 billion in retaliation. It was only when imminent retaliation activated exporter groups that enough senators found motivation to repeal COOL. The US prolonged the dispute through multiple legal stages, including appeal, compliance proceedings, and a retaliation threat before ultimately capitulating.

4.1.2.2 FEDERALISM Complexity in the legislative process is not the only way veto players obstruct policy reform. When the domestic implementation process is decentralized, even national-level efforts to comply with WTO decisions can fail. Federalism generates additional obstacles to compliance. For example, in a trade dispute brought by Japan and the European Union against Canada over its green energy program, Canada's federal structure was a key factor.

This dispute centered on two different areas of the WTO agreements: production subsidies and investment measures. The Agreement on Subsidies and Countervailing Measures restricts governments' ability to provide subsidies—financial contributions from public coffers—to targeted enterprises, industries, or regions. In particular, the WTO prohibits subsidies that are meant to boost export performance or are contingent on local content requirements—that is, rules that mandate the use of domestic rather than imported goods. These kinds of subsidies are explicitly prohibited because they are designed to affect trade and are thus likely to have adverse effects on other member states. Likewise, the Trade-Related Investment Measures (TRIMs) agreement aims to ensure nondiscrimination, transparency, and procedural fairness in how governments encourage investment. The TRIMs agreement specifically prohibits local content requirements, since such policies would discriminate against foreign suppliers. Together, these provisions advance the WTO's national treatment principle. But governments often disagree about the interpretation of treaty obligations on subsidies and investment.

Canada ran into problems in 2009 when the provincial government of Ontario implemented its Green Energy Act. This program built on Ontario's previous electricity policies but introduced several controversial new provisions. One part of the act established different price points—"feed-in tariff" rates—for different types of energy sources in a manner meant to encourage investment in renewable energy technology. Ontario's program was ambitious. The provincial government promised to create 50,000 new jobs through the Green Energy Act, especially in the construction of wind and solar energy infrastructure (Ontario Ministry of Energy 2011). Advocates of the program applauded it as a win for both the environment and the economy.

Nonetheless, the Green Energy Act drew foreign criticism. The central point of contention was the program's domestic content requirements imposed on electricity generation facilities. It required electricity companies use domestic solar and wind power technology in order to qualify for guaranteed prices offered under the Feed-In Tariff (FIT) Program. Japan and the European Union promptly sued. The complainants alleged that Ontario's program favored equipment purchases and contracts with renewable energy facilities in Ontario while excluding foreign suppliers.[29] This, they argued, ran afoul of the GATT provisions on quantitative restrictions and the TRIMs agreement. In addition, the plaintiffs said the Canadian government was providing price support to local industry, effectively granting a prohibited subsidy.

The Canadian government defended its program against Japan and Europe's accusations. Ontario officials noted that the FIT Program was "created for governmental purpose of securing electricity supply for Ontario consumers from clean sources, and *not* . . . with a view to use in the production of goods for commercial sale."[30] They also rebutted the characterization of the program as price support for an allegedly subsidized good. No physical products were at issue, they argued, since electricity is not a physical good.[31] The WTO panel was unpersuaded and largely rejected Canada's arguments, favoring Japan and Europe. The panel ruled the FIT Program violated the GATT and TRIMs agreement. They did not find support for the complainants' claims under the Subsidies Agreement, but this mattered little. Canada's program was a breach of the other WTO obligations.

The adverse ruling immediately provoked outcry from the provincial government of Ontario. Within Ontario, support for the program was mixed: initially the Liberal government defended the initiative, promising job creation in the province, while critics from the opposition urged repeal, blaming it for rising power costs.[32] Controversy at the national level further magnified obstacles to a speedy resolution. Ontario's energy minister denounced the international ruling, and industry groups pressed Ottawa to appeal. Commentators asserted that "in formal terms, the WTO decision is not binding on Ontario" (Hutton and Bremermann 2013).

Canada's appeal was unsuccessful. Some media sources criticized the federal government for being willing to accept the panel's verdict and said that it submitted "only a lukewarm appeal of the decision, which it subsequently lost" (Gipe 2013). The federal government had made only a half-hearted effort to advance Ontario's position, showing its ambivalence at best and pro-WTO sentiments at worst.

This was the first time Canada encountered a WTO ruling over provincial legislation and had to grapple with federalism in this context. At the federal level, the government was held by the Liberal party and largely favored complying with the WTO ruling. The government pressed Ontario to implement the policy reforms before the deadline in June 2014. Yet at the provincial level, the Ontario government largely favored defending the FIT Program and its support of domestic industries. In defense of the program, the provincial energy ministry cited the creation of approximately 31,000 jobs and billions of dollars in investment.[33]

The Ontario government proposed a new bill to modify the FIT Program. That legislation sought to remove domestic content requirements for future renewable energy generation projects.[34] The bill was dropped when Parliament dissolved for general elections in June 2014. It was renewed and passed the following month when the newly elected legislature convened. Shortly thereafter, the Ontario Power Authority terminated its contracts with large domestic suppliers.[35] By the end of July 2014, the provincial government of Ontario complied with the ruling through two implementation measures. First, it ceased to subject large renewable electricity procurements to domestic requirements. Second, it significantly lowered the domestic content requirements for small FIT procurement of wind and solar electricity under the FIT Program.[36] One of the complainants, Japan, argued that the delays had pushed Canada past the implementation deadline. After threatening to bring compliance proceedings, Japan ultimately dropped the matter. Ontario fell in line under threats of retaliation from both complainants and heightened pressure from the federal government, which generally favored compliance. Although the Canadian government ultimately secured cooperation at the provincial level, the process was fraught with dissent and significantly prolonged by officials in Ontario.

The Canadian green energy example is not an anomaly. Another instance where veto points from federalism posed an insurmountable obstacle to compliance is found in an Australian case on sanitary and phytosanitary (SPS) measures. In this case, the Australian government could not fully implement administrative measures mandated by a WTO ruling because subnational actors were unwilling to support them. A key feature of this example is that the constraints of federalism do not apply exclusively to legislation—they affect administrative measures as well.

In 1995, Canada sued Australia over salmon import inspection rules (DS18), which Canada alleged were in breach of the WTO agreement on SPS measures. The lawsuit arose after two decades of bilateral talks over the issue failed to progress (Taylor 2000; Gascoine 2000). The disputants sought a panel ruling in 1997. The WTO judges sided largely with the complainant, finding Australia to be in breach of its trade commitments. The ruling was upheld on appeal, so Australia was required to revise its import inspection rules. Formally, only administrative measures were needed to comply—the minister of trade would merely have to revise import guidelines implemented by the Australian Quarantine and Inspection Service. However, politics made compliance a far more complicated a process.

In its follow-up submissions to the WTO, Australia claimed that it fully complied by implementing new inspection guidelines before the July 1999 deadline. However, the Australian federal government encountered stout opposition from Tasmanian fishers and salmon cultivators (Taylor 2000, 481). Its revised policy aimed to assuage stakeholders in Tasmania and thereby fell short of Canada's expectations for compliance. Completely unconvinced the measures would restore fair trade practices, the Canadian government initiated compliance proceedings. It also requested authorization to impose retaliatory trade barriers worth CAD$45 million. Despite Australia's protestations, the WTO compliance panel determined that the government was continuing to violate the SPS rules.

In order to reach a bilateral settlement and avert retaliation, the Australian federal government had to reassure Canada it would bring Tasmanians into line. Yet this was not an easy feat. Under Australia's constitutional distribution of power, states and territories retain the capacity to apply quarantine restrictions affecting international trade over and above measures applied at the federal level (Gascoine 2000). Thus there was a question of whether Tasmania could even be required to abide by the terms of an international settlement struck by the Australian federal government. Reports indicate the Commonwealth was willing to use the domestic courts to induce compliance: "The federal Government has previously flagged High Court action against Tasmania if the ban continued."[37] Finally, in 2000, the disputants settled with revised import restrictions. However, this was far from what the WTO ruling had required. Some of the disputed Tasmanian restrictions on salmon remain in place to date, revealing full compliance was never achieved.

Federalism generates opportunities for domestic veto players to obstruct compliance with adverse WTO rulings. This case is particularly revealing because the struggle between national and regional preferences arose, in part, from divisions in authority over certain aspects of trade policy. Ultimately, the Australian federal government was only able to induce partial compliance due to obstacles from influential domestic groups and institutional checks.

4.1.2.3 PARTISAN DIVISIONS   While institutional divisions of authority form the core veto points in government, those institutional checks are amplified by multiple political parties that have divergent policy preferences (Tsebelis 1995, 2002). Partisan divisions and the pressure from interest groups that political actors respond to generate informal domestic constraints that also impede policy reform. Informal constraints indirectly bind political decision-makers through the downstream consequences they impose. As discussed in chapter 2, domestic groups can generate sufficient costs for political actors to the extent that policy reform simply becomes untenable. Numerous WTO disputes have been shaped by partisan divisions and the political influence of interest groups.

Examples of partisan dissent surrounding WTO disputes are plentiful.[38] An illustration comes from the Canadian dispute over magazines and other periodicals (DS31) mentioned briefly in chapter 2. This dispute arose over a Canadian tax and related measures on imported foreign magazines and "split-run periodicals," versions of American publications printed and sold in Canada. The Canadian government's tariff, tax, and postal rate scheme favored domestic publishers over their foreign counterparts—a move the government argued was intended to preserve culture in the face of overwhelming US media influence. The United States brought its complaint against Canada to the WTO, citing unfair protections of domestic industry. By July 1997, the WTO judges had been swayed by the United States' arguments and ruled that Canada had breached its free trade obligations.

To implement the ruling, the Canadian government announced that it would, by October 1998, repeal its relevant tariffs, eliminate a part of the tax, and restructure postal rates to ensure equal treatment of domestic and foreign publications.[39] This required executive, administrative, and legislative actions. While the former were completed in advance of the WTO's deadline, the legislative reforms proved difficult and politically incendiary.

The first effort took the form of Bill C-55, the Foreign Publishers Advertising Services Act, which preserved the benefits to the Canadian magazine industry. That bill provoked partisan controversy in Canadian Parliament.[40] On the one hand, domestic industry—especially the Association of Canadian Advertisers—applauded the effort to preserve Canadian heritage, and the Liberal Party took up these interests.[41] On the other hand, opponents warned that the US would make good on its retaliation threat should the bill pass in its original form, a point that the Conservatives (also known as Tories) found most persuasive. Despite the threat of sanctions, Canada's House of Commons passed the bill in March 1999. The US drew up a series of punitive tariffs on sensitive industries, including lumber, steel, plastics, and textiles. With an increasingly credible foreign threat and rising tensions between Conservative and Liberal Parties, the bill failed in the Senate where records reveal intense partisan debate.

Ottawa resumed talks with the US to chart out a revised version of the legislation. Per a bilateral agreement, Canada committed to pass an amended version of the bill, a version detractors referred to as "gutted." The new rules included limits on US ad sales that would incrementally be applied over a three-year period. In exchange, the US would seek no further recourse under the WTO or along parallel legal avenues—that is, NAFTA. This settlement was controversial. Tory senators said the deal was a betrayal and reflected Liberals' willingness to "cav[e] in" to American demands.[42] By October 2000, two full years after the deadline, Canadian Parliament approved Bill C-24, the Sales Tax and Excise Tax Amendments Act, which finally repealed the tax regime for split-run periodicals and brought Canada into compliance.

While the Canadian example highlights how partisan divisions in the legislature can thwart compliance, these factors can likewise impede the adoption and application of executive orders and administrative measures. In some instances where policies can formally be changed by unilateral acts, politicians may act strategically to maintain support from their parties or coalitions. Executives facing multiple veto players are at greater risk of interference when their preferred policy reforms contravene legislator preferences. For example, the US executive branch has authority to impose and remove safeguards. Yet Congress is permitted to issue a resolution of disapproval that can override safeguard determinations in certain circumstances, a power they are more likely to exercise under divided government.[43] Similarly, administrative measures are also subject to influence from veto players. A clear illustration can be found in a dispute between Viet Nam and the United States over antidumping measures on shrimp. When the US lost this WTO ruling, the US Department of Commerce and the US Trade Representative were tasked with implementation, yet their reforms were curtailed by Congressional committee oversight and required consultations with private sector advisory groups.[44] As these examples suggest, governments with more domestic veto players face a greater risk that executive or administrative reforms will be thwarted.[45] Thus even policy measures that appear to be under the control of a single head of state or administrative authority can be thwarted by opposition from other political actors.

4.1.2.4 FLEXIBILITY AND VETO PLAYERS Domestic constraints do not merely generate higher hurdles to compliance but also incentivize government leadership to use institutional flexibility to their advantage. Evidence suggests that governments prolong WTO legal proceedings in order to manage competing pressures from international and domestic sources. When respondent governments drag out disputes, they delay compliance and evade repercussions.

Opportunistic noncompliance is most plausible when interest groups exert considerable pressure on veto players. A noteworthy example comes from three parallel complaints filed against the European Union in May 2003 over the process for approving and marketing biotechnology, particularly genetically-modified organisms (GMOs).[46] The United States, Canada, and Argentina each alleged that EU policies had restricted the imports of agricultural and food products in manners inconsistent with obligations under the GATT, the Sanitary and Phytosantiary Agreement, and other WTO provisions. The complainants focused on a 1998 EC regulation (90/220) that imposed a de facto moratorium on new GMO approvals. Compounding the matter were France and Greece's commitment to block any vote in the EU Parliament for a rollback of this regulation and Austria's imposition of its own additional bans targeting Monsanto, a US firm. Across the EU member states, there was significant support for GMO restrictions. The lawsuit was complicated, and nearly five years elapsed before the DSM adopted the panel reports in November 2006. The panel resoundingly supported the complainants' claims against the EU.

Implementation of the ruling became contentious. At first, the European Union agreed that the reasonable period of time for compliance would expire in November 2007, but this deadline was extended to January 2008. As the January deadline approached, the Canadian and Argentinian governments and the EU again notified the WTO of an extension to June 2008. Subsequent extensions were incremental: August 2008, December 2008, and March 2009. At this point, Canada agreed to a bilateral settlement with the EU. The settlement entailed biannual diplomatic meetings on GMO trade issues but had no clear pathway toward compliance. Argentina continued to pursue the dispute, leading to further extensions of the implementation deadline: June and then December 2009, followed by January, then February, and finally March 2010. At that point, Argentina agreed to a bilateral settlement similar to the one Canada had, ending this seeming war of attrition on GMOs.

The United States followed a somewhat different tack in handling the EU's resistance. Upon the second extension to the deadline, in January 2008, the US requested remedies—that is, retaliation—under Article 22 of the Dispute Settlement Understanding. This move appeared to catalyze EU action. The European Food Safety Administration, responsible for approving biotechnology products, accelerated the GMO approvals in the following year. However, European Parliament remained divided, with Austria, Belgium, Denmark, and Luxembourg joining France and Greece in their efforts to block lasting reforms to the GMO restrictions; in other words, influential EU member states blocked compliance. To date, the US considers the dispute unresolved.

This GMO dispute illustrates how respondents can use the WTO's flexibility to balance pressure from international and domestic sources. All three complainants filed the same charges, and the EU faced consistent domestic pressures to resist. But the three complainant governments applied different degrees of international pressure. The EU delayed any substantive reforms to its WTO-inconsistent policies until Canada and ultimately Argentina, countries with a moderate stake in the export of GMO products, conceded to a meager settlement.[47] In dealing with the United States, which holds a substantial stake in the export of GMO products in particular, the EU made minor adjustments to stave off retaliation. Indeed, the United States' retaliation potential was greater than Argentina and Canada's. Across all three cases, the EU was able to accommodate the demands of the European member states and domestic groups that supported the restrictions on GMO products—that is, opposed compliance—while varying its use of institutional flexibility in relation to complainant pressure.

4.2 Systematically evaluating compliance

As the preceding examples have indicated, different sources of political constraints make it difficult for respondent governments to comply with WTO rulings. These examples highlight variation in the compliance process. In some instances, compliance hinged on governments passing new legislation, often amid partisan contention; in others, administrative measures or executive orders were needed to reform WTO-inconsistent policies. Pressure from international sources—especially powerful complainants—was a confounding factor. Are these cases representative of general patterns in the WTO? While the examples demonstrate the plausibility of my theory, a systematic test is needed. The remainder of this chapter provides that test. The empirical results that follow show that domestic constraints are associated with lower compliance rates, partial measures, delayed compliance, and engagement in more legal stages, suggesting that respondent states endeavor to use flexibility in the dispute process to delay compliance. The section that follows discusses the data collected for this analysis.

4.2.1 Why we cannot rely on WTO records

Measuring compliance with WTO rulings is not straightforward. The WTO system has no central agency responsible for enforcement of treaty terms. Governments need to monitor one another and pursue lawsuits against rule violators. Once the WTO DSM delivers an adverse ruling, the responsibility for tracking and verifying compliance lies in the hands of member states.

The WTO obtains information on compliance in two ways. First, it relies on voluntary reporting from respondent governments about their compliance status. Second, it relies on complainants to pursue violations until a satisfactory outcome is obtained, necessitating persistence on the part of the complainant. Neither source of information paints a complete picture.

Moreover, the WTO's official information may actually produce a biased account of compliance. For one thing, respondents routinely assert that they have implemented rulings. Yet they are not required to submit any evidence showing policy reform. This means some claims of compliance are merely "cheap talk." Many such declarations are followed by additional legal proceedings where the complainant supplies persuasive evidence that the respondent has not actually complied. A clear example is the dispute between the US and Mexico on antidumping measures for high fructose corn syrup.[48] Mexico reported to the WTO it had implemented the panel rulings, but a subsequent compliance investigation demonstrated the state remained in violation. Relying on WTO records would likely *overestimate compliance*, giving credit where it is not due.

A second reason that WTO records tend to generate a biased account is simply that plaintiffs give up. They drop disputes or accept settlements if litigation seems futile. Smaller economies with less retaliatory potential may be most easily deterred from pursuing obstinate defendants.

For example, Indonesia brought a complaint against the United States over its Family Smoking Prevention Tobacco Control Act of 2009 that banned clove cigarettes, one of Indonesia's lucrative exports.[49] Indonesia argued the ban violated WTO requirements on technical barriers to trade, among other issues. The panel and Appellate Body delivered split decisions, supporting Indonesia on only a minority of its claims. Nonetheless, the ruling required the United States to modify its policy by either reversing the ban or by extending it to similar domestic products, such as menthol cigarettes (Watson, 2014). Neither option would have garnered domestic support: the first would have provoked outcry from public health groups, while the second would have inflamed resistance from the domestic tobacco industry.[50] The US did neither, leaving the WTO-inconsistent policy in place well past the implementation deadline.

Indonesia requested retaliatory measures under Article 22, but before the request could be evaluated, the disputants reached a bilateral settlement.[51] Under the deal, the United States maintained its ban on clove cigarettes but promised to carve out an exception for Indonesian cigars and cigarillos. The settlement also entailed a promise that the US would refrain from suing Indonesia at the WTO regarding its controversial mineral ore export restrictions. This was seen as a satisfactory outcome for Indonesia, which lacked adequate economic clout to induce compliance from the far larger US.[52] The settlement clearly did not bring the US into compliance with the adverse ruling; at the same time, it contravened the most-favored nation principle foundational to the multilateral trade regime (Ballet, 2011).[53] Nonetheless, it was considered satisfactorily resolved by the WTO and there was no formal determination that the US had retained the contentious cigarette ban.

In short, many noncompliant behaviors are not identified as such by the WTO, particularly if disputants reach a post-ruling settlement. Institutional markers of noncompliance, such as the WTO awarding remedies, thus understate the prevalence of compliance problems.

4.2.2 Creating the WTO compliance database

In the absence of definitive WTO resources, I looked to primary sources for evidence. Across 155 cases, I sought out official statutory and regulatory measures passed by respondent governments. Regarding its dispute settlement goals, the WTO states, "the priority is for the losing defendant to bring its policy into line with the ruling."[54] Accordingly, I uncovered the tangible policy reforms governments made in order to comply with adverse rulings. My coding covers official legislation, administrative measures, and executive orders implemented by respondent governments. I evaluated governments' policy reforms, characterizing them as partial or complete in fulfilling the WTO requirements. I recorded the timing of those policy reforms, noting whether the reforms occurred before or after the WTO-mandated deadline. Bilateral settlements are also coded. I looked for evidence of partisan divisions over the policies and in several cases was able to link them to industry interests.

The result is a detailed account of 155 WTO disputes based on my evaluation of the legal record and multiple primary and secondary sources. The primary and secondary documents are in seven languages. In addition to English, the bilingual research assistants I worked with used sources in Arabic, Japanese, Korean, Mandarin Chinese, Portuguese, and Spanish. These cover the official languages of almost, but not all, respondent governments. There were four rulings against Indonesia, two against Thailand, and two against Turkey. Primary documents include a government's administrative and legislative measures, parliamentary debates, press releases, etc. The secondary sources include industry publications, newspaper articles, and case reports from lawyers and legal scholars. The database spans thirty-seven complainant countries and twenty-one respondent countries.

4.2.3 Comparison to WTO records

When I measure compliance in terms of policy reform, the results provide a very different picture than would be obtained from relying on WTO records. Complainants can bring compliance proceedings under Article 21.5 when they think a respondent has disregarded a ruling. This legal process recruits the same panel judges, where possible, and evaluates additional arguments and evidence from the litigants. It is rare for complainants to pursue their continued grievances through this process; complainants initiated Article 21.5 proceedings in 27 out of 155 (17.6%) disputes. Occasionally, the initiation is enough to precipitate a settlement and no ruling is reached. More often, the compliance panel reaches a legal decision that finds continued violations. Persistent violations were found in 19 out of those 27 cases, constituting about 12% of the over-all sample. But these few occurrences underrepresent actual noncompliance problems in the system.

My data collection, as discussed in the ensuing sections, uncovered 79 cases of noncompliance out of the 155 WTO disputes with adverse rulings. Over time, about half of those violations were belatedly corrected—that is, after the implementation deadline. In the other half, 36 cases, the respondents appear to have never complied. In the cases where I found persistent noncompliance, the WTO's own complainant-driven procedures detected merely eight instances of noncompliance. In other words, about four-fifths of the time, the institutional procedure for uncovering persistent violations falls short. Complainants, perhaps dissuaded by obstinate respondents or cognizant of their inability to summon enough market power to retaliate, dropped their lawsuits.[55]

Unpacking the discrepancies further, there are eleven cases in which a complainant obtained an Article 21.5 ruling of continued violations and the respondent ultimately complied. These can be thought of as "successes" for the DSM. They are examples of where the WTO did rectify long-standing breaches of the multilateral trade regime. The appendix for chapter 4 provides additional information on these failures and successes.

It bears emphasis that the WTO is deferential to litigants. Given the incentives of the typical complainant and respondent, the result is that the WTO underreports noncompliance and assumes a higher prevalence of compliance.

This is not the first study to argue that the WTO's Article 21.5 process is insufficient for identifying persistent noncompliance. Some other studies have collected data on compliance with WTO rulings. Busch and Reinhardt (2003) consider compliance with 101 adverse GATT judgments and 9 WTO disputes between the United States and Europe. My coding is consistent with the WTO cases Busch and Reinhardt assess. Davey (2005) looks at 58 disputes from the first ten years of WTO operation and finds that in 83% of cases, respondent governments report some form of implementation. However, Davey does not verify whether the respondent governments' reported implementation measures were sufficient to achieve partial or full compliance. Focusing exclusively on the United States and the European Union, Bruce Wilson (2007) evaluates compliance with 49 adverse rulings. But Wilson does not verify whether the US and EU's reported implementation measures were adequate to achieve compliance, nor does the study provide a systematic criteria for classifying dispute outcomes.

Other studies have examined variation across rulings against a single respondent. Notably, Brewster and Chilton (2014) evaluate the United States' compliance record by examining its policy reforms (if any). This study shows that complaints against the US over trade legislation, which inevitably invoke more veto players, lead to less compliance than disputes over administrative trade barriers. Likewise, Yildirim (2018) documents the EU's response to adverse WTO rulings. However, this latter study adopts a different approach, characterizing bilateral settlements as compliance, even when those settlements fail to implement specific recommendations contained in the panel reports or allow for discriminatory deals that are inconsistent with the most-favored national treatment principle.

The prior research advances our understanding of compliance with WTO rulings. Yet none of these studies examine outcomes for the entire set of disputant governments, nor do they offer the same degree of precision. As this chapter supplies a uniquely comprehensive account of compliance with adverse rulings, it provides a thorough appraisal of the DSM's performance. The following section details my coding methodology to demonstrate the variation and depth of sources used.

4.2.4 How disputes are resolved

4.2.4.1 LEGISLATIVE OR ADMINISTRATIVE COMPLIANCE   Several examples illustrate the variation in outcomes represented by these data. As noted, disputes with adverse rulings require that respondents remove or modify any trade barriers that violate WTO rules. Slightly fewer than half of these are resolved through complete and timely compliance.

In many cases, full compliance entails passing new legislation. For example, when the United States sued Canada over grain exports, the WTO panel determined that Canada had discriminated against foreign producers and thereby breached its trade commitments.[56] Canada was ordered to amend its Canada Grain Act to ensure equal treatment between domestic and foreign producers. It promptly amended the legislation to comply before the deadline.[57] In coding this case, I easily found unambiguous evidence in the legislation and parliamentary vote that the amendment satisfied WTO obligations.

But not all disputes are focused on legislation. Frequently, respondent governments need to implement new administrative measures. One illustration is the dispute where the European Union and Japan accused Canada of using motor vehicle tariffs to grant US automotive manufacturers preferential treatment.[58] This dispute concerned the US-Canada Auto Pact that permitted the US duty-free import privileges for automobiles while other foreign countries were subject to a 6.1% duty. The WTO panel ruled against Canada and ordered reform.[59] Despite resistance from major auto manufacturers, Canada's minister of finance repealed the tariffs to comply by the deadline.

I did not uncover instances in which governments exercised discretion over which type of measure—legislative or administrative—they could adopt. There were no apparent instances in which an administrative measure was challenged but the respondent government complied by implementing new legislation. Likewise, no disputes occurred in which the WTO struck down legislation but the government complied through administrative measures or executive orders. In other words, governments are rarely able to switch a policy's form. Once a government is tasked with implementing a ruling, it holds little control over how many domestic veto players are activated in a given case.

4.2.4.2 PARTIAL OR DELAYED COMPLIANCE   Respondents often adopt partial measures that do not completely satisfy a ruling. Other times, there are such significant delays that WTO-inconsistent policies are retained long after deadlines. The WTO system relies on persistent plaintiffs to highlight these cases. But because some cases of partial compliance go unchallenged, persistence is an imperfect measure. To evaluate these instances, I reviewed the actual reforms respondents enacted and compared them to substantive terms in the WTO recommendations.

A dispute the United States brought against Argentina over tariffs on textiles provides a clear example of partial compliance.[60] As is typical, the complainant won the judgment. Argentina complied only partially at first. Its Ministry of Economy, Public Works and Services passed a resolution that reduced import duties before the compliance deadline.[61] But it was not until months later that, under heightened pressure from and negotiations with the US, the Argentinian president enacted an executive order to resolve the dispute.[62]

To evaluate delayed compliance in each case, I compared the date at which the respondent revised or revoked WTO-inconsistent policies to the compliance deadline, the expiration of the "reasonable period of time." Delays may be brief or span many years. An example of a brief delay can be found in DS332. The WTO found that a Brazilian ban on retreaded tires—which Brazil argued was justified on the basis of health and safety—was an impermissible barrier to trade. Brazil was ordered to revoke the ban by December 2008. Ultimately, following an executive request, the secretary of foreign trade and the Ministry of Development, Industry and Foreign Trade, as well as a ruling from Brazil's highest court, brought the government into compliance in August 2009.[63]

4.2.4.3 NONCOMPLIANCE   My data also uncovers many clear cases of noncompliance. I identified persistent and unambiguous noncompliance in approximately 23% of disputes. These cases fall into two categories. The first is when the WTO institutional process deems the respondent noncompliant. This happens when the complainant prevails in noncompliance proceedings under Article 21.5 or succeeds in securing remedies under Article 22. An example of this type of case is a dispute where the United States and many Latin American nations sued the European Union over import duties on bananas. After determining the Europeans had not complied with the initial ruling, a WTO compliance panel authorized retaliations equivalent to approximately $200 million per year in 1999. The compliance panel then increased this value the following year. The standoff persisted for another twelve years. Finally, the parties negotiated a compromise that preserved some aspects of the original discriminatory trade policy.[64]

The second category is when the complainant initiates compliance proceedings but does not pursue further recourse and there is no evidence that the respondent complied. In these cases, it is likely that the complainant deemed the legal dispute futile. Or it is possible that the respondent offered some compensation to the complainant in order to retain WTO-inconsistent policies. One noteworthy example is a dispute between Indonesia and South Korea that remains unresolved.[65] This dispute began in 2004. Four years later, after an adverse ruling and continued resistance on Korea's part, the WTO compliance panel finally found that the government had failed to correct the initial violations. The Korean Trade Commission simply refused to adjust its antidumping decision[66] and Indonesian officials expressed dissatisfaction with this outcome. Korea issues periodic pro forma updates to the WTO with no change in status, and Indonesia has not pressed for further legal remedies. Thus the evidence strongly suggests that Indonesia ultimately dropped the dispute in response to Korea's persistent noncompliance.

It is fairly common for a complainant to drop a dispute against an obstinate respondent. Another example comes from the dispute the United States and Australia filed against the European Union that, as of this writing, remains unresolved. The complainants argued that the EU's requirements concerning the geographical origins of agricultural and food products violated equal treatment provisions under various WTO agreements, and the panel agreed. The EU declared that they had fully implemented the WTO ruling in time.[67] The US and Australia did not agree that the new regulations were sufficient. As of October 2008, the matter still appeared in the WTO dispute status reports as "unresolved," but the respondent refused to budge. Statements issued by the US and Australian officials indicate that neither complainant believes the EU has complied with the ruling. Likewise, in another example, the EU sued the US in 1999 over Section 211 of the Appropriations Act. Again, the panel ruling found the respondent had violated WTO obligations and set a compliance deadline of January 3, 2003. But the US took no steps to implement the panel ruling and requested multiple extensions of the deadline. After the fourth extension to June 2005, the case fell silent. The next development occurred in 2016 when a legislative amendment was introduced in Congress; this amendment failed to garner support and the dispute remains unresolved.

4.2.4.4 SETTLEMENT   The last coding category consists of disputes resolved through a formal compromise, a mutually agreed solution (MAS) between the litigant governments. In these instances, governments settle their dispute with some form of bilateral concessions. Settlements can occur any time during the dispute process. Most often, an MAS is signed before a panel ruling. But my focus is on post-ruling behavior, and here we do observe plenty of settlements. While the WTO is notified of each MAS, the specific terms of the settlement are not always disclosed. The bilateral agreement reports are usually brief and vague, alluding to substantive terms. I located information on the substantive terms whenever possible.

For example, a lengthy dispute between Viet Nam and the United States over the latter's antidumping duties on shrimp ended with a settlement. Viet Nam brought its complaint to the WTO. While the US was found to be in violation of trade obligations, it adopted only partial measures to comply, bowing to industry pressures (the Southern Shrimp Alliance). Viet Nam sued again and prevailed. Ultimately, the governments struck a bilateral agreement. According to their settlement, the US exempted one prominent Vietnamese exporter (Minh Phu) from its antidumping duties and refunded to that firm duties it previously paid. However, the US maintained its WTO-inconsistent duties on all other Vietnamese producers. As part of the settlement, the exempted firm had to certify that it was the sole producer and that other exporters were not circumventing the US order (according to a USTR press release of July 18, 2016). This post-adjudicative settlement did not entail compliance from the respondent but rather featured a preferential deal that assuaged the complainant. Nor did the settlement terms abide by the most-favored national treatment principle that is central to the multilateral trade regime. Importantly, the settlement terms were not part of the official WTO record. What this example highlights is that WTO records provide little (or no) information on MAS terms and whether those terms include compliance with rulings.

4.2.4.5 CODING LIMITATIONS   As with any cross-national study, there is a risk of bias in the data. The most salient form of bias relates to information availability. Governments with strong public reporting practices and a well-established record of transparency make evidence of compliance easily accessible. My coding of WTO disputes is likely to be most accurate for these respondent governments. The majority of litigants have transparent practices (e.g., the EU, the US, Canada, Australia, Japan, and South Korea). A few respondents have less transparent public sectors: Brazil and Mexico are noteworthy examples. I was still able to find in these jurisdictions detailed documentation of policy implementations and partial measures that fell short of full compliance. Even in governments with transparency, accountability, or corruption problems, there is usually adequate evidence to code compliance.

In a small but noteworthy number of countries, detailed policy information is difficult to find and evidence on compliance is sparse. The most important of these is China. The Chinese Communist Party tends to reveal little public information about its internal policy process, favoring instead unified final reports on WTO disputes. I employed native Mandarin Chinese speakers as research assistants to code these cases. They uncovered evidence of begrudging compliance on the part of the Chinese government within ministry reports and government-sanctioned news outlets. One example is the US complaint against China on Intellectual Property Rights (DS362). Regarding implementation, China reported that, in February 2010, the Standing Committee of the 11th National People's Congress had approved amendments to Chinese copyright law and, in March, the State Council had adopted the decision to revise the Regulations for Customs Protection of Intellectual Property Rights. Despite China's decision to comply with the rules, leadership has voiced "strong dissatisfaction" with the outcome of the lawsuit. China's then vice premier, Wu Yi, said the "USTR completely disregarded China's tremendous progress in the area of protecting intellectual property rights." In addition, Wang Xinpei, the spokesperson for the Ministry of Commerce, said China "regretted" that they allowed the United States to adjudicate the dispute through the WTO. The Chinese government's public tariff records also provided useful evidence on (non)compliance.[68] These reports are suggestive but not definitive. It remains plausible that the Chinese government has made superficial reforms to comply with WTO rulings but has also continued inconsistent practices that are obscured from public view.

Other respondent countries with inadequate reporting practices include Egypt (one adverse ruling) and Indonesia (four adverse rulings). In the complaint against Egypt (DS 211: Turkey v. Egypt—Steel Rebar), Egyptian officials, serving under then president Mubarak, declared to the WTO they had complied with the ruling in 2003 but supplied no evidence. Two years later, Egypt's Ministry of Trade and Industry appeared to have lifted the trade restrictions, but the dispute may not have been fully resolved until an MAS was signed in 2007. The Arabic-speaking research assistant I worked made inquiries to contacts in the ministry but was unable to discern the actual timeline or whether the compliance measures were, in fact, WTO consistent. These coding limitations were a concern in only a small number of disputes, but because they appear more often in nondemocratic regimes, they raise the possibility of bias.

On the one hand, the few countries with opaque reporting practices might lead me to overestimate compliance. When a government declared itself compliant, no further evidence was available to the contrary, and the complainant acquiesced, I coded the case as compliant. Governments with sparse public records were thus given the "benefit of the doubt." Compliance might be overestimated for countries that have poor reporting practices.

On the other hand, states with weak provisions about public information may be the very same ones that engage in—on average—more sincere reporting to the WTO. A widely recognized finding in the literature is that democratic governments engage in "optimal obfuscation" of trade policy (Kono 2006). The more accountable to the public a regime is, the more likely it is to implement its trade barriers though obscure, technocratic, and evasive policy devices. So more transparent regimes may, counterintuitively, hide their noncompliance more effectively. This means that compliance would actually be overestimated for governments with strong laws about public information. Altogether, the direction of bias from information gaps remains unclear. To help address this issue, I examine the compliance data in relation to a common transparency index and find no apparent correlation.[69]

4.3 Data

4.3.1 Dependent variable: compliance

I assessed all the WTO disputes that were initiated between 1995 and 2012 and resulted in an adverse panel ruling.[70] The unit of observation is the dispute: one or more complainants sue a single respondent government over a specific set of alleged trade barriers. Because each dispute can last several years, the sample is truncated in 2012 to allow five years to elapse before the outcomes are examined. The data are summarized in table 4.1.

The first and most striking point revealed by these data is that states are generally responsive to adjudication. In three-quarters of the disputes with adverse rulings, respondents reported some adjustments to their trade policies, although many of those efforts were only partial or delayed. In approximately two-thirds of the disputes, governments ultimately fully complied with their adverse rulings. However, those measures sometimes took effect after multiyear delays. In just under half of the disputes with adverse rulings, the respondent complied on time— that is, before the deadline established by the WTO. This means that the government adopted necessary policies before the implementation deadline and the complainant agreed that the policies were sufficient.

That nearly half of disputes produced timely compliance is an important finding. Even the largest economic powers routinely acquiesce to

TABLE 4.1 **Summary of WTO Disputes with Adverse Rulings**

	Dispute outcome				
	Compliance (any form)		No compliance		MAS[†]
Number (#)	119		36		35
Percentage (%)	76.7		23.3		22.6
Contested Policy (#)					
Administrative	112		31		30
Legislative	41		16		9
Both	34		11		4
Outcome Details	Full	On-Time	Resolved	Unresolved[‡]	
Number (#)	103	72	24	12	
Percentage (%)	66.5	46.5	15.5	7.7	

Note: [†]Twenty disputes ended with both MAS and compliance through policy reforms. [‡]Ongoing, dropped, or outcome unknown. Data cover 155 disputes with adverse rulings and this is the denominator used in percentage calculations

WTO rulings by modifying their policies, and they do so by the deadline set forth by the organization. This is striking because governments do so after engaging in a costly and sometimes prolonged legal battle. This is compelling evidence that the adjustments run contrary to the governments' preferences had the complainant not intervened by leveraging the WTO DSM.

Even when governments do not follow the WTO's prescriptions in their entirety, they do seem somewhat responsive. In another third of the disputes (47 out of 155), respondents made some policy adjustments. Either they delayed implementation past the WTO's deadline or they adopted partial measures. In the remaining disputes, just under one-quarter of the sample, there was no evidence of any movement toward compliance. In the case of many of these, the complaint was eventually dropped by the complainant without explanation or a settlement was struck that did not entail policy reforms consistent with the ruling; in each of these instances, there was a clear date when the dispute was deemed by the WTO to be "resolved." The remaining instances of noncompliance are unresolved, languishing for years on the WTO's docket without any update.

Table 4.1 also shows dispute outcomes by whether the contested trade policies were administrative, legislative, or both. There are many more adverse rulings that strike down administrative or executive measures than those that strike down legislative ones. A government is 1.4 times more likely to comply when a WTO ruling instructs a respondent to change administrative measures than when it is instructed to revise its laws. Some WTO rulings identify both administrative and legislative measures that constitute violations; in these cases, the rate at which the respondent implements any modifications to its trade policy is similar to the rate for legislative measures alone. Indeed, all else equal, governments tend to be more amenable to compliance when modifying the policies in question requires the consent of fewer domestic political actors.

The rates of bilateral settlements (that is, those that end in an MAS) are not significantly different across the types of contested policies. This dispels an important alternative hypothesis. One might speculate that respondents strike post-adjudicative settlements in an effort to skirt the difficulties they would face if they were to reform their trade policies. If this were the case, then the MAS rate when the contested policy is legislative would be higher than the MAS rate when the contested policy is administrative. The results in table 4.1 show no such pattern; the settlement rate for disputes over administrative measures is actually slightly higher.

Remedy disputes are somewhat more likely to lead to compliance than disputes over other trade barriers. Overall, discrepancies across the topics are not significant. Table 4.2 summarizes the compliance record by the dispute topic.

The second point revealed by the data is that WTO disputes are unlikely to serve as a mere facade for power politics. The most frequent users of the WTO dispute settlement system are the United States and the European Union. On the complainant side, they have respectively

TABLE 4.2 **Compliance and Settlement Record by Dispute Topic**

| Topic | Compliance | | | |
	Full	Partial	None	MAS[†]
Agriculture	12	0	11	20
Antidumping	18	7	8	18
Safeguards	15	1	1	14
Sanitary & Phytosanitary Measures	3	0	4	6
Subsidies & Countervailing Duties	27	2	9	33

Note: Number of disputes by trade barrier and agreement cited. [†]Settlements after adverse rulings only. Disputes span multiple topics.

filed thirty and thirty-one of the complaints that produced adverse rulings. Seventeen of the disputes were US complaints against the EU or
vice versa. On the respondent side, seventeen different countries in addition to the US and the EU have been implicated in adverse rulings.
These respondents span all parts of the globe and feature both democratic and nondemocratic regimes.

Table 4.3 describes the frequency of respondent governments involved
in disputes. The United States has complied in approximately three-
quarters of the cases where it has been found to have broken WTO obligations. The EU record is spottier, with an approximately even split
between full compliance and noncompliance. Canada stands out as approximately 90% compliant with adverse WTO rulings. Indeed, there is
substantial cross-country variation in compliance that has not been explained in prior research.

While no other equivalent data sets on compliance with WTO rulings exist, it is helpful to compare this evidence to related studies. In the
155 cases I evaluated—complaints brought by all countries (including the
US)—117 eventually had some progress toward compliance (albeit sometimes delayed by months or years), resulting in a "partial success" rate of
about 77%. For partial compliance measures adopted by the defendant
before the WTO-established deadline, the rate was somewhat lower at
63.4%. In my data, the United States' performance is right around the
full sample average. This is similar to findings by Davis (2012, 250), who
shows that for formal WTO complaints brought by the United States,
75.6% saw progress toward resolution. Likewise, Brewster and Chilton
(2014) report similar findings for complaints against the US. These rates
are informative. While the disputes did not always reach full compliance
in the specified time frame, they do reflect the WTO DSM's broader goal
of dispute resolution.

4.3.2 Explanatory and control variables

The first explanatory variable is domestic veto players in the respondent government (Tsebelis 1995, 2002; Henisz 2000). Veto points are
produced by institutional checks and partisan divisions. I measure *Veto
Points* using the Political Constraints Index (Henisz 2002). It accounts
for the number of independent branches of government, federalism, the
extent of partisan alignment across branches of government, and preference heterogeneity within each legislative body. Partisan alignment

TABLE 4.3 **Compliance Record by Respondent Government**

	Full	Partial	None	Veto points[‡]
Argentina	4	2	-	0.45
Australia	1	-	2	0.51
Brazil	2	-	-	0.40
Canada	9	1	1	0.45
Chile	-	2	1	0.65
China	8	-	2	0.00
Colombia	-	1	-	0.11
Dominican Rep.	2	-	-	0.28
Egypt	1	-	-	0.08
EU	13	-	14	0.47[†]
Guatemala	1	-	-	0.43
India	5	-	-	0.46
Indonesia	4	-	-	0.00
Japan	4	-	2	0.58
Korea	6	-	1	0.34
Mexico	4	2	-	0.33
Thailand	-	1	1	0.39
Turkey	1	-	1	0.41
US	38	7	11	0.40

Note: Number of disputes by respondent. Covers 155 disputes filed 1995–2012. [‡]Mean calculated for dispute start years. [†]EU uses weighted mean of country scores. Alternate coding by Yildirim (2018) sets the EU score at 0.85.

accounts for party composition and left or right preference which change over time. *Veto Points* range from 0 (least constrained) to 1 (most constrained). This metric is useful because it covers diverse governments, is widely accepted among political scientists (e.g., Mansfield and Milner 2012; Henisz and Mansfield 2006), and provides a unified summary of domestic obstacles. While the Political Constraints Index is updated yearly, many countries have a rather stable score over time, reflecting that the architecture of government is modified infrequently.

There are two versions of the veto points metric, similar except that *Veto Points II* accounts for an independent judiciary whereas *Veto Points I* does not. In this chapter, domestic veto points are assessed at two times: the year in which the dispute was initiated (start) and the compliance deadline (the reasonable period of time). When the European Union is the respondent, I use the weighted average of the veto points of the member countries, with membership updated year-by-year. The weights accord with each member state's vote share in the Council of the European Union. This weighting is intended to reflect that some member states hold greater sway over policy decisions in the EU. Many WTO disputes address EU-wide policies that require compliance efforts not only at the EU level but also proper implementation within the member states. This means the weighted average will tend to understate effective obstacles to compliance in the EU. To remedy this concern, I also used the EU-specific veto points measure created by Yildirim (2018) that accounts for political constraints unique to its supranational institutional structure.

While the veto points variable has clear benefits—its breadth of coverage and frequent use in related studies (e.g., Mansfield and Milner 2012; Henisz and Mansfield 2006)—there are also limitations. First, there is some conceptual and empirical overlap between veto players and regime type. Both concepts involve the extent of institutional checks and balances. And democracies have many more divisions of power than autocratic regimes, making the two difficult to separate empirically.

Nonetheless, there are important distinctions. Veto players theory accounts for institutional and partisan actors who must consent to policy changes. Veto points capture the agility of policy-making. By contrast, other features of government affect the regime type. Democracies are evaluated based on the rule of law, civil liberties, and the execution of elections, among other characteristics. Compliance with WTO rulings depends more on veto players than democracy. Stakeholders in international trade (e.g., firms and interest groups) are not thought to primarily influence trade policy directly through popular votes; rather, they tend to influence policy-making by lobbying legislators and shaping administrative decisions.

To address the empirical overlap, I conduct several statistical tests to probe the effects of democracy and veto players on compliance. The analysis below sometimes separately analyzes the subsample of democratic respondents. By comparing the subsample analysis to the full sample results, I show that variation in veto points among democracies matters.

The second limitation of the veto points measure in this context concerns its simplicity. By concisely measuring the joint impact of institutional checks and partisan divisions, the veto points variable might obscure two separate processes that give rise to noncompliance in WTO disputes. To address this concern, I investigate two related indicators. I account for the respondent's checks and balances (*Checks*), including those between legislative and executive branches of government. Legislative *Fractionalization* measures the number and distribution of parties in the legislature. These latter variables come from the Database of Political Institutions (Beck et al. 2001) and are expected to obstruct compliance through legislation.

The second explanatory variable in this analysis is the difficulty of reforming contested policy. Although governments encounter many varied factors that make some policy reforms more difficult than others, a key distinction is between administrative and legislative measures. I use an indicator variable to denote whether a contested policy was a *Legislative Measure*. Legislative measures are laws and amendments that require congressional or parliamentary consent to reform, while administrative measures include executive orders and regulations controlled by government agencies such as a ministry of trade, department of commerce, etc. Compliance is expected to be more difficult when legislative measures are at issue than when only administrative measures are concerned. In my sample, only democratic governments have been subjected to adverse rulings over legislative measures, presumably because the autocratic governments lack a legislative branch with meaningful authority over policy.

Several economic factors are likely to affect compliance. Respondents with larger economies may be better able to resist WTO rulings. I control for *Respondent GDP* in the year the dispute was initiated. The GDP data come from the World Bank and are log-transformed. To control for the complainant's economic clout, I account for the *Complainant GDP* in the year the dispute was initiated because complainants with larger economies have a greater capacity to penalize respondents that defy a WTO ruling.

I control for the number of *Third-Party* governments in disputes, coded from WTO records. Seven disputes have no third parties, 73 disputes have between one and five, and the remaining 75 have many third parties. Due to the skewed distribution, I use a log transformation in the regression analysis.[71] The number of governments entering the dispute as third parties could correlate with the scope of the dispute. Disputes with broad economic impact tend to attract the greatest attention from the broader membership of countries who participate as bystanders in the legal proceedings. By contrast, disputes that concern narrowly targeted trade barriers tend to attract fewer third-party countries. Third-party participation may also be associated with lower compliance rates, as argued in Kucik and Peritz (2021).

Certain attributes of WTO disputes could also predict compliance. I account for *Remedy* disputes over antidumping duties and countervailing measures. These cases are narrowly targeted at a particular industry and tend to activate fewer veto players. The *% Adverse Ruling* measures the percentage of legal claims found in favor of the complainant (Horn and Mavroidis 2008). Where rulings were appealed by governments, I count the claims that were sustained. In robustness checks, I also assess whether the claims cited in a given dispute were previously litigated in order to control for the accumulation of case law, using data from Kucik (2019).

In portions of the analysis, I also included an indicator variable for lawsuits against *Federal* governments, since these divisions of power could pose further obstacles to policy reform. For simplicity, the European Union is coded as a federal actor in the WTO. In some models, I include indicator variables for the European Union and United States separately as complainants and respondents.

Trade disputes differ in their economic scale. Some concern a wide array of products and large trade volumes; others address niche industries and small trade volumes. I account for the trade stakes in a case by measuring the product-specific disputed *Imports* into the respondent's market. This is calculated by taking the trade flow from the complainant country to the respondent country for the specific products named in the dispute (identified by the six- or four- digit Harmonized System codes), adding up those product trade flows, and then taking the natural log. Imports are calculated for the year the dispute commenced. These data come from a combination of data from the United Nations (2013) and Bown and Reynolds (2015). Trade stakes can be informative. At face value, it might seem that trade disputes with larger values might provoke more resistance from states. Conversely, narrow trade disputes that involve lower trade values might be more likely to lead to compliance, since respondent governments may be willing to capitulate. While this may seem like the ideal measure of trade stakes, there are, unfortunately, two limitations: It restricts the sample to only disputes where product trade can be observed, missing WTO cases on services, intellectual property, and broad points of policy contention. Moreover, product-specific trade data do not fully reflect retaliatory potential. Enforcement through trade retaliation can sometimes cut across industries.[72]

4.4 Results

To estimate the impact of domestic political constraints on compliance with WTO rulings, I fit a series of probit and ordered probit regression models. The probit model is appropriate for the analysis of binary outcome variables. I evaluate whether a government complied with a WTO ruling, measured as "ever comply" and "comply by deadline." Likewise, the ordered probit model is suitable for the analysis of ordered categorical variables. I evaluate whether a government complied completely, partially, or not at all. The following analysis examines the full sample of disputes, disputes over restrictions on trade in products, and a restricted sample of disputes in which the respondent is a democracy.

Throughout the analysis, standard errors are clustered by groups of related disputes, as determined by the WTO. This approach reflects the fact that sometimes multiple countries file separate complaints over the same allegations. For example, eight complaints were brought against the United States in 2002 regarding WTO-inconsistent steel tariffs. A single set of legal proceedings was conducted to address all these complaints. Clustering standard errors by groups of related disputes is preferable to doing so by respondent country. Countries encounter vastly different types of trade disputes featuring different plaintiffs, products, policy types, and so on, typically making their compliance decisions in one case unrelated to their compliance decisions in another. For example, the US decision to adjust its environmental standards for gasoline after Venezuela and Brazil brought complaints[73] was unrelated to the US decision to ignore the adverse ruling when the EU and other countries challenged its dumping and subsidies offset legislation.[74]

4.4.1 Eventual compliance

First, I evaluate whether the respondent ever complied, even after a lengthy delay. This is a lenient interpretation of compliance. Recall that WTO rulings are accompanied by an implementation deadline. But sometimes the respondent resists for several years before adjusting its trade policies to comply. Belated reforms still count as compliance in this portion of the analysis.

The government's veto points are measured at two points: the year in which the dispute began and the year of the compliance deadline—

TABLE 4.4 **Effect of Domestic Veto Points on Compliance**

	Did respondent ever comply? (1/0)					
	(1)	(2)	(3)	(4)	(5)	(6)
Veto Points I$_{Start}$	−1.66*	−2.70**				
	(0.87)	(1.35)				
Veto Points I$_{RPT}$			−3.02*			
			(1.73)			
Veto Points II$_{Start}$				−1.06		
				(0.65)		
Veto Points II$_{RPT}$					−1.22*	
					(0.74)	
Veto Points II$_{EU}$						−1.35*
						(0.76)
Legislative Measure		0.07	0.02	0.05	0.07	0.05
		(0.39)	(0.38)	(0.39)	(0.39)	(0.39)
Complainant GDP[†]		−0.10	−0.10	−0.11	−0.11	−0.12
		(0.10)	(0.10)	(0.10)	(0.10)	(0.10)
Respondent GDP[†]		0.01	0.04	0.08	0.08	0.09
		(0.10)	(0.11)	(0.11)	(0.11)	(0.11)
Imports[†]		0.04	0.04	0.04	0.05	0.05
		(0.06)	(0.06)	(0.06)	(0.06)	(0.06)
% Adverse		0.80	0.78	0.82	0.83	0.80
		(0.53)	(0.54)	(0.54)	(0.54)	(0.54)
Third Parties[†]		−0.59**	−0.68***	−0.61**	−0.62**	−0.60**
		(0.23)	(0.25)	(0.24)	(0.25)	(0.23)
Remedy		0.01	0.04	−0.01	0.02	0.02
		(0.34)	(0.34)	(0.33)	(0.33)	(0.33)
N	155	139	139	139	139	139
Log Likelihood	−81.92	−58.81	−58.74	−60.87	−60.65	−59.74

Note: Probit models estimated with R. Imports are bilateral trade flows from complainant to respondent for disputed products in year the dispute was initiated. Clustered standard errors by dispute group. Significance codes *p< 0.1; **p<0.05; ***p <0.01. [†]Log units. Intercepts not shown.

that is, when the reasonable period of time for compliance expired. I check this for both versions of the veto players metric: the original *Veto Points I* score and the alternative one that accounts for judicial independence, *Veto Points II*. The results are presented in table 4.4.

The first veto points measure shows consistent and statistically significant results (models 1–3). The first model considers all WTO disputes with adverse rulings initiated between 1995 and 2012, while the second includes the full set of control variables and therefore restricts the sample to disputes over import restrictions. The third model repeats the analysis, but instead uses domestic veto points the year of the implementation deadline (the reasonable period of time), typically 2–3 years after the initial legal compliant was filed. The estimated effect of domestic veto players on compliance is again significant.

The next set of models (4–6) uses the second measure of veto points, which accounts for an independent judiciary as a check on legislative and/or executive power. In few if any jurisdictions is judicial action required to implement WTO rulings; the judiciary is an irrelevant veto player. It is unsurprising that the second measure of veto points does not always have statistically significant effect on compliance. In the sixth specification, I use a measure of European Union veto points that additionally accounts for that institution's unique political constraints. These correlations reinforce the main results. Disputes over legislative measures do not have significantly different compliance rates than those over administrative trade policies.

The control variables behave largely as expected. The participation of third-party governments in disputes is associated with lower compliance rates. There are a couple possible reasons for this association. Third parties could complicate legal proceedings, voicing additional concerns and encouraging panel judges to issue more stringent rulings that respondents struggle to implement. Or disputes over the most wide-reaching and controversial trade policies that respondents are least willing to amend may attract more third-party participation (e.g., the US "zeroing" disputes). Bilateral trade in the disputed products, measured as the respondent's imports from the complainant, are not a significant predictor of compliance. This is consistent with findings by Bown and Reynolds (2015) that many disputes implicate only small amounts of trade; it is their political salience that drives countries to seek legal enforcement (Davis 2012; Chaudoin 2014). Nor is the extent of the adverse ruling a significant predictor, likely because panelists and Appellate Body judges exercise judicial restraint, ruling only on select claims (Busch and Pelc 2010; Steinberg 2004). I also checked complainant and respondent GDPs to assess the relative economic clout and found no significant association.

The veto points variable accounts for the joint impact institutional divisions and divergent preferences. To isolate the effects of these factors, I turned to two variables available from the Database of Political Institutions (Beck et al. 2001): institutional checks and legislative fractionalization. Because these measures pertain most clearly to the legislative processes, the analysis is restricted to the subset of disputes that required legislative measures (56 cases). Legislative disputes tend to vary widely in their complexity, so I additionally control for the number of legal claims raised in the complainant's initial legal submission.

TABLE 4.5 **Legislative Constraints on Compliance**

| | Did respondent ever comply? (1/0) | |
	(1)	(2)
Checks	−0.32	
	(0.28)	
Fractionalization		−4.69**
		(2.24)
Complainant GDP†	0.25	0.14
	(0.18)	(0.21)
Respondent GDP†	−0.33**	−0.23
	(0.16)	(0.16)
% Adverse	−0.27	−1.03
	(1.39)	(1.54)
EU Respondent	−0.85	−1.22
	(0.68)	(0.76)
Third Parties†	−0.24	−0.14
	(0.32)	(0.34)
Claim Count	−0.04	−0.08*
	(0.04)	(0.05)
Remedy	−0.03	0.03
	(0.50)	(0.51)
N	56	56
Log Likelihood	−22.56	−20.60

Note: Probit models estimated with R. Disputes concerning legislative measures only. Significance codes *p<0.1; **p<0.05. †Log units. Intercepts not shown.

Because the EU faces particularly staunch obstacles to legislative compliance through the European Parliament, I also include an EU dummy variable.

Table 4.5 shows that there is a weak association between institutional checks and noncompliance and a strong one between fractionalization and noncompliance. For disputes over legislative measures, the constellation of partisan power figures prominently. Where power is more evenly distributed among multiple parties—high fractionalization—legislatures face the highest hurdles in passing amendments or new policies to bring a government into compliance. By contrast, the legislative fractionalization variable is not a strong predictor of compliance in WTO disputes over administrative measures, consistent with my expectations.

Two other institutional factors complicate the veto players story. The first is federalism. Federal states face more complicated compliance processes than those with unified governments. As the above examples have shown, a federal government can adopt WTO-consistent policies but fail to see these policies come into full effect if subnational actors refuse to follow suit. Thus federalism could compound the obstacles to compliance already in place from domestic veto players. Special among these participants is the European Union, an inter-governmental organization comprised of dozens of states who have their own internal veto players. The EU is coded as a federation for the purposes of this analysis.

The second is democratic institutions. Prior research shows the importance of democracy to account for both patterns of which countries file complaints and which countries are targeted as respondents (Davis 2012). Likewise, democratic countries offer more opportunities for institutional contestation that would raise barriers to compliance. Clearly, democracies have more veto players than autocracies. Are democratic institutions, rather than veto players, the key driver of compliance activity in WTO disputes? Only a small number of nondemocratic states have been subjected to censure through adverse panel rulings during the years analyzed by this study. These countries are China, Indonesia, Egypt, and Thailand. Perhaps the difference between democratic and nondemocratic countries could be driving the results in table 4.4.

Table 4.6 investigates both possibilities. Control variables are included but not shown, and standard errors are again clustered by dispute group. The first model considers all disputes. It includes an interaction effect between veto points and whether the respondent government is federal. Respondents with more veto players continue to have a lower probability of complying with an adverse ruling; this effect appears to be stronger for federal respondents but not at a level of statistical significance. Federalism appears to magnify the obstacles from domestic veto players in perhaps a handful of disputes but this is not consistently a deciding factor.

The second model in table 4.6 looks at just the subset of democratic respondent governments—that is, it excludes the fifteen adverse rulings against nondemocratic regimes. Because there are so few observations of nondemocratic regimes, the subsample analysis is more informative than a model using an interaction term between veto points and the democracy indicator variable (Kam and Franzese 2007). The estimated effect of veto players is strengthened for the democratic subset. This lends support to the broader theory because it is in democratic countries that industry or other interest groups are best able to seek leverage over representatives in government.

The discrepancy in the magnitude of the coefficients between the full sample and democratic subset also suggests outlier observations may be

TABLE 4.6 **Evaluating Federalism, Democracy and Influential Countries**

	Did respondent ever comply? (1/0)					
	(1)	(2)	(3)	(4)	(5)	(6)
Veto Points I_{Start}	−2.42**	−6.32**	−3.55*			−2.05*
	(1.13)	(2.54)	(1.85)			(1.16)
Veto Points I_{Start} × Federal	−5.09					
	(5.78)					
Federal	2.58					
	(2.59)					
Veto Points II_{EU}				−8.01*	−1.54	
				(4.45)	(1.15)	
EU Complainant			0.79		0.70	
			(0.71)		(0.57)	
EU Respondent			−0.76**		−0.80**	
			(0.37)		(0.38)	
China Respondent			−1.09		−0.76	
			(1.09)		(1.16)	
Korea Respondent			−0.22		0.04	
			(0.59)		(0.58)	
Legislative Measure	0.08	−0.11	−0.08	−0.23	−0.09	0.28
	(0.42)	(0.46)	(0.38)	(0.46)	(0.39)	(0.39)
N	139	124	139	124	139	115
Democracy Subset?	No	Yes	No	Yes	No	No
Omit EU Respondent?	No	No	No	No	No	Yes
Controls?	Yes	Yes	Yes	Yes	Yes	Yes
Log Likelihood	−57.30	−50.11	−53.48	−49.58	−54.59	−40.58

Note: Probit models estimated with R. Clustered standard errors by dispute group. Significance codes *p<0.1; **p<0.05. Intercepts and control variables (GDPs, imports, % adverse, third parties, remedy) are included but not shown.

influencing the results. Using tests for statistical leverage, I determined that the most influential observations in the regression analysis came from the European Union, China, and South Korea. Thus model 3 repeats the analysis with dummy variables for those respondent governments. Together, these results suggest that the EU is an influential actor, featuring many domestic veto points and also driving down the WTO's overall compliance rates.

When nondemocratic countries are excluded from the sample, the EU's statistical influence is more pronounced. With this in mind, models 4 and 5 in the table examine the alternative measure of veto points, which accounts for the EU's dispute-specific veto players (Yildirim 2018). Comparing the democracy-only subset to the full sample (with an EU dummy variable) confirms that the supranational institution confronts special obstacles to compliance with WTO rulings. Finally, model

6 excludes all disputes in which the EU was the respondent. The coefficient on veto points is still significant but somewhat diminished in magnitude. This confirms that the EU is an influential participant in the WTO but not the sole driver.

On balance, the results confirm that the veto points result cannot be attributed to democratic institutions or influential countries alone. The checks and balances from democratic institutions are indeed contributing factors but cannot provide a complete story of why veto points tend to hinder compliance with WTO rulings.

4.4.2 Compliance timing

The timing of a trade dispute settlement matters. In some disputes, governments comply promptly, abiding by the WTO's deadline. Plaintiffs benefit from prompt resolution. Timely compliance means that the defendant lowers its import tariffs and the complainant's exporter firms enjoy market recoveries. But when the respondent drags out the process and delays any policy reform, the complainant bears the brunt. Its exporter firms may suffer, and the government will need to undertake additional legal proceedings. Defendants that are highly responsive to WTO rulings will tend to comply in a timely manner. Reluctant governments will prefer to wait until the deadline has passed and the complainant has threatened recourse before taking any action. The hypotheses laid out in chapter 2 indicate that domestic veto players should reduce the chance that a government complies by the implementation deadline.

To test this part of my theory, I look at whether respondent governments complied in a timely manner, before the WTO's deadline. This approach is more stringent because it considers only policy adjustments made before the reasonable period of time expired. I also constructed an ordinal measure of compliance that captures this timing by distinguishing between on-time, delayed, and no compliance. To guard against reverse-causality concerns, this part of the analysis considers only the veto points in the respondent government during the initial year of the dispute. Table 4.7 presents the results. Intercepts and control variables are included but not shown and standard errors are clustered by dispute group.

Using the *Veto Points I* measure, table 4.7, model 1, shows just the bivariate relationship between domestic political constraints and on-time compliance with WTO rulings. Model 2 controls for complainant and respondent economies, as well as the dispute-specific trade flows between

TABLE 4.7 **Timely Compliance**

	Did respondent comply by deadline? (1/0)				On-time, delayed, never (1/$\frac{1}{2}$/0)	
	(1)	(2)	(3)	(4)	(5)	(6)
Veto Points I$_{Start}$	-2.14**	-2.81***	-3.32*		-2.78***	
	(0.86)	(0.90)	(1.75)		(0.85)	
Veto Points II$_{Start}$				-1.15**		-1.18**
				(0.57)		(0.54)
Legislative Measure		-0.04	-0.25	-0.05	0.002	-0.03
		(0.30)	(0.32)	(0.31)	(0.27)	(0.28)
N	155	139	124	139	139	139
Democracy Subset?	No	No	Yes	No	No	No
Controls?	No	Yes	Yes	Yes	Yes	Yes
Model	P	P	P	P	OP	OP
Log Likelihood	-102.46	-87.50	-79.56	-90.95	-90.95	-135.09

Note: Probit and ordered probit models estimated with R. Clustered standard errors by dispute group. Significance codes *p<0.1; **p<0.05; ***p<0.01. Intercepts and control variables (GDPs, imports, % adverse, third parties, remedy) are included but not shown.

the complainant and the respondent. It has a smaller sample size because this omits disputes over issues such as government procurement, investment services, etc. The correlations here are stronger than those we saw above with the more lenient compliance measure.

Table 4.7 also reports results of ordered probit models where the dependent variable differentiates between on-time, delayed, and no compliance. Models 5 and 6 consider both versions of the veto points variable. Control variables are included but not shown in the table. Again, there are strong correlations between domestic veto points and the timing of compliance by the respondent government.

The effect is weaker when only democratic countries are considered— the coefficient in model 3 is statistically significant at only the 0.90 level. The second version of the veto points measure (including the judiciary) is also a strong predictor in model 4. Viewed alongside the results in table 4.4, this suggests that delays in compliance can be partly attributed to democratic institutions (that is, the contrast between democracy and autocracy). Eventual compliance, on the other hand, may be better explained by the constellations of political constraints within democracies. Autocracies tend to act quickly in response to adverse WTO rulings, adjusting policy, and democracies tend to delay. When they delay, the degree of domestic political constraints shapes whether or not the government ever complies.

Due to the complications that come from interpreting probit model estimates, I also convert them into marginal effects to demonstrate these contrasting results. Table 4.8 reports the marginal effects for corresponding models estimates, looking at *Comply ever?* and *Comply by deadline?* for both the full sample and the democratic respondent subsample. The marginal effects are calculated for the variables at their means. This shows that a change in veto points produces an approximately twofold increase in the probability of *eventual* compliance for democracies, as compared to the full set of respondent countries. When we consider *timely* compliance, the difference between the full set of countries and the democratic subsample is negligible.

Figure 4.1 illustrates the predicted effects from model 2 in table 4.7. The probability of timely compliance significantly diminishes with veto points in the respondent government. The shaded regions in the plot depict 90% and 95% confidence intervals associated with the point estimates. Moving from the 10th percentile of the veto points distribution to the 90th percentile brings about a decline in the predicted probability of timely compliance by 0.38. Translating these predictions into practical terms, this means that the Philippines in 2010 (*Veto Points* I_{start} = 0.11) had a 38% higher chance of complying with a WTO ruling before the deadline than did Australia in 2007 (*Veto Points* I_{start} = 0.50).

My theory also implies that a falling number of veto points should be associated with a greater likelihood of timely compliance. I considered whether rising, falling, or a stable number of veto points in a government affects the probability of compliance. Results suggest that rising veto

TABLE 4.8 **Marginal Effects Summarizing Full and Democracy-Only Samples**

	Ever comply? (1/0)		Comply by deadline? (1/0)	
Marginal Effects for Model:	(4.4.2)	(4.4.3)	(4.7.2)	(4.7.3)
Veto Points I_{Start}	−0.66*	−1.47*	−1.12**	−1.32
	(0.31)	(0.58)	(0.37)	(0.72)
Legislative Measure	0.02	−0.03	−0.02	−0.10
	(0.10)	(0.12)	(0.12)	(0.13)
N	139	124	139	124
Democracy Subset?	No	Yes	No	Yes
Controls?	Yes	Yes	Yes	Yes
Log Likelihood	−58.81	−50.11	−87.50	−79.56

Note: Probit model marginal effects estimated at variable means. Clustered standard errors by dispute group. Significance codes *p<0.1; **p<0.05. Controls (GDPs, imports, % adverse, third parties, remedy) are included but not shown.

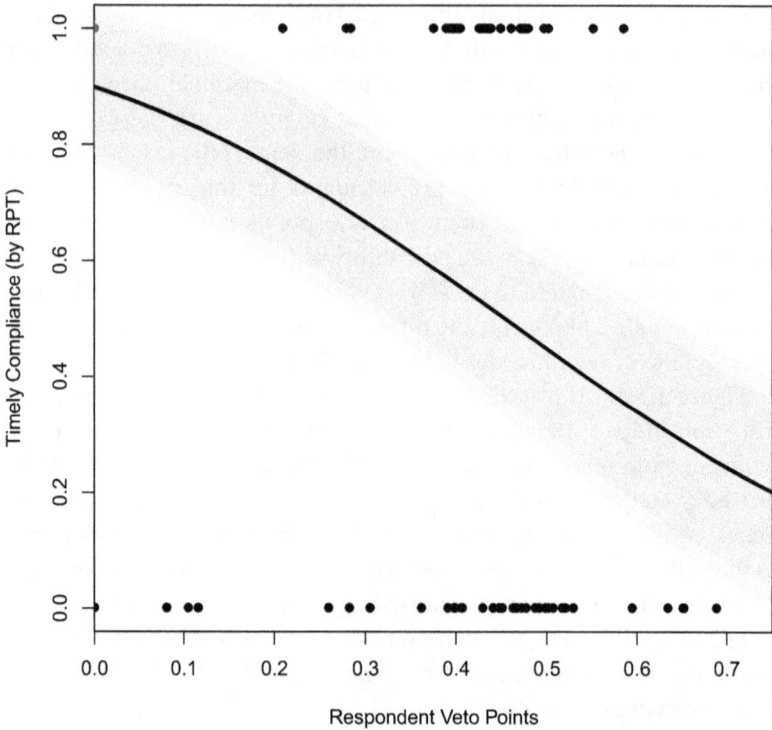

FIGURE 4.1. Predicted Probability of On-Time Compliance in WTO Disputes
Note: All predicted probabilities are calculated with the model in table 4.7(2) and control
variables held at their means. Timely compliance is indicated by whether the respondent
government adopted necessary policy reforms before the reasonable period of time expired.

points are associated with lower probability and declining veto points
are associated with higher probability of timely compliance, but the estimates are not statistically significant.[75] Relatedly, the theory suggests
that leadership turnover should be associated with compliance after a
period of noncompliance. Using data from Bobick and Smith (2016), I
assessed this possibility for a subset of WTO disputes (limited by the
years covered in leader turnover data) and found no strong correlation
there either.

4.4.3 Partial compliance

Full and timely compliance may simply be too high a bar for most respondent governments. In some cases, the ruling is too burdensome

to implement completely, but partial measures are feasible. To at least some observers, the WTO DSM will have still advanced the multilateral trade regime if it has encouraged governments to dismantle some barriers to trade, even if those efforts fall short of full compliance. And indeed, this may be a logical response to domestic veto players. If domestic actors stand in the way of full compliance, partial measures may be the only feasible pathway for government leaders.

In this section of the analysis, I distinguish between complete compliance, partial compliance, and noncompliance and examine the correlation to the respondent government's constraints. Because the dependent variable is ordinal, I use ordered probit models. Results are presented in table 4.9. Model 1 uses the full sample of observations to show that domestic political constraints are associated with less complete compliance. Model 2 introduces control variables, and model 3 looks specifically at

TABLE 4.9 **Complete, Partial, and Non- Compliance**

	Did respondent comply? Full, partial, none ($1/\frac{1}{2}/0$)					
	(1)	(2)	(3)	(4)	(5)	(6)
Veto Points I$_{Start}$	−1.81**	−2.68***	−3.47**			
	(0.92)	(1.01)	(1.45)			
Veto Points I$_{RPT}$				−2.16*		
				(1.14)		
Veto Points II$_{Start}$					−1.06*	
					(0.56)	
Veto Points II$_{EU}$						−1.23**
						(0.57)
Legislative Measure	−0.13	0.13	−0.02	0.07	0.10	0.10
	(0.27)	(0.32)	(0.34)	(0.32)	(0.32)	(0.31)
Complainant GDP[†]		−0.06	−0.05	−0.06	−0.06	−0.07
		(0.08)	(0.08)	(0.08)	(0.08)	(0.08)
Respondent GDP[†]		0.05	0.04	0.08	0.12	0.13
		(0.09)	(0.09)	(0.09)	(0.09)	(0.09)
Imports[†]		0.04	0.05	0.04	0.04	0.04
		(0.05)	(0.05)	(0.05)	(0.05)	(0.05)
% Adverse		0.65	0.73	0.64	0.67	0.65
		(0.50)	(0.53)	(0.49)	(0.50)	(0.50)
Third Parties[†]		−0.50**	−0.50**	−0.54**	−0.52**	−0.51**
		(0.21)	(0.22)	(0.22)	(0.22)	(0.21)
Remedy		−0.02	−0.18	0.04	−0.02	−0.0003
		(0.29)	(0.32)	(0.29)	(0.28)	(0.28)
N	155	139	124	139	139	139
Democracy Subset?	No	No	Yes	No	No	No
Log Likelihood	−130.87	−102.85	−95.16	−105.24	−105.64	−104.72

Note: Ordered probit models estimated with R. Clustered standard errors by dispute group. Significance codes *p<0.1; **p<0.05; ***p<0.01. [†]Log units. Intercepts not shown.

the subset of democratic respondent countries, showing strong results in both cases. Model 4 considers veto points in the year of the compliance deadline rather than the start of the dispute, while model 5 considers the second veto points measure that accounts for the constraints imposed by the judicial branch of government. The first measure of veto points yields stronger support than the second. To show that the results are not driven by the European Union—which has many veto points and a generally poor compliance record—I also repeated the analysis using the EU-specific coding of veto points in model 6. The estimated effect of veto points on compliance remains negative and statistically significant.

In disputes where more third-party countries participate, respondents are likely to adopt partial compliance measures that satisfy only portions of the ruling. This is consistent with arguments by Johns and Pelc (2018) that emphasize the distributional consequences of WTO rulings. When there are many bystander countries with stakes in the enforcement of WTO rules, governments may be especially reluctant to make sweeping concessions to achieve full compliance with adverse rulings. Instead, they opt for partial measures.

4.4.4 Uncovering opportunism

States appear to time their compliance activity in an opportunistic manner that evades international penalties while satisfying domestic stakeholders. It is impossible to know for sure whether governments are deliberately delaying in order to reap the benefits of institutional flexibility. However, several scholars have highlighted how states might take advantage of flexibility in the multilateral trade regime (Brewster 2011; Pelc 2013; Pelc and Urpelainen 2015), and certain empirical patterns are consistent with this explanation.

What behavior constitutes opportunistic noncompliance? Two empirical patterns would support the opportunism argument. The first concerns duration—the more domestic veto points in the respondent government, the longer the dispute is expected to last. By prolonging the dispute and delaying compliance, respondent governments could simultaneously satisfy domestic stakeholders and stave off retaliation from complainants. The second involves legal stages. The more access industry groups or other domestic interests have to influence politicians, the more legal stages I expect to be undertaken. Leaders in respondent governments who are beholden to domestic constraints might be more

TABLE 4.10 **Duration and Legal Stages**

	Compliance hazard			Number of legal stages		
	(1)	(2)	(3)	(4)	(5)	(6)
Respondent Veto Points I_{Start}	–2.09***	–2.17***	–3.10**	0.61**	0.51*	0.06
	(0.64)	(0.70)	(1.29)	(0.30)	(0.31)	(0.52)
Complainant Veto Points I_{Start}	–1.09	0.01	–0.75	–0.02	0.05	0.23
	(0.70)	(0.79)	(1.01)	(0.21)	(0.26)	(0.42)
Legislative Measure		–0.17	–0.25	0.25***	0.24**	0.24**
		(0.27)	(0.30)	(0.09)	(0.10)	(0.11)
Complainant GDP†		–0.11	–0.17**		–0.03	–0.04
		(0.07)	(0.08)		(0.03)	(0.04)
Respondent GDP†		–0.08	–0.18**		0.01	–0.01
		(0.08)	(0.09)		(0.03)	(0.04)
Imports†		0.004	0.05		0.01	0.01
		(0.04)	(0.04)		(0.02)	(0.02)
% Adverse		0.50	0.28		0.19	0.19
		(0.41)	(0.47)		(0.19)	(0.20)
Third Parties†		–0.65***	–0.69***		–0.02	–0.03
		(0.18)	(0.20)		(0.06)	(0.06)
Remedy					0.02	0.01
					(0.10)	(0.11)
N	154	136	108	153	137	117
Democracy Subset?	No	No	Yes	No	No	Yes
Compliance Events	117	108	83			
Model	CPH	CPH	CPH	Poisson	Poisson	Poisson
R2	0.07	0.20	0.25			
Log Likelihood				–251.51	–224.10	–193.10

Note: Survival and count models estimated with R. Covariates measured in year dispute was initiated. Imports are bilateral trade flows from complainant to respondent for disputed products only. Includes cases in which verdict was reversed on appeal. Significance codes *p<0.1; **p<0.05; ***p<0.01. †Log units. Intercepts not shown.

willing to appeal an adverse ruling, request an extension of the implementation deadline, or fight noncompliance accusations through legal means. If simple inertia were to blame, governments would not be expected to engage in additional legal procedures before the dispute is resolved. Together, a finding of prolonged disputes and more legal stages provides suggestive evidence of opportunism.

Evidence for the first point is presented in table 4.10, models 1 through 3. Dispute duration is measured as the number of months between the initial complaint and compliance (if ever). The table shows the results of a survival analysis using a Cox proportional hazard model where the "event" is compliance with the WTO ruling. The estimated coefficients indicate the risk of compliance: a positive coefficient indicates a higher risk, meaning the variable is associated with prompt compliance. A negative coefficient indicates a lower risk, meaning the variable is associated with prolonged noncompliance. Data are censored at January 2016; disputes in which the respondent never complies are modeled as surviving past the censor date.

The survival analysis shows that respondents with more veto points engage in prolonged disputes. The duration of noncompliance cannot be attributed to frictions within the complainant government—complainant veto points have little bearing on the persistence of the dispute. This helps to eliminate concerns that obstinate plaintiffs are to blame. The involvement of more third-party governments is associated with longer disputes. For the subset of disputes in which both the respondent *and* the complainant are democracies (model 3), the larger their economies, the more prolonged the dispute is.

The effect size is large. Suppose two disputes began in 1995, both between pairs of democratic states. In the first dispute, the respondent has only modest political constraints (0.11), while in the second, the respondent has many domestic constraints (0.69). Within ten years, the former has almost certainly complied; its predicted probability of survival is merely one in ten. The latter, by contrast, has a predicted probability of about one in two: the dispute is just as likely to remain in a persistent state of noncompliance as it is to be resolved. These predicted effects are displayed in figure 4.2. Estimates are from model 3 in table 4.10, using only the subset of disputes between pairs of democratic governments. Results are similar for the full sample.

Not only do respondents with many constraints engage in longer disputes but they also undertake more legal stages before reaching a resolution.[76] Models 4, 5, and 6 in table 4.10 present the results of Poisson models where the outcome variable is the number of legal stages undertaken.[77]

These models demonstrate that respondents with more veto points more often appeal panel decisions, negotiate extensions of the implementation deadline, and resort to noncompliance proceedings. I also repeated the analysis with the veto points measure that includes the judiciary. It too provides strong statistical support. This tendency is weaker for pairs of democratic governments (model 6).[78] It is plausible that democratic governments' behavior reflects a combination of intentional delays through additional legal proceedings and inadvertent delays relating to domestic institutions. Disputes over legislative measures lead to

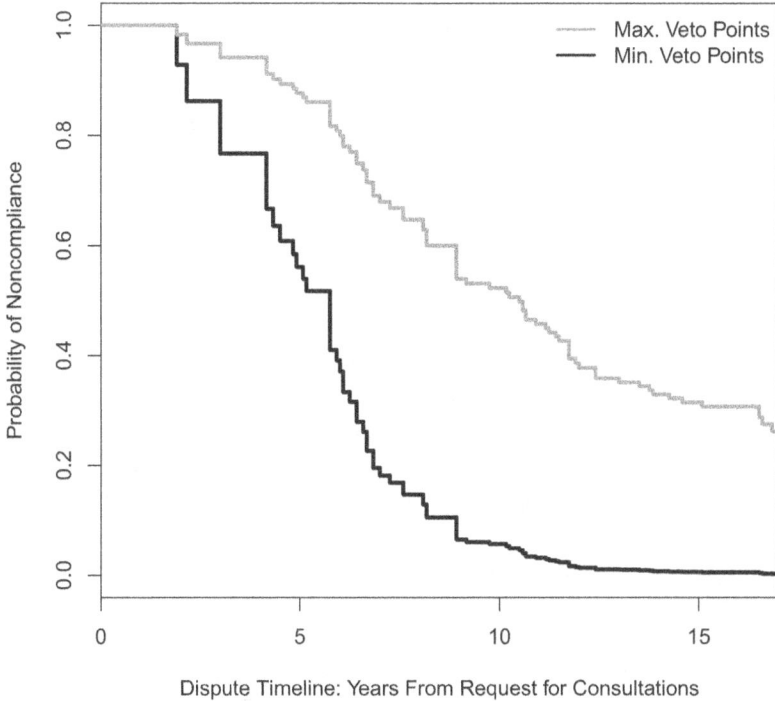

FIGURE 4.2. Predicted Hazard of Compliance for Respondents with Few and Many Domestic Veto Players
Note: All predicted probabilities are calculated with Cox proportional hazard ratios from model 3 in Table 4.10 with democratic disputant governments.

significantly more legal stages. Leaders who face a complex compliance process appear to lean more heavily on flexibility in the dispute settlement process.

The association between legal stages and domestic constraints suggests that, in general, more than mere institutional inertia is at play. Governments appear to engage in additional legal actions in order to buy time during which they maintain the WTO-violating policies. This enables governments to manage domestic pressure. Delays appear to be within the control of some savvy governments that may use institutional flexibility to prolong periods of noncompliance. In this sense, respondents with the the domestic *incentives* may opportunistically use the WTO's remedy gap (Brewster 2011) to their advantage.

4.4.5 Firm influence and selection into rulings

The above analysis has demonstrated that respondents with many domestic constraints comply less often, adopt partial measures, delay compliance efforts, and undertake more legal stages in WTO disputes. Domestic stakeholders have every incentive to persuade veto players to
block the adoption of policies that are disadvantageous to them. Many
firms—on both sides of WTO disputes—lobby government officials on
trade policy. Firms in complainant states with trade grievances urge officials to enforce WTO rules, often through adjudication (Shaffer 2003;
Bagwell and Staiger 2005). Likewise, firms in respondent states and industries targeted by complaints urge government officials to resist
these enforcement efforts. If the respondent has a WTO-inconsistent
trade barrier in place, respondent-side firms have nothing to gain from
(timely) compliance and every incentive to preserve the status quo. But
because private stakeholders channel their advocacy through government, it is ultimately the structure of that government that affects the
policy outcomes.

This raises two important concerns. The first has to do with stakeholders' political influence during the dispute process. Nearly 60% of
WTO disputes are resolved without litigation. The parties reach a settlement or the complainant drops its charges, so the WTO panel never
delivers a ruling. Firms, for their part, have incentives to lobby government officials intensively once a WTO dispute begins. As Ryu and
Stone (2018) argue, firms encourage reluctant government officials to in-
vest time and resources in a case, which improves the prospects for a
resolution that is favorable to the firms' interests. Under pressure from
these private stakeholders, governments are less likely to settle early and
therefore less likely to compromise on those interests. This creates a potential selection problem. If the disputes attracting the most intensive
engagement from firms are more likely to proceed to a panel ruling, then
perhaps respondents' compliance decisions are driven directly by stakeholder interests and veto points are irrelevant. In other words, are the
above results driven by selection bias arising from firms' influence?

The second concern has to do with government officials' sensitivity to
political influence over time. Research shows that *complainant* governments initiate WTO disputes at times that are politically beneficial (Bobick and A. Smith 2016; Chaudoin 2014)—for example, during election
years—and that when elections bring ideological turnover, governments

are more likely to renege on existing free trade commitments (Gray and Kucik 2017). Thus it is also plausible that when *respondent* government officials are facing reelection, they might be particularly attentive to stakeholder demands. If election years brought significantly elevated risk of noncompliance for governments with many domestic veto players, then perhaps the structure government is an inadequate explanation. Are the above results driven by electoral pressures?

To evaluate both concerns, I analyzed WTO disputes, including those that never proceeded to a panel ruling. Compliance outcomes are only observed in disputes that had an adverse panel ruling. Early settlements are censored, as are the very few disputes in which the WTO panel found no violations or the contested policy expired during the legal proceedings so the respondent was not required to take further action. To analyze these data, I use a series of two-step Heckman selection models. In this portion of the analysis, the selection variable is whether or not the dispute had an adverse ruling. The outcome variable is whether the respondent government complied by the WTO-established deadline, subsequent to an adverse ruling. In addition to the respondent's domestic veto points, the main variables of interest are: the number of firms expressing stakes in either side of the dispute, the intensity of lobbying or campaign contribution activity, and whether the disputant governments are facing election in the upcoming year.

This portion of the analysis incorporates data from Ryu and Stone (2018), who provide the most comprehensive record to date of major multinational firms' involvement in WTO disputes. While the data are extensive, this does limit the sample size to the first 406 disputes. The authors identified the major firms involved in each WTO dispute. They started with all firms in the *Fortune* Global 500 list during the period of study, then matched firms to disputes using a text-mining algorithm and a comprehensive library of WTO documentation, supplemented with a sample of newspaper articles. They aggregated firm activity on the pro-complainant and pro-respondent sides.[79] This yielded two variables counting the number of firms indicating stakes on either side of the dispute. In addition, Ryu and Stone used lobbying disclosure requirements in the US to measure the intensity of firms' political activities related to each WTO dispute. These data measure the amount of lobbying expenditures by the United States and foreign firms targeted at US federal agencies (in millions of dollars). For example, during the US-EU disputes over aircraft subsidies, the data include average lobbying expenditures by Boeing and Airbus. Unfortunately, no comparable lobbying data can be assembled for the full scope of countries that engage in WTO disputes. Complainant and respondent election year data are also drawn from the same dataset. These are indicator variables coded 1 if a legislative election is approaching within the next twelve months, and 0 otherwise.

Several other factors shape the progression of WTO disputes. As discussed in chapter 3, the European Union and the United States are the most likely to engage in prolonged disputes with rulings, whereas countries with smaller economies tend to settle early. Disputes with broader participation by third-party countries overwhelmingly proceed to a panel ruling, as are disputes addressing issues of systemic concern to the membership (Busch and Reinhardt 2006; Reinhardt 2001). For this latter variable, I read WTO complaints and third-party submissions to hand-code the systemic indicator following the same coding rules as prior work. Likewise, disputes over politically sensitive issues like health and safety regulation (e.g., sanitary and phytosanitary disputes), technical barriers to trade that serve as disguised protectionism, and agricultural issues also tend to prompt panel rulings (Busch and Pelc 2010). As Johns and Pelc (2014) highlight, complainants can manipulate the chance of early settlement by restricting third-party country participation (Article XXII). Remedy disputes have been a frequent sticking point for the US in particular with respect to zeroing rules and are also predictive of rulings. These variables enter into the selection equation.

Table 4.11 presents the results of the Heckman selection models. The selection stage is whether there was an adverse panel ruling and the outcome stage is whether the respondent complied by the WTO deadline.[80] The models are identified by a systemic dispute indicator variable and firm involvement on the complainant side. These variables are highly predictive of the WTO reaching a ruling. Neither, however, is predictive of compliance.

Model 1 in table 4.11 provides baseline estimates without the control variables. In the selection equation, firm engagement, especially on the complainant side, and systemic issues both reduce the chance of early settlement and are more likely to lead to a panel ruling (which is almost always adverse). When accounting for the selection stage, the correlation between the respondent's veto points and noncompliance remains strong. Model 2 includes the full set of control variables for both the selection and outcome stages. It also includes in the selection stage four

TABLE 4.11 **Heckman Selection Models with Firm Influence**

Outcome stage:	Did respondent comply on time? (1/0)				
	(1)	(2)	(3)	(4)	(5)
Veto Points I_{Start}	−0.90***	−0.87***	−0.86***		−0.82***
	(0.27)	(0.27)	(0.27)		(0.29)
Legislative Measure	−0.06	−0.06	−0.07	−0.44***	−0.06
	(0.08)	(0.08)	(0.09)	(0.13)	(0.08)
Complainant GDP†		−0.01	−0.01	−0.07*	−0.01
		(0.02)	(0.02)	(0.04)	(0.02)
Respondent GDP†		−0.01	−0.01	−0.17	−0.003
		(0.03)	(0.03)	(0.36)	(0.03)
%Adverse		0.28**	0.28*	0.50**	0.31**
		(0.14)	(0.14)	(0.19)	(0.15)
Third Parties†		−0.10	−0.11	0.08	−0.11
		(0.06)	(0.07)	(0.09)	(0.07)
Remedy		0.11	0.11	0.19	0.10
		(0.08)	(0.09)	(0.14)	(0.08)
Firms (Respondent, count)‡			−0.01	0.03	
			(0.03)	(0.07)	
Lobbying (US Respondent)‡				−0.01	
				(0.01)	
Veto Points I_{Start} × Election					−0.49
					(0.79)
Respondent Election‡					0.30
					(0.34)

Selection stage:	Was there an adverse panel ruling? (1/0)				
Firms (Complainant, count)‡	0.47***	0.50***	0.49***	0.46***	0.49***
	(0.11)	(0.12)	(0.11)	(0.12)	(0.11)
Firms (Respondent, count)‡	0.25**	0.27**	0.27**	0.35**	0.27**
	(0.11)	(0.12)	(0.12)	(0.14)	(0.12)
Article XXII	−0.21	−0.21	−0.17	−0.41*	−0.17
	(0.18)	(0.19)	(0.19)	(0.22)	(0.19)
Third Parties†	0.94***	1.02***	0.96***	0.68***	0.96***
	(0.11)	(0.12)	(0.12)	(0.14)	(0.12)
Remedy	0.10	0.20	0.08	0.29	0.08
	(0.18)	(0.21)	(0.20)	(0.23)	(0.20)
Systemic	0.46**	0.42*	0.41*	0.61**	0.40*
	(0.21)	(0.23)	(0.22)	(0.25)	(0.22)
Complainant GDP†		−0.24***	−0.07	−0.19***	−0.07
		(0.09)	(0.05)	(0.06)	(0.05)
Respondent GDP†		0.11	0.002	−0.08	0.01
		(0.08)	(0.05)	(0.06)	(0.05)
SPS/TBT		−0.12	−0.21	−0.09	−0.23
		(0.27)	(0.27)	(0.29)	(0.27)
Agriculture		−0.04	0.04	0.04	0.04
		(0.25)	(0.24)	(0.27)	(0.24)
Complainant Election‡					−0.09
					(0.22)
Respondent Election‡					0.15
					(0.21)

N	406	405	405	108	405
EU and US Dummies?	No	Yes	No	No	No
US Respondent Only?	No	No	No	Yes	No
R²	0.07	0.12	0.12	0.38	0.13
Inv. Mills Ratio	0.11 (0.08)	−0.02 (0.11)	−0.04 (0.13)	0.15 (0.17)	−0.05 (0.12)

Note: Selection models estimated with R. Significance codes *p<0.1; **p<0.05; ***p<0.01. †Log units. ‡Firm count, lobbying, and election year data are from Ryu and Stone (2018). Intercepts not shown.

indicator variables for whether the European Union and the United States were complainants or respondents in the dispute. Complainant status is associated with a higher probability of the dispute proceeding to an adverse ruling; respondent status is not significant for either the US or the EU. The correlation between respondent veto players and non-compliance remains statistically significant. The Heckman correction is a useful one and uncovers somewhat smaller but more precise estimates of the main effect.

Model 3 further evaluates the number of multinational firms involved in the respondent side of the dispute. Although more stakeholder firms are negatively associated with compliance—as one might expect—the correlation is not statistically significant. The estimated effect of domestic veto points remains robust. This model supports my theory. It indicates that stakeholder firm involvement on either side of the dispute can increase the chance that governments escalate to litigation and obtain a panel ruling. Yet once the WTO panel issues a ruling, firms cannot directly influence compliance. They must work through existing institutions to delay or block compliance. Domestic veto players are a crucial step in the pathway between policy preferences and policy outcomes. This interpretation is reinforced by model 4, which examines the effect of lobbying expenditures by stakeholder firms on the US government's compliance. Lobbying at the WTO panel stage is not a significant predictor. Note that because US veto points vary only modestly over time, depending on the partisan composition of government, the variable was excluded from model 4.

Legislative electoral timing seems to have little bearing on the resolution of WTO disputes. Model 5 shows that upcoming elections in neither the complainant nor the respondent government significantly alter the chance that the dispute goes to a panel ruling. The negative effect of veto points on timely compliance is not significantly different for respondents in election years as compared to other years. This helps to dispel the idea that governments adjust their compliance decisions around broader electoral pressures. Finally, the inverse Mills ratio indicates that for the first model, selection bias is present and the Heckman correction is warranted. In the other model specifications where the full set of variables is used, selection bias is not nearly as significant.

In summary, large multinational firms are often key stakeholders in WTO disputes. They influence the dispute process chiefly by decreasing the odds of early settlement and increasing the chance that an adverse panel ruling is reached. This forces the trade dispute into the spotlight, drawing attention from pro- and anti-compliance groups in the respondent state. Firms themselves cannot directly affect compliance decisions at this point but rather must solicit support from political actors. Political actors, in turn, can exercise veto power to block the adoption of compliant policies. Even accounting for the selection effects with the Heckman correction, the evidence shows that domestic veto points in respondent governments remain a robust predictor of compliance with panel rulings.

4.4.6 Alternative explanations

The core contribution of this chapter is a detailed and systematic account of the policy reforms governments make in WTO disputes. I have traced the legislative and administrative measures states enact, the timing of reforms, and whether they satisfy the full portfolio of demands made by the WTO. Using these data, I have demonstrated that governments with more veto players comply less often, less fully, and more belatedly with the court's judgments.

The most important potential objection to the findings concerns coding bias. Perhaps the compliance measure reflects variation in government transparency. Democracies are, on the whole, more transparent than nondemocratic regimes, and they reveal a wealth of information that makes it possible to identify cases of noncompliance. For nondemocratic countries, it is far more difficult to find reliable information about compliance. Autocratic regimes often hide their missteps from international audiences and are emboldened to misreport. If these governments tend to provide misleading information about their trade policies, then I may have erroneously coded them as compliant. This might attribute to domestic political constraints an effect that is actually due to policy transparency practices.

Fortunately, this is unlikely to be a concern. When coding the dependent variables, I accounted for (but did not completely rely upon) many different sources, including the *complainant* government's assessment of the respondent's compliance measures. Complainants are vigilant and not easily deceived. Their domestic audiences, including industry groups within complainant countries, help to discern whether a respondent's policy reforms are sufficient. Moreover, chapter 5 takes up this concern by focusing on the downstream economic effect of rulings. While governments have varying levels of transparency, trade flows are tracked and reported systematically by several international bodies. They tend not to be vulnerable to systematic reporting bias—at least not in ways that would alter my assessment of product-level trade recoveries following WTO rulings. Chapter 5 shows the economic effect of rulings remains strongly correlated with domestic veto players.

A second potential objection concerns the use of the WTO system. When do plaintiffs turn to an international legal body to intervene in trade disputes? As discussed in chapter 3, not all prospective plaintiff governments are equally likely to pursue litigation. Some governments initiate litigation in order to send a costly signal to key domestic audiences at home that they are taking a hard stance against foreign barriers to trade (Davis 2012). If plaintiffs perhaps turn to the WTO more often when the defendant government has more domestic constraints *and* compliance is less likely, this selection process could generate bias relevant to my results. It is nearly impossible to identify all opportunities for dispute initiation in all countries over the twenty years evaluated in this study, making a decisive empirical test impractical. However, Davis (2012) offers a significant step forward by documenting US investigations into foreign trade barriers. I analyzed these data and found the US government's decision to litigate is uncorrelated with the prospective defendant's domestic politics. Because the US is the major user of WTO adjudication, these null results are reassuring. It is unlikely that the results reported above are due to this form of selection bias.

A third and related objection is that perhaps government preferences over trade policy, not domestic political constraints, are driving compliance behavior. According to this contention, perhaps the governments with the most domestic veto players tend to be the same states holding protectionist preferences. Because they tend to favor more trade protection, they routinely fail to conform with free trade commitments, they are more often hauled before the WTO as defendants, and they are the least likely to abide by trade-liberalizing rulings.

The European Union is frequently challenged at the WTO for violations. According to this third potential objection, it is staunch European support for policies like aircraft subsidies and bans on hormone-treated meats that explain noncompliance with WTO rulings; the EU's complex internal institutional structure for policy-making is merely coincidental. Whether the European Parliament, the Council, or the Commission participate in the compliance process and whether member states abide by EU-level mandates would be irrelevant in explaining outcomes.

While unyielding protectionist preferences may certainly drive some long-standing infractions of WTO rules, this argument is an unsatisfactory systematic explanation for (non)compliance behavior. It is widely argued—and empirical evidence shows—that democratic governments hold more free trade preferences than nondemocratic regimes (Milner 1999). For example, Mansfield, Milner, and Rosendorff (2002) argue democratic countries' greater free trade preferences originate in electoral mechanisms and voters' willingness to punish politicians for unfavorable economic conditions. Milner and Kubota (2005) highlight how democratization induces trade liberalization in developing countries, building on the Heckscher-Ohlin and Stolper-Samuelson theorems. Mansfield, Milner, and Rosendorff (2000) demonstrate that the ratification responsibilities of the legislature in democratic states leads pairs of democracies to set lower trade barriers than mixed or autocratic country pairs. Democratic countries, of course, feature more internal veto players than autocracies do. If underlying trade preferences were the main driver, then we should see *more*, not less, compliance with WTO rulings from countries with many veto players. The correlations would be precisely the opposite of the above findings.

4.5 Conclusion

The WTO Dispute Settlement Mechanism is widely used by governments to resolve trade disputes. By using a legalized process, governments can stave off costly trade wars. The DSM also insulates governments from the pressures of domestic industry groups and helps to promote early settlements. Yet once a WTO panel renders a verdict, the responsibility lies with the disputant governments to implement the ruling. Losing respondents must reverse protectionist policies, and they are frequently met with resistance at home. That resistance is borne out through the political process, and the more political constraints a respondent has, the less likely it is to comply with an adverse ruling. At the same time, that government is more likely to prolong the legal dispute, possibly to buy time with domestic audiences while abiding by WTO rules. In this respect, respondents can take advantage of flexibility in the DSM to manage domestic political constraints alongside international pressure to cooperate.

This chapter has offered a first hard test of compliance in the WTO. I have examined the ways governments reform their policies to address adverse rulings. A key finding of this chapter is that WTO rulings can be effective in promoting policies that restore cooperation between disputing governments. Placing this finding in context, there is reason to believe the WTO might enjoy a higher success rate than other international courts. WTO disputes activate domestic tension between stakeholders precisely because some stand to gain from adherence to multilateral trade rules. When a respondent country is confronted with a choice over compliance, in addition to anti-compliance voices, there are firms, industry groups, and politicians that want to preserve access to foreign markets, avert retaliation, or maintain predictable open trade relations. By contrast, other types of international disputes may provoke uniform resistance from defendant states. For instance, the International Court of Justice often adjudicates territorial disputes at the behest of democratic leaders (Huth, Croco, and Appel 2011). Yet because they address fundamental sovereignty concerns, territorial disputes are widely thought to be the most intractable of conflicts. In these disputes, the losing state may have few pro-compliance domestic stakeholders.

What remains unexplored are the economic ramifications of WTO rulings. When a government corrects its violations and adopts compliant policies, is there a trade impact? Do rulings ultimately help to restore market share for the complainant state and firms within it? The next chapter takes on precisely these questions by examining the fluctuations in trade flows for disputed products in the wake of WTO rulings. The analysis that follows shows that compared to expected trade levels, the governments in a dispute often experience subsequent trade recoveries. It provides a strong case that compliance does translate into deeper cooperation for members of the multilateral trade regime.

This chapter empirically demonstrates that domestic constraints are associated with less frequent and incomplete policy compliance. Governments are less likely to adjust their trade policies to comply with adverse WTO rulings when they face more domestic political constraints. Also consistent with my theory is the finding that governments are less likely to adjust legislative measures to comply than to correct administrative measures. When appraising the success of the WTO, one must account for conditional effectiveness of the DSM. Among governments that have relatively unified authority, adverse rulings can prompt substantive policy reforms that reinforce cooperation according to the obligations set forth under the WTO treaties. This effect is particularly pronounced for democracies, presumably because it is in these countries that competing interest groups can vie for influence over trade policy.

This chapter has pointed to a broader implication of institutional design. Despite the seeming inefficiencies of the DSM, those features may actually provide a flexibility that helps stabilize the multilateral trade regime. If losing respondent governments can use dispute procedures to manage their domestic political constraints and buy time, then they may be less likely to reject the international legal system altogether. These implications are explored in chapter 7.

CHAPTER FIVE

Trade Cooperation in WTO Disputes

The preceding chapters presented a theory of government compliance with international rulings and the limiting role of domestic political constraints. By collecting a record of governments' policy reforms in the wake of World Trade Organization disputes, I found strong empirical support for this theory. Governments are far more likely to abide by adverse rulings when there are fewer domestic veto players. The evidence suggests that the WTO does successfully encourage countries to enact consistent trade policies. But the goals of the multilateral trade regime do not end there. The WTO was crafted to promote deeper multilateral trade *cooperation*. By constraining the trade policies of member states, the institution aims to promote trade flows among countries and deliver corresponding efficiency gains. To that end, adverse rulings should help disputing countries recover trade.

This chapter tests the theory by considering the economic impact of WTO rulings. The economic consequences are critical (Bechtel and Sattler 2015; Bown and Reynolds 2015; Chaudoin, Kucik, and Pelc 2016). Plaintiffs use adjudication to confront defendants over trade restrictions and push for deeper market integration, even though this need not be the sole aim.[1] Building on the expectation that a key goal is the restoration of trade flows, this chapter shows that domestic political constraints in defendant countries shape trade recoveries in the wake of adverse rulings.

As with many domains of international affairs, compliance with adverse WTO rulings does not necessarily translate into deeper cooperation. Some defendant governments implement policies that contain only superficial revisions. Others remove one WTO-inconsistent trade barrier only to sidestep the ruling by substituting another to achieve a similar trade-restricting impact (Bown 2004a, 74). Policy substitution undercuts the cooperative aims. The mismatch between compliance and cooperation need not be driven by deliberate government activity. Even when respondents do comply, trade may not be restored due to firms and markets adjusting to the previous violation. Thus if countries routinely enact compliant policies without deepening their trade cooperation, they undercut the WTO.

The WTO's impact on state cooperation can be measured with an economic indicator: trade flows. Adverse rulings require defendant governments to remove trade barriers—most often import restrictions—that violate WTO obligations. When a defendant does so correctly and completely, it typically prompts an increase in imports. Conversely, when a state does not comply at all with the WTO recommendations on a contested import restriction, there would rarely be a corresponding recovery in trade for the disputed products exported from the complainant to the respondent. This chapter estimates the effect of adverse WTO rulings on the trade flows of disputed products between disputing countries. The estimated economic impact of adverse rulings are indicative of whether interventions by the Dispute Settlement Body have restored substantial cooperation.

Estimating the effect of WTO interventions on countries' trade flows is a methodologically challenging task. This chapter leverages statistical tools for causal inference. In an ideal world, researchers would be able to specify what product-level trade flows between disputing countries would have been in the absence of the panelists' intervention. In other words, researchers would ideally be able to specify the correct "counterfactual" (Rubin 2005). By comparing the counterfactual to the actual realized trade flows, the causal effect of the ruling could be calculated and this quantity, in turn, would be an excellent measure of whether the institution promoted cooperation.

Of course, short of this fictitious world, we must make do with observed trade patterns and use these to *estimate* the counterfactual. The method of synthetic case control created by Abadie and Gardeazabal (2003) and extended by Abadie, Diamond, and Hainmueller (2010,

2015) provides the best statistical approach for estimating causal effects in this context. I use this method to estimate a precise counterfactual that represents what product-level trade would have been without the WTO's legal verdict in each individual trade dispute. For each dispute, I identify the affected products and collect data on the trade flows of just those products. I examine the complainant's trade flows to other countries and the actual disputant countries' trade flows in the years surrounding the WTO dispute. Using the other countries' trade flows, I create a weighted average that closely resembles the disputants' trade in the years prior to the lawsuit—this is the estimated counterfactual. Then, by comparing actual trade to the estimated counterfactual trade flows, I determine whether trade in the disputed products increased beyond ordinary fluctuations. Relative deviations indicate the approximate causal effect of an adverse WTO ruling. When I detect positive deviations, I infer that the defendant government lowered trade barriers and cooperated. Using this approach, I measure post-ruling cooperation in 120 WTO disputes (1995 to 2011) where defendants imposed import-restricting trade barriers.

This synthetic control method is preferable to alternative statistical methods in this context. For instance, matching would not be appropriate because it does not account for temporal trends. Traditional regression would not be appropriate because these data include many thousands of observations of product-level trade flows but merely 120 cases subjected to an adverse ruling. The results show that in the majority of WTO disputes with adverse rulings, trade flows are restored and defendants demonstrate deeper cooperation with the multilateral trade regime.[2]

But, as the preceding chapter showed with respect to compliance, trade cooperation is not evenly restored in all disputes. Some rulings from the WTO Dispute Settlement Mechanism prompt marked increases in trade, while others have no detectable effect. The variation is systematically linked to domestic politics. The more veto players in a defendant government, the lower the chance that trade flows are substantially recovered. The unevenness of the economic impact is meaningful. Some scholars have puzzled over the seemingly insignificant effect of WTO disputes on trade. This chapter helps to resolve the puzzle by showing there is a substantial heterogeneity in dispute outcomes that is obscured when one examines the record on average. The results buttress this book's broader argument that international dispute settlement is not uniformly effective or ineffective but rather dependent on the domestic political constraints within governments.

5.1 Assessing the economic impact of WTO rulings

An ideal test of the WTO DSM, with respect to its effect on international cooperation, would compare disputes to the development of the same trade conflict where the institution did not exist. Absent a randomized experiment, one reasonable empirical approach might entail comparing the record of disputant countries' trade cooperation to similar countries that held the same trade grievances but were not members of the WTO and therefore did not have access to its legal apparatus. But because nearly all countries are members of the WTO and have been for some time, it is impossible to construct such a comparison from the actual empirical record. One can still examine the DSM's effectiveness by focusing on a narrower but revealing aspect of the institution: whether its *adverse rulings* restore trade cooperation for those particular disputant countries in a given conflict.

Adverse rulings require losing defendant governments to remove their WTO-inconsistent trade barriers. Many different forms of trade barriers are challenged in these disputes. Consider the alcoholic beverages tax disputes discussed in the previous chapter. In each, the defendant state imposed a higher tax on foreign products than like domestic products constituting a barrier to trade. The adverse rulings in each case have required the defendant to equalize the taxes applied to equivalent domestic and foreign products. If a defendant lowers the tax on imported goods to match the tax on its domestic equivalents, this should prompt an increase in the imported goods. It is also possible imports would similarly rise if the taxes were raised on the domestic goods. Either way, the removal of a trade barrier can lead to increased imports from the complainant to the respondent country for the affected products. That trade impact points to deepened cooperation.

Many other trade barriers fit a similar logic. If a respondent country were to lower antidumping duties on certain foreign goods from a complainant country, this too could induce an increase in those disputed imports. Certain import bans, quantitative restrictions, and technical barriers to trade can also follow this pattern. In each instance, if the trade barrier is removed, the respondent's imports in the affected products should increase. The empirical challenge is to correctly identify these increases and understand when they are more or less likely to apply.

Yet other WTO disputes center around treaty violations that do not have clear implications for imports. For instance, if a respondent country revokes a trade policy that violates most-favored nation principles, that could lead trade from countries other than the complainant to fill the market. Imports from the complainant to the respondent for disputed products would not, in this instance, recover, even though there was compliance. Relatedly, disputes over a defendant government's subsidies or various export-promoting policies would not be expected to induce recovery in imports. Other disputes concern non-merchandise trade (e.g., gambling services) and cannot be evaluated in this manner. Finally, some disputes do not hold substantial economic stakes and are instead pursued to further political or legal aims.

The section that follows discusses the strategy for measuring the trade impact of adverse WTO rulings in the subset of disputes that center on import restrictions targeting specific products. While I cannot cover the full range of treaty violations, the majority of adverse rulings do pertain to import restrictions. It is for these disputes that I estimate the impact on trade flows and infer whether WTO intervention ushered along deeper trade cooperation between complainant and respondent states.

5.1.1 Measurement strategy

In the study of international organizations, it is rare that a researcher can conduct a randomized experiment to accurately measure the causal effect of an institution on state behavior. Instead, one must infer causal effects from observational data using the best statistical tools available. I estimate the causal impact of an adverse WTO ruling by comparing trade between disputing countries to an approximate counterfactual that represents what trade would have been without the ruling. I use this estimated counterfactual to measure the adverse ruling's effect on relevant trade flows and thereby assess whether the WTO's intervention promoted cooperation between the disputing countries. Although adverse rulings are not randomly assigned and true treatment effects cannot be obtained, casting the analysis in a causal inference framework is informative. In this chapter, I use the language of causal inference, referring to the adverse ruling as the *treatment* and post-ruling trade as the *outcome*.

The key is to correctly control for changes in trade that occur for reasons unrelated to the WTO dispute. Disputes may be prompted by economic trends that cannot be reversed, even when the defendant government complies completely with a ruling. For example, complainants sometimes initiate disputes when their exports for a product are declining, even though the decline is partly driven by forces exogenous to the defendant's trade barrier. To mitigate this problem, I use a synthetic control method (Abadie and Gardeazabal 2003) to estimate a control from trade flows following a parallel trend, as explained below. Estimating the causal effect of an adverse WTO ruling entails choosing the appropriate control unit for comparison. Thus I must ensure that the increase or decrease I detect is calculated *relative* to the appropriate baseline.

Another challenge is that the unit of analysis is a country's trade with another partner country. When evaluating just a few aggregate entities, a combination of comparison units often does a better job reproducing the characteristics of the unit of interest than any single comparison unit alone (Abadie, Diamond, and Hainmueller 2015). The synthetic control unit is constructed from a weighted average of all potential comparison units. This means that in choosing the appropriate control unit for comparison, I am not limited to finding a single similar country with similar trends in product-level trade to the defendant country. The approach leverages a weighted average of many other countries' trade to construct a reasonably well-matched comparison unit.

Before applying the synthetic control method to measure the trade impact of WTO rulings, I describe the approach. Figure 5.1 illustrates two hypothetical scenarios for WTO disputes. In both, trade is decreasing over time and a WTO dispute yields an adverse ruling (treatment). Observed trade (outcome) continues to decrease after the ruling (post-treatment). Did the ruling prompt the defendant government to restore trade cooperation? This depends on what trade *would have been* after the WTO dispute if there had not been an adverse ruling.

When trade for the treated unit exceeds trade for the control unit, as measured by a positive average yearly deviation after the treatment, I infer the defendant cooperated (figure 5.1[a]). Conversely, when trade for the treated unit does not exceed trade for the control unit, I expect the respondent did not cooperate in a meaningful way, either by failing to comply or side-stepping the ruling (as discussed above). Because trade data are noisy, I aim to avoid false negatives. Thus I infer the ruling failed to advance cooperation only when I detect a negative average yearly deviation (figure 5.1[b]).

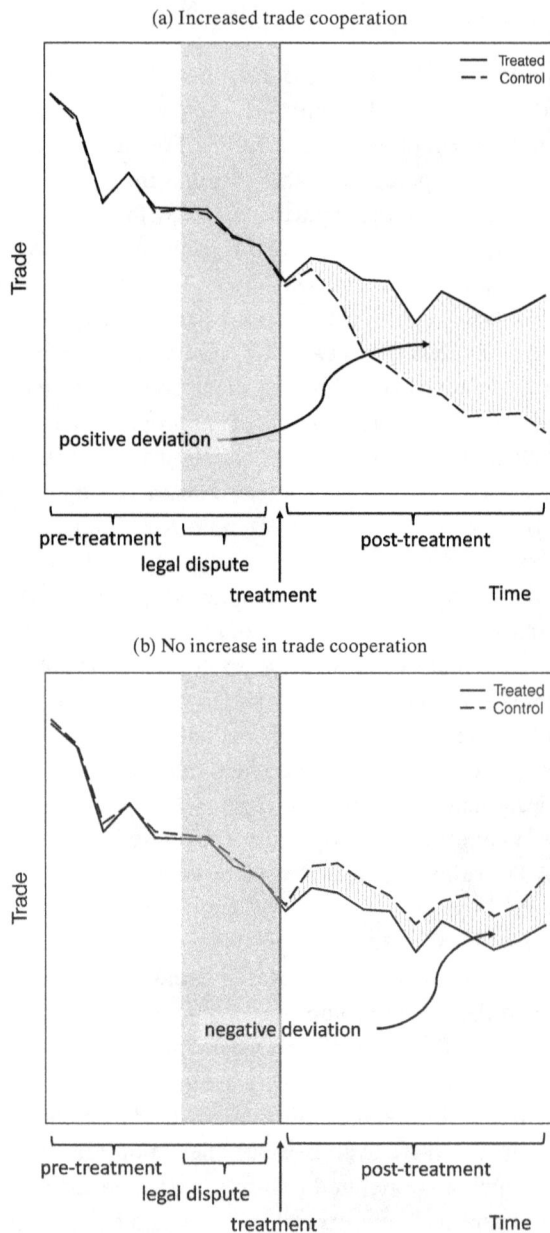

FIGURE 5.1. Hypothetical Trade Patterns for Evaluating Cooperation after Adverse Ruling
Note: Hypothetical disputes where trade is trending down over time. (a) illustrates cooperation trade pattern, indicated by a positive average deviation. (b) illustrates a trade pattern where cooperation did not increase. The shaded area denotes the duration of the legal dispute and the vertical line indicates the implementation deadline.

Measuring cooperation with trade flows prioritizes the economic impact of WTO rulings. Like any metric, it involves judgments about cases
that occupy a gray area. Governments sometimes settle WTO disputes
through compensation schemes where the losing respondent offers a
payment to the complainant in lieu of prompt implementation, according to Article 22.1 of the WTO Dispute Settlement Understanding.

Although the WTO endorses temporary arrangements along these
lines, such cases do not count as trade cooperation per my methodology. This measurement decision reflects the WTO's stated objectives.
The central goal of the WTO is to liberalize trade policy in order to promote free and fair trade flows between countries. Article 22.1 specifies
that "compensation and the suspension of concessions . . . are temporary
measures available in the event that the recommendations and rulings
are not implemented within a reasonable period of time. However, neither compensation nor the suspension of concessions . . . is preferred to
full implementation" of panel decisions. The WTO does not regard such
compensation or retaliation to be suitable substitutes for the overarching
goal of restoring trade cooperation. Thus my trade-based measurement
reflects the organization's goal.

5.1.2 Using product-level trade flows for each dispute

This chapter evaluates the trade impact of WTO rulings in 120 disputes.
The criteria for inclusion are as follows: First, the dispute must have
reached an adverse ruling between 1995 and 2011—that is, the panel delivered a ruling that favored the complainant on at least one legal claim.
In any case where the ruling was completely overturned on appeal, that
case is excluded from my analysis. Many disputes take several years to
reach resolution. I truncate the sample at rulings issued up to 2011 to ensure more than five years have elapsed before evaluating trade impacts.
Second, the dispute must address import restrictions. This includes
trade barriers such as tariffs, countervailing duties, antidumping measures, safeguards, quantitative restrictions, discriminatory tax schemes,
etc. When respondent governments have import restrictions in place and
then remove those barriers, imports into their market for the affected
products are expected to increase. By contrast, I exclude disputes over
export-promoting measures such as subsidies because the bilateral trade
implications are not as clear.[3]

WTO disputes target specific products and services. I identify which products were at issue and then collect annual bilateral trade data, aggregating when multiple products are cited in a given dispute. Only the trade flows for disputed products enter the analysis. Where possible, six-digit Harmonized System (HS) codes are used. If disputes cite products at the four- or two-digit level or have insufficient coverage, I use the highest level of precision available.[4] Data are from the UN Commodity Trade Statistics Database, the UN Service Trade Statistics Database, and the European Commission's Eurostat database on international trade. When analyzing the European Union's trade flows, I use aggregates across the entire bloc, updating EU membership by year. For each dispute, the complainant's annual exports of the disputed product to the respondent (directed dyad-year) is measured. The comparison trade flow, the counterfactual *control unit*, is formed from a weighted average of the complainant's annual exports of the disputed product to other countries that were not engaged in the dispute.

Disputes involve vastly different trade values. Some concern products with high trade volume and value (e.g., gasoline) while others reflect only small export markets (e.g., preserved peaches). To ensure trade values are comparable across different disputes, I measure the *export share*, defined as the complainant's annual exports of disputed products to the respondent or other country, divided by its total annual exports of the products to the world. A large export share means the respondent's market was very important to the complainant. Export shares improve comparisons between countries. For instance, one can say that in the case of the European Union's alcoholic beverages exports in a given year, about 7% were exported to the United States, 5% went to Japan, 3% went to Singapore, etc. Export shares similarly improve comparisons within countries over time by accounting for price fluctuations and variation in the complainant's export volumes.[5]

For each dispute and in each year t, the complainant exports disputed products to the respondent and to other countries. Let $j = 1$ denote the respondent and let $j = 2,3, \ldots J$ denote the other countries. Then the complainant's export share to country j in year t is

$$ExportShare_{jt} = \frac{Complainant's\ Exports\ of\ Product\ to\ Country_{jt}}{Complainant's\ Exports\ of\ Product\ to\ World_{t}}$$

Export shares are compositional data. When the respondent's share of the complainant's exports increases, other countries' shares necessarily decrease. This creates interference between units, violating a key assumption for the causal inference model. To remedy this problem, I adopt a common practice of transforming compositional data with a log-arithm ratio (Tomz, Tucker, and Wittenberg 2002). In each dispute, each country's export share is divided by the *ex ante* largest trade partner among control countries, and I then take the logarithm of that quotient. The transformation factors out the proportional component from the treated and control units, isolating the independent variation and satisfy-ing the noninterference assumption. The transformed unit of analysis is

$$y_{jt} = log\left(\frac{ExportShare_{jt}}{ExportShare_{2t}}\right), \quad for \; j \in \{1, 2, 3...J\}$$

where $j = 2$ denotes the control country (in $j = 2, 3, \ldots J$) with the largest export share. This transformation is an effective way to ensure that if the respondent's share of the complainant's exports increases, that change does not affect other countries' shares. The log-ratio-transformed data enters into all synthetic control calculations below.

5.1.3 Synthetic control method

I use the synthetic control method (SCM) to estimate the counterfac-tual—a synthetic control unit—and infer the approximate causal effect of an adverse WTO ruling (Abadie and Gardeazabal 2003; Abadie, Dia-mond, and Hainmueller 2010, 2011).[6] As with the hypothetical approach above, I compare the synthetic control unit to actual trade flows and use that comparison to determine whether trade significantly increased in the post-ruling period, relative to the expected trade flows. This yields an estimate of the causal effect of an adverse ruling on trade. For each dispute, my estimate is valid when (1) the control units are subjected to the same systematic factors as the treated unit—save the WTO ruling and covariates—and (2) there is no interference between units.

For each of the 120 disputes, I use a sample of up to fifteen coun-tries observed over twenty years. The respondent country is the *treated unit*, while other countries form the *donor pool*, the potential compari-son units used to approximate the counterfactual. The donor pool con-sists of countries (1) whose markets are similarly important to the com-plainant as measured by the export share, (2) that have adequate data, and (3) that are not engaged in similar WTO disputes. Several countries from the respondent's geographical region are included because they are apt to experience the same systematic factors as the respondent country.

Each WTO ruling has an implementation deadline that splits the sample into a *pre-treatment period* and a *post-treatment period*. The pre-treatment period is the years leading up to the complainant's request for consultations and the year(s) the dispute has commenced but prior to the deadline for implementing the panel ruling. The post-treatment period begins with the implementation deadline—in WTO parlance, the expiration of the reasonable period of time to comply with the ruling. This post-treatment window lasts five years.

I chose a five year post-treatment period based on trends in compliance activity and in order to balance two research priorities. The majority of WTO disputes with any compliance experience those policy reforms within about five years of the ruling. This makes it a suitable time for observing a trade impact.[7] There are also practical reasons. On the one hand, more years of post-treatment data provide greater certainty about a trade impact. This could strengthen claims about the longevity of the impact of rulings on cooperation. On the other hand, fewer years in the post-treatment period mean more recent WTO disputes can be included in my analysis. Fewer years also mean external events unrelated to the trade dispute that occur after the ruling are less likely to confound the inferences. Of course, this is not a perfect solution. Longer or shorter periods might be more appropriate for evaluating the trade impact in individual disputes since some trade barriers predate measurement (a chronic issue) whereas others represent a new policy imposed to limit trade. However, it is preferable to have a standard time period for the sake of consistency in the research.[8]

SCM entails a two-part optimization process (Abadie, Diamond, and Hainmueller 2011) using countries' product-level trade flows measured in log-ratio export shares (the outcome variable) and a number of relevant covariates. First, each country in the donor pool receives a weight that optimizes the similarity between the respondent and the weighted average of the donor pool countries on the covariates in the pre-treatment period (that is, before the deadline). Second, each covariate receives a weight that minimizes the discrepancy in the pre-treatment period between the respondent's trade and the synthetic control, using the country-weights from the first step. Covariates that are important predictors of the respondent's trade receive more weight. The optimal solution entails a set of country-weights and covariate-weights.

To guide the weighting of countries from the donor pool, I rely on a variety of control variables that are generically predictive of trade flows.

Potential defendant countries impose trade barriers on specific products depending on a constellation of economic and political factors, especially during economic downturns, at times when particular industries garner clout, and at times when political conditions are receptive to particularistic interests. Some of these conditions are driven by exogenous shocks; others are systematic. The systematic part that can be uniformly modeled across all disputes includes features of the defendant's economy and political system. For the economic factors, I choose covariates that predict intensity of trade in various sectors of the economy and relative reliance on foreign commerce. These are GDP; GDP per capita; annual GDP growth; value added in agriculture, industry, manufacturing, and services; trade dependence; and the unemployment rate (World Bank 2013). Covariates for the European Union are averages across member states, with membership updated by year.

Political institutions also shape the trade violations that lead to WTO disputes; the factor most widely accepted as relevant in a country's political institutions is the country's level of democracy. Thus in my robustness checks, I include democracy as measured by Polity IV as a covariate (Marshall and Jaggers 2012). This also captures a clear systematic predictor of trade.

I use the general macroeconomic indicators and level of democracy to ensure consistent coding across all disputes in my dataset. As with the decision about the five-year post treatment window, the decision to use a standard set of covariates is a practical one. Each dispute might be more precisely modeled with product-specific covariates suited to the individual countries and trade barriers in question. However, doing so would introduce difficulties in the second stage of the analysis where comparisons are drawn across disputes. Moreover, in selecting a donor pool of comparison countries, I ensure that they trade at similar levels with the complainant country in the disputed products as does the defendant state. If there are other unmodeled political-institutional differences between the defendant government and the donor pool that affect product-level trade with the complainant country, then this would lead to noisier estimates of the trade impact of rulings.[9]

The synthetic control unit—the weighted average of donor pool countries—is accurate when its trade matches the respondent's in the pretreatment period. It is then projected into the following five years to approximate the counterfactual: the trade the respondent would have had in the absence of the WTO ruling. This estimated counterfactual is compared to the respondent's actual trade. If the respondent and synthetic control trade follow parallel trends—that is, they are subjected to all the same systematic factors and shocks, save for the WTO ruling—this approach identifies the average treatment effect on the treated.[10]

The goal is to create an estimated counterfactual—a synthetic control—from a weighted average of countries in the donor pool. The estimate is accurate when the export share for the synthetic control matches the respondent's export share in the pre-treatment period. The result is a synthetic control unit with trade patterns that closely resemble the respondent's actual trade in the pre-treatment period.

The average yearly difference between the respondent's actual and expected trade in the post-treatment period minus the average yearly difference in the pre-treatment period, is summarized with a trade score S. A positive score indicates the respondent's trade after the deadline was higher than would be expected had the WTO not intervened with an adverse ruling. This suggests the defendant government removed the trade barrier or reformed its practices to deepen trade cooperation with the complainant country. Otherwise, I infer no change in cooperation. The standard deviation of these yearly measurements in the pre-treatment period d captures the stability of the estimator and, in this respect, the quality of the synthetic control fit.

Trade scores S are approximately normally distributed between −0.29 and 0.24 with a mean of -0.004. On the upper bound, a trade score of 0.24 indicates the ruling helped the complainant recover nearly one-quarter of its export market in the disputed product. For the typical dispute, this export share translates into roughly $80 million in recovered trade per year. The sample mean indicates that on average, however, the effect of adverse rulings on trade may be negligible.

On the other hand, many disputes had a negative score. This suggests continued noncooperation—the defendant government ignored the WTO ruling or adjusted its trade barriers in ways that retained import restrictions. Negative scores could also point to market adaptation—exporters in the complainant country secured other overseas consumers while the respondent country never recovered demand for the imported goods targeted by the WTO-inconsistent policy. Whether driven by government strategy, market adjustments, or both, these are cases where the ruling did not prompt deeper trade cooperation between the disputants.

Two of the contrasting examples discussed in the previous chapter also illustrate this method. Recall that the European Union sued both South

Korea and Japan over each country's tax scheme for alcoholic beverages in the early years of the WTO DSM. In both cases, the WTO ruled in favor of the EU. In both, the defendant governments were urged to reform by applying equal tax rates for equivalent domestic and foreign products; this involved legislative reform. Korea promptly complied, while Japan resisted for several years after the WTO deadline before eventually taking steps to modify its tax scheme. The two disputes also show different trajectories in terms of the trade recoveries prompted by the rulings. Figure 5.2 displays the trade patterns for these WTO disputes.

In the first example, the European Union's alcohol exports to South Korea increased relative to expected trends in the absence of the ruling. Figure 5.2(a) shows bilateral trade rose relative to the synthetic control after the implementation deadline, yielding a positive trade score. This suggests that Korea deepened its trade cooperation with the EU in the wake of the ruling. To estimate the trade flows that would have occurred in the absence of the WTO intervention, I use the synthetic control trade. The corresponding table shows country- and variable-weights for the synthetic control unit. The counterfactual is constructed from a weighted average of the EU's alcohol exports to Thailand, Singapore, the United States, and China. Those countries' agriculture value added, GDP, and GDP growth were the most important predictors for creating the weighted average. These trade patterns are consistent with Korea's prompt compliance; policy reform lowered barriers to trade, and trade flows intensified.

In the second example, Japan was resistant to the ruling. It took many years for Japan to reform its tax system, long after the WTO's deadline for implementation had passed. Figure 5.2(b) demonstrates Japanese imports of European alcoholic beverages did not recover relative to the expected trends. The trade score is negative and significant.

The corresponding table shows the synthetic control construction. Here, the counterfactual is a weighted average of US, Brazil, and China's alcohol imports from Europe. The US contributes significantly to the counterfactual estimates. This is sensible because no other countries imported alcohol as intensively from the EU in the years leading up to the WTO ruling. While Japan and the US differ in countless ways, the comparison in figure 5.2 is specifically made with respect to imported European alcohol products and therefore any skewing in the comparison group is not especially worrisome. That comparison reflects the importance of the relative affluence of Japanese consumers, economic growth,

DS75: Synthetic Control

Covariate	Weights
GDP	0.32
GDP growth	0.18
GDP per capita	0.01
Agriculture VA	0.49
Industry VA	0.00
Manufacture VA	0.00
Services VA	0.00
Trade %	0.00
Unemployment	0.00

Comparison Country	Weights
Argentina	0.00
Australia	0.00
Brazil	0.00
Canada	0.00
China	0.07
Mexico	0.00
Indonesia	0.00
India	0.00
Singapore	0.35
Thailand	0.48
USA	0.09

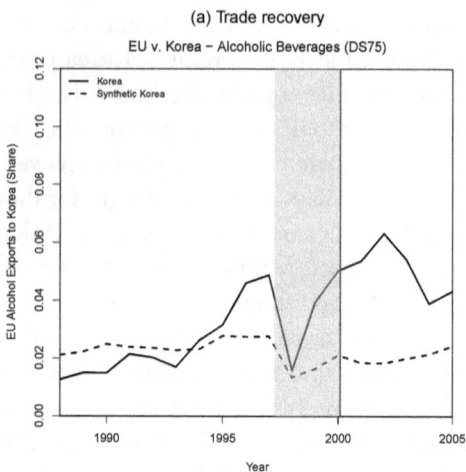

(a) Trade recovery

EU v. Korea – Alcoholic Beverages (DS75)

DS8: Synthetic Control

Covariate	Weights
GDP	0.01
GDP growth	0.18
GDP per capita	0.35
Agriculture VA	0.15
Industry VA	0.03
Manufacture VA	0.04
Services VA	0.04
Trade %	0.20
Unemployment	0.01

Comparison Country	Weights
Argentina	0.00
Australia	0.00
Brazil	0.16
Canada	0.00
China	0.01
Mexico	0.00
Indonesia	0.00
India	0.00
Singapore	0.00
Thailand	0.00
USA	0.83

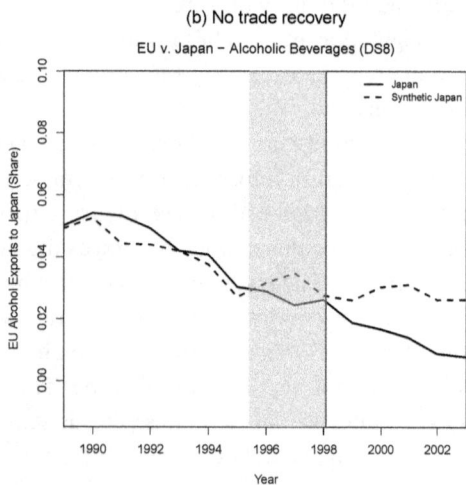

(b) No trade recovery

EU v. Japan – Alcoholic Beverages (DS8)

FIGURE 5.2. Synthetic Controls for WTO Disputes with Trade Cooperation and No Increase in Trade Cooperation
Note: (a) illustrates trade cooperation, and (b) illustrates no increase in cooperation.
Vertical shaded areas cover the dispute duration from the request for consultations to the implementation deadline (bold vertical line). Estimates created with "synth" package in R.
Tables show covariate and comparison country-weights for each case.

the agricultural sector, and the countries' overall trade dependence. These trade patterns suggest Japan did not restore trade cooperation for some time. In both examples, the country-weights and variable-weights align well with reasonable expectations about Korean and Japanese appetites for alcohol imports from Europe.

5.1.4 Methodological advantages

SCM has several advantages over alternative approaches, including matching and regression. First, and unlike matching, SCM creates a counterfactual based on pre-treatment trends in the outcome of interest. This mitigates the problem of time-varying confounders. As Abadie, Diamond, and Hainmueller (2010) explain, SCM "extends the traditional linear panel data framework, allowing that the effects of unobserved variables on the outcome vary with time" (494). Many exogenous factors affect multiple countries in similar ways—for example, a worsening drought impacts an entire region over time. Where unobserved, time-varying factors affect the donor pool in the same way they do the treated unit, and SCM controls for them, reducing the risk of omitted variable bias. In constructing the counterfactual, I choose a donor pool that is likely subject to the same systematic factors. For example, if an economic shock affected the treated country's entire geographical region at a given time, one would not have to directly observe or model that shock to estimate an appropriate counterfactual. Using a donor pool of comparison countries from the same geographical region would control for the shock.

Second, SCM creates more similar controls than standard matching techniques can achieve with a small, heterogeneous set of units. When a sample consists of few aggregate units, matching can be ineffective because treated units cannot be paired to control units without sometimes drawing very dissimilar comparisons. The matching criteria can also heavily influence the conclusions drawn (Jeffrey Smith and Todd 2005; Imai and Ratkovic 2014). By contrast, SCM creates composite control units that better reflect heterogeneous entities like countries.

Third, SCM is transparent and flexible, allowing for the direct analysis of similarities between cases of interest and the synthetic control.[11] It is transparent because it makes explicit the contribution of each comparison unit. It is flexible because it allows each WTO dispute to have a separate covariate-weighting that reflects the products and industries involved. For example, in a dispute over computer chips, South Korea's exports to the European looked much like its exports to Japan.[12] The co-variates for GDP and industry value added received the most weight. In a dispute over cigarettes, Honduras's exports to the Dominican Republic looked like a combination of Honduras's exports to Canada and Costa Rica[13] and the key covariate was agriculture value added. These weightings comport with reasonable expectations about the sectors at stake in each dispute. Whereas conventional matching techniques impose the same covariate-weight for all cases, SCM gives each case its own optimized covariate-weighting reflecting the specific characteristics of the case at hand.

This method safeguards against extrapolation outside the support of the data. Synthetic control units are computed as weighted averages (convex combinations) of the control units, so all estimates are based on interpolation.

Moreover, this measure of trade cooperation is reliable. It is unlikely to produce "false positives." There were twelve WTO rulings between 1995 and 2011 in which the respondent prevailed.[14] In each, the panel determined that either the complainant's claims were without merit or the policy in question had expired before a judgment could be reached. In some, an initially adverse panel ruling was revered on appeal. These disputes can be thought of as placebo tests: there were no adverse rulings for the respondents to implement. I repeated the SCM estimate technique on each of these cases. None indicate trade patterns indicative of deeper cooperation. This provides reassurance that where SCM detects a positive effect of a ruling on bilateral trade flows, that effect is real—not merely the result of noise in the data.

It is informative to compare this measurement of trade impact to my evaluation of compliance in the preceding chapter. Does policy compliance lead to restored cooperation? In slightly over half of the disputes, compliance corresponded to trade cooperation: where policy reforms took place, significant trade increases followed, and where no policy reforms were implemented, no trade increases followed. In nearly all disputes where there was a discrepancy, it was because formal policy reforms were implemented but did not result in a measurable increase in trade flows in the disputed products. This pattern is largely consistent with the canonical literature that observes states may formally comply but take actions that fall short of deep cooperation (Downs, Rocke, and Barsoom 1996).

My trade cooperation measurement can similarly be compared to other scholars' work that examines responses to WTO rulings. Several prior studies have also evaluated whether governments reported or made substantial efforts to implement adverse rulings through policy reform.[15] In the most complete of these prior studies, Brewster and Chilton (2014) examine US compliance from 1995 to 2012. In the majority of the cases in which the United States complied, I uncover trade recoveries indicative of deeper cooperation. Conversely, in most cases of noncompliance, there was little evidence of restored trade flows. Again, where discrepancies arise, it is because Brewster and Chilton found nominal compliance but no significant trade recovery resulted. This is likely when a respondent implements superficial policy reforms that do little to restore affected markets.

5.2 Analysis and results

5.2.1 Variables

Turning now to the domestic politics portion of the analysis, I consider whether, like compliance, trade cooperation hinges on a respondent country's internal veto points. The dependent variable, trade cooperation, is measured from trade flow patterns in the wake of a WTO ruling. I use the score S, the difference between actual and expected trade in the five years after the implementation deadline minus the difference in years before. While the direction is reliable, the magnitude is sensitive to data availability and is therefore noisy. I transform the trade cooperation score S and associated standard deviation d according to two alternative coding rules.

Under the first coding rule, *Trade Cooperation$_A$* is a binary variable. A positive score $S > 0$ denotes disputed trade flows increased over expected levels, which occurs in 47% of the cases (56 of 120). Under the second coding rule, *Trade Cooperation$_B$* is an ordinal variable that accounts for the point estimate and associated uncertainty.[16] The standard deviation d provides a simple estimate of the precision in the match between the actual trade flows and the expected trade flows and thus the reliability of the score. Small standard deviations indicate the synthetic control unit precisely fits the observed data in the pre-treatment period and produces a more reliable trade cooperation score. The case is coded as cooperation (2) if the score is positive and larger than the standard deviation, no cooperation (0) if the score is negative and larger in magnitude than the standard deviation, and inconclusive (1) otherwise. This indicates strong evidence of trade recoveries in 31.7% of cases (38 of 120) and no trade recovery in 48% of cases (58 of 120).

The explanatory variable is domestic veto players in the respondent government. I measure this as the respondent's *Veto Points* using the Political Constraints Index (Henisz 2002). This is the first index discussed in chapter 4. I assess the veto points at the start of the dispute. Recall that this measure accounts for the number of independent branches of government, the extent of partisan alignment across branches of government, and preference heterogeneity within each legislative body. Partisan alignment accounts for party composition left-right preference, a component which varies over time. Veto points range from 0 (least constrained) to 1 (most constrained). This metric has broad coverage and is widely used in related studies.

The Political Constraints Index does not provide values for the European Union, which participates in the WTO as a single entity. When the EU is the respondent, I use two different measurement strategies. First, I take the weighted average of national governments' veto points, with weights corresponding to those states' vote share on the EU Council, updated by year. This will tend to understate the veto players because many EU-wide decisions must then be implemented by national governments. Second, I use the coding of EU veto points from Yildirim et al. (2017). This second measure accounts for political constraints generated by the European Parliament, the European Commission, and the Council of the European Union and their corresponding alignment.

As in chapter 4, I evaluate federalism as another contributing factor to a government's domestic political constraints. I use an indicator variable for federal respondents, treating the European Union as federal. For instance, when the Canadian federal government urged compliance in a dispute over renewable energy technology, it needed support from Ontario's provincial authorities.

Two control variables help to account for international pressure in a given dispute. I control for the number of *Third Party* countries (Horn and Mavroidis 2008; Kucik and Pelc 2016); seven disputes included in this portion of the analysis have no third parties, fifty-nine disputes have between one and five, and the remainder have many third parties. This variable is log-transformed to account for the skewed distribution, with a zero used when no third-party governments participate. I use the *Com-*

plainant GDP in the year the dispute was initiated and a dummy variable indicating whether the EU or the US was a complainant, as complainants with larger economies have a greater capacity to retaliate.

Additional controls include the *Respondent GDP*. The GDP data come from the World Bank and are normalized to improve comparability. I account for the percentage of legal claims found in favor of the complainant, *% Adverse Ruling*. If the governments appeal the ruling, I count the claims that were sustained. I include a dummy variable for the twenty-two cases where the European Union is the respondent because its participation in the WTO as a supranational block likely introduces more obstacles to trade cooperation. A dummy variable to denote whether the dispute concerned *Legislative* measures is also included since these disputes tend to implicate many products and demand more substantial reforms and are subject to more veto players. Finally, I account for trade *Remedy* disputes since they may activate fewer veto players.

5.2.2 Results

Across all model specifications, veto points are associated with a lower probability of substantial trade recovery. Table 5.1 shows probit regression results with *Trade Cooperation$_A$*. The *Veto Points* variable has a negative coefficient, statistically significant at conventional levels.[17]

The coding of EU veto players from Yildirim et al. (2017) yields similar results (model 3). Defendant governments that are federal are less likely to display trade recoveries (model 4). This is consistent with the domestic constraints argument: even compliant policies enacted at the national level may fail to produce trade recoveries if subnational actors do not adequately implement those directives.

Next, I consider the role of the European Union, a unique participant in the WTO. Model 5 omits lawsuits against the EU and verifies the unique institution is not driving the results. Although the EU has a low rate of compliance and faces significant domestic obstacles to policy implementation, its trade recovery across disputes is similar to the sample average. In approximately 45% of the merchandise disputes, the EU displayed significant trade recoveries over expected levels, whereas for the overall sample, that rate was 46%.

Two additional tests focus on democratic institutions. Model 6 looks exclusively at disputes where the respondent country is democratic. For this subset of cases, variation in veto players remains a meaningful predictor of trade cooperation. The statistical significance of veto players and federalism diminishes slightly, suggesting some of the variation in trade cooperation is attributable to democratic institutions. The subsample analysis is more meaningful here than an interaction effect using the full sample of countries because there are so few disputes implicating nondemocratic countries. Moreover, it is possible that the trade data are more accurate for countries with stronger transparency standards—typically democracies. The few autocracies may make a modest contribution to the statistical results or they may simply have less reliable data.

In model 7, I examine the role of democracy by including the Polity score as a predictor in my synthetic control calculations. This means that when the counterfactual trade flows were estimated in each dispute, the level of democracy was a contributing factor to the weighting of comparison countries. The same other covariates (GDP, industry value added, GDP growth, etc.) were also included in the SCM calculations. To the extent that a defendant government's Polity score was strongly predictive of its trade flows, that means that other democratic countries' trade flows were assigned more weight than autocratic countries' in the synthetic control unit. This approach controls for level of democracy at the first stage of the analysis, the calculation of dispute-specific trade recovery. It obviates the need to control for level of democracy at the second stage. The main results hold here as well.

The number of third-party countries participating as bystanders in a dispute is positively associated with trade recovery. The extent of an adverse ruling is positively associated with trade cooperation as well but falls short of statistical significance. Legislative measures are not systematically associated with trade recoveries. Chapter 4 showed that legislative measures are vulnerable to more veto players that can obstruct compliant policy reforms. Yet those same disputes also tend to address broader trade policies with more sweeping effects on trade flows. Considering this null effect alongside the findings in chapter 4 suggests that while it is more difficult to achieve legislative compliance, those few cases do tend to deliver deeper trade cooperation.

Complaininat and respondent countries' GDP are not strongly predictive of merchandise trade recoveries. Once governments engage in litigation, their relative economic power does not appear to be the main driver of outcomes. This reinforces WTO advocates' claim that the legal

TABLE 5.1 **Impact of WTO Rulings on Trade Cooperation, Binary Measure**

	(1)	(2)	(3)	(4)	(5)	(6)	... with democracy (7)[‡]
			Trade cooperation$_A$				
Veto Points	-2.07**	-2.33**			-2.02*	-2.84*	-2.81**
	(0.98)	(1.05)			(1.12)	(1.59)	(1.15)
Veto Points$_{EU}$			-2.24**				
			(1.05)				
Federal				-0.58*	-0.62*	-0.55	-0.38
				(0.34)	(0.36)	(0.41)	(0.36)
Legislative		0.37	0.37	0.21	0.06	0.30	0.72**
		(0.32)	(0.32)	(0.32)	(0.38)	(0.35)	(0.34)
Complainant GDP		-0.73*	-0.73*	-0.57	-0.13	-0.22	-0.69
		(0.44)	(0.43)	(0.42)	(0.15)	(0.15)	(0.44)
Respondent GDP		0.07	0.07	0.21	0.29	0.12	0.13
		(0.17)	(0.17)	(0.19)	(0.20)	(0.18)	(0.20)
% Adverse Ruling		0.02	0.02	0.12	0.93*	-0.02	-0.001
		(0.44)	(0.44)	(0.44)	(0.50)	(0.55)	(0.45)
Third Parties[†]		0.37**	0.37**	0.38**	0.28	0.23	0.30*
		(0.18)	(0.18)	(0.18)	(0.19)	(0.18)	(0.18)
Remedy		-0.21	-0.21	-0.22	-0.63*	-0.30	-0.20
		(0.27)	(0.27)	(0.27)	(0.32)	(0.31)	(0.28)
EU Respondent		-0.13	0.72	-0.31			-0.06
		(0.37)	(0.60)	(0.37)			(0.38)
EU or US Complainant		1.25	1.25	1.00			1.03
		(0.90)	(0.90)	(0.88)			(0.91)
N	120	120	120	120	98	99	120
Democracy subset?	No	No	No	No	No	Yes	No
Exclude EU?	No	No	No	No	Yes	No	No
Log Likelihood	-80.53	-76.48	-76.66	-77.62	-59.12	-62.39	-73.57

Notes: Probit models estimated with R. Trade cooperation is coded using SCM with annual bilateral trade data for disputed products. Significance codes *p<0.1; **p<0.05; ***p<0.01. †Log units. ‡Cooperation is coded using Polity IV as covariate. Intercepts not shown.

process has an equalizing impact on the relations among countries, reducing the importance of power politics.

Figure 5.3 shows the predicted effect of veto points on compliance. As veto points increase, the predicted probability of a measurable trade impact decreases. Estimates use the probit model with all controls held at their means. Most disputes involve respondent governments with a moderate number of veto points.

Several examples are plotted. When Mexico was sued in 2004 over its imposition of antidumping duties, it had few veto points (0.284). Institutional constraints on the executive were modest. The Partido Acción Na-

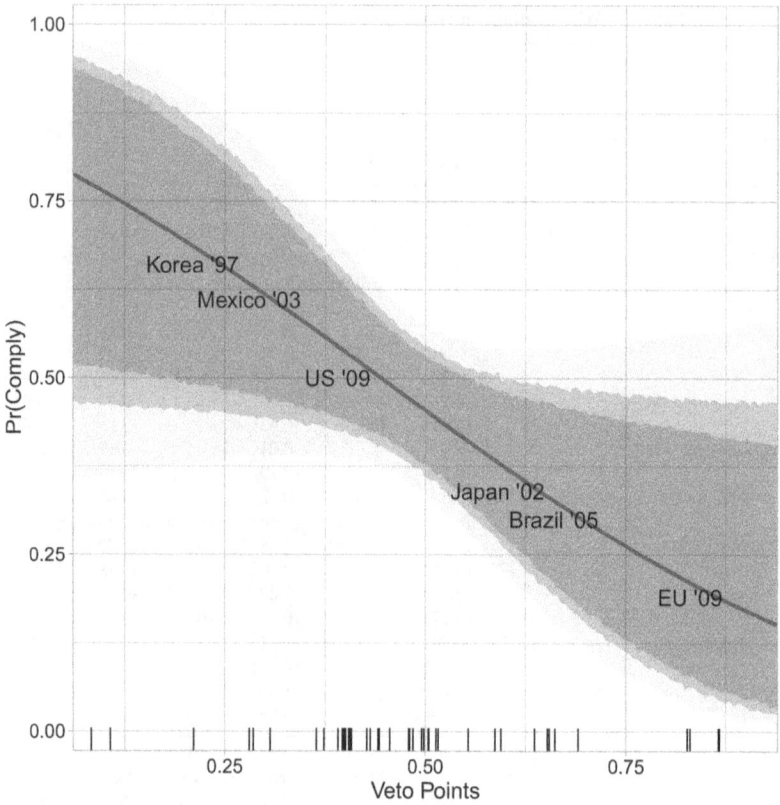

FIGURE 5.3. Predicted Effect of Veto Points on Trade Impact of Adverse Ruling
Note: Shading denotes 90% and 95% confidence intervals. Examples of veto points for selected
country-years are plotted. The rug shows the distribution of observations. Predictions are based
on model 3 in table 5.2, with controls held at their means.

cional (PAN) held the presidency and had pluralities in both houses of
the legislature.[18] Mexico's predicted probability of a recovery in the disputed trade was high ($\approx$ 0.6), and in this instance, it did demonstrate
significant recoveries in imports of the disputed products. By contrast,
when Brazil was sued in 2005 over import barriers on automobile tires,
it had many veto points (0.684). This reflects its many municipalities and
a coalition government.[19] Brazil's predicted probability of trade recovery
was low ($\approx$ 0.2), and it did not show any notable increase in imports over
expected levels. Most of the variation in veto points is across countries,
due to fixed institutions. There is some modest variation within individual countries over time, due to partisan shifts. For instance, in 2009, the

US had fewer veto points (0.397) than it did in 2011 (0.414), when the Republican Party gained a majority of seats in the House of Representatives while the Democratic Party maintained control of the Senate and presidency.

To examine the strength of the results, I repeat the analysis using the alternative coding rule that accounts for uncertainty. Table 5.2 shows results from ordered multinomial probit models using the *Trade Cooperation*$_B$ variable.

Table 5.2 confirms that defendant governments with more veto points are significantly less likely to respond to adverse rulings by deepening their trade cooperation with respect to disputed products. The results also hold when I repeat the analysis using the level of democracy as an additional covariate in the SCM calculations (model 7). This indicates that the variation in trade impact cannot be attributed to the level of democracy alone; veto points still carry explanatory power. By accounting for democracy in the measurement of compliance and federalism in the regression analysis, these results show that the veto players explanation remains strong. Finally, I use the trade scores directly in the regression (8) and confirm there is a tendency, albeit statistically insignificant, for countries with more veto points to comply less. The predicted effects are large. If an average respondent increased its domestic veto points from the least to the most, its predicted probability of trade recovery *decreases* by 0.44.[20]

5.3 Selection into trade disputes and rulings

While WTO rulings do often promote recovery in disputed trade, this step constitutes the last in several stages of international cooperation. At each step of a trade dispute, there are selection forces that either encourage or discourage its continuation. At the outset, not all countries are equally likely to implement trade barriers that prompt disputes. Likewise, selection forces may increase the chance that certain types of disputes move forward into formal lawsuits at the WTO or that an adverse ruling is reached. As argued in chapter 3, only some selection forces will be relevant to the empirical results regarding domestic veto players. This section considers salient potential forms of selection and offers evidence that they are not driving the findings presented in chapter 5.

First, one might consider whether veto players affect the WTO vio-

TABLE 5.2 **Impact of WTO Rulings on Trade Cooperation, Ordinal Measure**

	(1)	(2)	(3)	(4)	(5)	(6)	... with democracy (7)[‡]	Trade score (s) (8)
			Trade cooperation$_B$					
Veto Points	−2.16**	−2.49**			−2.32**	−2.71*	−2.25**	−0.06
	(0.90)	(0.98)			(1.03)	(1.42)	(1.00)	(0.05)
Veto Points$_{EU}$			−2.42**					
			(0.97)					
Federal				−0.63**	−0.67**	−0.56	−0.66**	0.001
				(0.31)	(0.33)	(0.37)	(0.32)	(0.02)
Legislative		0.47	0.47	0.30	0.29	0.42	0.45	0.01
		(0.29)	(0.29)	(0.29)	(0.34)	(0.32)	(0.30)	(0.02)
Complainant GDP		−0.56	−0.56	−0.40	0.01	−0.10	−0.50	−0.001
		(0.40)	(0.40)	(0.39)	(0.13)	(0.14)	(0.40)	(0.02)
Respondent GDP		−0.003	−0.004	0.15	0.23	0.08	0.12	−0.01
		(0.15)	(0.15)	(0.18)	(0.18)	(0.17)	(0.18)	(0.01)
% Adverse Ruling		−0.25	−0.25	−0.13	0.66	−0.26	0.06	−0.02
		(0.41)	(0.41)	(0.42)	(0.46)	(0.51)	(0.42)	(0.02)
Third Parties[†]		0.31*	0.32*	0.33**	0.30*	0.22	0.26	0.002
		(0.16)	(0.16)	(0.16)	(0.18)	(0.17)	(0.16)	(0.01)
Remedy		−0.17	−0.17	−0.18	−0.59**	−0.24	−0.07	0.01
		(0.25)	(0.25)	(0.25)	(0.29)	(0.28)	(0.25)	(0.01)
EU Respondent		0.003	0.93*	−0.18			0.15	0.02
		(0.35)	(0.56)	(0.34)			(0.34)	(0.02)
EU or US Complainant		1.18	1.18	0.92			0.93	0.01
		(0.84)	(0.84)	(0.81)			(0.83)	(0.04)
N	120	120	120	120	98	99	120	120
Democracy subset?	No	No	No	No	No	Yes	No	No
Exclude EU?	No	No	No	No	Yes	No	No	No
Log Likelihood	−121.48	−117.24	−117.41	−118.67	−92.77	−95.92	−116.91	
Cooperation Measure	(0/1/2)	(0/1/2)	(0/1/2)	(0/1/2)	(0/1/2)	(0/1/2)	(0/1/2)[‡]	continuous
Model	OP	OP	OP	OP	OP	OP	OP	OLS

Notes: Ordered probit and linear models estimated with R. Trade cooperation is coded using SCM with annual bilateral trade data for disputed products. Significance codes *p<0.1; **p<0.05; ***p<0.01. [†]Log units. [‡]Cooperation is coded using Polity IV as covariate. Intercepts not shown.

lations that emerge in the first place. As discussed earlier, theory is mixed as to which domestic political factors—veto players included— lead countries to initially violate their trade obligations. In this context, there is reason to expect that the selection of trade violations would lead me to underestimate the size of the effect of veto players on post-ruling cooperation.

Consider the possibility that veto points don't obstruct all policy changes equally. Rather than being purely neutral, veto points are held by actors with particular preferences over trade policy. This leads to two possible scenarios. On the one hand, suppose that veto points are controlled by protectionist actors, such as a political party that supports additional trade barriers. These veto points would not be used to block the initial protectionist measures (i.e., first-order noncompliance). Thus no selection effect exists because these protectionist measures would be easily adopted regardless of the number of veto points. In this scenario, my findings with respect to the trade impact of rulings would thus reflect the hypothesized impact of veto players. In short, if protectionist interests control veto points, the selection of trade policies that violate WTO commitments could not possibly explain the above results.

Suppose, on the other hand, that veto points are controlled by liberal actors. Then veto points would be used to block the initial protectionist measures. Fewer WTO violations would occur, and only the protectionist measures that garner widespread support would ever be put into place. However, if these veto points are controlled by liberals, they should not be used to obstruct second-order compliance—and consequently should not produce second-order results with respect to the trade impact of rulings. In short, if liberal interests control veto points, the selection of trade policies that violate WTO rules would lead me to underestimate the size of the results. Therefore, depending on who controls the veto points—protectionist or liberalizing interests—either there is a selection effect but no second-order results or no selection effect and second-order results.

It is well-established that a range of domestic political factors shape a government's tendency to violate free-trade obligations in the first place (e.g., Rickard 2010; Gray 2014; Mansfield and Milner 2012). Yet selection effects arising from veto players at this stage do not provide a compelling explanation of the results presented above.

A second potential form of selection bias concerns the generation disputes. Governments choose whether and when to file a WTO complaint based on their own political and economic conditions (Bown 2005b; Davis and Shirato 2007). Davis (2012) demonstrates that the US government tends to resort to WTO adjudication—rather than bilateral negotiations—to solve its trade conflicts when there is greater domestic political pressure and when trade with the target partner state is significant. Selection bias could arise if the governments targeted in WTO complaints differ systematically from those states that commit equivalent trade violations but are not sued.

This type of selection could affect conclusions about trade cooperation. On the one hand, strategic restraint suggests that complainant states would bother to file WTO cases only when they anticipate low resistance from the respondent states (Davis 2012, 130). This implies that disputes against respondents with fewer veto points might be more often pursued to the point of litigation. On the other hand, resistance on the part of a potential respondent in initial talks about a trade barrier might push the case to adjudication. This would mean that prospective plaintiff states would tend to engage in bilateral negotiations with respondents that are willing to strike a deal and do not need to contend with many domestic constraints. At the same time, those plaintiffs prefer to bring formal WTO complaints against governments with many domestic veto players because escalation and appeal to legal remedies buttress their position. Then WTO disputes might overrepresent defendants with a high number of veto players as well as instances in which trade recoveries are least attainable.

To evaluate this form of selection, I compare trade disputes adjudicated at the WTO to those that are not. It is nearly impossible to obtain a representative, cross-national sample of trade grievances that were addressed through adjudication versus other bilateral means. Nonetheless, as the most active user of WTO dispute settlement and a major actor in international trade politics, the United States presents an informative case. Davis (2012) collected comprehensive data on the United States' response to foreign trade barriers.[21] These data reflect annual reports by the US Trade Representative on trade barriers that are harmful to the US export interests. These barriers represent a set of potential cases for WTO adjudication against the major trade partners of the US—the prospective respondents—and cover both regulatory and statutory trade barriers. Nine major trade partners are covered: Canada, the European Union, Japan, Mexico, Korea, Brazil, Malaysia, Singapore, and India. If the USTR disproportionately pursued WTO complaints against countries with high numbers of veto players and negotiated with countries with low numbers of veto players, especially in cases with similar grievances, the evidence would reinforce concerns about selection bias.

Drawing on replication data from Davis (2012), I evaluate whether a US trade partner's domestic veto players correlate with the decision to initiate a formal WTO complaint over a given trade barrier. There are 322 trade barriers in Davis's data with sufficient overlap for my analysis, and in 41 of them, the US initiated a WTO complaint. For such trade barriers leading to adjudication, the average veto points of the respondent governments was 0.447. For the remaining 281 trade barriers where the US did not pursue adjudication, the average number of veto points of the trade partners was 0.450. The difference between the two samples is negligible, as confirmed by a simple t – test of difference in means. Domestic veto points in the partner government do not predict the United States' initiation of WTO disputes.

Next, I build on the regression analysis in Davis (2012, 134) to examine this potential selection effect. Davis models the USTR decision to file a WTO complaint for each industry-specific trade barrier in the National Trade Estimate Reports. Davis finds that industries that exert more political influence see a stronger chance of trade barriers being challenged at the WTO. I adapt this analysis in Table 5.3. The table presents the results from several probit models for the initiation of WTO disputes by the United States.[22] The dependent variable is whether or not the US filed a formal complaint in response to a foreign trade barrier.[23] The explanatory variable is domestic veto points in the prospective respondent (target) government. The control variables in this analysis are from the portion of Davis's book *Why Adjudicate?* (2012) I am replicating. *US Political Contributions* accounts for the demand side of trade adjudication. *Section 301* indicates cases deemed to have had sufficient merit and pursued under this export promotion tool in the US Trade Act. The US industry size, measured in terms of production and export values, are other important controls, alongside industry stakes for the trade partner (i.e., the prospective respondent country). Data on import penetration ratio (share of imports in GDP) for the trade partner industry serve as a proxy for the market stakes in the dispute (see Davis [2012, 131] for discussion of *MPEN*). This analysis accounts for the form of the trade barrier in question (*Import Policy*, and whether it carries a distortionary effect on trade), progress toward resolution of the trade complaint, and the duration of the dispute.

The number of domestic veto points in the partner country (i.e., the potential respondent) is *not* a significant predictor of the US decision to file a WTO complaint. The null result holds in the full sample (model 1), with all controls (model 2), and for the democratic respondent subset (model 3). At the same time, the other variables behave largely as shown in the prior research. There is one exception that pertains to *US Political Contributions*, which falls short of statistical significance in this specification. This suggests the internal features of the prospective respondent

TABLE 5.3 **Initiation of WTO Complaints by the United States**

	File WTO complaint? (1/0)		
	(1)	(2)	(3)
Veto Points	0.57	0.17	0.56
	(0.89)	(1.09)	(1.35)
US Political Contributions	0.11	0.31	0.15
	(0.10)	(0.20)	(0.20)
Section 301	1.31***	1.43***	1.72***
	(0.29)	(0.33)	(0.43)
Production Value		0.03	0.34
		(0.30)	(0.36)
Exports Value		0.29*	0.22
		(0.17)	(0.22)
MPEN (Partner)		0.01	0.01
		(0.01)	(0.01)
Import Policy	0.70***	0.70**	0.95***
	(0.24)	(0.28)	(0.34)
Distortion	0.70***	0.62**	1.10***
	(0.23)	(0.26)	(0.36)
Progress	−0.43**	−0.38*	−0.51**
	(0.17)	(0.20)	(0.25)
Duration	0.25***	0.24***	0.30***
	(0.07)	(0.09)	(0.11)
Trade Barriers (N)	322	249	205
Democrcy subset?	No	No	Yes
Log Likelihood	−82.69	−61.74	−41.46

Notes: Probit models estimated with R. Replication of Davis (2012) including respondent veto points. Data are industry-specific trade barriers listed in the US National Trade Estimate Reports 1995-2004. Significance codes *p<0.1; **p<0.05; ***p<0.01. Intercepts not shown.

government and the political contributions by the industry are moderately collinear. Trade partners with many domestic veto points tend to impose trade barriers that attract particular attention from US industry stakeholders.

This analysis demonstrates that the trade partners the United States challenges at the WTO look very much like the partners it engages through negotiations. Whether other potential plaintiff countries may respond differently remains an open question. But for the WTO's most active litigant, the United States, there is no evidence for this particular form of selection bias.

A third concern is that selection bias could arise from the early settlement of WTO disputes. Governments have incentives to reach bilateral settlements before resorting to an adverse panel ruling. While officially

prohibited under the WTO's most-favored nation principle, discriminatory settlements that benefit the complainant are well documented
(Kucik and Pelc 2016). At the same time, disputes can be lengthy, with
costs rising should litigation be required. When a respondent has violated WTO obligations, complainants strive to extract a settlement deal
and end the conflict as quickly as possible. Approximately half of the
disputes (in the years examined) were settled early without a ruling. The
remaining half persist, and countries resort to litigation and, thus, a ruling. If the selection of disputes into litigation is correlated with domestic veto players in the respondent government, the estimates presented
above could be biased. Most plausibly, complainants that confront the
most obstinate of respondent governments—those with many domestic
constraints—may fail to extract early settlements and resort to a panel
ruling. The same intractable disputes would produce a lower chance of
trade recovery. By analyzing the trade impact of only those disputes with
adverse rulings, I could obtain a biased estimate of the effect of domestic constraints.

To evaluate this possibility, I model a two-stage process using a series
of Heckman selection models (Heckman 1979, 1990; Dubin and Rivers
1989). The first stage, the selection equation, estimates the probability
that governments fail to resolve their dispute during consultations and
go on to receive an adverse ruling. Because almost all cases that go to
litigation receive some form of adverse ruling, the selection stage closely
approximates selection into litigation. The second stage, the outcome
equation, estimates the probability that respondent governments deepen
their trade cooperation, conditional on litigation and an adverse ruling.
Table 5.4 presents the two-stage analysis.

As in the preceding chapter, I rely on several variables to identify the
models. When one or more third-party countries enter the proceedings
by citing systemic interests, the cases are much more likely to be litigated
and produce adverse rulings (Johns and Pelc 2014; Busch and Pelc 2010;
Busch and Reinhardt 2000a). The correlation between systemic interests
and adverse rulings is strong (correlation 0.565, selection stage). *Systemic
Interest* is almost entirely unrelated to trade cooperation in response to
those rulings (correlation 0.063, outcome stage), satisfying the exclusion
criteria. To improve identification, I also model the selection stage by
indicating disputes that addressed politically sensitive issues: the WTO
agreements on *Agriculture, Sanitary and Phytosanitary* measures, or

Services, or those that potentially implicate *All Products*. Respondents may tend to settle politically sensitive topics behind closed doors before litigation heightens public scrutiny.

Other variables in the selection stage improve the fit. I use the discrepancy in policy preferences between the complainant and respondent governments, measured as the distance between their United Nations General Assembly vote ideal point estimates (*ideal point distance*) (Bailey, Strezhnev, and Voeten 2017). The greater the disputants' ideal point distance, the more likely they are to litigate and the less likely they are to resolve their disagreement through negotiated settlement. I include the *exchange rate* between the complainant and respondent to capture relative strength of their markets (Przeworski and Vreeland 2000). Complainant government characteristics also influence the selection process but are not predictive of the outcome stage. I account for whether the complainant government is initiating the dispute during an election year (legislative or executive) and, the complainant's electoral system (proportionate representation). These factors might increase the time-sensitivity of the dispute and lead the complainant to capitulate sooner. Also considered are the complainant's minimum winning coalition size and the strength of its economy. Each of these variables clearly satisfies the exclusion restriction and improves the selection model.

Table 5.4 shows that the results are robust to this form of selection. In the outcome stage, the coefficient on the respondent's veto points remains negative and statistically significant. Respondents with more domestic political constraints are less likely to display trade recoveries. The magnitude of the coefficient declines somewhat as compared to the single-stage estimates. This suggests that disputes with adverse rulings tend to involve more constrained respondents and weaker trade recoveries. In the selection stage, disputes in which one or more third-party countries cite systemic interests are least likely to settle. Disputants with vast discrepancies in their policy preferences, the ideal point difference, are also more likely to resort to litigation that produces an adverse ruling. The exchange rate between the disputant governments and the complainant's electoral system, election year, and coalition size are not significant predictors of litigation.

In additional checks, I confirmed that the respondent's domestic political constraints are *not* a significant predictor of litigation. For disputes settled early, the average veto point score is 0.418 while the average for litigated disputes is 0.409, a difference that is statistically insignificant. A

TABLE 5.4 **Heckman Selection Models for Trade Impact of WTO Ruling**

Outcome equation:	Trade cooperation$_A$ (1/0)	
	(1)	(2)
Veto Points	−0.78**	−0.79**
	(0.35)	(0.35)
Third Parties†	0.07	0.07
	(0.11)	(0.11)
% Adverse	0.05	0.05
	(0.17)	(0.16)
Respondent GDP†	−0.003	−0.01
	(0.05)	(0.05)
Complainant GDP†	−0.06	−0.06
	(0.05)	(0.05)
Remedy	−0.07	−0.08
	(0.01)	(0.01)
Legislative Measure	0.17	0.13
	(0.12)	(0.12)
Selection equation:	**Was there an adverse ruling? (1/0)**	
Systemic Interest	1.03***	1.10***
	(0.20)	(0.21)
Third Parties†	0.94***	0.98***
	(0.12)	(0.12)
Ideal Point Distance	0.22**	0.15
	(0.09)	(0.09)
Complainant GDP†	0.01	0.16
	(0.13)	(0.10)
Complainant Election Year	−0.05	
	(0.24)	
Complainant PR	0.22	
	(0.21)	
Complainant MWC	0.95	
	(0.96)	
Exchange Rate Ratio	−0.00002	
	(0.0001)	
All Products		−0.64*
		(0.39)
Agriculture		−0.06
		(0.29)
Services		−1.08*
		(0.60)
Sanitary and Phytosanitary		−0.70*
		(0.37)
N	311	325
Adverse rulings	118	120
R^2	0.16	0.15
Inv. Mills Ratio	−0.08 (0.17)	−0.08 (0.17)

Notes: Selection models estimated with R. Trade cooperation coded using SCM with annual bilateral trade flows for disputed products. *p<0.1; **p<0.05; ***p<0.01. †Log units. Intercepts not shown.

simple t – test fails to support a difference in means (p-value = 0.484). The respondents also look similar when measured on their level of democracy: the average polity score for respondents that settle early is 8.30, while the average for governments that receive an adverse ruling is 8.56, with no significant difference in means.

The selection hazard is summarized by the inverse Mills ratio. It reflects the possibility that respondents with many veto players tend to resort to litigation, so the expected value of trade cooperation in settled disputes is no longer 0.5—that is, there is an equal chance that there will be trade recovery and that there will be no effect on trade. The fact that it is not statistically different from zero suggests that the single-stage estimation approach is sufficient. This form of selection bias is plausible but does not appear to be a serious problem for the analysis either. While WTO disputes involve many strategic interactions among countries and many points at which selection forces act, the key stages investigated above do not substantially alter the main findings.

Finally, one might ask whether endogeneity bias arises in which international trade disputes affect domestic politics. Scholars have shown that trade affects domestic political cleavages (Rogowski 1989) and that international conditions can force a country to adapt its trade policy process (e.g., US fast-track negotiating authority). This form of reverse causality is not a serious concern. Trade disputes occur over a short time frame—approximately five years. Changes in trade policy have a rapid impact on trade flows. By contrast, domestic veto points usually change slowly. They reflect (1) the institutional separation of power that is altered only a few times over the course of a country's modern lifespan and (2) partisan divisions that are determined by unrelated and powerful macro-political issues. WTO disputes and the alteration of trade flows they prompt are unlikely to affect a respondent's veto points.

5.4 WTO rulings, compliance, and cooperation

While the WTO's Dispute Settlement Mechanism is central to the multilateral trade regime, relatively little is known about its effectiveness in restoring trade cooperation among countries in individual disputes. Governments comply with adverse rulings, and these policy changes affect trade cooperation. Disputing countries routinely display recoveries in trade flows for the products cited in the WTO complaint in the years following a ruling.

This chapter has leveraged the method of synthetic case control to identify the trade impact of adverse WTO rulings. By constructing an approximate counterfactual against which to gauge trade fluctuations, I have identified the trade impact for the specific disputant states and products in question. An increase in actual trade relative to expected trade indicates a respondent government responded to a ruling by deepening its trade cooperation with the complainant. Using this methodology, this chapter assessed cooperation for each of 120 WTO disputes with adverse rulings between 1995 and 2011 wherever adequate merchandise trade data were available. Adverse legal rulings deliver trade recoveries for disputants, helping plaintiffs recover some of their foreign markets.

Those wins for plaintiffs are uneven. Many disputes prompt substantial increases in trade, while others have no discernible effect. Domestic political constraints in respondent governments explain this variation. Conditional on violating a treaty, the more domestic veto points a government has, the less likely it is to restore bilateral trade flows that point to deeper cooperation. Combined with the results in the preceding chapter, the evidence is clear that WTO rulings are less successful in promoting compliance and cooperation when defendant governments encounter more domestic political constraints. The results are robust across model specifications, coding schemes, and tests for selection effects.

The empirical findings concerning the WTO support my theory. The findings also have important implications for the study of international dispute settlement. Many scholars have highlighted the advantages of flexibility mechanisms that provide a safety valve to countries facing acute domestic pressure to defy their international commitments; governments are less likely to abandon an institution altogether when they are permitted temporary transgressions (Rosendorff and Milner 2001; Carrubba 2005; Rosendorff 2005; Johns 2014). The models that link the WTO's flexibility to stability typically treat states as unitary actors that can violate rules and then easily return to their international commitments. Chapters 4 and 5 have indicated that returning to compliance may not be so simple; multiple veto players can obstruct the process leading to weaker recoveries in trade. This implies a potential hazard of institutional flexibility in the multilateral trade regime. When veto players lock in treaty violations, flexibility mechanisms may fail to restore cooperative economic relations between countries, even after the temporary pressure to violate trade rules has passed. For these cases, flexibility mechanisms may be less successful in generating long-term stability. International courts may be particularly vulnerable due to the public nature of litigation which forces the government into a fraught domestic political process. At this point, treaty violations become difficult to reverse.

Two key aspects of my theory remain underexplored: First, do the lessons from the WTO extend to other highly legalized regimes? The ECJ provides an excellent test case for probing the generalizability of the preceding findings. Second, are domestic veto players driving noncompliance, or does this conflate other political factors within the defendant government? To further unpack the mechanism, I separately consider the institutional checks and balances and partisan conflicts that contribute to veto points. The European Union, whose member states are all democracies but have varying degrees of domestic institutional and partisan constraints, provides an appropriate test case. Chapter 6, the final empirical portion of this book, turns to the ECJ for answers.

The ECJ and Domestic Constraints on the Single Market

The preceding chapters presented a theory of international courts, compliance, and domestic politics and then tested that theory at the World Trade Organization's Dispute Settlement Mechanism. Three questions remain unresolved: First, can we be sure that the observed compliance patterns are driven by domestic political constraints rather than other political or economic circumstances? Perhaps powerful plaintiffs are able to force defendants to comply with international legal rulings while weaker plaintiffs cannot. Or perhaps a defendant country's exposure to international trade better explains its willingness to implement legal rulings from an international entity.

Second, which aspects of domestic political constraints—institutional checks, partisan divisions, or capture by special interests—exert influence over international economic disputes? WTO litigants are diverse. The majority are consolidated democracies, while others have middling institutions, and some are autocratic. Institutional checks and balances may matter most in certain contexts. In others, divisions in power among political parties form critical veto points. To unpack these forms of political constraints, it would be informative to compare a selection of countries that share broadly similar political institutions and evaluate nuanced differences between them. By looking at variations among democracies, one can better determine which forms of domestic constraints matter most in the context of international economic cooperation.

Third, are the findings generalizable beyond the purview of the WTO? The preceding chapters tested the theory with the multilateral trade regime but left unexplored wider applications. Current political events challenge the durability of the WTO, especially as governments flout its legal rulings. If similar compliance problems plague other international organizations, the domestic political obstacles to cooperation among states may be more pervasive.

6.1 Turning to the ECJ

I turn to the Court of Justice of the European Union (ECJ) to find answers.[1] The first reason this chapter examines the ECJ is to dispel competing explanations for compliance patterns. A major part of the ECJ's work is adjudicating infringement disputes. Infringement disputes are a category where the European Commission prosecutes member states for alleged breaches of EU law. As Tallberg (2002*b*) notes: "in its position as international prosecutor, the Commission initiates a staggering number of infringement proceedings each year," many of which escalate to litigation (636). Unlike WTO disputes, all ECJ infringement disputes are brought by the same plaintiff—the Commission. By examining these cases, I am able to rule out an alternative explanation for compliance patterns across disputes; the plaintiff's clout is held "constant." By eliminating the plaintiff's own leverage over the defendant as a possible explanation of compliance patterns, I am better able to isolate the role of domestic politics in the defendant country. This research design is not the perfect solution. The European Commission does choose its infringement cases based on the urging of member states and nongovernmental actors. And those petitioners may supply the Commission with information to guide its investigations. Nonetheless, these requests are processed through the Commission in a centralized vetting process that ensures broad consistency across disputes.

At the same time, the European Union's ambitious agenda of regional economic integration makes it an excellent test case. All EU nations are obligated to enact European policy on a host of other economic issues including their relationship to the external, global market. This means exposure to international trade is held largely constant across states. Many infringement disputes are over states' failure to implement EU policy on internal market integration. States vary in how responsive they are to pro-integration rulings from the ECJ. Because *external* market forces are largely held constant, we can better isolate the effect of member states' domestic politics and ECJ rulings on the *internal* market. In summary, infringement disputes provide an excellent setting to test my theory because (1) the plaintiff is held constant across all disputes and (2) many features of the economic environment are held constant across countries.

This leads to the second reason I examine the ECJ: to unpack the domestic political constraints mechanism. The WTO's membership features both autocratic and democratic states, hailing from vastly different political histories. By contrast, all members of the European Union are democracies. Compared to the WTO's membership, the EU member states are a politically homogeneous group. Still, EU states vary in their domestic veto players. Some have more institutional checks and balances, such as semi-presidential and bicameral systems; some have fewer institutional checks. Partisan divisions that constrain decision-makers vary, as does the access interest groups have to those political actors. By testing my theory in the European context, I am able to break apart the veto players mechanism into its constituent parts and provide a finer-grained account of the different sources of political constraints.

The third motivation for scrutinizing the ECJ is to show that the arguments in the preceding chapters are generalizable. The WTO is not the only setting in which legal rulings induce international economic cooperation between states. Similar patterns appear in infringement disputes over European economic integration. When European states lose numerous rulings on trade-related disputes, they demonstrate a larger subsequent boost in their imports from the rest of the EU. Those trade patterns suggest they have—on average—reformed their policies in order to comply with the rulings. The parallels between the WTO and ECJ in this respect also highlight the range of enforcement strategies employed by international organizations. Whereas the WTO relies on decentralized, state-based enforcement, the infringement procedure at the EU leverages a centralized process by the Commission. Both approaches appear to prompt deeper economic ties among member states in the wake of disputes, highlighting the range of institutional design that can advance international cooperation.

The WTO Dispute Settlement System is not unique in seeing less compliance from defendant governments that have many domestic veto players. European states with more internal political constraints are also less responsive to the ECJ when they lose infringement disputes in terms of trade impact. The findings suggest that domestic politics within states undercut the performance of international economic courts more generally. The ECJ has become famous for its political power and is often credited with driving the integration of Europe through its jurisprudence (Martinsen 2015b; Slaughter, Stone Sweet, and Weiler 1998; Alter 2001). Yet even the ECJ depends on the acquiescence of domestic political actors to execute its decisions. Politics within member states can counteract the court's legal efforts to enforce European integration. Thus the court provides a crucial extension for testing my theory and supports broader claims about the cross-cutting effects of domestic veto players on international cooperation.

6.2 Domestic constraints on economic integration

Recent decades have brought major shifts in the European Union. The organization has expanded is purview, regulating a broader scope of issues and placing far more demanding requirements on its member states. All these obligations serve the goal of deepening regional integration, especially with respect to the internal market.

According to many scholars, the process of European integration has and continues to be fraught due to resistance from some member states. Each time the EU has expanded its membership—and today, as it continues to evaluate new applicants—it has encountered opposition (Schneider 2014). Likewise, some states have been reluctant to consent to deeper legal obligations. Domestic politics within member states are often the source of roadblocks in each stage of EU negotiations. Some governments have faced the highest hurdles in securing consent from their national parliaments (Benz 2004). Pahre (1997) explains that partisan competition within member states' parliaments constrained diplomatic negotiations over the EU. Moreover, parties have formed governing coalitions and established oversight institutions within their respective parliaments to curb the decision-making authority of the EU. These domestic constraints have not only constructed roadblocks in the negotiation process but have also shaped the bargaining strategies adopted by member states (McKibben 2015).

On economic issues, these domestic obstacles have been pronounced. The European single market is constituted by four fundamental freedoms or "pillars": the free movement of goods, services, people, and capital. Each of these pillars has fueled controversy at various points in EU history. For example, domestic dissent is especially acute today in the case of the United Kingdom's decision to withdraw from the Euro-peawn Union. By a close margin, British citizens decided that continu-ing to abide by the terms of integration were too onerous, with the free movement of people being a point of heated debate (Horan 2016). In-deed, Theresa May's government has long insisted that free movement of people from the European Union to Britain must end after "Brexit." And yet the precise terms of Britain's departure remain, as of this writ-ing, unspecified because of discord both between parties and within the Labour Party. Domestic dissent has thus complicated and—at times—undercut member state cooperation with the economic obligations of the EU.

Domestic actors often hold widely divergent preferences on the other pillars of European integration as well. The free movement of goods requirement—unfettered trade within the community—also serves as a nexus for controversy. Some industry groups favor technical barriers to trade that diminish competition from other firms in the European mar-ket; others prefer policies that facilitate intra-EU commerce. These di-vergent preferences can produce cleavages between industries or along other lines. For instance, many seemingly peripheral regulatory issues concerning social and environmental standards are actually about mar-ket protections. ECJ rulings on these issues often aim to ensure govern-ments cannot use these standards as disguised trade barriers.[2] Likewise, as Carbone (2010) documents, within many European nations, pro- and anti-integration cleavages have tended to fall along class and party lines. These divergent preferences matter for policy-making.[3] As detailed in the preceding chapters, when a government has many formal divisions of power, it is more likely that interest groups will manage to find a sym-pathetic ear in government (Ehrlich 2011) and thus will have a better chance to sway policy toward to their liking. In many cases, this means that domestic interest groups can use their leverage to impede the single European market.

Whether or not these domestic political factors affect government ad-herence to EU obligations remains a point of debate. Once governments successfully negotiate the terms of EU integration, they confront differ-ent roadblocks to enacting policies that give their treaty terms effect—for example, correctly adopting EU law, regulations, and directives.

Sometimes the incomplete adoption of EU law reflects demands for targeted economic policy. For instance, Rickard (2018) offers a close look at subsidies in the EU, a major source of noncompliant national economic policies that undermines the single market. This research shows that a state's electoral system and its geographical distribution of industry jointly affect the allocation of subsidies and can thus drive its government's failure to embrace EU economic integration.

Incomplete adoption of EU law also reflects the structure of domestic government and its tendency toward policy stability. Veto players theory predicts that the more political constraints a government has, the more difficulty it encounters in passing new policies. In his canonical work, Tsebelis (1995, 2002) demonstrates that veto players can inhibit policy reforms in a wide range of institutional contexts across European countries. In particular, veto players strongly predict policy stability on a range of macroeconomic issues, from taxation to budget deficits. By extension, the same factors can explain European states' adoption of policies to enact EU economic integration. Governments with more internal divisions of power and divergent preferences among constituents face higher hurdles to implementing EU obligations.

As discussed in chapter 2, my argument extends classic veto players theory. Veto players are traditionally thought to inhibit the adoption of new legislation. The same insights can be applied to *informal* veto players that inhibit policy-making beyond the legislative context. Even the adoption of administrative measures can be thwarted when there are sharp partisan divisions in domestic government. Once new EU-consistent policies are in place, governments with more domestic veto players are less likely to reverse course. States with substantial domestic political constraints should be less likely to renege and should thus be more apt to *first-order comply* with EU law, whether those policies have been enacted through domestic legislation or administrative measures.

With respect to European integration, empirical support for veto players theory is mixed. Some studies uncover clear evidence that domestic constraints hinder the adoption of EU obligations. Thomson (2009) finds that states with more decentralized political systems are less likely to adopt EU-compliant policies in a timely manner. Börzel, T. Hofmann, and Panke (2012) find that domestic constraints significantly increase persistent noncompliance, measured by the stages of infringement proceedings undertaken. Relatedly, Haverland (2000) examines the effect of veto points and policy mismatch on the adoption of EU environmental directives and finds that subnational actors (e.g., regional authorities) are pivotal in generating compliance.

Other studies cast doubt on the adequacy of domestic political constraints to explain state compliance with EU obligations. Mbaye (2001) finds that veto points do not predict initial infringements of EU law. Falkner, Hartlapp, and Treib (2007) report that in only six countries that are particularly beholden to domestic political controversy do veto points explain failures to implement EU labor law. In particular, they identify Austria, the United Kingdom, Belgium, Germany, the Netherlands, and Spain as especially vulnerable to veto players in this domain. Yet formal veto points are not always salient, and in many other instances, the transposition of EU directives on labor remains an administrative process that is isolated from political influence. Börzel et al. (2010) examine whether veto points compound implementation problems in already–inefficient bureaucracies; this study finds no significant effect on the infringement rate, suggesting that domestic veto players are not a meaningful predictor of state compliance with EU obligations.

The disparate results in the literature can be explained by considering two issues. First, many studies measure institutional and partisan constraints in a single composite score that risks obscuring meaningful variation (König and Luetgert, 2009). This methodological approach is sensible but leaves unexplored the possibility that states encounter widely different obstacles to compliance. For instance, if a government relies heavily on regional authorities to implement EU law, institutional divisions may be the primary obstacle. In contrast, partisan constraints may be more salient if a government is politically polarized and parliamentary approval is required to implement EU law. Therefore, multiple measures of political constraints help to capture this variation and shed light on the range of obstacles governments face. Second, the disparate findings reflect ambiguity about when domestic constraints are activated. EU integration does not always provoke opposition, and on uncontroversial matters, institutional and partisan constraints matter little. By contrast, when EU integration is the source of a legal dispute, the calculus changes. For infringement lawsuits, compliance is often controversial. These are cases in which the Commission sues states for allegedly failing to ensure first-order compliance. Lawsuits isolate exactly the instances in which EU integration is most fraught.

These are precisely the cases, according to a growing scholarship, that are most likely to be fraught with controversy. Through successive legal decisions, the ECJ incrementally expanded its authority to press for European integration, sometimes counter to state preferences. Burley and Mattli (1993) argue that the ECJ has quietly extended the scope of EU law, advancing European community goals over the immediate interests of member states. Slaughter, Stone Sweet, and Weiler (1998) further argue that national courts have been instrumental in facilitating the ECJ's pro-integration agenda. When the court rules a government is in breach, that defendant is obligated to correct the initial violation: *second-order compliance.* These legal decisions shine a spotlight on the divergence between the ECJ's efforts to promote integration and national governments' reluctance to follow suit.

There are also practical reasons to think adverse ECJ infringement rulings highlight instances of divergent preferences. The multistage infringement procedure helps to resolve violations of EU law that arise from simple reporting failures (König and Mäder 2013). Only the most intractable cases persist long enough to go before the ECJ. In other words, an ECJ dispute only arises when a government rebuts Commission allegations; otherwise, the conflict would most likely have resolved earlier in the infringement procedure. Second-order compliance decisions are especially vulnerable to domestic political constraints because these are precisely the cases where influential domestic groups stand in the way. As with the WTO, adverse rulings in ECJ disputes identify cases in which a state—or politically influential constituencies within its borders—is reluctant to abide by EU law.

Beyond identifying points of contention, adverse rulings can exacerbate controversy. ECJ rulings on economic integration carry distributive implications. They produce divergent domestic consequences for different groups (Rogowski 1989; Hiscox 2002). For instance, when the court orders a state to dismantle its barriers to intra-EU trade, it is asking the state to rescind special protection for a target industry. That hurts the industry by precipitating sudden adjustments to a more competitive EU-wide market. Thus ECJ rulings fuel disagreement over compliance (Garrett, Kelemen, and Schulz 1998).[4] By highlighting the "difficult" cases for international economic integration—that is, second-order compliance decisions—this chapter extends the insights of the classic veto players theory. I argue that adverse trade rulings isolate cases in which important constituencies within states do not want to comply and domestic controversies are particularly acute. It is in this context that domestic political constraints lock in violations of EU commitments and inhibit economic integration.

Counter to this perspective is a growing scholarship that sees the ECJ working in cooperation with member states and key domestic actors to facilitate integration. Alter (2014) shows how legal rulings affect domestic politics, activating support from "compliance partners" who then reinforce the court's authority; state delegation of power to international courts undermines "governments' monopoly power to determine for itself what international law requires and allows international legal norms to become politically salient in ways that may not be directly servicing national interests defined by governments" (340). This scholarship indicates a different role for veto players, suggesting that domestic actors that face national institutional constraints in altering policy might instead work through the European supranational legal system to obtain legal rulings and usher along the changes they desire. By extension, this scholarship implies that governments with more domestic veto points would more frequently become engaged in infringement disputes.

6.3 Illustrating the mechanism

6.3.1 Formal constraints

There are two main mechanisms through which domestic political constraints can impede compliance with adverse legal rulings from the ECJ. First, governments face *formal obstacles* to policy reform, making it more difficult for them to comply with rulings (Börzel, T. Hofmann, and Panke 2012; König and Luetgert 2009). Institutional divisions of power are widely acknowledged by the European Commission as impediments to compliance. For example, in its 1988 report, the Commission observed that "cases where judgments have not been complied with . . . are [often] due to the slowness of domestic legislative procedures."[5] Of Italy in particular, the Commission reported many instances were due to "problems of administrative infrastructure [and] . . . the length of Parliamentary procedures.[6] Likewise, Tallberg (2002b) highlights how Italy and Sweden have encountered significant legislative obstacles to compliance.

Moreover, formal institutional factors are compounded by party politics—for example, strong opposition parties (Mbaye 2001). The more partisan divisions in government, the more opportunities for domestic stakeholders—interest groups that stand to lose from the ruling—to demand their representatives block policy reform.

An example can be found in a 1990 lawsuit over the United Kingdom's patent law, which arose from the country's compulsory patent licensing provisions. Licensing requirements made it nearly mandatory for companies to produce the patented goods in Britain rather than in other parts of Europe. The Commission sued the government, asserting that the rules "encourage the patentee to manufacture in the national territory rather than to import from the territory of other Member States and . . . [have] equivalent effect to quantitative restrictions on imports."[7] Compulsory licensing formed a barrier to intra-European trade because it favored domestic production at the expense of equivalent producers outside the UK's borders.

Britain rebutted the Commission's claims in two ways: First, the UK disagreed that its patent law constituted a barrier to trade. Britain argued that "contested provisions do not prevent or restrict imports."[8] Second, and more fundamentally, the UK challenged the EU's authority. The government argued that authority to create patent licensing rules lay "within the exclusive competence of the national legislature."[9] The EU could not legitimately overturn a member state's own national legislature, the UK argued.

As it has in the majority of infringement lawsuits, the ECJ sided with the European Commission. It concluded that UK patent law "necessarily reduces imports of the patented product from other Member States and thus affects intra-Community trade"[10] and ordered the UK to amend its legislation.[11] This ruling was quickly followed by a closely related preliminary reference judgment on the same compulsory license provisions on pharmaceutical patents, *Generics (UK) Ltd. v. Smith Kline.*[12] This latter judgment reinforced the court's conclusion that EU law held supremacy (Tudor 2012).

The ruling was controversial in that it fueled resistance from the pharmaceutical industry, a group with significant political clout. Pharmaceutical industry interests were well recognized and represented in Parliament, making it hard to pass any legislative amendments. During the parliamentary proceedings, one MP highlighted "the effectiveness, profitability and success of the pharmaceutical industry . . . [with] a record trade surplus of £1.1 billion in 1990. The UK pharmaceutical industry was the third largest positive contributor to the nation's balance of trade . . . What then should the Government be doing? They should

adopt the posture of supporting their industries."[13] Heated debate between the parties and legislative deadlock ensued. The debate over patent law amendments pitted pro-EU integration proponents directly
against those supporting the pharmaceutical industry, a crucial stakeholder in the UK economy. The ECJ ruling highlighted antagonism between domestic interests.

Given the political stakes, the UK refused to budge on its patent law.
Several years elapsed. The UK drafted new legislation but made little
movement toward passage. In the 1995 annual report on compliance
with ECJ rulings, the Commission dismally noted, "The UK has notified the Commission of draft legislation. The Commission is awaiting its
enactment. Progress."[14] It wasn't until nearly seven years after the ruling,
when the Labour Party wrested control from the Conservatives to con-
solidate its power, that Parliament finally passed revisions to UK patent
law. The revisions brought the UK into compliance.[15] What this fraught
process illustrates is that when governments have many domestic political constraints—in this instance, legislative divisions—there is ample opportunity for stakeholders to obstruct compliance. Here, the pharmaceutical industry had a stake in maintaining compulsory licensing and
successfully urged MPs to impede compliance.

In light of Brexit, it might come as no surprise that the United Kingdom has been especially resistant to the ECJ. And yet the country is not
alone in its obstinacy. Many other states that are seemingly more amenable to EU authority have also struggled to comply with adverse infringement rulings. Often, these compliance problems can be traced back to
domestic institutional veto points. This is especially noticeable where
interest groups wield strong regional influence and are able to pressure
legislators.

Another illustration comes from a dispute brought by the European
Commission against Germany in 2005. The Commission challenged a
decades-old German law that protected Volkswagen, the car manufacturer (C-112/05).[16] The lawsuit followed a multiyear enforcement effort
by the Commission.[17] The Volkswagen law was thought to be a "glar-
ing example of a European country's protecting its industrial champion
from foreign ownership" and the court case was widely expected to have
an "important impact on the pace of integration in the single European
market," according to a *New York Times* report.[18]

The Commission argued the Volkswagen law infringed on the freedom of establishment and movement of capital in the European Union—

two requirements of the single market. The law placed constraints on shareholder voting rights and effectively granted special privileges to the German state of Lower Saxony (Blauberger 2014, 463). It prevented foreign buyers (especially from the United Kingdom) from obtaining significant shares. In a 2007 judgment, the court sided with the Commission and ordered Germany to amend its law. The adverse ruling was delivered at a sensitive time "when Germany [was] increasingly nervous about foreign investors, particularly wealthy state-owned investment funds and hedge funds, buying into what it [deemed] strategically important industries."[19]

Germany did not respond favorably to the ruling. Conflicting regional and corporate interests within Germany fueled legislative divisions in the Bundestag. On the one hand, complying with the court's judgment by completely abolishing the law would clear the way for a competing auto manufacturer, Porsche, to obtain controlling shares of Volkswagen. This side captured attention of legislators from the German state of Baden-Württemberg, where Porsche was headquartered. On the other hand, defying the ECJ and preserving the law favored a major employer in Lower Saxony with thousands of jobs on the line. Trade unions saw political influence through the huge company as a guarantor of jobs. Political tension over the law intensified as Germany's previous chancellor, Gerhard Schröder, accused the EU interfering in member states' own business.[20] Nearly a year of legislative holdup ensued. By late September 2008, the two states continued to "squabble in the Bundesrat, but the chamber then voted its blessing to the Merkel government's reform law."[21] This reform entailed minor modifications; Germany retained the provisions of the original law that protected regional stakeholders, arguably the most controversial part of the historical Volkswagen law.[22]

The Commission deemed the revised law noncompliant—a continued breach of EU obligations. Several more years elapsed before the Commission pursued a second lawsuit aiming to establish Germany's continued noncompliance (C-95/12).[23] The Commission sought two penalties against Germany: First, they requested €31,114 per day from the 2007 ruling until the state complied. Second, the Commission sought a €282,725 daily fine from the date of a ruling in the second case until the Volkswagen law was revised to satisfy EU rules.[24] The court delivered its verdict in October 2013. It sided with Germany, recognizing the state's argument that Volkswagen was a strategic national asset that needed to be protected. It absolved the member state of any further compliance burden. In this case, legislative veto players prolonged the dispute, and

the German government was ultimately able to make only minor amendments in order to sufficiently satisfy the court.

6.3.2 Informal constraints

National parliaments are not the only sources of domestic political constraints. Informal constraints can also pose obstacles to compliance with
ECJ rulings. Some court decisions strike down national administrative
rules for being inconsistent with the European single market. And while
an executive order or rule modification might be all that is needed to
come into compliance, there are potent political pressures that complicate the seemingly simple process. Politicians face informal constraints
from influential interest groups. Those groups, which often rely on market protections struck down by the ECJ, can punish politicians. And
even when a government formally adopts compliant policies on the
books, these groups can make implementation far more difficult.

An example is the dispute over Greece's subsidies to its own airline
industry. For years, Greece generously subsidized Olympic Airways
and ultimately ran afoul of state aid rules. Under EU law, state aid—
government subsidies that distort competition or the free market—is
considered unlawful unless the European Commission grants a member
state an explicit exemption. The Commission investigated Greece and,
finding obstacles to competition in the EU internal market, urged the
state to reform.[25] Greece largely ignored the decision, and in 2003, the
Commission brought its complaint to the ECJ (C-415/03). The court determined that the aid, which took the form of loan guarantees, debt re-
ductions amounting to GRD 427 billion, capital injections totaling GRD
40.8 billion, and other benefits, was "incompatible with the common
market within the meaning of Article 87(1) of the EC Treaty"[26]

In order to comply with the court's adverse ruling, Greece would
have had to end the program and Olympic Airlines would have had to
repay the aid. This, of course, presented enforcement obstacles. Greece
informed the Commission that it anticipated significant difficulties
"regard[ing] . . . the national procedures for recovery of the aid at issue"
(C-369/07).[27] In other words, the Greek government saw practical obstacles to inducing compliance from the airline itself. Instead of recovering
the years of EU-inconsistent aid, Greece imposed a modest tax.

Why was it so challenging for Greece to reverse its subsidies and recover aid money? The Ministry of Transport and Telecommunications

and the Ministry of National Economy were the two government agencies responsible for carrying out compliance efforts. Neither was vulnerable to the usual checks and balances that regularly foil legislative compliance. The answer appears to lie in the strength of the airline unions and the political access they enjoyed. Featherstone and Papadimitriou (2007) argue that "the relationship between government and the unions of [Olympic Airlines] . . . reflected the complexity, clientelism, corruption and conflict evident in the wider system of Greek labor relations" (47). The case study highlights:

> [Union leaders] lobby directly government ministers and party bosses with whom they enjoyed open channels of communication through their party-political affiliations . . . Union strength was evident in their strike capacity and successive governments had acted in fear of them. Moreover, given the record of failed attempts at reform, the unions could rationally adopt a skepticism towards the will and capability of fresh government projects. The Olympic unions were, in short, *perceived by government as veto-players* . . . The net effect, in strategic terms, was of the contest between ministers and the unions. (emphasis added)[28]

With the government ministries beholden to interest group politics, Greece made little progress toward compliance. These domestic stakeholders effectively blocked government reform, using their political leverage over government ministers.

The Commission brought a second lawsuit in August 2007, under Article 228 EC, alleging Greece's continued noncompliance. The ECJ ruled that Greece remained in violation of EU obligations. The court upheld the requirements set forth in its first ruling and imposed additional penalties. Specifically, it ordered a "penalty payment of EUR 16,000 for each day of delay in adopting the measures necessary to comply with the [first] judgment" and ordered Greece "to pay to the Commission of the European Communities . . . a lump sum of EUR 2 million."[29] Subsequent reports from the Commission in 2014 indicate Greece had taken only partial steps to recover the state aid.[30] This case demonstrates that domestic stakeholders can leverage their political influence over a government's administrative agencies to obstruct compliance with court rulings.

The influence of domestic stakeholders need not take the form of such obvious obstructionism. Veto players can foil implementation even when compliant policies have been officially adopted (Haverland 2000).

Subnational actors (e.g., regional authorities) have to cooperate in order to give practical effect to EU-compliant policies. Those same political actors may be sensitive to local interest groups that oppose compliance.

Federal member states tend to blame recalcitrant subnational authorities that are in charge of implementing European law for their compliance problems (Börzel 2003, 207). Especially when subnational enforcement is weak, firms in one region might flout single-market policies. The more political constraints in government and the more political influence those groups wield, the more likely it is that they can block enforcement of policies already in place (Falkner et al. 2007). The Commission recognizes that firms can obstruct compliance in this way. In its 1986 annual report, the Commission explained, "while the obstacles to trade which still exist are to some extent due to resistance on the part of Member States to dismantling neo-protectionist borders, it is also clear that . . . private citizens and firms . . . help to significantly maintain this state of affairs."[31] In short, import-competing interest groups and other nongovernment actors can effectively undercut ECJ rulings. Even if a government implements policies that comply with the court, such groups can limit the ruling's economic impact.

This mechanism is clearly illustrated in an agriculture dispute known as the "Spanish strawberries case."[32] Here, the French government tacitly allowed barriers to trade. The controversy began when French farmers started destroying imported fruits and vegetables and intimidating retailers. The farmers' reasoning was that Spain—then a recent admit to the European Union—was flooding the European market with low-priced produce. Through these tactics, the farmers tried to curb competition. For over a decade, the Commission had received complaints that French authorities were passively ignoring the issue. Private individuals and French farmers continued to commit violent acts directed against agricultural products from other member states.[33]

The Commission frequently reminded the French government of their obligations under the treaty with respect to the free movement of goods. The reminders had little effect. The French government ignored the matter, tacitly permitting private individuals to obstruct agricultural imports. French authorities made only superficial formal efforts to comply with the court by, for example, vaguely stating their intention to comply. Spain continued to urge the European Commission to investigate. Faced with an impending intringement investigation, "the French Government stressed that it had adopted all the measures open to it in order to ensure the free movement of goods in its territory and . . . substantially contained the number of acts of violence."[34] Regardless, the Commission determined that the French government's measures were insufficient. According to the Commission, "the French Minister for Agriculture stated that, although he disapproved of and condemned the violence by the farmers, he in no way contemplated any intervention by the police in order to put a stop to it."[35] Escalating the dispute, the Commission subsequently brought a formal complaint to the ECJ.

Meanwhile, the French government defended its position as an antidumping measure. It argued that "the dissatisfaction of French farmers is due to the considerable increase in exports of Spanish products since the accession of the Kingdom of Spain, which has led to a substantial fall in prices magnified by . . . dumping prices charged by Spanish producers. The French market for fruit and vegetables was seriously disrupted by the fact that the transitional [accession] period . . . had not been accompanied by any mechanism for monitoring the export prices charged by Spanish producers."[36] The Court was not persuaded. In December 1997, the ECJ ruled that France had imposed a de facto barrier to trade by failing to enforce community law.

France continued to resist. Farmers had long formed an influential interest group (T. Hofmann 2013) with a strong presence in the National Assembly (F. Wilson 1987, 112). They exerted considerable pressure on the Senate to represent their interests. With polarized domestic politics, it was unlikely that even an executive push for compliance would be effective against this powerful constituency (Hall and Keeler 2001). Farmer influence waned between the ruling and the early 2000s as the farmer population precipitously declined by a third. With weakening farmer interests, the political climate shifted, making compliance more feasible. The case remained unresolved until 2005, when France finally demonstrated that its agriculture ministry had enforced the rules (European Commission 2004, 16).[37] This dispute demonstrates how resistance to ECJ trade-liberalizing rulings can arise not only from formal channels but also from private stakeholders who wield political influence.

In summary, divisive politics can hinder compliance with ECJ rulings by making it more difficult to implement new policies, legislative and administrative alike, and enforce those policies already in place. These examples show that domestic veto players can arise from formal institutional checks within legislatures. They can also arise from informal means: access points that enable interest groups to exert political influence. Consequently, interest groups—broadly defined—can either deter government agencies from implementing compliant policies or deter the enforcement of policies on the books.

As these case studies suggest, compliance problems have undercut the goal of achieving a single regional market. The first case likely impacted the production and sales of pharmaceuticals, impeding imports across the United Kingdom's borders. The second case highlighted regional interests and showed how German support to Volkswagen violated multiple aspects of the goal of the single market. The third case showed that market distortions created by Greek subsidies favored the domestic Olympic Airways at the expense of comparable competitors. Finally, the fourth case showed an impact on trade in agricultural goods—specifically, fruits and vegetables imported into France. Each showed how compliance problems are, at least in part, attributable to political constraints in member states.

These are only a few instances in which trade-related ECJ rulings have impacted European economic integration. Many additional cases have spanned a wide range of goods and services whose production and sales help to drive the European economy. While each dispute may carry rather small trade stakes when evaluated on its own, there may be important cumulative effects. Each state has been involved in dozens of these lawsuits. If a member state routinely loses ECJ rulings on economic issues and tends to comply with those rulings, we should expect to observe aggregate effects. That is, we should expect that state to show deeper economic integration with the European market, all else equal.

A government that loses numerous trade-related lawsuits is obligated to remove barriers to EU commerce. When governments remove many such barriers—for example, revising intellectual property rules, revoking airline subsidies, deregulating transportation, and enforcing free trade rules for agricultural goods—there should be a cumulative effect on their integration into the European economy. One way a government achieves deeper economic integration is when it enables more imports from other nations within the community. A government that complies with judicial orders should experience an increase in intra-EU imports over previous levels. In other words, the more frequent the court's admonition, the greater the subsequent trade boost should be *if the member state complies*. Conversely, a government that is frequently found in breach but routinely disregards those pro-integration rulings, should display smaller increases—if any—in its imports from the rest of the EU.

As we have seen in the preceding chapters, states vary widely in their response to rebuke from the WTO's Dispute Settlement Body. Similar expectations hold for the ECJ. The more domestic constraints a government has—both institutional and partisan—the less likely it should be to comply with adverse rulings. Less compliance should then lead to smaller trade boosts from these rulings, all else equal. In other words, domestic constraints should dull the effects on intra-European trade that we would have expected to observe in the wake of the ECJ's interventions. Thus on average, the *interaction* of domestic constraints and trade-liberalizing rulings should be associated with smaller boosts in intra-EU imports into defendant states.

A systematic test of the argument requires (1) identifying observable implications of compliance and noncompliance in ECJ disputes, (2) isolating the ECJ cases that carry clear implications for European economic integration, and (3) differentiating among the different forms of domestic political constraints that are expected to impede compliance.

Before turning to a systematic empirical test of the theory, two caveats must be noted: First, it is possible that actors who care most about a ruling do not enjoy political access. Perhaps only organized interest groups—pharmaceutical companies, airline unions, or farmers—can exert sufficient political pressure to block policy. In order to address this concern, the empirical tests that follow measure multiple dimensions of the domestic environment: divisions within the legislature, between different branches of government, and in the ideological positions of parties. Second, not all infringement disputes are about deregulation, where a state must dismantle barriers to EU imports in order to comply; some disputes are about reregulation. So ECJ rulings require governments to establish different policies to achieve common market standards. Reregulation disputes should also be sensitive to domestic constraints. When the ECJ orders a state to reregulate in order to establish the free movement of goods, it is asking for revised policy. Revised or new policies are still vulnerable to veto players, so the argument should still apply.

6.4 Data and model

6.4.1 Trade and economic integration

A major challenge for understanding European economic integration is determining whether governments abide by the legal decisions of the

ECJ. The European Commission and scholars alike struggle to identify whether and when governments correctly adopt legal decisions in
the thousands of infringement disputes the court has adjudicated. Official compliance statistics are incomplete because they hinge on effective monitoring (König and Mäder 2014), and the Commission struggles
to detect complex trade barriers. The Commission has long recognized
that many infringements involve "obstacles to free movement for both
industrial and agricultural products. [They] are taking more sophisticated forms and are often deliberate" (European Commission 1983, 7).
Moreover, even when single-market policies are formally implemented,
states may not consistently enforce them. The Commission notes: "beyond the formal incorporation of Community directives into national
law, there is the problem of how the rules are actually applied by the national authorities."[38] If these kinds of problems are common, the Commission might routinely overlook noncompliance by member states.

Once the ECJ delivers an adverse ruling, member states are given
significant leeway to correctly implement that decision. As the examples above demonstrate, governments often fail to implement unfavorable legal rulings. The Commission's ability to track implementation is
imperfect at best, and it is likely that many instances of persistent noncompliance go undetected, or at least unchallenged (Andersen 2012;
Taborowski 2012).

Detection problems are compounded by the fact that governments are
savvy at evading unfavorable legal decisions. Andreas Hofmann (2018b)
finds that it is not at all uncommon for "national policy-makers, admin-
istrations and the judiciary [to] fail to comply with individual rulings"
from the ECJ (285). Member state authorities, Hofmann argues, "have
developed multiple strategies to limit the practical effect of controversial
lines of ECJ case-law," and they have devised numerous "work–arounds"
to evade ECJ decisions (285). Similarly, Batory (2016) argues that member states sometimes enact symbolic or superficial measures to appear
compliant with EU law while resisting substantial reforms they deem too
costly. Batory explains, "symbolic and creative compliance occur when
an addressee, in this case a member state, pretends to align its behaviour
with the prescribed rule or changes its behaviour in superficial ways that
leave the addressee's original objective intact" (889). In other words, a defendant government might formally abide by the court's judgment but resist the corresponding policy effect that deepens economic cooperation.

An example of this can be found in an ECJ dispute over an allegedly discriminatory Danish tax law on spirits. In this case, the court struck down the tax law as a thinly veiled import barrier (Case 171/78).[39] A case study by Rasmussen (1986) demonstrates that while the Danish government eliminated the policy in question, it recreated the protectionist environment through a different tax law (also see Carrubba and Gabel 2015, 79n47). Denmark effectively preserved its barrier to imports, ignoring the aim of the ruling to deepen economic cooperation. As this example highlights, neither the ECJ nor the Commission nor any other EU authorities can reliably construct an accurate record of whether member states comply with adverse judgments and whether any measures taken have the intended effect.

Scholars have previously approached this empirical problem by focusing their attention on detailed case studies where the process and compliance outcomes can be traced. For example, in examining environmental and social policy disputes concerning Germany, Panke (2007) shows that ECJ judgments sometimes fail to induce compliance by member states. Likewise, Martinsen (2015a) highlights crucial cases in which member states failed to comply with rulings on labor market regulations. Other research on compliance in the EU takes a similar case study approach (Slaughter, Stone Sweet, and Weiler 1998).

However, the literature has yet to systematically identify second-order (non)compliance with ECJ rulings across the wide range of infringement cases and member states. In other words, no EU scholarship of which I am aware assembles an equivalent dataset to that presented in chapter 4 with respect to the WTO. There is good reason for this void. Whereas there were only about 150 WTO disputes where second-order compliance was at issue, the ECJ has ruled on several hundred trade-related infringement disputes alone since the late 1980s, when the Single European Act went into effect. There have been nearly a thousand ECJ rulings in that same time period if we include cases that affect other aspects of economic integration (e.g., labor conditions and the free movement of workers). Thus a direct measure of *policy compliance* may be prohibitively difficult to create.

Instead, this chapter focuses on the observable *economic consequences* of (non)compliance. Trade-liberalizing rulings from the ECJ should have a direct bearing on a government's economic integration within the EU. When a government faithfully complies with trade-liberalizing rulings, it dismantles explicit or tacit barriers to trade. At least in theory, with fewer barriers, intra-European imports into that country should expand. A government that loses ECJ rulings and complies is expected—on average—to increase its reliance on commerce with the remainder of the European community. Conversely, if the ruling did little to sway national policy or practice, a government's economic integration within the community should change little, all else equal. Therefore, intra-EU trade patterns provide an imperfect yet informative measure of whether that country has deepened its economic ties with the rest of the EU in response to adverse rulings. Fluctuations in trade following trade-liberalizing ECJ rulings should track a country's economic integration. Therefore, it should track a country's general tendency toward compliance with the court.

There are several reasons that intra-EU trade is meaningful and informative measure of deep cooperation in the EU (Carrubba 2005). First, a trade-based metric reflects the EU's founding goal of dismantling internal barriers to commerce. By the institution's own assertion, the original purpose of the EU was to foster peace through economic cooperation: "the idea being that countries who trade with one another become economically interdependent and so are more likely to avoid conflict" (European Commission 2017). Changes in intra-EU trade track countries' progress toward dismantling those barriers to commerce. Additionally, reliable trade data are reported annually for all EU members so that comprehensive information is available.

Second, using trade to measure the economic consequences of compliance can be more revealing than examining the actual policies that create or dismantle barriers to trade within the EU. As argued in previous chapters, measuring compliance alone would fail to distinguish between superficial and substantively meaningful actions that advance international cooperation. Just because a government formally implements EU law through policy does not mean that it has properly applied those policies, nor does it mean that the targets of those policies—subnational actors, firms, etc.—follow suit. The French government's noncompliance in the Spanish strawberries case illustrates this point exactly. If we only considered policy compliance, superficial policy concessions governments make to follow ECJ rulings would be indistinguishable from substantial efforts that dismantle barriers to the single market. Trade flows, by contrast, indicate the economic consequences of pro-integration policy reforms. They should only follow substantial policy concessions that promote deeper international cooperation.

Third, infringement disputes are a crucial tool the Commission uses to broadly enforce the single market. At face value, it might appear that infringement disputes are very narrowly focused and would only have very small effects on trade. For example, an infringement dispute might address whether French wine is imported into Germany. Yet this is not the full story. The infringement process is set up to be far more inclusive than a single ruling on a single sector might suggest. Through the active use of precedent, the ECJ generates rulings that strike down obstacles to the European single market. The Commission, in seeking out infringement disputes, and the court, in constructing its legal decisions, both craft the course of European integration (Carrubba 2005; Carrubba, Gabel, and Hankla 2008). So even though a country's compliance in individual disputes may have only a small impact on aggregate trade patterns, fluctuations in trade will reflect a broader trend toward economic integration that is forced through litigation. Measuring integration with aggregate EU trade flows reflects how ECJ litigation is actually used.

However, there are problems with relying on intra-EU trade flows as a consequence of compliance with ECJ trade rulings. Governments may make good-faith efforts to reform policy to comply with adverse rulings only to find that firms and markets are resistant to adaptation. As shown in chapter 5, compliance may be a necessary condition for pro-integration economic impact, but will not always produce those changes in trade. Reverse causality is a related concern. Some scholarship has indicated that member states that trade more with the rest of the European Union find themselves running afoul of EU law less often, at least in certain sectors (König and Luetgert 2009; Perkins and Neumayer 2007). This may result in fewer ECJ disputes. According to this logic, then, countries that expand trade with the EU increase their dependency on the community and have weaker incentives to evade single-market rules. They subsequently experience fewer trade-liberalizing rulings from the ECJ. Yet other research suggests an inverse relationship: high levels of intra-EU trade correlates with less compliance (Börzel et al. 2010). By using time lags and over-time trends—trade in the years following adverse ECJ rulings—the research design ameliorates some endogeneity concerns. This is addressed in greater detail below.

6.4.2 Explanatory variables: ECJ rulings and domestic constraints

The first explanatory variable is whether the Commission sued a state over trade-related infringements and prevailed. This counts one or more trade-liberalizing rulings for each country and year, 1987 to 2012. In contrast to previous scholarship, this study covers years since the European single-market initiative has come into full effect. This is an important update because pressing challenges to EU economic integration have arisen in the last two decades (e.g., the global financial crisis of 2008, which strained the Eurozone). I analyze all EU-15 states that have been EU members over this period. This distinguishes the current analysis from previous studies that have focused exclusively on the six core members (Carrubba 2005). The broader scope is critical: EU expansion has brought new challenges in harmonizing deeply dissimilar economies (Meunier and McNamara 2007), especially related to differences between the original members and newer admits.

To create the first explanatory variable, I only count ECJ rulings that are relevant to trade. This includes disputes over the internal market, taxation and the customs union, competition policy, freedom of enterprise, and financial affairs. Policies that inhibit the free movement of goods, taxation schemes that encourage consumers to buy local instead of imported goods, and technical standards that affect competition, for example, are all trade-related. These are the disputes that are likely to have a measurable impact on intra-EU trade. In an extension to the analysis, I separately consider agriculture infringements to trace sector-level effects.

I exclude rulings that are unrelated to trade. The Commission also prosecutes violations of EU law on environmental and social protection, labor standards, health and safety, administrative and budgetary matters, information technology and media, legal services, education, transportation, and energy policy. I do *not* count any of these cases because they do not have clear implications for trade.

In fact, sometimes these policies create a direct conflict with the internal market. For example, when the European Union raises environmental standards, complying with those same provisions could interfere with the free movement of goods.[40] Although these disputes are critical for EU integration, their economic impact varies widely.

The following analysis relies on two data sources. The first is the Database on Infringement Incidents in the European Union (Börzel and Knoll 2012), which identifies the subject and legal outcome of each infringement. From this database, I selected infringements that were (1) trade-related, (2) prosecuted at the court, and (3) ruled to be violations of EU law. The data cover rulings from 1987 to 1999. Second, I created a database from ECJ records for adverse trade rulings from 2000 to 2012, as discussed in Peritz (2018). I identified all cases in which the Commission sued a state under the infringement procedure (Article 258 of TFEU). If the Commission prevailed on at least one legal claim, the ruling was coded as "adverse." I read each of these 825 judgments to determine whether the case was trade-related, counting only the categoriesnoted above. This produced 261 qualifying cases of adverse trade-liberalizing rulings. I did not find any cases where the Commission sought to limit imports.[41]

In some years, governments experienced no trade-liberalizing rulings. But in others, they confronted several. Austria, Luxembourg, and Sweden had the fewest incidents; Belgium, France, and Italy had the most. In one single year, France lost nine lawsuits over trade-related issues. In a typical year, Italy lost two or three.

The statistical analysis uses a binary indicator to denote one or more rulings because sometimes a country would face multiple closely related infringements. I expect to observe a positive correlation between adverse trade rulings and the subsequent import share. The expectation is that all else equal, countries that are challenged by adverse trade rulings have been advised to dismantle barriers to intra-EU trade. If they meaningfully follow through, then such countries will see an uptick in intra-EU imports in the following year(s). However, there is another way to think about the relationship between intra-EU trade and adverse trade rulings: perhaps countries with a lower baseline level of intra-EU imports have more barriers in place and are subjected to more adverse trade rulings. To guard against this possibility, as discussed further below, I run my analysis with country random effects, which control for each country's baseline trade and thereby isolates the relevant deviations.

The other explanatory variable is domestic political constraints in the defendant government. To capture the range of political constraints that may affect compliance, I use five alternative measurements (Beck et al. 2001; Keefer and Stasavage 2003): The first variable is *Veto Points*, which accounts for formal checks and partisan divisions in countries over time (Henisz 2002). The veto points variable uses a spatial model of political interactions among government branches by measuring the number of independent branches with veto power and the distribution of political preferences across these branches. As noted before, the variable ranges from 0 to 1, with a higher number denoting more constraints. I use the version that accounts for the role of the judiciary, since some ECJ infringement rulings have been challenged by national courts. Recall from the previous chapters that veto points partly reflect a country's democratic institutions. Since all EU-15 states are full democracies, the countries included in this chapter vary far less in their veto points than those in the WTO.

Second is the formal institutional checks in government, *Checks*, which ranges between 2 and 16, with higher numbers denoting more constraints. The third is partisan *Fractionalization* in the legislature. Ranging from 0 to 1, fractionalization measures the probability that two legislators picked at random will be from different parties. Fractionalization increases with the number of parties, particularly when they are of similar size.

Fourth, *Polarization* measures the maximum gap between the ideological orientation of the executive party and the four principle parties of the legislature, using information on party platforms. Despite certain weaknesses (e.g., Esteban and Schneider 2008), this metric captures divergent policy preferences.

The fifth variable is the *Effective Number of Parties* in government. Following convention, this is measured as the reciprocal of the sum of the squared seat shares of all parties in the government, or equivalently, one divided by the Herfindahl-Hirschman concentration index (Laakso and Taagepera 1979; Neto and Cox 1997). Compared to legislative fractionalization, this measure is somewhat less sensitive to the presence of small parties. Correlations between the variables are in the appendix for chapter 6.

I expect the interaction between adverse trade rulings and domestic political constraints to be negatively correlated with import shares. As discussed below, the statistical analysis includes country random effects to control for each country's baseline intra-EU imports. Thus the analysis asks: if the country had been subjected to adverse trade rulings but had fewer domestic political constraints, would the subsequent intra-EU import share have been higher? The counterfactual is the country's own baseline trade levels when it was subjected to adverse rulings but in the alternate scenario where its domestic constraints differ.

6.4.3 Control variables

Numerous other factors shape a country's imports. First, I control for economic predictors of intra-European trade (World Bank 2013). Gross domestic product (*GDP*) should be positively correlated with import share because the largest economies are highly integrated. *GDP per capita* is included because affluent countries tend to import more goods. *Export* dependence (measured as share of GDP) is included because some trade violations boost export-oriented industries, potentially confounding the estimated effects. Table 6.4 controls for the *Agriculture* value added.

Second, I control for legal factors that mediate the impact of adverse trade rulings. Legal tradition is thought to matter (Carrubba and Murrah 2005; Mattli and Slaughter 1998): under constitutional monism, international treaties are directly applicable as national law whereas under dualism, treaties must be transposed to take effect. This implies that *Dualist* states face greater difficulties implementing EU law. Some governments tend to neglect EU legal obligations at the outset. The *Transposition Deficit*, the percentage of EU internal market directives that are incorrectly transposed each year (König and Mäder 2013), should be positively correlated with intra-EU trade. Conflicts over EU integration have been litigated both through the preliminary reference system and the infringement procedure. For each country and year, I count the number of trade-related *Preliminary References* on which the ECJ delivered a judgment. This should be positively correlated with intra-EU trade.

Third, I control for political factors. To account for a defendant's ability to comply with ECJ rulings, I rely on two measures (Holmberg and Rothstein 2012). *Government Effectiveness* is a composite index that captures quality of public services, political capture of civil services, policy implementation, and the credibility of a government's commitment to such policies (Kaufmann, Kraay, and Mastruzzi 2010). Effective governments are better equipped to implement rulings, deepening EU economic integration. *Government Debt* controls for the possibility that highly indebted governments tend to suffer from bureaucratic inefficiencies (Kaufmann and Kraay 2015) and are ineffective. I control for whether a member state has a bicameral legislature, *Bicameralism*, which could exacerbate political obstacles since legislation adopted by a lower house need not pass in the upper house.

Other political controls address a defendant's willingness to comply. Falkner et al. (2007) argue that EU governments with less leverage over EU decision-making—in the Council, for example—are more likely to oppose integration through noncompliance rather than challenge the proposals during the law-making process: "opposition through the back door" (452). A government's clout in EU institutions is one proxy for whether a government obtains EU directives that align with its preferences. I control for each state's voting power in the Council of the European Union using the Shapley-Shubik Index, *SSI council* (Bräuninger and König 2005; Schneider 2011; Shapley and Shubik 1954). I expect states with more voting power to comply more often, leading to greater economic integration. Last, governments may be willing to comply when there is popular support for EU membership, which I measure using Eurobarometer survey data (European Commission 2016).

6.4.4 Statistical model

This analysis aims to answer two questions: Did a country demonstrate higher trade integration after an adverse ECJ ruling, as compared to its own prior levels? And if so, was the boost in integration smaller for countries with more domestic political constraints? The data for this analysis are in a time-series cross-sectional format, with observations by country and year. Because the analysis relies on panel data and is concerned with country responses to ECJ rulings, it is useful to include country random effects to isolate how each country's intra-EU imports differ from its own baseline levels over time.

The dependent variable, intra-EU import share (Y_{jt}), follows an approximately normal distribution, and a linear regression model is a reasonable first step for the analysis. However, the import share is a bounded dependent variable—it must fall between 0 and 1. It is useful to explicitly account for this attribute. Thus in robustness checks, I also use a generalized linear model (beta regression) and find that my results hold.

The statistical analysis uses the following model:

$$Y_{jt} = \alpha_j + \beta_1 Adv.Rulings_{j,t-1} + \beta_2 Constraints_{j,t-1}$$
$$+ \beta_3 Adv.Rulings_{j,t-1} \times Constraints_{j,t-1} + \beta_4 X_{j,t-1} + \varepsilon_{j,t-1}$$

Coefficients estimate the effects of adverse trade rulings, domestic constraints, and their interaction. I expect β_1 to be positive and β_3 to be negative. The controls are denoted X and the error ε.

The model includes country random effects to account for omitted variables that differ between countries and over time. Each country j

receives an intercept α_j; the intercepts are normally distributed. Random effects are more appropriate than fixed effects, as indicated by a Hausman test (see the appendix for chapter 6).

The explanatory and control variables are lagged by one year. This reflects the delay between the ruling and policy reform and the policy's delayed impact on trade. I selected the one-year lag based on findings in prior research. Gabel et al. (2012) examine the effect of pro-commission ECJ rulings on intra-EU imports with an autoregressive distributed lag model. For a subset of the rulings considered, they find a positive effect on intra-EU imports when evaluating one- and two-year lags; the latter was of greater significance, reflecting a cumulative effect as time progresses (Gabel et al. 2012, 1133).[42] I employ a one-year lag to isolate the impact of rulings issued immediately prior without confounding the estimates from multiple years of prior rulings. I also checked a two-year lag and found nearly identical results (see appendix).

A brief note on the statistical approach is warranted. The structure of the data in this analysis of ECJ rulings differs from that in the preceding empirical chapters on the WTO. This follows differences in the two courts' enforcement activity. In the WTO, there were a small number of adverse trade rulings with different plaintiffs, respondents, trade barriers, and products in question. Each individual dispute's trade impact could be estimated by comparing the disputants' trade to trade among countries that were similar but otherwise uninvolved in the dispute at hand.

By contrast, that statistical design is not possible in the context of ECJ infringement rulings. The ECJ has ruled on many hundreds of trade-related infringement disputes, with multiple rulings per defendant country per year. The sole plaintiff is the European Commission, and the trade flows in question comes from all other member states— the disputed imports cannot be attributed to any single exporter country. Likewise, many of these disputes affect a wide range of products, making it untenable to use the same fine-grained, product-level trade data employed in chapter 5. Instead, in this chapter, the unit of analysis is the country-year: panel data where EU countries are subjected to multiple adverse ECJ infringement rulings on trade each year. This data structure reflects the frequency of ECJ enforcement and the fact that the Commission brings lawsuits on behalf of the broader EU membership. To address heterogeneity across countries, I use country random effects.

6.5 Results

Countries that lose infringement lawsuits deepen their economic ties to the European Union. This finding suggests that, on average, the ECJ can push member states toward deeper economic integration and that governments tend to abide by judicial demands. The more trade-related infringement rulings a government loses, the larger its subsequent increase in intra-EU trade, all else equal. Yet all is not equal; domestic politics within member states intervene. When a country has many domestic constraints, the effect of ECJ rulings on economic integration is diminished.

6.5.1 Trade-related infringements

Table 6.1 presents results with the different measures of political constraints and economic controls. Four of the five measures provide statistically significant support for my theory. There is a positive direct association between adverse trade rulings and EU import share. The interaction term has a statistically significant negative coefficient for institutional checks in a government, fractionalization of its legislature, political polarization, and its effective number of parties. Using the *count* of adverse trade rulings, rather than the binary indicator, produces similar results.

However, the veto points variable is not a significant predictor.[43] When states are subjected to adverse trade rulings, their veto points have little bearing on whether or not they report subsequent increases in intra-EU imports. The likely explanation is the relative similarity of EU-15 member states. All are robust democracies and, with the exception of Greece, vary only modestly in terms of their veto points (ranging from 0.7 to 0.9). In comparison, the WTO disputants display a far wider range in veto points, even among democratic countries (0.3 to 0.9).[44] The Henisz (2000) measure of veto points may be too coarse to capture relevant variation among EU members. More nuance among democracies is captured by the checks variable, which accounts for the constellation of majority and minority parties in government.

Because the domestic political constraints variables in this analysis have different scales and distributions, it is useful to visualize their impact in terms of marginal effects. Figure 6.1 illustrates the estimated marginal effects for four measures of political constraints: *Checks*, legislative *Fractionalization*, *Polarization*, and the *Effective Number of*

TABLE 6.1 **Impact of Trade Rulings and Political Constraints on Import Share, Economic Controls**

	Intra-EU import share$_{jt}$				
	(1)	(2)	(3)	(4)	(5)
Adverse Tr. Ruling × Veto Points	0.03				
	(0.06)				
Veto Points	−0.06				
	(0.06)				
Adverse Tr. Ruling × Checks		−0.01**			
		(0.004)			
Checks		−0.001			
		(0.003)			
Adverse Tr. Ruling × Fractionalization			−0.13**		
			(0.05)		
Fractionalization			−0.02		
			(0.07)		
Adverse Tr. Ruling × Polarization				−0.01**	
				(0.01)	
Polarization				0.01**	
				(0.01)	
Adverse Tr. Ruling × Effective No. Parties					−0.01**
					(0.01)
Effective No. Parties					−0.01
					(0.01)
Adverse Tr. Rulings	−0.03	0.02	0.08**	0.01	0.01
	(0.04)	(0.02)	(0.04)	(0.01)	(0.01)
GDP[†]	0.07***	0.08***	0.08***	0.07***	0.07***
	(0.01)	(0.01)	(0.01)	(0.01)	(0.01)
GDP per capita[†]	−0.09**	−0.10**	−0.09**	−0.09**	−0.09**
	(0.04)	(0.04)	(0.04)	(0.04)	(0.04)
Export Share GDP[†]	−0.11***	−0.11***	−0.12***	−0.11***	−0.11***
	(0.02)	(0.02)	(0.02)	(0.02)	(0.02)
N	342	341	333	343	343
Countries	15	15	15	15	15
Log Likelihood	522	517	512	523	523
Std. Dev. (Intercept)	0.21	0.22	0.23	0.23	0.23

Note: Models estimated with R. All specifications include country random intercepts. Explanatory variables are lagged by one year. Significance codes *p<0.1; **p<0.05; ***p<0.01. [†]Log units.

Parties. Because the marginal effect for the veto players composite variable is null, it is not shown. These figures show how increases in domestic political constraints tend to undercut the trade-promoting effect of adverse ECJ rulings. Importantly, the plots show the distribution of the variables, demonstrating the range in which we can be confident about the statistical association.

Figure 6.1(a) demonstrates that the positive association between adverse trade rulings and imports is diminished when a government has many checks. Most EU member states featured a moderate number of checks in the years the analysis examines. The small number of countries with the highest number of checks at certain times—Denmark in the 1990s, Ireland from the late 1990s to early 2000s, and Netherlands in the early 2000s—are influential in driving the correlations. For these countries and time periods, more parties are needed in the government coalition to maintain a majority. In the remainder of country-years, domestic checks appear less influential in steering the negative correlation.

Figure 6.1(b) confirms a similar pattern for highly fractionalized legislatures. Here, the distribution of observations is far more even. There is a consistent negative correlation across the range of this variable, indicating that no particular countries are driving the negative marginal effect. Thus party fractionalization is consistently related to obstruction.

Also shown in the plots are estimated marginal effects for low, medium, and high levels of political constraints. The estimates are based on a linear model. Marginal effects at each level suggest the linearity assumption is reasonable. Had we observed a non-monotonic ordering, then we would have doubted the suitability of the linear regression model. Likewise, the sample distributions indicate satisfactory support across the range of moderating variables (Hainmueller, Mummolo, and Xu 2016). If the sample distributions revealed that only high-constraints country-years experience adverse rulings while low-constraints observations experience none, then one should doubt the estimated marginal effects. The distributions alleviate this concern.

Figure 6.1(c) shows the marginal effect of political polarization and 6.1(d) shows estimates for the effective number of parties. While these two measures demonstrate a negative effect, there is evidence of nonlinearity (polarization) and a skewed distribution of observations (effective number of parties), suggesting that the estimates may be somewhat vulnerable to model dependence.

Predicted effects illustrate the substantive significance of the findings. Suppose a government has few domestic constraints, as with Portugal's securely dominant Socialist and Social Democratic Parties. If Portugal were subjected to adverse rulings, its EU-import share would be expected to increase the next year by approximately 0.3%, roughly translating to nearly €97 million in imports.[45] Conversely if the Dutch government, with its many political constraints, were subjected to adverse trade rulings, one would not expect a positive effect on imports. While predicted effects are not precise, they do show that the impact of adverse trade rulings hinges on domestic politics.

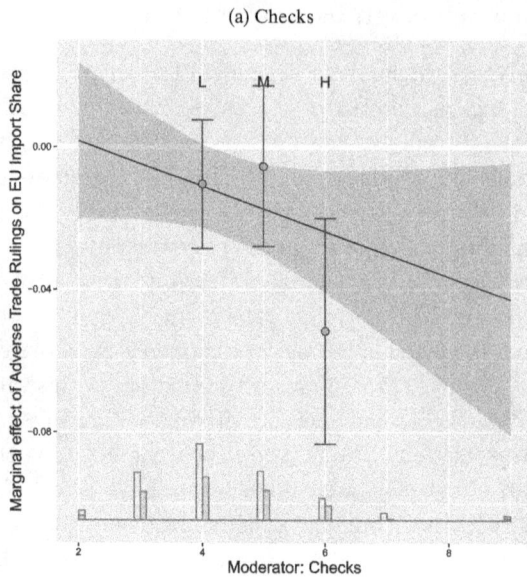

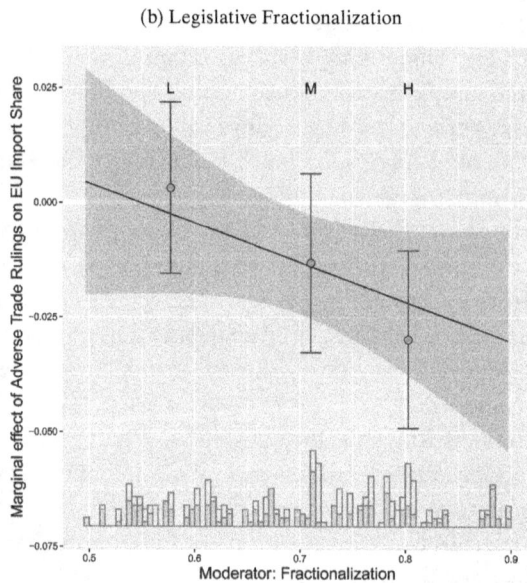

FIGURE 6.1. Marginal Effect of Adverse Trade Rulings on EU Import Share, Moderated by Political Constraints

Note: The marginal effects are based on estimates from Table 6.1, models 1–3 and 5. Shaded areas denote 95% confidence intervals and histograms show the sample distributions. Also shown are binning estimators for low, medium, and high levels of political constraints. The marginal effect of veto points is insignificant and not shown.

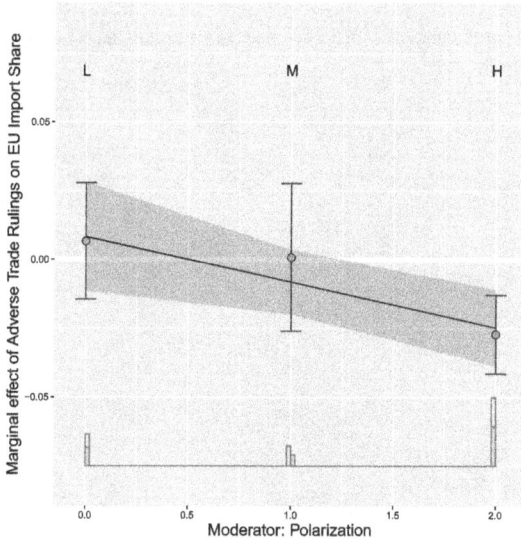

(c) Polarization

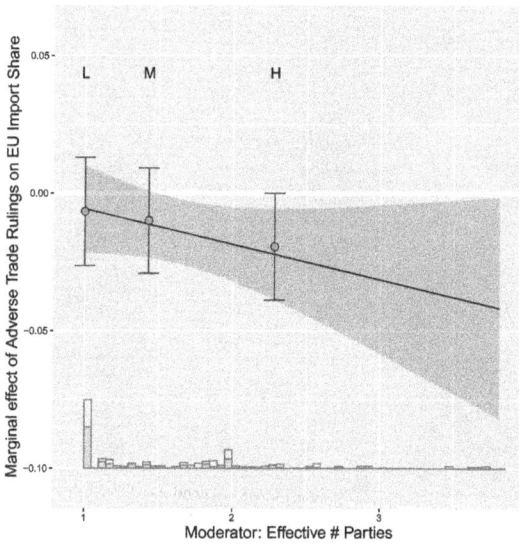

(d) Effective Number of Parties

TABLE 6.2 **Impact of Trade Rulings and Political Constraints on Import Share, Legal Controls**

	Intra-EU import share$_{ji}$				
	(1)	(2)	(3)	(4)	(5)
Adverse Tr. Ruling × Veto Points	−0.07				
	(0.06)				
Veto Points	0.01				
	(0.06)				
Adverse Tr. Ruling × Checks		−0.01***			
		(0.004)			
Checks		−0.01*			
		(0.004)			
Adverse Tr. Ruling × Fractionalization			−0.12**		
			(0.05)		
Fractionalization			−0.12*		
			(0.08)		
Adverse Tr. Ruling × Polarization				−0.01*	
				(0.01)	
Polarization				−0.001	
				(0.006)	
Adverse Tr. Ruling × Effective No. Parties					−0.01*
					(0.01)
Effective No. Parties					0.001
					(0.01)
Adverse Tr. Rulings	0.04**	0.07**	0.01	0.04	0.01
	(0.02)	(0.04)	(0.01)	(0.05)	(0.01)
GDP[†]	0.02***	0.03***	0.03***	0.03***	0.03***
	(0.002)	(0.002)	(0.003)	(0.002)	(0.002)
Dualist	−0.05	−0.05	−0.06	−0.05	−0.06
	(0.05)	(0.05)	(0.06)	(0.05)	(0.05)
Bicameralism	−0.09*	−0.09	−0.10*	−0.09*	−0.09*
	(0.05)	(0.05)	(0.06)	(0.05)	(0.05)
Transposition Deficit	0.02***	0.02***	0.02***	0.02***	0.02***
	(0.002)	(0.002)	(0.002)	(0.002)	(0.002)
# Preliminary References	−0.001	−0.001	−0.001	−0.001	−0.001
	(0.001)	(0.001)	(0.001)	(0.001)	(0.001)
N	238	238	233	238	238
Countries	15	15	15	15	15
Log Likelihood	386	388	385	384	383
Std. Dev. (Intercept)	0.090	0.096	0.104	0.093	0.092

Note: Models estimated with R. All specifications include country random intercepts. Explanatory variables are lagged by one year. Significance codes *p<0.1; **p<0.05; ***p<0.01. [†]Log units.

The results hold when legal and political controls are included. Table 6.2 accounts for legal factors while table 6.3 brings in political controls. Estimates using institutional checks, legislative fractionalization, and polarization are statistically significant. Estimates using the effective number of parties are somewhat weaker. I find scant evidence that veto

TABLE 6.3 **Impact of Trade Rulings and Political Constraints on Import Share, Political Controls**

	Intra-EU import share$_{ji}$				
	(1)	(2)	(3)	(4)	(5)
Adverse Tr. Ruling × Veto Points	−0.04				
	(0.05)				
Veto Points	0.002				
	(0.05)				
Adverse Tr. Ruling × Checks		−0.01***			
		(0.004)			
Checks		0.003			
		(0.004)			
Adverse Tr. Ruling × Fractionalization			−0.09**		
			(0.04)		
Fractionalization			−0.10		
			(0.07)		
Adverse Tr. Ruling × Polarization				−0.01**	
				(0.01)	
Polarization				0.001	
				(0.01)	
Adverse Tr. Ruling × Effective No. Parties					−0.004
					(0.004)
Effective No. Parties					−0.001
					(0.01)
Adverse Tr. Rulings	0.02	0.04**	0.06*	0.01	−0.003
	(0.04)	(0.02)	(0.03)	(0.01)	(0.01)
GDP†	0.01***	0.01***	0.02***	0.02***	0.01***
	(0.003)	(0.002)	(0.003)	(0.002)	(0.002)
Government Debt Share GDP	−0.0001	0.0002	−0.004	−0.003	−0.001
	(0.02)	(0.02)	(0.02)	(0.02)	(0.02)
Government Effectiveness	0.07***	0.06***	0.06***	0.06***	0.07***
	(0.01)	(0.01)	(0.01)	(0.01)	(0.01)
Public Opinion of EU	−0.03	−0.02	−0.04	−0.03	−0.02
	(0.03)	(0.03)	(0.03)	(0.03)	(0.03)
SSI Council	0.02***	0.02***	0.02***	0.02***	0.02***
	(0.002)	(0.002)	(0.002)	(0.003)	(0.002)
N	216	216	211	216	216
Countries‡	14	14	14	14	14
Log Likelihood	388	388	383	388	383
Std. Dev. (Intercept)	0.151	0.152	0.161	0.155	0.152

Note: Models estimated with R. All specifications include country random intercepts. Explanatory variables are lagged by one year. Significance codes *p<0.1; **p<0.05; ***p<0.01. †Log units. ‡Austria omitted due to inadequate data.

points per se matter. In summary, the analysis demonstrates that fragmented policy-making diminishes the effect of trade-liberalizing rulings on intra-EU trade.

The control variables corroborate the findings in the literature. States with larger economies are more integrated into the EU market. Export-oriented economies are more reliant on imports from outside the EU. Affluence is associated with less EU trade, possibly reflecting a larger appetite for foreign goods. The transposition deficit has a positive effect that mainly reflects the Netherlands and Greece, which are, respectively, more and less diligent in reporting the transposition of directives and less and more reliant on intra-EU trade. A dualist legal tradition, bicameralism, and the number of trade-related preliminary references are not significant factors. Effective governments, as measured by the Kaufmann, Kraay, and Mastruzzi (2010) index, are more integrated, presumably due to their capacity to implement pro-liberalizing European policy. Political power in the Council, measured by the Shapley-Shubik Index, is associated with more intra-EU trade. Even if politically weaker states tacitly resist by failing to implement directives, this does seem to diminish economic integration. Government debt and public opinion are not significant.

Many infringement disputes touch on multiple sectors of the economy—for instance, the regulation of commercial transport. They affect intra-European commerce in everything from raw materials to finished goods. Other disputes target certain sectors. It is possible that the trade impact of these narrow disputes is too modest to detect in aggregate data and that other features of the defendant governments drive the results. I address this concern by focusing on the agricultural sector, which remains a contentious aspect of community law. Each year, states are found to have placed illegal restrictions on trade of agricultural goods through transport and inspection requirements, technical barriers to trade, and other means.

6.5.2 Agriculture-related infringements

Do adverse rulings on agriculture prompt an increase in intra-EU agriculture imports? I collected data on each state's imports of agriculture goods from within the EU as a share of its total imports agricultural goods from the world. Agriculture products are identified by Harmonized System (HS) code at the two-digit level. I selected adverse rulings on agriculture, as classified by the Commission and my reading of ECJ

TABLE 6.4 **Impact of Agriculture Rulings and Political Constraints on Agricultural Import Share**

	Intra-EU agricultural import share$_{jt}$				
	(1)	(2)	(3)	(4)	(5)
Adverse Ag. Ruling × Checks	−0.004				
	(0.004)				
Checks	−0.01***				
	(0.003)				
Adverse Ag. Ruling × Fractionalization		−0.10**			
		(0.05)			
Fractionalization		−0.06			
		(0.06)			
Adverse Ag. Ruling × Polarization			−0.01*		
			(0.01)		
Polarization			−0.003		
			(0.004)		
Adverse Ag. Ruling × Veto Points				−0.10**	
				(0.05)	
Veto Points				0.04	
				(0.04)	
Adverse Ag. Ruling × Effective No. Parties					−0.01
					(0.01)
Effective No. Parties					0.001
					(0.01)
Adverse Ag. Ruling	0.04**	0.09**	0.03***	0.09***	0.04***
	(0.02)	(0.04)	(0.01)	(0.04)	(0.01)
Agriculture Value Added Share GDP	0.01***	0.01***	0.01***	0.01***	0.01***
	(0.003)	(0.003)	(0.003)	(0.003)	(0.003)
N	260	255	260	260	260
Countries	15	15	15	15	15
Log Likelihood	485	478	482	485	481
Economic controls?	Yes	Yes	Yes	Yes	Yes
Std. Dev. (Intercept)	0.136	0.134	0.132	0.135	0.134

Note: Models estimated with R. All specifications include country random intercepts. Explanatory variables are lagged by one year. Significance codes *p<0.1; **p<0.05; ***p<0.01. Only adverse agriculture rulings are included. Economic controls are GDP per capita, exports share of GDP, and government debt share of GDP.

judgments, and repeated the analysis. Instead of controlling for each country's GDP, I instead account for agriculture value added as a portion of GDP to more accurately capture this sector of the economy. The corresponding analysis is presented in table 6.4. Note that the regression models include but do not show the economic controls. The economic control variables are GDP per capita, exports, and government debt. I also checked political control variables: the transposition deficit, government effectiveness, and SSI council and found similar results.

The agriculture-sector results buttress the main argument. When defendant governments lose agriculture lawsuits at the ECJ, they subsequently increase their agriculture imports. This effect is diminished when the government has many domestic constraints. Fractionalization, polarization, and veto points are statistically significant at conventional levels. However, the *Checks* variable loses significance, likely reflecting the fact that agriculture policy is usually set by a single agency, such as a ministry of agriculture. While partisan politics influence agriculture policy, formal institutional checks may have little bearing.

These statistical results echo the broader concerns around a politically charged sector. The European Union has long wielded a heavy hand in managing agricultural markets within the community.[46] The Common Agricultural Policy (CAP) is a staple of European integration; among many other market interventions, the EU subsidizes food production. Integration of agriculture has been a point of contention, particularly during points of expansion (Anderson and Tyers 1995). Likewise, controversial overhauls have exacerbated dissent both between net producer and net consumer member states, as well as among domestic groups within those states.[47] To this end, one of the Commission's major goals is dismantling CAP-inconsistent subsidies and other obstacles to the free movement of agricultural goods by pursuing infringement disputes and ECJ lawsuits.

6.5.3 Time effects

While states are obligated to promptly implement rulings, there may be delays before policy reforms impact trade. As noted above, Gabel et al. (2012, 1135) find the peak impact two years after a ruling. In an extension to the main analysis, I examine time effects. I introduce an additional one-year lag between the adverse ruling and the trade outcome such that the intra-EU import share at time t is predicted by political constraints at time $t - 1$ and adverse trade rulings at time $t - 2$. This allows for an additional one-year delay between when the court issues its ruling and when the defendant government adjusts its policy to comply.[48] I also include a simple time index to adjust for system-wide temporal trends in trade.[49] Results are presented in the appendix for this chapter. The additional one-year lag magnifies the negative impact of political constraints and adverse trade rulings on intra-EU imports: coefficients on the interaction terms are negative and highly significant for all measures of political constraints except veto points.

6.5.4 Robustness

A first potential objection might be that a single group of countries may be driving the results, limiting the explanatory power of my theory. According to some scholarship, Austria, Belgium, Germany, the Netherlands, Spain, and the United Kingdom, are thought to be most vulnerable to clashes between domestic interests and EU law (Falkner, Hartlapp, and Treib 2007; Thomson 2009). Do similar patterns hold for ECJ rulings? To assess this, I repeated the analysis using a multilevel model where each country received a different coefficient on the interaction term *Adverse trade ruling× Constraints t – 1*. This analysis showed that no single country or group is driving the results.

Another concern is reverse causality: perhaps imports cause infringement rulings, particularly for states with few constraints. Prior research has found a positive correlation between intra-EU trade and initial violations of EU law, suggesting a causal link (e.g., Bergman 2000; Huelshoff, Sperling, and Hess 2005; Mbaye 2001; Sverdrup 2004; but see Perkins and Neumayer 2007). More violations could lead to trade-liberalizing ECJ rulings. This is unlikely to be a serious problem for this analysis. The temporal lag in the regression rules out simple endogeneity. Moreover, a reverse-causality argument would require an unrealistic set of conditions: a state trades within the EU, the Commission investigates a possible infringement targeting states with the most intra-EU imports that the state ignores or resists, the Commission sues, and the ECJ reaches a verdict. To account for my results, the Commission would have to target states that it anticipates will have few domestic constraints in the future.

Relatedly, some potential infringements are resolved earlier in the process before even reaching the ECJ. It is possible that this selection mechanism reflects the domestic politics of the defendant government. While my data only cover infringement disputes that advanced to an ECJ decision, Börzel et al. (2010) examined the full set of violations of EU obligations from 1978 to 1999. The authors considered all suspected infringements and determined whether they reached the "reasoned opinion" stage of the infringement process. Recall, the reasoned option stage is when the European Commission officially reports serious cases of noncompliance but has not yet brought those concerns to the court. Then, the authors determine whether those infringements are referred to the ECJ, the next stage of enforcement. Börzel et al. (2010, 1375) compare infringement patterns to the same veto points index by Henisz (2000) that I employed. Political constraints are not a significant predictor of an infringement investigation proceeding to a reasoned opinion. Nor does this variable predict the referral of a dispute to the ECJ for adjudication (see Börzel et al. 2010, 1377). Although these data do not cover more recent years of infringement disputes, they provide compelling evidence that political constraints are not driving selection into adjudication.

Third, previous research has argued that in order to maintain legitimacy, the ECJ is reluctant to rule against governments when it anticipates defiance. To the extent that this produces selection bias, it does not explain my results. The strategic-court logic implies there will be fewer adverse rulings against governments that are stymied by domestic politics. The data do not support this: political constraints differ little between country-years with adverse rulings and those without.

Table 6.5 presents the sample average for each measure of political constraints for country-years with and without adverse trade rulings. The samples are well balanced: t – tests show no statistically significant difference in means at the conventional level (p – value < 0.05). To examine the data a different way, I plotted the rate of adverse rulings against the different measures of political constraints and found no correlations whatsoever. To the extent the ECJ delivers adverse rulings against certain countries more frequently, that decision is not guided by the countries' domestic political constraints.

TABLE 6.5 **Sample Averages with and without Trade-Liberalizing Rulings**

	Sample average (μ)	
	With adverse trade ruling	Without adverse trade ruling
Veto Points	0.777	0.763
Checks	4.370	4.397
Legislative Fractionalization	0.693	0.705
Polarization	1.299	1.322
Effective No. of Parties	1.766	1.860

Note: Sample averages for each political constraints variable measured by country-year (j,t). t-tests show no significant difference in means, p>0.05.

Finally, there may be concerns with model dependency, given the bounded distribution of the dependent variable. The import share is constrained to fall between 0 and 1, meaning a distributional assumption of the linear model is not strictly satisfied. To check this possibility, I reran the analysis using a beta regression explicitly designed for bounded dependent variables. The substantive results were nearly identical, alleviating concern that the findings are model dependent.

6.6 Implications

The ECJ is widely recognized as a driver of European legal integration. Key to its success is its ability to supersede national political strife, avoiding narrow interests that could undermine European cooperation. EU legal doctrine ensures that when there is a conflict between national and supranational law, it is the European law that must be applied, and that ECJ rulings can be enforced in national courts. With respect to preliminary reference cases, these provisions have effectively linked ECJ rulings to binding domestic ones (Carrubba and Murrah 2005). Yet for infringement cases, which are decided at the international level and implemented via domestic policy, the record is spottier. Supremacy, direct effect, and enforcement mechanisms have not been sufficient for the ECJ to force all reluctant governments to enact meaningful economic integration. Infringement rulings leave ample opportunity for domestic politics to intervene.

This chapter has demonstrated a link between trade-liberalizing rulings and domestic politics on the one hand and European economic integration on the other. Countries that face adverse rulings on trade-related issues expand their intra-European imports, but divisive domestic politics diminish this effect. Governments that are highly constrained by institutional checks or partisan divisions have difficulty adopting and enforcing policies mandated by the ECJ, as revealed through intra-EU trade. The results are consistent across multiple models.

The results in this chapter lend support to the claim that domestic political constraints can obstruct compliance with international legal rulings across different international settings. This pattern is not an anomaly of the World Trade Organization alone. Even if one cannot explicitly measure compliance in every ECJ case, the prevailing effect of compliance with trade-liberalizing rulings is to deepen economic integration.

Domestic politics appear to hinder this process, undercutting the economic value of a ruling.

A couple key points can be gleaned, then, from the ECJ analysis. First, there is important variation in state responses to trade-liberalizing rulings. This variation cannot be attributed to differences among plaintiffs or geopolitical circumstances because all infringement rulings share a common plaintiff, the Commission. Likewise the international political and economic conditions member states experience are very similar by virtue of the EU's common external policies. Holding these other factors fixed helps isolate the effect of domestic politics. This ECJ analysis buttresses the findings in the preceding chapters.

Second, this chapter has shown that even strong international courts face intractable domestic hurdles when pursuing their legal mandate. Scholars have long recognized that increased legalization of international organizations can have mixed effects on cooperation among states (Abbott and Snidal 2000; Goldstein and Martin 2000). Strong courts such as the ECJ work well when they rule on precise law and are nested within a broader political structure—here, the European Union—making exit from the regime costly (Johns 2015; Phelan 2015). While strong courts can increase the likelihood of compliance, they may also force compliance controversies back into the battleground of domestic politics. Domestic groups that oppose integration may see ECJ rulings as an ingress for tacit resistance. By obstructing compliance through domestic avenues—for example, vetoing policies or inhibiting their local enforcement—these groups can diminish the economic consequences of European legal integration.

These findings lend insight into the conditions under which international courts can or cannot solve compliance problems in international or regional economic organizations. Diversity of interests *across* states is an evident obstacle to forming a cooperative economic regime. At the same time, diversity of interests *within* member states—especially among influential groups with obstructionist aims—pose a significant barrier to successfully enforcing that community. Whether the WTO and the ECJ strike the right balance in enforcing deep economic cooperation among their members amidst domestic divisions is the focus of the final chapter.

CHAPTER SEVEN

Reshaping International Economic Courts

7.1 Backlash against international legalization

International economic relations are more legalized than ever before (Abbott et al. 2000). Treaties establish rules for many aspects of the global economy with increasing precision, and states agree to substantial international obligations. Many governments delegate authority to multilateral organizations to administer those rules and adjudicatory bodies to resolve conflicts. While some international institutions are merely shells of what their founders envisioned (Gray 2018), others, including the World Trade Organization and the European Union, have grown to serve more countries on a wider range of issues. Once predominantly a resource for industrialized democratic states, the WTO Dispute Settlement Mechanism now serves a broad range of countries seeking to address their trade disputes. States dedicate money and political capital to the process and appear to value WTO legal rulings. Likewise, expanding beyond the original six-member European Coal and Steel Community, the Court of Justice of the European Union adjudicates disputes among its now twenty-seven member states. The European Commission, the main body tasked with enforcing EU integration, holds states accountable through ECJ lawsuits. States regularly engage in adjudication and appear to behave as if the rulings of international courts matter.

Despite this broad trend toward international legalization, recent

years have also revealed instances of acute backlash. For the WTO
DSM, one noteworthy source of resistance is the United States. Shortly
after assuming office, the Trump administration sidestepped WTO obligations and commenced a spiraling trade war with China and other key
partners. Had the US followed WTO rules, it would have instead pursued legal dispute resolution and refrained from unauthorized retaliation. This was seen as a serious rejection of the multilateral trade regime: "The Trump administration has led the United States in stepping
back from its traditional role at the head of global institutions like the
WTO, creating a vacuum in leadership and throwing their future into
question."[1] The administration went beyond merely ignoring its obligation to use WTO legal channels. It also blocked the appointment of new
WTO Appellate Body judges. When the terms of some judges expired
at the end of 2019, the body lacked sufficient personnel to conduct appeals cases.[2] This action thwarted dispute settlement. With the shift in
US leadership to the Biden administration, the US renewed its support
of the WTO DSM.[3] Yet, for now, the long-term consequences for the
WTO's authority remain unclear.

Backlash against international legalization is also evident in the
United Kingdom's contentious exit from the European Union. For supporters of Brexit, the overriding political objective was to reestablish UK
sovereignty over its own affairs. In campaigning for Brexit, Prime Minister Johnson criticized the ECJ for overreaching and promised an end to
the court's jurisdiction. A key feature of Johnson's withdrawal plan was
extricating the UK judiciary from ECJ rulings: even lower UK courts
could overturn ECJ decisions as they saw fit.[4] Post-Brexit, Johnson declared that goal complete: "We have taken back control of laws and our
destiny . . . the jurisdiction of the ECJ will come to an end" (B. Johnson 2020). The broad popular support for Brexit, and the smoldering re-
sentment of the EU in other member states, shows just how entrenched
these sentiments have become. As some scholarship highlights, backlash
against the institutions of economic globalization is driven by domestic
political polarization and dissent from the people left worse off by the
integration of global markets (Walter 2021; Colantone and Stanig 2018).

These events highlight how international economic organizations
occupy a precarious position in world affairs. Countries may disregard
their international promises when those obligations become too onerous. Some states go further to obstruct operations or even exit the regime when the clash between international authority and national sov-

ereignty is insurmountable. Importantly, it would seem that some of the most powerful founding members—the US in the WTO and the UK in the EU—are also the most emphatic critics. Their rejection risks unraveling the regimes. This book helps to make sense of the recent backlash.

First, my book delineates the limits on international legalization. By focusing on hard cases where governments have preferences that counter their international obligations—and nonetheless do comply and cooperate—I demonstrate that ICs can fulfill their mandate. I show that domestic political constraints help determine whether states abide by IC rulings or resist their authority. Popular preferences, partisan agendas, and political leadership may fan the flames of anti-globalization sentiments, but these factors fluctuate over time. My research demonstrates that compliance problems are systematically linked to the domestic political structures that give anti-compliance groups leverage. Thus to explain why international legalization is under fire, scholars should not be overly invested in the idiosyncrasies of Donald Trump vis-à-vis the WTO, Boris Johnson vis-à-vis the ECJ, or others leaders; they should devote their attentions to political institutions. States resist ICs when salient domestic players oppose cooperation and, crucially, leverage their political standing to realize their policy aims.

Backlash can be traced back to the winners and losers in today's globalized economy and the structures those groups operate within. In some respects, economic globalization may be a victim of its own success. Intensive trade specialization has grown the global pie. But the shares have become increasingly unequal, especially within the industrialized Western democratic countries that pioneered the WTO. The stakeholders who suffer most acutely from economic globalization have limited avenues to express their discontent. It is nearly impossible for a handful of aggrieved workers, unions, and industry groups to undo the deeply ingrained structures of free trade or global value chains. Likewise, it is difficult to disentangle current policy from the multilateral trade regime.

But globalization's discontents can carve out slightly larger slices of the pie. This may mean retaining the few trade protections they do enjoy by preventing the rollback of those highly valued policies. When WTO rulings strike down trade barriers, anti-compliance stakeholders can make their preferences known and ask domestic veto players to block policy reform. They can encourage their political representatives to throw a wrench into the gears of the WTO's legal machinery. After the United States' obstruction of WTO dispute settlement operations, its new leadership has promised a tune-up (Congressional Research Service 2021). Reinvigorated interest in the rule of law for international trade relations will likely prove inadequate if the US, the EU, and other major players do not address these domestic sources of backlash.

Second, my book illuminates the fundamental tension between international and domestic institutions. Different states can utilize international legal apparatuses to varying degrees, and their incentives to do so reflect domestic politics. My findings suggest that international economic courts may need to be fine-tuned to address the evolving needs of member states. Institutional flexibility, especially in the multilateral trade regime, allows for tolerated noncompliance under certain circumstances (Kucik and Reinhardt 2008; Pelc 2009, 2016; Rosendorff 2005). Flexible international courts give countries more leeway to avoid the enforcement of adverse rulings. A key remedy—if not the only viable solution—is to build greater flexibility into ICs to specifically accommodate domestic political constraints within member states.

At the WTO, the most sophisticated users of the DSM are the richest democracies with the greatest capacity to bend the rules to their liking. These countries prolong legal proceedings and evade compliance in a way that balances competing political pressures at home and from abroad. They do so largely out of necessity (Rodrik 2011). Leaders of democratic governments with the most political constraints are least able to force an agenda of international cooperation. Their ability to abide by international rulings waxes and wanes with the support of domestic stakeholders. By contrast, an autocratic government with few domestic constraints—China, for example—can establish a clearer plan for when and how to abide by WTO agreements and execute that agenda with greater precision. When international adjudication becomes excessively rigid, and when the bar for cooperation imposed for states is too high, ICs will struggle to remain relevant. Countries—especially democracies—will circumvent and disregard their rulings, undercutting the institution's authority.

In this respect, the WTO has done itself few favors. The Appellate Body has pushed for greater legalization through its increasing reliance on legal precedent (Pelc 2014). Despite the fact that precedent is proscribed in WTO agreements, judges tend to apply prior rulings and even interpret them in ways that expand countries' trade obligations (Kucik and Puig 2021). The United States' recent resistance to the Appellate

Body is a pointed protest against WTO legal overreach (US Library of Congress 2021). Precedent removes the ambiguity in treaties that states deliberately incorporate via "incomplete contracts" in order to preserve flexibility (Koremenos 2005; Rosendorff and Milner 2001; Horn, Maggi, and Staiger 2010). Sharpening of the legal teeth of an international court can eliminate exactly the flexibility many countries rely on. As political and economic circumstances change, states often need to readjust the balance among different domestic political pressures and may wish to reinterpret their international commitments accordingly. Rigid applications of international law make it more difficult for democratic governments to strike this balance and comply with IC rulings. Domestic political constraints within the United States, the European Union, and other key WTO member states are not changing anytime soon. If the WTO wants to have a viable future, it likely needs to roll back its approach to precedent. The final section of this chapter details some possible WTO reforms in this vein.

7.2 Summary of contributions

This book makes two main contributions to the scholarship on international organizations. The first is good news. This book provides systematic evidence that international economic courts are, indeed, effective. Both the World Trade Organization's Dispute Settlement Mechanism and the Court of Justice of the European Union have advanced international cooperation in concrete ways. Chapter 4 demonstrated that WTO rulings have encouraged policy reforms in reluctant states. Governments comply with rulings by passing new trade policies and modifying old ones in at least a large portion of cases. Compliance matters for economic relations between states. Chapter 5 showed that WTO rulings deliver significant trade recoveries for disputing governments. Adjudication ultimately furthers the WTO's agenda of promoting free and fair trade relations around the globe. At the ECJ, the impact of legal rulings on economic relations is also apparent. When judges rule that member states' policies obstruct the single market, those governments expand EU commerce. Chapter 6 demonstrated that legal decisions do, on average, prompt countries to deepen economic ties with the rest of the EU.

My findings are significant and, for many IO skeptics, will come as a surprise. Canonical literature argues that governments self-select into legal commitments that align with their existing preferences (Downs and Rocke 1995; Downs, Rocke, and Barsoom 1996). But ICs offer an important window into IO effectiveness. They isolate instances where governments do not want to cooperate but sometimes, under the right nudge or threat from the court, do actually reform their policies and practice. The most revealing examples come from powerful defendant states that comply despite enjoying economic clout that allows them to ignore legal rulings and plaintiff demands. Examples from the WTO include when the United States acquiesced in a complaint from Antigua and Barbuda and the European Union twice acquiesced in complaints from Thailand. As for the ECJ, the compliance record appears quite strong from even large economies such as Germany and the Netherlands. International economic courts are more than a mere facade for power politics.

With respect to the WTO, some scholars have puzzled over the seemingly insignificant effect of legal rulings on trade flows (Chaudoin, Kucik, and Pelc 2016; Bown and Reynolds 2015). Others have highlighted that the track record of formal compliance is mixed, at least with high-profile disputes (Davey 2009; Brewster and Chilton 2014; Busch and Reinhardt 2003). I show the WTO DSM induces compliance and delivers trade benefits. My findings advance the literature by rigorously demonstrating both the policy and economic impacts of international adjudication; both are indicators of IO effectiveness.

Likewise, scholars have argued that ECJ judges are wary of backlash from reluctant states. They may sometimes curtail their rulings to avoid these problems (Carrubba, Gabel, and Hankla 2008; Gabel et al. 2012). Even so, ECJ rulings do prompt states to reform in ways that expand commerce in the community. The literature on preliminary rulings indicates that the ECJ relies on national courts to give its judgments bite and to enforce its pro-integration agenda (Carrubba 2005; Carrubba and Murrah 2005). I show that the ECJ does not need to rely on national courts to do its bidding. Infringement rulings, long thought to face pervasive enforcement problems (Börzel et al. 2010), also facilitate European economic integration. These empirical results mark an advance in the literature.

For the diplomats who crafted these IOs and continue to work within them, my findings should come as reassurance. International law wields a degree of normative authority, differentiating between acceptable and unacceptable state conduct. To the extent that countries behave as if their international legal obligations matter, they reinforce that authority. In turn, they will use the legal resources at their disposal to ensure other countries follow mutually beneficial rules. More frequent compliance with international legal rulings begets a stronger regime.

The second key contribution of this book is to provide a systematic explanation for why international courts fail to induce economic cooperation among certain countries. The success of these courts hinges on domestic political institutions and the preferences of different domestic actors within member states.

International relations scholarship has long recognized that domestic veto players limit a government's agility in international affairs. Governments with many domestic veto players find it difficult to join international agreements. They face a higher barrier to entry, so only treaties garnering the most widespread support are ever ratified. Once a government with many domestic veto players does enter an international agreement, its commitment is thought to be a more credible promise for future compliance. Veto players decrease the risk that a country exits the agreement since more actors would have to coordinate in order to abandon it. Yet this constraint is far from perfect. Sometimes short-term incentives lead governments to break their international commitments. Domestic actors that hold formal veto power might permit these breaches. For example, an executive facing an upcoming election might refrain from vetoing trade protection policies crafted by the legislature.

Throughout this book, I have offered systematic evidence that once governments break their international commitments, formal and informal domestic veto players can lock in those violations, making it more difficult to return to compliance. Veto players lock in violations because international economic cooperation carries domestic distributive consequences: one group's gain is another group's loss. Divisions of political authority matter because there are stark divisions in preferences. When ICs ask governments to reverse policies, they disrupt the domestic balance and exacerbate the conflict between stakeholders.

My findings advance scholarly efforts to explain the relationship between domestic politics and international adjudication. Research has demonstrated that *plaintiff* governments initiate lawsuits with an eye toward domestic audiences (Davis 2012; Allee and Huth 2006; Chaudoin 2014). They may aim to curry favor from certain domestic groups or at times of political turnover (Gray and Kucik 2017; Bobick and A. Smith 2016). This book has unpacked the domestic politics in *defendant* governments that are involved in international litigation.

By understanding the defendant government's calculations, potential plaintiffs can discern whether lawsuits will deliver policy reform and economic benefits. Plaintiffs can deploy their legal resources with finer-tuned aims and may expect greater rewards for their litigation expenditures if they target consolidated governments. For instance, the European Commission might choose to time a lawsuit around national partisan realignment in a member state. It could seek an ECJ judgment when political power in the target state is more concentrated in the hands of one party or a tight coalition. Likewise, when a country sues a federal state before the WTO, it might focus its complaint on policies that are administered by national rather than state or provincial governments. Policies controlled at the federal level might activate fewer veto players than those that also require consent of multiple actors at the regional level. With more savvy use of their legal resources, plaintiffs can address their international grievances when defendant governments are most receptive to foreign legal intervention. And they can avoid futile lawsuits that will inevitably result in noncompliance, knowing that when a defendant persistently ignores rulings it undercuts the credibility of the IC.

More broadly, this book has shown that the checks and balances that are fundamental to democracy generate challenging conditions for international cooperation (Mansfield, Milner, and Pevehouse 2007). Throughout much of the WTO's and the European Union's histories, the most avid supporters of legalization have been countries with robust democratic institutions and strong traditions of international economic engagement. Recent backlash calls this tendency into question. An unintended consequence of international legalization is that these governments then find themselves doubly entangled: constrained by international laws abroad and veto players at home. The logic of a two-level game articulated by Putnam (1988) decades ago bears out in the context of international courts. But unlike diplomatic interactions, which may leave little opportunity for anyone to craft rules of negotiation, ICs can be cleverly redesigned to account for this quandary.

7.3 Implications for the design of international courts

While the future of international legalization may not be as sanguine as it once appeared, international courts can be modified to accommodate changing times. Strong ICs can be redesigned to include more flexibility mechanisms—opportunities for tolerated defection. More flexibility encourages governments to remain in the international regime rather than abandon it altogether (Johns 2015; Gilligan, Johns, and Rosendorff 2010). But, as this book has demonstrated with respect to the WTO, governments are keen to exploit informal sources of flexibility. Under pressure from domestic constituents, governments prolong lawsuits through appeal, deadline extensions, and compliance proceedings, and they evade judgments. Some governments then hide behind their domestic political constraints to avoid international enforcement. Consequent trade losses are difficult to recover as markets and firms adjust to protectionist policies.[5] Too much informal flexibility may foster problematic policies that undercut international cooperation.

The WTO DSM can be made more effective. I offer three recommendations.[6] First, flexibility mechanisms could be explicitly targeted at states' domestic political conditions. WTO trade rules allow only for exceptions under narrowly defined emergencies (e.g., economic crisis), when states cite competing values (e.g., environmental concerns, health and safety, or security), and other limited conditions. Exceptions could be expanded to include domestic political and economic conditions that demonstrably obstruct compliance. For instance, a state could be granted additional leeway when there is an upcoming election, rising unemployment in certain industries, or other temporary obstacles.

Modifications along these lines would need to be paired with increased oversight and partial compliance benchmarks. DSM procedures could evaluate particular obstacles in order to differentiate between appropriate and opportunistic use of flexibility mechanisms. Panel decisions could establish partial compliance steps for defendant governments to meet, with the long-term goal of full implementation. Lessons from the design of trade agreements could be incorporated more fully into the WTO's dispute settlement procedure itself (Pelc 2009; Johns 2014; Johns and Peritz 2015). Under the current WTO system, if a defendant government fails to implement an adverse ruling, it can negotiate with the plaintiff and arrange for compensation pending full implementation.[7] These steps could be incorporated earlier into the dispute process. Defendants would need to present evidence that electoral circumstances or institutional barriers hinder compliance, such as resistant districts in a federal country. WTO panelists, rather than the plaintiff government, could establish a timeline for incremental compliance steps and proportionate penalties. Given existing WTO panel deliberations and efforts at fine-tuning the implementation deadline, these added responsibilities would not entail a major expansion in capacity.

More stringent reporting procedures would help. Under the current system, defendant governments are required to report on their progress toward compliance but do not need to provide any evidence. States rarely supply details. The WTO does not verify their reports. Instead, panelists and plaintiffs could regularly report at WTO meetings to ensure defendants are achieving their partial compliance targets and following through on prescribed penalties. Governments that fail to achieve their targets could be penalized. The additional verification would help to close loopholes in the dispute settlement process and resolve the remedy gap (Brewster 2011). By moving more decisively toward a compensation-based system, the WTO could alleviate some of the problems arising from over-legalization. Such an arrangement might reduce the lock-in effect of domestic veto players, allowing governments to phase out popular trade protections. While returning to some of the deficiencies of the old GATT system, this kind of flexibility could entice the US and other major players to work within the multilateral regime rather than abandon it altogether.

The second recommendation involves rethinking the role of legal precedent in international courts. Johns (2015) argues that when strengthening ICs, designers should also increase the precision of the law on which those courts rule. In the evolution from the GATT to the WTO, stronger enforcement was paired with an increasing precision of rules. For example, the WTO established more precise rules on government procurement, the calculation and application of countervailing duties, the application of health and safety exceptions, etc. But the WTO has also sought to make the rules more precise by incorporating legal precedent into panel and Appellate Body decisions, taking legal reasoning from prior decisions and invoking them to guide subsequent rulings in separate disputes (Pelc 2014). In its most incendiary form, which has provoked outcry from the United States, precedent applications can *extend* countries' obligations under WTO rules (Kucik and Puig 2021; Kucik, Peritz, and Puig, forthcoming). While many international courts, including the WTO DSM and the ECJ, behave as if prior rulings should guide current ones, they formally reject legal precedent (Payandeh 2014; Shahabuddeen 2007; Verdier and Voeten 2014). Countries widely agree that precedent impinges on their sovereignty and that they should not be held accountable for interpretations from international judges that were applied to other states in other contexts.

The WTO DSM should follow its mandate to interpret and apply the treaty obligations to cases at hand without reliance on precedent. When the Appellate Body reviews panel reports, it should evaluate them on the substance of the case without invoking prior decisions. This would allow for more customized judgments that move away from a strict interpretation of the law and more toward a compensation system that accounts for each government's obstacles to compliance. States may find that additional negotiation rounds are eventually needed to increase the precision of WTO rules, especially as the international economy evolves. For instance, the agreement on intellectual property rights might need to be revisited as national intellectual property law grapples with the newest computer technology. Diplomats appointed by their respective governments, rather than international judges, need to be the ones who refine and sharpen the trade rules.

With a greater precision in their legal obligations, ICs can more effectively serve the diverse population of member states. At the WTO, this means leveling the playing field between high- and low-capacity states. Governments often become embroiled in prolonged and intricate trade disputes. Wealthier states with greater legal capacity are better equipped to persuade panel or Appellate Body judges on unchartered aspects of the WTO treaties. States with less capacity tend to settle their disputes early. This may come from less powerful states' greater uncertainty about the outcome of litigation or their reluctance to enter prolonged legal matches where they will be ultimately overpowered. When precedent reshapes the rules, it is unlikely to do so in ways that advantage the less powerful WTO members. Fine-tuning WTO rules through negotiations will give less powerful states standing to advocate for obligations that work for them. Although a partial solution at best, greater precision of the law may help to ameliorate the power politics that cast a shadow over ICs.

Third, the WTO could take lessons from the ECJ about centralized enforcement. After the European Commission struggled for years with noncompliance problems, the EU's 1992 Maastricht Treaty reforms introduced new enforcement instruments. When a state persistently disregards ECJ rulings, the Commission may bring the case before the court, requesting a penalty to be paid by the member state concerned. The

ECJ can then grant, modify, or reject that request.[8] The fines are calibrated to be large enough to encourage compliance: proportionate to the severity and duration of the violation and, importantly, the wealth of the member state. Penalties are increased for states with the largest economies in order to incentivize compliance. The Commission enjoys discretion to pursue long-standing infringements by recommending appropriate penalties. This discretion can be used to level the playing field between wealthy and poorer states (Falkner 2018; A. Hofmann 2018a).

Centralizing certain aspects of the enforcement process might improve WTO dispute settlement. Under current WTO procedures, a plaintiff can request retaliation against defendants that do not implement rulings. WTO judges must evaluate that request and then authorize the penalties for persistent noncompliance.[9] While proportionate retaliation may be a reasonable solution to an immediate trade dispute, the system is apt to replicate power politics and have an uneven effect on compliance. Retaliation is only persuasive if a plaintiff has a large enough economy or a defendant government's leadership cares about the sector in question. Instead, the WTO judges could authorize penalties for persistent noncompliance in proportion to not only the magnitude of the violation but also the size of the defendant's economy. Perhaps in some instances, third-party governments that side with a plaintiff could also participate in retaliation, albeit to a lesser degree. The DSM could coordinate this process such that enforcement does not strictly rely on the persistence and market power of plaintiffs. This would emulate some of the more successful features of the ECJ without requiring the deep economic integration that makes the European Union unique.

International economic courts face a delicate balancing act. These courts are established to promote the rule of law, yet they operate within a fundamentally anarchic international environment. They are in place to advance the collective goals of member states: international trade cooperation and economic integration. Yet sovereign states are not eager to acquiesce to international legal decisions. Governments grapple with domestic political constraints that tie leaders' hands, limiting their ability to follow through on their international promises in meaningful ways.

While this book has focused on state compliance with and the effectiveness of international economic courts, and the domestic political conditions within states, some of the lessons hold for international organizations more broadly. IOs can be better designed to reflect the range of domestic political interests and institutional barriers in member states. Additional flexibility measures can be incorporated to accommodate these domestic political obstacles, especially when international cooperation generates domestic distributive conflict. Enforcement efforts can be targeted more effectively in view of states' internal obstacles. At the same time, IOs can do more to publicize and shine light on both compliant and noncompliant behavior without resorting to formal legal enforcement. More information may ultimately help to level the playing field between powerful and weaker states, guide decisions about litigation, and shape the incentives of states and the political actors within them. By accounting for the cross-cutting effects of domestic political constraints, IOs can better promote lasting cooperation among countries.

Acknowledgments

Years ago, I sat in a creaky seat in the lecture room of Cornell University's McGraw Hall while a light but steady snow fell outside. Somewhat on a whim, I had enrolled in a course on global governance and human rights. The professor was a captivating speaker. The lectures illuminated the horrific tragedy of the Rwandan genocide, more than a decade prior and half a world away. The international community's tepid response made the mission of the International Criminal Court seem all the more pressing. This class left me with a sense of pessimism. International efforts at uncovering truth and applying restorative justice seemed to fall short. And yet the promise of international law fascinated me. I wondered whether international organizations in general, and courts in particular, could do more to avert political conflicts before they erupted and to facilitate reconciliation once conflicts occurred. A meandering academic path eventually brought me to international economic organizations. But a common theme remains. Can international courts meaningfully promote cooperation between sovereign states? This is the broader question my book tackles. In the domain of international trade, I can now say the answer is (often) yes.

This project developed over many years, beginning with my graduate studies at the University of California, Los Angeles. The support and feedback from my PhD advisors was invaluable. I am indebted to Leslie Johns, who mentored and supported me every step of the way. I cannot thank Leslie enough for taking a chance on a new graduate student and opening the door to this fascinating career for me. Arthur Stein molded my thinking about international conflict and cooperation and inspired me as a scholar. Our conversations over the years sparked so many more research projects than I could ever complete. I thank Jeffrey Lewis,

Ronald Rogowski, and Richard Steinberg, whose feedback shaped my research, broadening my theory and deepening the methodological rigor of my work. I also owe a debt of gratitude to the informal mentors who took the time to offer advice on my dissertation: Christina Davis, Songying Fang, Julia Gray, Jeffrey Kucik, Krzysztof Pelc, Peter Rosendorff, Christina Schneider, and Jana von Stein. Beyond my dissertation committee, many other faculty at UCLA supported my studies. In particular, I thank Kathleen Bawn, James DeNardo, Miriam Golden, Chad Hazlett, Mark Handcock, Michael Ross, Michael Thies, Robert Trager, and Lynn Vavrek. My UCLA graduate colleagues were a tremendous source of camaraderie and motivation. I am fortunate to have shared my graduate school experience with Sarah Brierley, Rebecca DiBennardo, Sebastián Garrido de Sierra, Kristen Kao, Paasha Mahdavi, Felipe Nunes, George Ofosu, Steve Palley, Francesca Parente, Andrea Vilán, Ryan Weldzius, and Anne White.

The broader scholarly community provided valuable feedback on various iterations of my research. I am grateful to Leo Baccini, Michael Bechtel, Timm Betz, Tanja Börzel, Renee Bowen, Chad Bown, Lawrence Broz, Ruth Carlitz, Clifford Carrubba, Stephen Chaudoin, Adam Chilton, Courtenay Conrad, Cosette Creamer, Tobias Hofmann, Kosuke Imai, Barbara Koremenos, Edward Mansfield, Michaela Mattes, Helen Milner, Noel Pereyra-Johnston, William Phelan, Tonya Putnam, Stephanie Rickard, Alastair Smith, and many others. Philippa Yasbek provided incisive comments from a policy perspective. I presented portions of my book in various conferences and department talks including the American Political Science Association; the Workshop on New Approaches to International Security and Cooperation in Bozeman, MT; the Browne Center Young Scholars in IR Conference; the International Political Economy Society; the International Studies Association; McGill University; the MIRTH workshop at the University of California, Berkeley; New York University; the Political Economy of International Organizations; the University of California Conference on International Cooperation; the University of Michigan; the University of Pennsylvania; the University of Southern California; and Vanderbilt University. Feedback from these audiences helped me to refine and extend my arguments and empirical tests.

This book involved substantial data collection that would not have been possible without the diligent and thoughtful work of my research assistants. I thank Sarah Chung, Ireen Litvak-Zur, Tzu-Ping Liu, Yuree Noh, Marissa Ramirez, Nahrain Rasho, Harunobu Saijo, Evan Sandlin, Amy Skoll, Mei Yu, and Yirong Abigail Zhao. Tanja Börzel, Christina Davis, Jeffrey Kucik, Krzysztof Pelc, Jeheung Ryu, Randall Stone, and Aydin Yildirim generously shared their replication data. This book reflects the cumulative efforts to understand the World Trade Organization and the Court of Justice of the European Union.

This project was made possible by generous funding from the National Science Foundation doctoral dissertation research improvement grant #1421326; the University of California, Davis Social Science Institute; the University of California, Los Angeles Graduate Division; and the University of California Institute for Global Cooperation and Conflict. I was fortunate to be awarded a fellowship for the 2016–17 academic year to visit Princeton University's Niehaus Center for Globalization and Governance. This incredible community of scholars pushed my research in new directions. The NCGG program gave me the time to immerse myself in my research and write much of the manuscript.

I have found a welcoming academic home at the University of California, Davis. I thank Amber Boydstun, Erik Engstrom, Chris Hare, Adrienne Hosek, Bradford Jones, Daniel Kono, Heather McKibben, Jeanette Money, Shalini Satkunanandan, John Scott, and Lauren Young for reading drafts and providing invaluable advice on this book. It is a pleasure to work with such a bright and enthusiastic group. A special thanks goes to Hillary Goldsher for supporting me as I bring this research project to publication.

Portions of the book have appeared elsewhere, and I am grateful to the publishers of these earlier articles for allowing me to draw upon them here. An abbreviated version of chapter 5 appeared in "When Are International Institutions Effective? The Impact of Domestic Veto Players on Compliance with WTO Rulings" in *International Studies Quarterly*, January 2020, 61(1): 220–34. Portions of chapter 6 appeared in "Obstructing Integration: Domestic Politics and the European Court of Justice" in *European Union Politics*, April 2018, 19(3): 427–57.

At the University of Chicago Press, Chuck Myers encouraged the project and helped me to focus on the core question of why international economic courts matter during a time of backlash against globalization. I am fortunate to have benefited from Chuck's editorial wisdom and guidance in this process. Erika Barrios and Caterina MacLean ably oversaw the production. I appreciate the excellent suggestions from two anonymous reviewers. Their comments pushed me to revise the book in several directions, and it is much stronger as a result.

Most importantly, I thank my family for their unconditional love and support.

Appendix for Chapter 4

AI.I Measurement

This appendix justifies my data collection effort. The full dataset and code book are available in the online supplementary materials. Measuring compliance with WTO rulings is not straightforward. For each of the disputes, I sought out official statutory and regulatory measures passed by defendant governments—that is, tangible policy changes in the wake of rulings. The coding reflects official legislation and administrative measures implemented by defendant governments.

The WTO itself does not track or verify compliance. Instead, it relies on (1) voluntary reporting from defendant governments and (2) complainants that pursue violations until a satisfactory outcome is obtained. Defendants usually declare compliance before the deadline but do not routinely provide supporting evidence or specifics. This means that many instances of noncompliance go undetected.

Table AI.I demonstrates that the WTO rarely detects persistent compliance problems. In many cases where the respondent failed to enact any policy reforms, the WTO had no formal record of this negative outcome. In the few instances where the WTO did have a formal record of compliance problems and the plaintiff pressed for resolution, the respondent did eventually comply. Table AI.2 shows cases where respondents eventually corrected their violations.

WTO Rarely Detects Compliance Problems

Dispute	Complainant(s)	Respondent	Comply ever?	Did WTO detect noncompliance?
18	Canada	Australia	0	Yes
26	US	EU	0	–
27	Ecuador, Guatemala, Honduras, Mexico, US	EU	0	Yes
34	India	Turkey	0	–
48	Canada	EU	0	–
126	US	Australia	0	Yes
136	EU	US	0	–
141	India	EU	0	Yes
160	EU	US	0	–
162	Japan	US	0	–
174	US	EU	0	–
176	EU	US	0	–
207	Argentina, Australia, Brazil, Chile, EU, India, Indonesia, Japan, Korea, Thailand	Chile	0	Yes
222	Brazil	Canada	0	No
231	Peru	EU	0	–
234	Canada, Mexico	US	0	No
245	US	Japan	0	Yes
265	Australia	EU	0	–
266	Brazil	EU	0	–
283	Thailand	EU	0	–
285	Antigua and Barbuda	US	0	Yes
290	Australia	EU	0	–
291	US	EU	0	–
292	Canada	EU	0	–
293	Argentina	EU	0	–
312	Indonesia	Korea	0	Yes
316	US	EU	0	–
322	Japan	US	0	–
336	Korea	Japan	0	No
363	US	China	0	–
371	Philippines	Thailand	0	–
381	Mexico	US	0	–
404	Viet Nam	US	0	–
406	Indonesia	US	0	–
413	US	China	0	–

Note: Empty cell "–" indicates that no WTO compliance investigation took place.

TABLE A1.2 **Where WTO Detects Noncompliance, the Respondent Eventually Corrects Violation**

Dispute	Complainant(s)	Respondent	Comply ever?	Did WTO detect noncompliance?
46	Canada	Brazil	1	Yes
103	US	Canada	1	Yes
108	EU	US	1	Yes
113	New Zealand	Canada	1	Yes
132	US	Mexico	1	Yes
257	Canada	US	1	Yes
264	Canada	US	1	Yes
267	Brazil	US	1	Yes
268	Argentina	US	0.5	Yes
277	Canada	US	1	Yes
294	EU	US	0.5	Yes

Note: 1 denotes respondent fully complied eventually; 0.5 denotes partial compliance.

Appendix for Chapter 5

A2.1 Applying the synthetic control method

This portion of the appendix describes the statistical approach and computation for the synthetic control method. It draws directly on Abadie, Diamond, and Hainmueller (2010, 2015, 2011), using language and mathematical representations from their original publications. I summarize the methodology and explain how it is applied to measure the impact of WTO rulings on trade.

The synthetic control method (SCM) begins with a sample of units (countries, j) observed over multiple time periods (years, $t= 1,2, \ldots T$). The case of interest, the unit exposed to the intervention, is the "treated unit" ($j = 1$). Other units constitute the "donor pool," the population of potential comparison units that may be used to approximate the counterfactual of the case of interest without the intervention ($j = 2,3, \ldots J$). The donor pool contains units with outcomes that are thought to be "driven by the same structural process as the unit representing the case of interest and that were not subject to structure shocks to the outcome variable during the sample period of the study" (Abadie, Diamond, and Hainmueller 2011, 4). The goal is to closely match the pre-intervention characteristics of the treated unit by using a combination of untreated units.

The "treated unit" is the respondent country that experienced an adverse WTO ruling. The "donor pool" consists of countries other than the respondent. These countries are selected to be roughly similar to the respondent in terms of several economic characteristics. All countries are observed annually for several years before a WTO ruling—the "pre-intervention period"—and several years after—the "post-intervention period."

The synthetic control is defined as the *weighted average* of units in the donor pool, represented by a column vector of weights:

$$W = (w_2,...,w_{j+1})' \text{ wherein:}$$
$$0 \le w_j \le 1 \text{ for } j = 2,...,J \tag{1}$$
$$\text{and } w_2 + ... + w_J = 1$$

The weights minimize the difference between the pre-intervention characteristics of the treated unit and the synthetic control. Vector W summarizes the "unit-weights."

The pre-intervention characteristics are the variables that describe each country's economy in the years leading up to the dispute. The variables include GDP, unemployment rate, industry share of GDP, and so on, as described above. I assign unit-weight to each donor pool country to ensure their unit-weighted average (the synthetic control) looks very much like the respondent country (the treated unit) in the years before the ruling.

Optimal weights are found as follows: Suppose there are k variables representing the different characteristics of interest. Let X_1 be a $(k \times 1)$ vector of values for the pre-intervention characteristics of the treated unit and X_0 be a $(k \times (J-1))$ matrix with values for the same variables for units in the donor pool. The best vector of unit-weights, the synthetic control W^*, minimizes the size of the difference $X_1 - X_0 W$. The optimization problem is to find the W^* that minimizes:

$$\| X_1 - X_0 W \| V = \sqrt{(X_1 - X_0 W)' V (X_1 - X_0 W)} \tag{2}$$

where V is a $(k \times k)$ symmetric and positive semidefinite matrix of weights for the variables in X_1 and X_0. I refer to the matrix V as the "covariate-weight" matrix and describe it below. The vector of unit-weights W reflects the relative importance assigned to each donor unit (country) when measuring the difference $X_1 - X_0 W$. Countries with large predictive power on the outcome receive greater unit-weight.

For example, suppose the WTO rules against China in a dispute. I compare China to India, Japan, and the United States in the pre-intervention period. If China's economic characteristics—GDP growth rate, unemployment rate, etc.—look more like India's than Japan's or the United States', then India would get a larger unit-weight. Which economic characteristics are most important in determining India's similarity to China? To make this determination, SCM also identifies optimal covariate-weights.

To compute the best covariate-weight matrix V^*, one must optimize over all reasonable covariate-weighting schemes V according to some optimization criteria. The "synth" package in R minimizes the mean squared prediction error (MSPE) of the outcome variable in the pre-intervention periods. Specifically, let Y_1^{pre} be the $(T_p \times 1)$ vector of values for the outcome variable for the treated unit in the pre-intervention periods. Note that $1 \leq T_p$ is the number of pre-intervention periods over which the MSPE is minimized. For example, if we have data for China during the ten years leading up to the adverse ruling, then $T_p = 10$ and the vector Y_1^{pre} is China's trade in those ten years. Let Y_0^{pre} be the $(T_p \times (J - 1))$ analogous matrix for the $(J - 1)$ units in the donor pool. Using the example where the donor pool consists of India, Japan, and the United States, the Y_0^{pre} matrix has ten rows and three columns. The values of the matrix are the countries' yearly trade. These data are used to compute an optimal covariate-weight matrix. So V^* is chosen to minimize:

$$arg \min_{V \in V} (Y_1^{pre} - Y_0^{pre} W * (V))\,'(Y_1^{pre} - Y_0^{pre} W * (V)) \qquad (3)$$

V is the set of all positive definite and diagonal matrices of covariate-weights. The unit-weights for the synthetic control are given by W^* as discussed above. Because the matrix V^* is positive diagonal, it ensures all covariates receive non-negative weights that directly predict the outcome variable and there are no covariate interactions.

In summary, the synthetic control method solves a nested optimization problem that minimizes equation 3 for the $W^*(V)$ given by equation 2. It selects an optimal vector of unit-weights W^* and an optimal matrix of covariate-weights V^*. The unit-weights W^* correspond to each country's contribution to the synthetic control unit and the covariate-weights V^* correspond to each covariate's contribution to the similarity determination.

The synthetic control unit is used to estimate the treatment effect. The treatment effect is estimated by comparing post-intervention outcomes for the treated unit to those for the synthetic control unit (which is not exposed to the intervention). In the example above, we interpolate what China's trade *would have been* in the years following the WTO dispute had it not actually been "treated" with an adverse ruling. The interpolation is based on a combination of what India, Japan, and the United States' actual trade was in the post-dispute years. Since the vector of unit-weights W^* placed the most weight on India, the "synthetic-China" trade pattern looks a lot like India's actual trade pattern. I compare China's *actual* trade and the synthetic-China *interpolated* trade to estimate the treatment effect.

To calculate the treatment effect, I compare the post-intervention outcomes for the treated unit to the synthetic control unit for every year in the post-intervention period. Let Y_{jt}^{post} be the outcome of unit j at time t. So Y_{1t}^{post} is the vector of post-intervention values of the outcome for the treated unit. In the example, this is China's trade in the post-dispute years. The matrix of post-intervention values of the outcome for the donor pool is denoted Y_{jt}^{post} where $j = 2, \ldots ,J$. The matrix Y_{jt}^{post} contains Indian, Japanese, and US trade in the post-dispute years.

The synthetic control estimator of the effect of the treatment is given by:

$$\hat{\alpha}_{1t} = Y_{1t}^{post} - \sum_{j=2}^{J} w_j^* Y_{jt}^{post} \tag{4}$$

(Abadie and Gardeazabal 2003; Abadie, Diamond, and Hainmueller 2010). This is the difference between the vector of post-intervention values for the treated unit minus the unit-weighted average of post-intervention values for the donor pool. In summary, this technique establishes a synthetic control unit that has similar behavior to the case of interest during the time period prior to the intervention and interprets the discrepancy in the outcome variable following the intervention as produced by the intervention itself. Trade cooperation is then measured with a summary statistic and associated uncertainty. Denote the time of treatment to be $t = \tilde{t}$. The synthetic control estimator of the effect of the treatment is given by equation 4 for the post-treatment period, $t > \tilde{t}$. Similarly, I define a goodness-of-fit estimator for the pre-treatment period by:

$$\hat{\alpha}_{1t}^{pre} = Y_{1t}^{pre} - \sum_{j=2}^{J} w_j^* Y_{jt}^{pre} \ for \ t \leq \tilde{t} \tag{5}$$

The trade cooperation score S is calculated as the difference in means. This is the average effect of the treatment in the post-intervention period minus the average goodness-of-fit in the pre-intervention period:

$$S = \frac{1}{(T-\tilde{t})} \sum_{i+1}^{T} \hat{\alpha}_{1t} - \frac{1}{\tilde{t}} \sum_{1}^{i} \hat{\alpha}_{1t}^{pre} . \tag{6}$$

The standard deviation is computed for the $\hat{\alpha}_{1t}^{pre}$ values. It denotes how good a fit the synthetic control was. If the synthetic control unit was very similar to the treated unit in all years of the pre-intervention period, then the two should vary over time together and the standard deviation will be small. The compliance score should be quite trustworthy. If the synthetic control unit, on the other hand, is very dissimilar to the treated unit in some of the pre-intervention years, then the standard deviation will be large. When the standard deviation is large, the cooperation score is less reliable. Thus together the cooperation score and standard deviation capture the extent of cooperation and the reliability of the metric.

A2.2 Trade flows used in SCM

This section provides additional information about the trade flows that are used in the synthetic control analysis. Other countries enter WTO disputes as third parties, but this is not a serious source of bias. Third-party countries often side with the complainant because they are typically concerned with exports to the respondent (Bown 2005a). When the respondent complies, third parties should similarly benefit: their exports to the respondent should increase. Figure A2.1 shows a schematic of the trade flows used to create the counterfactual. Because I estimate the counterfactual from the complainant's exports to other countries— *not* other countries' exports to the respondent—I avoid trade flows that concern third parties. Nevertheless, to guard against possible bias, I exclude third-party governments from the donor pool.

Because the trade flows are compositional data, I follow the standard practice of transforming the data with a log ratio. I divide each unit's trade share by the *ex ante* largest control unit and take the natural logarithm of this quantity. The log-ratio transformation helps ensure there is no interference between the units, an important assumption for applying the synthetic control method.

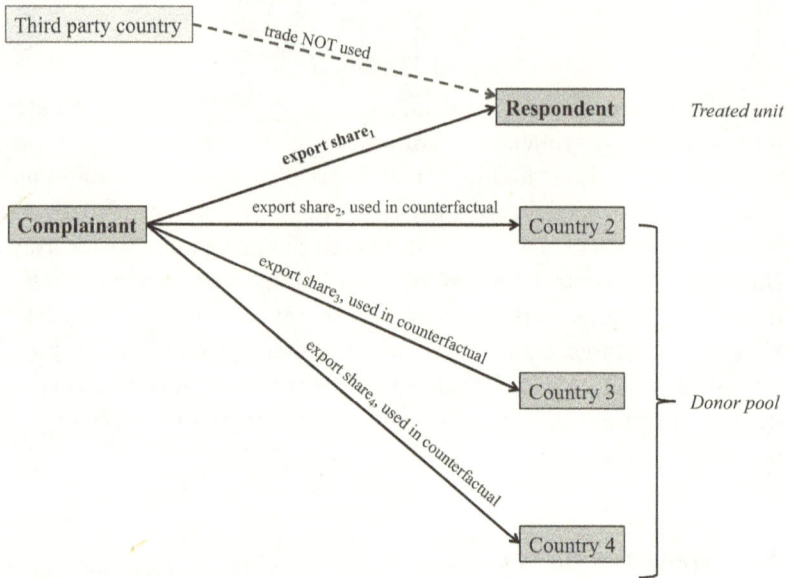

FIGURE A2.1. Schematic of Trade Flows
Note: Exports from the complainant to other countries are used to estimate the counterfactual. Third-party countries export to the respondent, but these trade flows are not used. All trade flows are measured in log ratio units.

A2.3 Robustness of regression results

Table A2.1 presents robustness checks using additional legal, political and economic controls. The complexity of the dispute and the number of legal claims (*# Claims*) could impede compliance and thereby diminish the trade impact. Experience with the legal process could strengthen either the complainant's or respondent's positions so I control for each government's past dispute in their respective roles—*Comp. Past Disputes* and *Resp. Past Disputes.* The respondent's history of past disputes is a significant predictor of trade impact. The most active users of the WTO may also be the most resistant to its authority. For the complainant, I control for the value of *Complainant Exports* and *Complainant Imports,* each as a share of GDP. Another control is *Respondent Exports* because exporters may push their governments to remove WTO-violating import restrictions in order to avoid retaliation from abroad. The relative size of disputants' economies is also included as the *GDP Ratio,* with higher numbers denoting that a complainant's economy is larger than its respondent's.

TABLE A2.1 **Probit and Ordered Probit Models for WTO Disputes with Control Variables**

	Trade cooperation$_A$			Trade cooperation$_B$		
	(1)	(2)	(3)	(4)	(5)	(6)
Veto Points	−2.47**	−2.78**	−2.67**	−2.58**	−3.21***	−2.73**
	(1.24)	(1.29)	(1.19)	(1.11)	(1.19)	(1.06)
Third Parties[†]	0.41**	0.36**	0.40**	0.42**	0.34**	0.38**
	(0.21)	(0.18)	(0.19)	(0.19)	(0.16)	(0.17)
% Adverse Ruling	0.38	0.39	0.58	0.05	0.11	0.23
	(0.53)	(0.50)	(0.51)	(0.49)	(0.47)	(0.47)
Respondent GDP[†]	0.39*		0.15	0.42*		0.12
	(0.23)		(0.18)	(0.22)		(0.16)
Complainant GDP[†]	−0.38		−0.16	−0.22		−0.02
	(0.26)		(0.14)	(0.23)		(0.13)
Federal Respondent	−0.57	−0.64*	−0.52	−0.63*	−0.65*	−0.58*
	(0.39)	(0.37)	(0.39)	(0.35)	(0.34)	(0.35)
Legislative Measure	0.41	0.34	0.34	0.50	0.49	0.49
	(0.36)	(0.34)	(0.34)	(0.32)	(0.31)	(0.31)
EU Respondent		0.53			0.55	
		(0.51)			(0.47)	
Comp. Past Disputes	0.01			0.01		
	(0.01)			(0.01)		
Resp. Past Disputes	−0.01			−0.01*		
	(0.01)			(0.01)		
# Claims	−0.01			−0.01		
	(0.02)			(0.02)		
GDP Ratio		−0.004			0.004	
		(0.01)			(0.01)	
Complainant Imports[†]		−0.01			−0.01	
		(0.03)			(0.03)	
Complainant Exports[†]		0.01			0.003	
		(0.03)			(0.03)	
Respondent Exports[†]		−0.02			−0.02	
		(0.02)			(0.02)	
Comp. Election Year			−0.44			−0.47
			(0.32)			(0.30)
Resp. Election Year			−0.34			−0.29
			(0.29)			(0.26)
N	113	113	113	113	113	113
Cooperation measure	(0/1)	(0/1)	(0/1)	(0/1/2)	(0/1/2)	(0/1/2)
Log Likelihood	−68.04	−70.11	−67.61	−105.32	−107.13	−105.48

Note: Probit models are calculated with R. Cooperation is coded using SCM with annual bilateral trade data for disputed products. [†]Log units. Significance codes *p<0.1; **p<0.05; ***p<0.01. Intercepts not shown.

These controls do not alter the findings. Drawing from the partisan business cycle literature, I control for *Election Year* in both litigants during the first year of dispute. Neither affects the veto players result.

A2.4 Single-step linear regression

The methodology in chapter 5 relies on a two-step approach to evaluate whether the respondent's domestic veto players diminish the ability of WTO rulings to recover trade between governments. The first step uses SCM. Product-level trade flows for each dispute are used to estimate trade recovery in the wake of an adverse WTO ruling. This step employs numerous controls that describe a respondent's and its comparison countries' economies. This group of countries can be labeled "partner" countries that import disputed products from the complainant country. The result is a fine-tuned measure of trade recovery in each individual dispute. Then the second step uses a probit regression to test the hypothesis that respondents with more domestic veto players are less apt to deliver trade recovery. This latter step brings in several litigant- and dispute-level controls.

An alternative approach models both steps in a single linear regression with two expectations. The first expectation is that there should be an overall recovery in product-level trade for the respondent after the adverse ruling (that is, after the implementation deadline) compared to the other partner countries and compared to pre-ruling trade. Second, the respondent's veto points are associated with smaller product-level trade recoveries, all else equal. Recall that product-level trade, the respondent, and the implementation deadline are specific to each dispute. This requires a linear interaction model of the form:

$$Y_{jtd} = \beta_0 + \beta_1 Vetopoints_{1td} \times T_{jtd} + \beta_2 T_{jtd} + \beta_3 Vetopoints_{1td} + \beta_4 X_d \times T_{jtd} + \beta_5 X_d$$
$$+ \beta_6 Z_{jt} + \varepsilon_{jtd}$$

The export share for the disputed products (d), from the complainant to the partner country (j) in year t, is denoted by dependent variable Y_{jtd}. The treatment indicator for respondent country ($j = 1$) in the period after the adverse ruling (specifically after the implementation deadline) is T_{jtd}. So in a given dispute d, if a respondent country $j = 1$ was required to implement an adverse ruling in year $t = 2000$, the treatment indicator takes on a value of 1 when $j = 1$ and $t \geq 2000$ and 0 otherwise. Note that the treatment indicator reflects the dispute d according to which country is the respondent and when the implementation deadline occurs. The expectation is that β_1 is negative and significant while β_2 is positive and significant.

The dispute controls are denoted X_d. This includes the *% Adverse Ruling,* the number of *Third Parties,* etc. We are only interested in their interaction with the treatment indicator T_{jtd} because they are irrelevant for non-respondent partner countries ($j \neq 1$) and the time period before the adverse ruling. We have the various trade controls Z_{jt} that were previously employed in SCM calculations. Those controls are used to predict export shares Y_{jtd} for all partner countries ($j = 1,2,3 \ldots$) and all years ($t = 1988,1989,1990 \ldots$)—both before and after the WTO ruling implementation deadline. Standard errors are clustered by dispute.

Model A2.2(1) shows the regression analysis with basic trade controls and no dispute controls. There is a statistically significant increase in export shares for respondent governments in the post-treatment period, as denoted by the positive coefficient on the treatment indicator. This effect is significantly diminished when respondent governments have more veto points, as denoted by the negative coefficient on the main interaction term. Model A2.2(2) introduces additional trade controls for the partner countries. Model A2.2(3) introduces basic dispute characteristics. Model A2.2(4) brings in additional dispute characteristics, including whether the dispute is over controversial issues such as agricultural trade or health and safety measures.

This analysis shows the substantive findings are not an artifact of the two-step methodology. As expected, the results are weaker and harder to interpret. This is because the linear model forces all the trade covariates to carry the explanatory power across all disputes, whether those disputes pertain to steel tariffs, bans on hormone-treated beef, lumber, textiles, or apples (to name a few) and whether the respondent is a major economic power or a small market. SCM has the distinct advantage of fine-tuning covariate-weights to reflect the particular attributes of the dispute and constructing a synthetic control unit that looks most like the respondent government, even when that country has no perfect single "matched country." The linear regression has hundreds of "control" units for just 120 treated units, making the weighting approach in SCM all the more suitable. Finally, the single step approach does not distinguish individual disputes as producing cooperation or not, effectively obscuring a substantively important outcome. In summary, the results in table A2.2 confirm the basic substantive findings of chapter 5 while reinforcing the advantages of SCM.

TABLE A2.2 **Linear Regression of Disputed-Product Export Share for WTO Disputant and Non-Disputant States, 1988 to 2012**

	Disputed product export share$_{jtd}$			
	(1)	(2)	(3)	(4)
DISPUTE VARIABLES				
Respondent Veto Points × Treated	−0.164*	−0.163*	−0.193*	−0.128
	(0.085)	(0.085)	(0.109)	(0.117)
Respondent Veto Points	0.021	0.021	0.016	0.006
	(0.019)	(0.019)	(0.019)	(0.019)
Treated	0.085**	0.085**	0.196**	0.170*
	(0.040)	(0.040)	(0.089)	(0.088)
Third Parties[‡] ×Treated			−0.055*	−0.054*
			(0.029)	(0.028)
Third Parties[‡]			−0.003	−0.005*
			(0.003)	(0.003)
% Adverse Ruling × Treated			−0.018	−0.011
			(0.065)	(0.064)
% Adverse Ruling			0.007	0.007
			(0.007)	(0.007)
Legislative Measure × Treated			−0.006	−0.019
			(0.041)	(0.042)
Legislative Measure			0.003	0.005
			(0.006)	(0.006)
EU Respondent × Treated			−0.062	−0.046
			(0.043)	(0.043)
EU Respondent			0.035	0.032
			(0.048)	(0.048)
Agriculture × Treated				0.008
				(0.027)
Agriculture				0.005
				(0.007)
Sanitary & Phytosan × Treated				−0.106*
				(0.055)
Sanitary & Phytosan				0.014*
				(0.007)
TRADE CONTROLS				
Complainant GDP[†]	−0.007***	−0.007***	−0.009***	−0.009***
	(0.002)	(0.002)	(0.003)	(0.003)
Partner GDP[†]	0.058***	0.058***	0.058***	0.058***
	(0.006)	(0.006)	(0.006)	(0.006)
Partner agriculture	−0.001***	−0.001***	−0.001***	−0.001***
	(0.0003)	(0.0004)	(0.0003)	(0.0003)
Partner industry	0.0004	0.0004	0.0004	0.0004
	(0.0003)	(0.0003)	(0.0003)	(0.0003)
Partner manufacturing	0.00005	0.0001	−0.0001	−0.0001
	(0.0004)	(0.0004)	(0.0004)	(0.0004)
Partner unemployment	−0.002**	−0.002**	−0.002**	−0.002**
	(0.001)	(0.001)	(0.001)	(0.001)
Partner Polity Score	0.001**	0.001*	0.001*	0.001*
	(0.0004)	(0.0004)	(0.0004)	(0.0004)
Partner GDP growth		0.0001		
		(0.0002)		
Partner GDP per capita[‡]		−0.001		
		(0.003)		

Partner trade dependence[‡]		-0.002		
		(0.006)		
N	19,578	19,562	19,578	19,578
Disputes	120	120	120	120
Years	24	24	24	24
R^2	0.275	0.275	0.283	0.286

Note: Models are calculated with R. Standard errors clustered by dispute. Significance codes *$p<0.1$; **$p<0.05$; ***$p<0.01$. Intercepts not shown. [†]Normalized. [‡]Log transformed.

A2.5 Veto players in the EU

The European Union participates in the WTO as a single entity. The measure of veto players by Henisz (2000) is only available for countries. Therefore, one cannot directly measure EU veto players using existing data.

I use two approaches to measuring veto players in the EU. First, I use a weighted average of national veto players, with weights according to Council vote shares. This likely undercounts the true veto players because even when the EU institutions are the decision makers, key actors in the national governments may fail to consent to policy reforms. Second, I use data from Yildirim et al. (2017) that provide a veto points score for the EU institutions, including the Commission, Council, and Parliament, by applying Henisz's Political Constraints Index methodology. The EU is coded as having a higher veto points score (EU mean=0.86, sd=0.02) than the weighted national average (EU mean = 0.47, sd = 0.01). My results are robust to this alternative coding.

Further still, one can assess whether the coding of EU veto players ultimately affects the substantive findings. How severe would bias have to be to change the results? I conducted a simple sensitivity analysis to extremely low and extremely high veto points values. No matter what value of veto points I assign to the EU, the regression coefficient is negative. For any hypothetical value of EU veto points greater than 0.2, the negative regression coefficient is statistically significant at the $p < 0.1$ level. The negative correlation between veto points and noncompliance is robust to any plausible value for EU veto points. It is helpful to place this result in context. In 1995, Malaysia's veto points score was 0.295, and in 2006, Colombia's veto points score was 0.110. Malaysia and Colombia's political systems are far less constrained than the EU, not least because of their weak democratic institutions. Thus a value of 0.2 for the EU is unrealistic; surely the EU veto points score is much higher. For any higher EU scores, my regression results are robust.

A3

Appendix for Chapter 6

A3.1 Description of data

The following section describes data used in chapter 6, including measurement details, coverage, sources, and descriptive statistics.

A3.1.1 Dependent variables

Import share: Total value of imported goods to country j from other EU-15 countries as share of total imported goods to country j from the world in a given year t. Measured for each EU-15 country annually with complete coverage for years 1989–2013.[1,2] (European Commission, 2019).

Import share in agriculture: Value of imported agricultural goods to country j from other EU-15 countries as share of total imported agricultural goods to country j from the world, classified as HS 02–12 and 14–18.

Figure A3.1 illustrates the trends in intra-EU imports over time by country. Panel (a) shows that the import values, measured in logged euros, have steadily increased. Panel (b) shows the import shares, the portion of a country's total imports that come from the EU-15. This is the dependent variable in the main analysis.

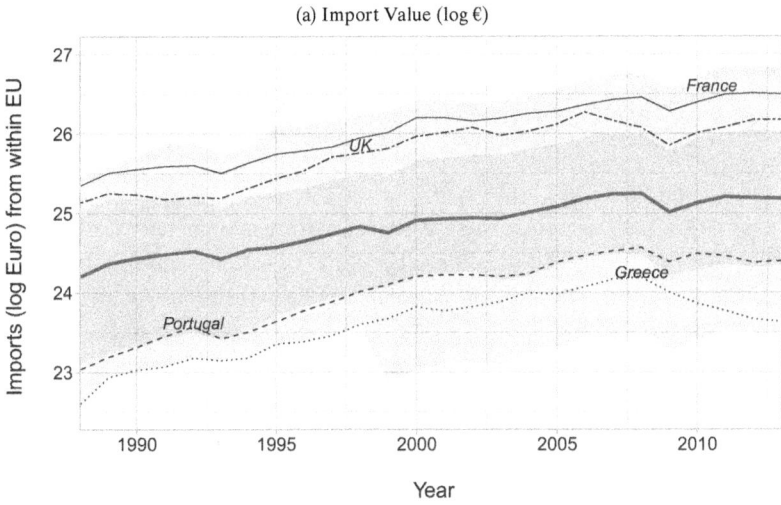

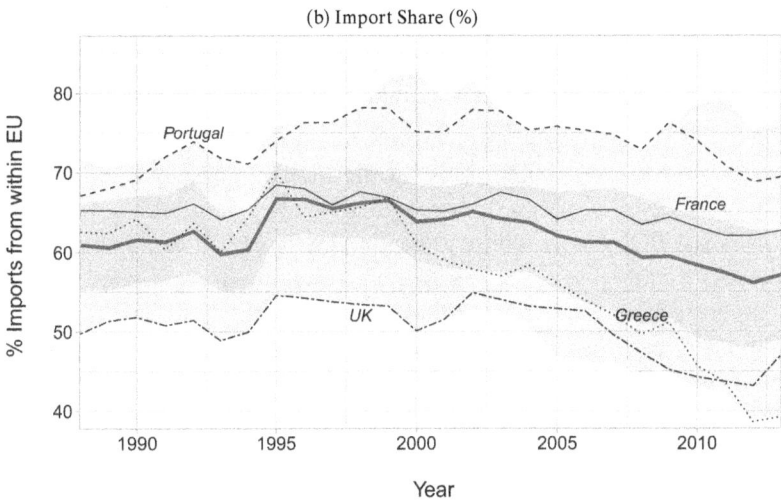

FIGURE A3.1. Intra-EU Imports over Time by Country
Note: Data from EuroStat. Import values are reported in logged euros. Import share is the portion of a country's total imports that come from the EU-15. Example countries are plotted with lines. Shaded areas indicate the minimum, first quartile, third quartile, and maximum country values. The mean is indicated with a bold line in each plot.

A3.1.2 Explanatory variables

Adverse trade ruling: Indicator variable where 1 denotes a country lost one or more trade-related infringement lawsuits at the ECJ in a given year. These data are recorded by the year of the ruling. They are assembled in two parts:

  i. *Years 1988 to 1999*: These data are extracted from the Database on EU Infringement Proceedings by Börzel and Knoll (2012), http://www .infringement-db.jmce.org/Index.html. Infringements are counted if they satisfy both criteria: (1) the ECJ ruled in favor of the Commission (that is, against a member state) and (2) the policy sector is coded as "internal market," "taxation and customs union," "competition," or "enterprise." For agricultural infringements, I selected rulings with the policy sector code "agriculture" (all other extraction criteria remain the same).
  ii. *Years 2000 to 2012*: I code these data from the court's own records, http:// www.curia.europa.eu/, according to the following procedure.

First, I searched for all ECJ lawsuits where the parties were *Commission v. [Member State]*. I downloaded all rulings issued since 2000. Second, I selected only lawsuits the Commission brought to the court under Article 258 of the Treaty on the Functioning of the European Union (TFEU) or its predecessor grounds (Article 226 EC or Article 169 of the EC Treaty). Third, and aided by the policy sector coding indicated by the court, I reviewed each ruling for trade-related topics. I included only those rulings that pertain to "internal market," "taxation and customs union," "competition," or "enterprise." Fourth, I read the judgment to determine whether the Commission prevailed. For rulings with multiple legal claims, I counted the outcome as "adverse" if the Commission prevailed on at least one substantive claim. For agricultural infringements, I instead selected rulings on "agriculture" and at least one of the trade-related criteria listed above (all other coding criteria remain the same). In the end, I produced a database of 826 rulings in which 261 were adverse trade-related infringements and 35 were adverse infringements relating to agriculture in the single market.

The following examples illustrate the coding criteria. In a first example, a lawsuit over country-of-origin labeling (C-325/00), the ECJ found that a German labeling requirement created a barrier to trade that violated EU law. The 2002 judgment noted:

"The contested scheme has . . . restrictive effects on the free movement of goods between Member States. Such a scheme, set up in order to promote the distribution of agricultural and food products made in Germany . . . may encourage consumers to buy the products with the [German] label to the exclusion of imported products. Germany has failed to fulfill its obligations under Article 30 of the Treaty."

I count this case as an adverse trade ruling.

By contrast, in a lawsuit over quantitative restrictions on the imports of trailers for motorcycles, Italy prevailed (C-110/05). This judgment noted:

"The Commission claims that the effect of . . . [Italy's] Highway Code is to prevent the use of trailers lawfully produced and marketed in the [other] Member States . . . and to hinder their importation into, and sale in, Italy. The Court hereby dismisses the action [and] orders the Commission of the European Communities to pay the costs."

Although this case addressed barriers to intra-EU trade, the ruling favored the defendant government and so it does *not* count in my dataset.

There are numerous cases unrelated to trade. For example, Greece lost many infringement rulings over its failure to fulfill environmental obligations (e.g., C-103/00, C-83/02, C-352/02, and C-119/02). Austria lost many infringement disputes over health and safety standards, especially in the workplace (e.g., C-150/00, C-111/00, C-110/00, C-473/99, and C-424/99). These types of cases are *not* counted either.

Table A3.1 summarizes the data on adverse trade rulings.

Checks: Institutional checks and balances. Measured for each country annually with complete coverage years 1988–2012 Source: Keefer and Stasavage. (2003). The *Checks* variable is incremented by one in parliamentary regimes for every party in the government coalition so long as the parties are needed to maintain a majority and for every party in the government coalition that has a position on economic issues closer to the largest opposition party than the executive. The *Checks* variable is incremented by one in presidential systems if the chief executive's opposition controls the legislature, for each chamber in the legislature, and for each party that is allied with the president's party but has an ideological orientation closer to the opposition. There are other details described in the DPI codebook.

TABLE A3.1 **Adverse Trade Infringement Rulings by Country**

Country	Adverse trade rulings per year			Total
	Median	Mean	Maximum	
Austria[‡]	1	0.78	3	14
Belgium[†]	1	1.72	7	43
Denmark	0	0.52	2	13
Finland[‡]	0	0.28	1	5
France	1	1.88	9	47
Germany	1	1.36	3	34
Greece	1	1.64	6	41
Ireland	1	0.96	4	24
Italy	2	2.48	7	62
Luxembourg[‡]	0	0.36	1	5
Netherlands	1	0.68	3	17
Portugal	0	1.12	4	28
Spain	1	1.56	4	39
Sweden[‡]	0	0.33	3	6
United Kingdom	0	0.44	2	11

Note: Infringement disputes on trade matters where the ECJ favored the Commission, 1988–2012. [†]Count includes Luxembourg 1988–1998. [‡]Covers 1999–2012 only.

Effective number of parties: Calculated as the reciprocal of the Herfindahl-Hirschman index of party concentration (1/HHI). The Herfindahl-Hirschman index is the sum of the squared seat shares of all parties in parliament. Measured for each country annually with complete coverage years 1988–2012. Source: Beck et al. (2001).

Legislative fractionalization: The probability that two deputies picked at random from the legislature will be of different parties. Measured for each country annually with complete coverage years 1988–2012. Source: Beck et al. (2001).

Polarization: Polarization is the maximum difference between the chief executive's party's ideological position and the values of those of the three largest government parties and the largest opposition party. Measured for each country annually with complete coverage years 1988–2012. Source: Beck et al. (2001).

Veto points: Measure of political constraints that estimates the feasibility of policy change based on the number of veto players in government. I use the "POLCONV" version that accounts for the judiciary. It is based on a spatial model of political interaction to derive the extent to which any one political actor or the replacement for any one actor—the executive or a chamber

TABLE A3.2 **Variances and Correlations between Measures of Political Constraints**

	Variance	Correlations			
		Checks	Legislative Fract	Polarization	Veto points
Checks	1.757				
Legislative fractionalization	0.011	0.537			
Polarization	0.740	0.490	0.700		
Veto points	0.008	0.145	0.339	0.306	
Effective # parties	1.008	0.277	0.823	0.508	0.368

Note: Variances and correlations are for complete observations entering into the regression analysis.

of the legislature, for example—is constrained in his or her choice of future policies. Measured for each country annually with complete coverage years 1988–2012. Source: Political Constraint Index (POLCON) Dataset v.2012, Henisz (2002).

Table A3.2 presents the variance for each measure of political constraints and their corresponding correlations. *Checks* and *Veto Points* are the least correlated, while *Legislative Fractionalization* and *Effective Number of Parties* are highly correlated. The legislative fractionalization index and the effective number of parties differ slightly in that the latter is less sensitive to the presence of small parties or independent legislators who claim no party affiliation.

A3.1.3 Control variables[3]

Bicameralism: Indicator for whether country's legislature is unicameral (0) or bicameral (1). Source: author's coding.[4]

Dualism: Indicator for whether country's legal system is monist (0) or dualist (1). Source: author's coding.

Exports: Value of country's exports of goods and services as percentage of its GDP. Measured annually by country, 1988–2012. Source: World Development Indicators (WDI) (World Bank 2013).

GDP: Gross domestic product in constant 2010 US dollars. Logged units. Source: WDI (World Bank 2013).

GDP per capita: GDP per capita in constant 2010 US dollars. Logged units. Source: WDI (World Bank 2013).

GDP growth: Annual percentage growth in GDP. Source: WDI (World Bank 2013).

Government debt: Government debt as percentage of GDP. Measured annually by country with coverage for years 1995–2012 and 21.4% of observations missing. Source: Organisation for Economic Co-operation and Development, http://www.data.oecd.org. The World Bank's database is also missing many observations.

Government effectiveness: Index measuring perceptions of the quality of public services, civil service and the degree of its independence from political pressures, policy formulation and implementation, and the credibility of the government's commitment to such policies. Annual coverage 1996–2012 for all EU-15 countries. Source: Worldwide Governance Indicators Database (Kaufmann and Kraay 2015).

Preliminary reference rulings: Preliminary reference rulings issued by the Court of Justice on the following topics: "taxation," "free movement of goods," "competition," and "internal market principles," as classified by the court. Measured as annual count of rulings by referring country. I code these observations by the year the judgment was issued. Source: Author's coding from ECJ records, http://www.curia.europa.eu. Data are lagged one additional year to capture the possibility that an unresolved dispute is taken up through a related infringement lawsuit, coverage for all countries, 1986–2011.[5]

Public opinion of EU: Eurobarometer survey question asked respondents whether they thought their country benefited from EU membership. Fraction of respondents that answered "yes." Measured semi-annually, from 1988 to 2011 for all EU-15 countries except Austria. I used the earlier of the two survey waves each year, typically conducted in March or April. Unfortunately, Eurobarometer did not have a survey question specifically about *economic* benefits of membership. Source: Eurobarometer (European Commission 2016).

SSI council: Shapley-Shubik voting power index for Council of ministers of the European Union (%). Source: Indices of Power (Bräuninger and König 2005) and extending calculations by Schneider (2011).

Sector value added: Value added for agriculture, industry, or manufacturing sectors, each measured as a percentage of the country's GDP. Some missing observations. Source: WDI, (World Bank 2013).

Transposition deficit: The transposition deficit shows the percentage of Single Market directives not yet notified to the Commission in relation to the total number of directives that should have been notified by the deadline. The indicator can be considered as a measure of policy coherence between the EU and the Member States. Annual coverage for years 1997–2012 for most countries with 38.7% of observations missing. Source: European Commission, 2019.

A3.1.3.1 WHY FOCUS ON INTERNAL TRADE? Article 28 of the TFEU states, "The Union shall comprise a customs union which shall cover all trade in goods and [prohibit] between member states customs duties on imports and exports and charges having equivalent effect." Complementing this "pillar" are freedoms of exchange in services, capital, and labor, which aim to create a single market. Labor or capital mobility could reveal other critical dimensions of the single market. Policy convergence or cultural dimensions could reveal other ways that the ECJ has had an impact on European integration. Each of these dimensions warrants future study.

A3.1.3.2 WHY FOCUS ON INFRINGEMENT DISPUTES RATHER THAN PRELIMINARY REFERENCES? In preliminary references, the plaintiffs vary widely and can include individual citizens, corporations, industry groups, and so on, so it is difficult to consistently map rulings onto pro-integration policies or compare across lawsuits. Infringement disputes, by contrast, have the same plaintiff: the European Commission. I control for the number of preliminary references countries undertake each year.

A3.1.3.3 ARE ALL AGRICULTURE DISPUTES EXPECTED TO IMPACT TRADE? Some agriculture rulings are only indirectly related to trade. For example, several disputes address food inspection where the defendant government failed to apply community fees to domestic producers, giving them an unfair market advantage (e.g., C-214/98). To the extent that such cases are irrelevant, this should bias my results toward a null finding.

A3.2 Robustness of regression results

A3.2.1 Random effects

Statistical tests recommend the use of random effects in the regression analysis. I first checked whether there was evidence of individual (country) effects, using the Breusch-Pagan test for heteroscedasticity. The test is decisive that there are individual effects in the linear models for all political constraints metrics except veto points. Either random or fixed effects are needed to correct for heteroscedasticity.

I conducted a Hausman test to determine whether fixed effects or random effects are preferable (Hausman 1978). I checked this for each measure of political constraints and the baseline regression model (without controls). The null hypothesis is that random effects are preferred due to their higher efficiency. The alternative hypothesis is that the individual (country) effects are correlated with regressors in the model, raising the risk of bias and making fixed effects the better choice. For each of the five measures, the χ^2 test statistic is smaller than the critical value ($\chi^2 = 7.814$ for three degrees of freedom), leading me to fail to reject the null. Random effects are preferable: it is safe to choose the more efficient model because the risk of bias is small enough. See table A3.3.

The test results agree with conventional wisdom. Fixed effects are preferred when the omitted variables differ between individuals but are constant over time. This is because fixed effects absorb differences between individuals, allowing only changes over time *within* individuals to predict the dependent variable. Random effects tend to be preferred when omitted variables not only differ between individuals but also vary

TABLE A3.3 **Hausman Test Justifies Random Effects**

	Hausman test		
	χ^2	p-value	Interpretation
	(Crit.val. 3 df. $\chi^2 = 7.81$)		
Checks	0.16	0.98	Fail to reject H0 → Use random effects
Legislative fractionalization	2.07	0.56	Fail to reject H0 → Use random effects
Polarization	0.36	0.95	Fail to reject H0 → Use random effects
Veto points	0.68	0.88	Fail to reject H0 → Use random effects
Effective # parties	2.87	0.41	Fail to reject H0 → Use random effects

Note: All test statistics calculated from regression of *Import share* on *Adverse trade ruling×constraints*, *Adverse trade ruling* and *constraints* without controls.

TABLE A3.4 **Regression of Intra-EU Import Share on Adverse Trade Rulings and Political Constraints with Two-Year Lag**

	(1)	(2)	(3)	(4)	(5)	(6)	(7)	(8)	(9)	(10)
	Intra-EU import share$_{it}$									
Adv. Tr. Ruling$_{t-2}$ × Checks$_{t-1}$	−0.01** (0.003)					−0.01** (0.003)				
Checks$_{t-1}$	−0.004 (0.003)					−0.002 (0.003)				
Adv. Tr. Ruling$_{t-2}$ × Fractionalization$_{t-1}$		−0.15*** (0.05)					−0.09*** (0.04)			
Fractionalization$_{t-1}$		−0.02 (0.06)					−0.07 (0.06)			
Adv. Tr. Ruling$_{t-2}$ × Polarization$_{t-1}$			−0.02*** (0.01)					−0.01 (0.004)		
Polarization$_{t-1}$			0.01*** (0.005)					−0.003 (0.004)		
Adv. Tr. Ruling$_{t-2}$ × Veto Points$_{t-1}$				−0.01 (0.06)					−0.08 (0.05)	
Veto Points$_{t-1}$				0.004 (0.06)					0.02 (0.05)	
Adv. Tr. Ruling$_{t-2}$ × Effective No. Parties$_{t-1}$					−0.01** (0.01)					−0.01* (0.004)
Effective No. Parties$_{t-1}$					−0.01 (0.01)					0.01 (0.01)
Adverse Trade Ruling$_{t-2}$	0.03* (0.02)	0.11*** (0.03)	0.02** (0.01)	0.01 (0.05)	0.02** (0.004)	0.03* (0.01)	0.07*** (0.03)	0.01 (0.01)	0.06 (0.04)	0.01 (0.01)
N	338	330	340	339	322	247	242	247	247	247
Time Trend?	Yes	Yes	Yes	Yes	Yes	Yes	Yes	Yes	Yes	Yes
Economic Controls?	Yes	Yes	Yes	Yes	No	No	No	No	No	No
Political and Legal Controls?	No	No	No	No	No	Yes	Yes	Yes	No	Yes
Log Likelihood	546	539	549	547	512	479	475	478	482	477
Std. Dev. (Intercept)	0.069	0.072	0.071	0.071	0.073	0.095	0.099	0.098	0.095	0.095

Note: Models are calculated with R. Control variables are lagged by one year. Significance codes *$p<0.1$; **$p<0.05$; ***$p<0.01$. Specifications include country random intercepts and control variables, not shown.

over time. They allow differences *between* individual to also predict the dependent variable. In the present case, there are almost surely unobserved factors that shape both the over-time trends in intra-EU imports as well as country differences, making random effects the better choice.

A3.2.2 Time effects

I examined the possibility that the effects of adverse (pro-Commission) trade rulings are not exhibited immediately. Gabel et al. (2012) suggest a two-year lag leads to the peak effect on trade. Results are in table A3.4. Columns 1 to 5 include economic controls. The additional one-year lag appears to magnify the negative impact of political constraints and adverse trade rulings on intra-EU imports: coefficients on the interaction terms are negative and highly significant for all measures of political constraints except veto points. Columns 6 to 10 include political and legal controls. Results are generally robust with the exception of *polarization*, which is weaker—polarization may follow a trend over time that correlates with trade but does not adequately explain it.

Notes

Chapter 1

1. The tariffs were applied under Section 232 of the Trade Expansion Act of 1962.

2. The EU participates in the WTO as a single entity.

3. David Lawder, "Steel Industry Groups Urge Biden to Keep Tariffs in Place After EU Truce," *Reuters*, May 19, 2021.

4. Ohio and Pennsylvania have competitive Senate and House races that are critical for implementing the Biden administration's agenda.

5. Julia Manchester, Niv Elis, and Morgan Chalfant, "Biden Faces Dilemma on Trump Steel Tariffs," *The Hill*, May 27, 2021, https://thehill.com/policy/finance/trade/555647-biden-faces-dilemma-on-trump-steel-tariffs/.

6. To this point, former WTO director-general Roberto Azevêdo has warned, "if the member countries simply begin to take matters into their own hands, disregarding all these principles . . . the global economic environment could deteriorate very fast. . . . These measures tend to exacerbate nationalistic sentiments [and] intolerance" (Goodman 2018).

7. The court was formerly known as the European Court of Justice, commonly abbreviated ECJ.

8. Abbott et al. (2000) define legalization with three components: First, governments *delegate* greater authority to international institutions. Second, those institutions entail more *obligation*: states are beholden to deeper commitments. Third, the rules governing behavior are increasingly *precise*, leaving less ambiguity as to what constitutes permissible and impermissible conduct.

9. Davis (2012) demonstrates that one reason plaintiffs sue at the WTO is to broadcast a costly signal of support to domestic stakeholders. If judgments had no impact on defendants, lawsuits would be perceived as "cheap talk."

10. Calculations based on data from Romano (1998) and author's updates. Some of these courts have ceased functioning but never officially declared termination.

11. See Alter (2014) for the most comprehensive account of international courts to date. Alter identifies multiple functions ICs can perform, of which enforcement tends to be the most challenging.

12. Examples of these other institutions include the International Center for Settlement of Investment Disputes, the International Humanitarian Fact-Finding Commission, and the International Criminal Tribunal for Rwanda.

13. "Understanding on Rules and Procedures Governing the Settlement of Disputes," World Trade Organization, 1995.

14. "Consolidated Texts of the EU Treaties as Amended by the Treaty of Lisbon: Section 5," Europa (website), European Union, 2009.

15. "The Court in Figures," Court of Justice of the European Union, updated December 31, 2020, https://curia.europa.eu/jcms/jcms/P_80908/en/. In 2017, 736 cases were initiated, slightly higher than previous years.

16. Scholars contrast de jure and de facto interpretations of international law (Kelsen 1941; Schultz 2014).

17. American Convention on Human Rights entered into force in 1978 and the court took effect the following year.

18. The arguments would not necessarily apply to courts that prosecute individual political leaders such as the International Criminal Court (United Nations General Assembly 1998). The ICC aims to hold former leaders accountable for past crimes; ousted leaders may no longer have any supportive constituents remaining in their countries.

Chapter 2

1. Sovereignty is broadly defined as the legitimate power of a governing body over itself, although scholarship (e.g., Krasner 1999) has delineated multiple forms of sovereignty, recognizing complexity in the term.

2. Stein (1982) distinguishes between coordination and collaboration dilemmas. The former involve common interests such as setting shared standards. The latter involve avoiding common aversions by which a self-interested action leads to uncooperative outcomes.

3. Following the literature, I use the term "international institutions" to encompass all formalized versions of international cooperation including treaties and organizations (Abbott and Snidal 2000). The term "international organizations" refers specifically to those institutions with centralized bureaucracy and independent decision-making capabilities (Abbott and Snidal 1998).

4. For a comprehensive account of the many different forms and functions of international courts, see Alter (2014).

5. International rulings are also thought to guide the development of norms and shape community perceptions of what constitutes legal or illegal behavior,

as many constructivist scholars have highlighted (Finnemore 1993; Finnemore and Sikkink 1998; Barnett and Finnemore 1999).

6. I focus on treaty-based international law, setting aside *customary* international law, the universally applicable norms and obligations to which governments are thought to be bound. In the terminology of Abbott and Snidal (2000), my focus is "hard law" which is so prevalent in international economic relations.

7. "United States and Japan Sign Antitrust Cooperation Agreement," U.S. Department of Justice, October 7, 1999, www.usdoj.gov/opa/pr/1999/October/470at.htm.

8. For instance, a government might lower its tariffs on foreign automobiles only to restrict the importation of crucial engine components, thus using policy substitution to retain protective aims (Berry, Levinsohn, and Pakes 1999).

9. Goldsmith voiced concerns in an interview included in the report "Investigation into the Office of Legal Counsel's Memoranda Concerning Issues Relating to the Central Intelligence Agency's Use of Enhanced Interrogation Techniques on Suspected Terrorists," Department of Justice, Office of Personal Responsibility, July 29, 2009.

10. See Cole (2009), Amnesty International (2004), Jeffrey Smith (2004), and the United Nations Committee Against Torture (2013).

11. Some studies examine governments' choices to impose legal versus illegal trade protection that ultimately provoke a dispute (see, e.g., Bown 2004c), but these measurable instances represent a small subset of cases.

12. A complicated link exists between the effectiveness of international courts, on the one hand, and each of the criteria courts might be assessed on—judgment compliance, usage rates, and impact on state conduct—on the other (Shany 2012).

13. Simmons (1998) also highlights the value of this distinction for empirical studies: "The study of first-order compliance raises difficulties of establishing an underlying 'rate' of compliance, since it is far from clear how to conceptualize a denominator for such a rate . . . Studies of second-order compliance can often more convincingly establish such a rate, as well as narrow the range of behavior that would constitute compliance by focusing on a particular, often precisely rendered, decision" (78).

14. Export-oriented industries sometimes push policy in the opposite direction (Gilligan 1997).

15. "Magazines Fight for Life as Ad Revenue Weakens," *Toronto Star*, January 27, 1990. "Magazine Industry Urges Laws to Stem Foreign Competition," *Toronto Star*, February 9, 1993.

16. The Stolper-Samuelson theorem specifies these conflicting preferences. Dani Rodrik (2008) describes a generalized version of the theorem. "Regardless of the number of goods and factors, at least one factor of production must experience a decline in real income from trade as long as trade induces the relative price of some domestically produced good(s) to fall (and as long as the pro-

ductivity benefits from trade are restricted to the traditional, inter-sectoral allocative efficiency improvements, about which more later). All that this result requires is a very mild assumption, namely that goods be produced with varying factor intensities (that is, using different combination of factors). The stark implication is that someone will lose, even if the nation as a whole becomes richer."

17. Whereas Davis (2012) focuses on the domestic factors that incentivize plaintiff governments to litigate, I look at the flip side of international legal disputes. I ask how defendant governments respond to litigation and whether that response is conditional on their domestic political institutions. Thus my theory complements this prior work. Davis (2012, 88–92) does address the propensity of democratic defendant governments to litigate but compliance with adverse rulings is not evaluated.

18. See "Magazine Bill Angers Senate; Tories Say Liberals Trying to Shove Legislation Through," *Hamilton Spectator*, Ontario, June 1, 1999.

19. The GSM-102 export credit guarantee program in question was authorized under the Agricultural Trade Act of 1978, 7 U.S.C. § 5622. Two other programs cited in Brazil's original WTO complaint, the GSM-103 program and Supplier Credit Guarantee Program, were eliminated by congress in 2008.

20. In his podcast, Nate Silver explained exactly this dynamic: "Generally, we think of developed democracies as requiring a reliance on norms and restraint and you don't always do what you have the power to do because of threats of retribution and that you kind of keep each other in check and show restraint in order to uphold the democratic norms and ideals . . . are we quickly approaching a place where that is out the window?" Nate Silver. "Politics Podcast: What Comes Next in the Fight to Fill Ginsburg's Seat," September 21, 2021, in *FiveThirtyEight*, podcast, MP3 audio, 1:01:01.

21. Guzman and Simmons (2004) find that having meager legal resources means that developing countries can only afford to launch targeted complaints aimed at the largest markets.

22. WTO disputes DS26 and DS48, European Communities—Measures Concerning Meat and Meat Products (Hormones).

23. 285 Parl. Deb. H.C. (6th ser.) (1996) cols. 152–5.

24. This argument is specific to international trade. Scholars have demonstrated that pro-compliance groups can mobilize quite effectively in the domains of environmental cooperation (Dai 2005) and human rights (Simmons 2009).

Chapter 3

1. An example of an international court that is *not* permanent is the International Criminal Tribunal for the Former Yugoslavia. Other courts, initially constructed to be permanent, have dissolved. For example, the Appeals Board

of the Western European Union was disbanded in 2011 when the Lisbon Treaty of the European Union entered into force.

2. Activity is a crucial first criteria. As Gray (2018) highlights, many international organizations wither into uselessness.

3. EU members that do not use the euro and therefore maintain separate monetary policy are Bulgaria, Croatia, Czech Republic, Denmark, Hungary, Poland, Romania, and Sweden. The United Kingdom maintained a separate currency when it was an EU member.

4. In a recent innovative study, Conrad and Ritter (2019) assess state compliance with human rights treaties. Their insights could be applied to understand compliance with legal rulings from human rights courts.

5. This is unsurprising since countries with the largest GDP typically have more diversified and self-sufficient economies.

6. WTO dispute DS250, United States–Equalizing Excise Tax Imposed by Florida on Processed Orange and Grapefruit Products

7. Todd Benson, "International Business; Brazil Resolves Complaint on Florida Juice Import Tax," *New York Times,* May 29, 2004.

8. A complainant can also drop accusations entirely.

9. WTO dispute DS281, US–Anti-dumping Measures on Cement from Mexico.

10. Martin Crustinger, "Mexico, US Solidify Cement Accord," *Houston Chronicle*, March 4, 2006; Elisabeth Malkin, "US Cuts Duty on Cement from Mexico," *New York Times,* January 20, 2006.

11. Typically, three or four of the standing members of the Appellate Body are citizens of developing countries.

12. Mexico was found to have violated the WTO Dispute Settlement Understanding, Article 6.2 when it submitted its complaint.

13. In DS62, the Appellate Body found that, contrary to panel recommendations, the European tariffs were actually consistent with GATT art. II:1.

14. In the following eight cases, the AB overturned the panel's original adverse ruling: DS60, DS62/67/68 (combined proceeding), DS315, DS320/321 (combined proceeding), and DS360.

15. "Memorandum from John M. Andersen, Acting Deputy Assistant Secretary for Antidumping and Countervailing Duty Operations to Ronald K. Lorentzen, Acting Assistant Secretary for Import Administration on Issues and Decision Memorandum for the Final Results of Proceeding Under Section 129 of the Uruguay Round Agreements Act: Antidumping Measures on Stainless Steel from Mexico (DS344)," A-201–882 Section 129 Proceeding Public Document AD/CVD Operations, April 3, 2009.

16. See World Trade Organization, "United States—Anti-Dumping Measures on Certain Hot-Rolled Steel Products from Japan: Request for Modification of the Reasonable Period of Time," No. WT/DS184/18, 2004.

17. Art. 10 of the Dispute Settlement Understanding states that any member country having "a substantial interest in the matter" can submit a report to the panel.

18. See "The EU Single Market: Policy Framework," *Europa* (website), European Union, http://ec.europa.eu/internal_market.

19. The ECJ has interpreted the Commission's responsibilities very broadly. It has authority to play an active role in eliminating barriers to trade, per EEC Treaty art. 30 (*Official Journal of the European Union*, 1990, 13).

20. For a parallel argument in the context of the GATT/WTO, see Bowen (2013).

21. The analysis in chapter 6 covers the following core member states: Austria, Belgium, Denmark, France, Finland, Germany, Greece, Ireland, Italy, Luxembourg, the Netherlands, Portugal, Spain, Sweden, and the United Kingdom for the years 1987 to 2012. Austria, Finland, and Sweden joined the EU in 1995, so their coverage is limited. More recent admits to the EU do not have enough data to conduct the quantitative analysis in chapter 6.

22. Some scholars argue that the ECJ system has been emulated in the more recent Andean Tribunal (Alter, Helfer, and Saldias 2012; Alter and Helfer 2010). If not unique, then, the EU's preliminary ruling system is certainly unusual.

23. In preliminary references, the plaintiffs vary widely and can include individual citizens, corporations, industry groups, etc. So it is difficult to consistently map rulings onto pro-integration policies or compare across lawsuits. Infringement disputes, by contrast, all have the same plaintiff: the Commission. It is therefore easier to associate infringement rulings with pro-integration policies and compare one lawsuit to the next.

24. Sanctions are meant to be large enough so as to have a deterrent effect (TFEU art. 260; Euratom Treaty art. 106a). They are calculated in proportion to the severity of the breach as well as the size of the country's economy with the goal of inducing compliance.

25. "No Action against France for Months in Beef Row," *Journal*, Newcastle, UK, March 14, 2002.

26. If the ECJ adjusts its rulings to reduce the risk of unilateral noncompliance, it does so quite imperfectly: we still observe defiance.

27. For simplicity, this can be thought of as a country setting its tariff below (following) or above (violating) an allowable threshold. In reality, the range of policies that could abide by or violate treaty terms are far more nuanced, ranging from antidumping duty calculations to transportation regulations to trade restrictions directed toward health and environmental issues.

28. Many studies have cast doubt on the adequacy of this theorem to explain empirical patterns (Feenstra 2015; Davis and Mishra 2007). Nonetheless, for the purposes of my argument, it provides a helpful framework for understanding the distributive implications of trade.

29. Note that compared to the foundational work by Milner (1997) and Milner and Rosendorff (1997), the roles of the legislator as agenda setter and executive as ratifier are reversed. This is because my argument focuses on adherence to and defection from existing international agreements rather than the formation of new international agreements.

30. See Olson (1965) for a foundational treatment of collective action and political mobilization.

31. Other research shows that the responsiveness of legislators to protectionist versus liberalizing trade interests hinges on the electoral system in place (e.g., Rogowski 1987; Grossman and Helpman 2005; Rickard 2012) and the reciprocal trade interests of domestic stakeholders (Betz 2017).

32. The conventional wisdom on constituency size and trade policy preferences has been called into question, notably by Karol (2007) and Ehrlich (2009). Further, Bailey (2001) has highlighted how diffused trade liberalizing interests can also sway legislators.

33. In this discussion, I assume that a first-order treaty violation involves some positive action—the government passes a policy that violates the treaty. A more general model could allow that some treaty violations are "status quo" policies. In this alternative scenario, the first-order compliance dynamics would be simplified and the second-order compliance dynamics would remain the same.

34. Another contributing factor is term limits. Some Executives may never have to face the consequences of their noncompliance if their tenure in office is ending.

35. Emily Cochrane and Alan Rappeport, "Democrats to Unveil Up To $3600 Child Tax Credit as Part of Stimulus Bill," *New York Times*, February 7, 2021.

Chapter 4

1. "Japan—Customs Duties, Taxes, and Labeling Practices on Imported Wines and Alcoholic Beverages," GATT Report of the Panel, November 10, 1987 (L/6216).

2. WTO dispute DS8, Japan—Taxes on Alcoholic Beverages, June 21, 1995.

3. WTO dispute DS75, Korea—Taxes on Alcoholic Beverages, April 2, 1997.

4. "Commission Calls for WTO Talks on South Korean Alcohol Tax," *European Report*, April 2, 1997.

5. 57 Panel Report, Japan—Taxes on Alcoholic Beverages, WT/DS8/R, WT/DS10/R, WT/DS11/R, circulated 11 July 1996, DSR 1996:I, 125, para. 6.33, 6.35.

6. "Tax Ruling Boosts Whiskey Hopes," *Herald*, Glasgow, Scotland, January 19, 1999.

7. The Japanese and Korean political circumstances are also mentioned in

Mansfield and Milner (2012), who show that veto players impact a country's ability to form preferential trade agreements.

8. "S. Korea's Most Popular Drink under Fire: Government Must Raise Excise Task on Soju and Cut Import Tariffs on Whiskey," *Vancouver Sun*, British Columbia, October 23, 1999.

9. "Agreement on the 72% Tax Rate for Soju and Whiskey: Whiskey Prices Fall and Imports are Likely to Surge," *Maeil Business Newspaper*, November 30, 1999. Translation by research assistants.

10. Liquor Tax Act, No. 6055, and partial amendment of Education Tax Act, No. 6050, December 28, 1999.

11. "EU, S. Korea Becoming Closer, More Interdependent," *Korea Herald*, October 16, 2000.

12. Also see Mansfield and Milner (2012, 60).

13. See "WTO Ruling Pushes Shochu Makers to Reinvent Product," *Nikkei Weekly*, March 31, 1997.

14. "Japan Fails to Remove Whiskey Tax," *Scotsman*, Scotland, November 23, 1996.

15. WTO Document No. 97–0558, February 14, 1997.

16. World Trade Organization, *The WTO Agreements Series: Technical Barriers to Trade*, 13. Geneva: World Trade Organization, 2014.

17. Food, Conservation, and Energy Act of 2008, H.R. 2419, 110th Congress, introduced May 22, 2007. Section 11002 set forth the COOL requirements.

18. Farm, Nutrition, and Bioenergy Act of 2007, H.R. 2419, 110th Congress, introduced July 26, 2007, H8687–H8699.

19. In addition to challenging the COOL provisions in the 2008 Farm Bill, Canada and Mexico's complaints referred to other US rules that aided the implementation. They were the 2008 Interim Final Rule (AMS), the 2009 Final Rule (AMS), and the Vilsack Letter, instruments that, along with the COOL provisions, formed one single trade discriminatory measure. See Panel Report, WT/DS384/R.

20. See Panel Report, WT/DS384/R, 180.

21. Arbitration Report, WT/DS384, 384–24 4/12/12, 12.

22. U.S. 78 Fed. Reg. 31367.

23. Cool Reform Coalition, "Letter to the Members of the United States Senate," May 14, 2015, https://businessdocbox.com/Agriculture/85327492-May-14-2015-to-the-members-of-the-united-states-senate.html.

24. On June 10, 2015, the House passed, with a vote of 300 to 131, the Country of Origin Labeling Amendments Act of 2015 (H.R. 2393), which repealed beef, pork, and chicken from the COOL statute.

25. See Senate amendment S. 2920, introduced in June 2015.

26. Voluntary Country of Origin Labeling (COOL) and Trade Enhancement

Act of 2015 (S. 1844). Senate bill S. 1844 amends the Agricultural Marketing Act (7 U.S.C. x1621) as well.

27. I thank Timm Betz for raising this point.

28. See US Department of Agriculture Press Release No. 0345.15 of December 18, 2015, and 81 Fed. Reg. 10755; Consolidated Appropriations Act 2016, Public Law No. 114–115.

29. WTO dispute DS412, Canada–Certain Measures Affecting the Renewable Energy Generation Sector. Japan, joined by the European Union and the United States, alleged that by boosting renewable energy generation facilities using local equipment, Canada had granted a subsidy to domestic suppliers, imposed a quantitative restriction on foreign goods, and violated its investment obligations.

30. Panel Report, DS412 and DS426, December 19, 2012. Emphasis added.

31. Panel Report, DS412 and DS426, December 19, 2012.

32. See "Ruling Threatens Ontario Green Energy Jobs," *Toronto Star*, May 7, 2013; "Final Appeal Fails, Forcing Ontario to Plan for Green Energy Act Changes," *Globe and Mail*, May 7, 2013.

33. "Final Appeal Fails, Forcing Ontario to Plan for Green Energy Act Changes," *Globe and Mail*, May 7, 2013.

34. Ontario Bill 153, Complying with the International Trade Obligations Act, 2013.

35. Ontario Energy Board Act 1998, Regulation 578/05 Prescribed Contracts Re: Section 78.4 and 78.4 of the Act, revoked on January 1, 2015 (O.Reg. 295/14, ss.1,2).

36. Bob Chiarelli, Ontario Minister of Energy, Letter to Mr. Colin Andersen, Chief Executive Officer of Ontario Power Authority concerning "Administrative Matters Related to Renewable Energy and Conservation Programs," August 16, 2013, http://www.ontla.on.ca/library/repository/mon/27008/323760.pdf.

37. "Canberra Casts for Truce in Salmon War," *Australian*, May 18, 2000.

38. For example, DS50 and DS79, US and EU v. India—Patents; DS 108: EU v. US—Foreign Sales Corporations; DS265, DS266, and DS283, Australia, Brazil and Thailand v. EU—Export Subsidies on Sugar.

39. Canada needed to make four changes: (1) repeal the existing custom tariff (code 9958) prohibiting split-run foreign magazine imports and foreign magazines with more than 5% of their advertisements directed at the Canadian market through executive order; (2) eliminate a part of the Excise Tax Act on Canadian advertising in split-run magazines through a legislative amendment; (3) restructure the postal subsidy program to make payments directly to magazine publishers' accounts through administrative action by the Department of Canadian Heritage and Canada Post; and (4) harmonize commercial postal rates for domestic and foreign publications.

40. James Baxter, "Liberals Face Backbench Rebellions over Contentious Magazine Bill," *Ottawa Citizen*, February 23, 1999.

41. Stewart (2010) explains that on November 17, Sheila Copps, the Liberal Party minister of Canadian heritage, clashed with Reform Party members of Parliament in a committee meeting, saying that "the only opponents to the legislation tend to be American companies" and that it was "sad that a Canadian party is more interested in speaking out for its American bosses than it is for Canada." She said Canada faced a perennial choice of "the state or the United States" and that non-American cultural identities were threatened by a global "monoculture." The Reform Party represented a far-right populist position and in 2000 merged into the Canadian Alliance.

42. See "Magazine Bill Angers Senate; Tories Say Liberals Trying to Shove Legislation Through," *Hamilton Spectator*, Ontario, June 1, 1999.

43. See Congressional Research Service, "Safeguards: Section 201 of the Trade Act of 1974," December 21, 2018.

44. See "DS429: United States Antidumping Measures on Certain Shrimp from Viet Nam, Recourse to Article 21.3(c), Written Submission of the United States" October 15, 2015, page 8; WT/DS426/12 "Award of the Arbitrator," pages 15–16 and 18–19; and the "Agreement between the Government of the United States and the Government of the Socialist Republic of Viet Name on Antidumping Duty Order on Certain Frozen Warmwater Shrimp from Viet Nam," July 18, 2016.

45. Poletti and DeBievre (2014) highlight the constellation of domestic obstacle faced by the EU in WTO disputes.

46. WTO dispute DS291/292/293.

47. In 2003, Canada's agriculture exports to the European Union constituted approximately 0.089% of its GDP. Argentina's exports of agriculture products to the EU constituted 1.39% of its GDP.

48. WTO dispute DS132: Mexico–High Fructose Corn Syrup.

49. WTO dispute DS406: United States–Clove Cigarettes.

50. See US Congressional Record Extensions of Remarks, April 21, 2009 E913.

51. See Memorandum of Understanding between the Government of the United States of America and the Government of the Republic of Indonesia, signed October 3, 2014.

52. See "Discrimination Is Indonesia's Best Case in the Clove Cigarette Dispute," *Jakarta Globe*, 2014, accessed Sept. 21, 2016, http://jakartaglobe .beritasatu.com/opinion/discrimination-is-indonesias-best-case-in-the-clove -cigarette-dispute/.

53. Also see "Indonesia Announces Deal with US on Clove Cigarettes Trade Dispute," *Bridges Weekly*, October 9, 2014.

54. "What is the WTO? Understanding the WTO," accessed December 1, 2021, https://www.wto.org/english/thewto_e/whatis_e/tif_e/tif_e.htm.

55. An interesting exception can be found in the Antigua and Barbuda law-

suit against the United States concerning gaming technology. The far smaller complainant could not effectively retaliate through import barriers against the larger US economy. The WTO authorized cross-sectoral retaliation against copyrighted material in the US movie industry. Hollywood, an influential interest group, eventually pressured the US to strike a bilateral settlement with the Caribbean nation that fell short of compliance.

56. WTO Dispute DS276, US v. Canada—Measures Relating to Exports of Wheat and Treatment of Imported Grain.

57. The reasonable period of time to comply expired August 1, 2005, and Bill C-40 quickly passed through parliament and took effect May 19, 2005.

58. WTO disputes DS139 and DS142, Japan and EU v. Canada—Autos.

59. To be in compliance, Canada needed to repeal the Motor Vehicles Tariff Order of 1998 and its provisions for special remission orders, and the deadline was set as February 19, 2001.

60. DS56, US v. Argentina—Textiles and Apparel.

61. Resolution 806/98 went into effect October 3, 1998, before the January 1999 deadline.

62. President Menem's Executive Decree 109/99 entered into force May 30, 1999.

63. This was the only WTO dispute in which I found evidence that the judiciary played a role, but it appeared to be a mere formality

64. WTO dispute DS27, Ecuador; Guatemala; Honduras; Mexico; US v. European Communities (Union)—Bananas. The Geneva Agreement on Trade in Bananas was negotiated in 2008–2009, finalized in December 2009, and approved by the European Parliament on February 3, 2011, and by the European Council on March 7, 2011. The US was not a party to the agreement and signed a separate agreement. All parties finally agreed the case was settled on November 8, 2012.

65. WTO dispute DS312, Indonesia v. Korea—Paper.

66. Korean Trade Commission Antidumping Decision 2003-22 issued on Sept. 24, 2003. Translation by research assistant.

67. Council Regulation (EC) No. 510/2006 was implemented a few days in advance of the April 3, 2006, deadline.

68. See DS394/395/398, US, EU and Mexico v. China—Raw Materials.

69. I use the Country Policy and Institutional Assessment (CPIA) database "transparency in the public sector rating" for the years comprehensive data are available (2005–2016), matching by the compliance deadline.

70. If the panel ruling was reversed on appeal, then no compliance activity was required, and I did not include the dispute.

71. The main results are the same as when a simple count is used.

72. An additional concern has to do with endogeneity. Disputes may be initiated precisely because trade flows are lower as a result of the respondent's bar-

riers. Using lagged trade values does not completely remedy the problem, since some trade barriers are in place for many years prior to a dispute and complainant's timing of dispute initiation is demonstrated to be sensitive to political circumstances apart from trade losses (Davis 2012; Chaudoin 2014; Brutger 2017).

73. WTO dispute DS2/4, United States—Standards for Reformulated and Conventional Gasoline.

74. WTO dispute DS217, United States—Continued Dumping and Subsidy Offset Act of 2000 (Byrd Amendment).

75. Note that the calculation of rising and falling considered the time between the dispute initiation and the expiration of the reasonable period of time for implementation.

76. Judges on WTO panels sometimes consider the respondent's political circumstances when crafting a ruling and may account for the difficulty of passing legislation on politically charged issues (Creamer 2017; Busch and Pelc 2016).

77. The legal stage count ranges from 1 to 6. The following stages are included: the panel report is adopted, the appellate body report is adopted, the reasonable period of time for compliance is extended, remedies/retaliation are requested (but not necessarily applied), Article 21.5 compliance proceedings are conducted, and second recourse to Article 21.5 proceedings are conducted.

78. For OECD respondent countries, multiple legal stages are also associated with more avenues for access by special interest groups (Ehrlich 2011). With more opportunities for industry influence, these governments appear to exploit multiple legal stages in the WTO dispute process to delay compliance.

79. Firms were coded as involved if they were mentioned in the complainant's brief or subsequent WTO documentation, including panel rulings, or if they were linked to the dispute by news articles.

80. Similar results hold when the outcome variable measures whether the respondent ever complied.

Chapter 5

1. Recall that some countries use WTO adjudication as a costly signal to domestic stakeholders, while others aim to set precedent in the interpretation of WTO rules (Davis 2012; Pelc 2014).

2. This chapter draws on Peritz (2020) and contains more complex statistical content than the other portions of the book. Some readers may prefer to skip section 5.1.

3. All disputes are categorized as either import-restriction cases or export-promoting cases. In the appendix for this chapter, I include in the sample the twenty-four disputes over export-promoting measures like subsidies. The findings hold for the larger sample.

4. These data are of a finer grain than those used in similar prior studies such as Bechtel and Sattler (2015), which uses one-digit SITC sector codes.

5. By contrast, standardizing relative to the respondent's imports may generate biased results because in many WTO disputes, the respondent imposes a trade barrier against all imports, regardless of the country of origin.

6. See the appendix to this chapter for technical details.

7. In robustness checks, I varied the window from two to ten years and found the results to be stable.

8. Some disputes take longer than five years to resolve. At the time of the coding, some defendants remained noncompliant. In these instances, my coding of noncompliance may be uncertain because the defendant could implement very belated compliance measures. Nonetheless, very belated compliance measures are still very similar to noncompliance from a dispute settlement perspective. In such an instance, the defendant retained a violation policy for a prolonged period, accruing economic benefits to the disadvantage of the plaintiff.

9. To the extent that these general covariates lead to poorer estimates of the trade impact, they would introduce more uncertainty in the regression analysis below.

10. Trade diversion, the increase (or reduction) in trade some countries may experience when another country imposes (or removes) trade barriers, introduces a measurement obstacle which I mitigate in two ways: First, the log-ratio transformation helps reduce the risk of interference between units insofar as trade is diverted homogeneously. Second, the macroeconomic and industry-specific covariates—GDP, agriculture, industry, unemployment, etc.—help explain possible diversion.

11. Abadie, Diamond, and Hainmueller (2010) explain: "because a synthetic control is a weighted average of available control units, [SCM] makes explicit: (1) the relative contribution of each control unit to the counterfactual of interest and (2) the similarities . . . between the unit affected by the event or intervention of interest and the synthetic control" (494).

12. WTO dispute DS299, European Communities–Countervailing Measures on Dynamic Random Access Memory Chips from Korea.

13. WTO dispute DS302, Dominican Republic–Measures Affecting the Importation and Internal Sale of Cigarettes from Honduras.

14. Several additional cases with findings of no violation dealt with broad trade policies or non-merchandise disputes so product-level trade flows could not be measured in these cases.

15. Busch and Reinhardt (2003) examine compliance with GATT-era rulings and nine WTO rulings. Davey (2005) and Bruce Wilson (2007) evaluate high-profile disputes but do not disclose case-by-case coding.

16. I adopt a simple approach, rather than a bootstrap estimate of uncertainty, because Abadie and Imbens (2008) demonstrate biased results occur when boot-

strapping is applied to matching estimators. New approaches to estimating uncertainty for synthetic controls are developed in Xu (2017).

17. Where random measurement errors arise in coding compliance, results attenuate the coefficient on the explanatory variable and therefore underestimate the magnitude of the effect (Cox and Snell 1989).

18. In 2003, the PAN held 38.11% of the seats in the senate and 38.24% of the seats in the lower house compared to smaller shares held by the main opposition party.

19. The Brazilian Constitution treats its 5,570 municipalities as parts of the federation, each with an autonomous local government.

20. This estimate uses table 5.2(6) and conditions on a transition from the ambiguous outcome to cooperation.

21. For a complete discussion of these data, see Davis (2012, 123–26).

22. Note that these data contain only eighteen disputes with adverse rulings over import restricting trade barriers—cases for which I calculated a trade cooperation score. Therefore, estimating a three-stage Heckman selection model is statistically untenable.

23. The unit of analysis here is the foreign trade barrier; by contrast Davis (2012) assembles panel data to examine the US treatment of these trade barriers over time.

Chapter 6

1. This chapter draws directly on Peritz (2018).

2. For example, an Austrian infringement dispute over transportation pollution standards pitted environmentalists against industry groups benefiting from lower shipping costs. See European Commission v. Republic of Austria, C-320/03.

3. Also see Seikel (2015).

4. But see Tobias Hofmann (2018), who argues that the power of interest groups diminishes over the course of infringement proceedings.

5. Commission of the European Communities, *Sixth Annual Report to the European Parliament on Commission Monitoring of the Application of Community Law*, 1988, 89/C 330/01.

6. Commission of the European Communities, *Fifth Annual Report to the European Parliament on Commission Monitoring of the Application of Community Law*, 1987, 88/C 310/01.

7. Judgment of February 18, 1992, Commission of the European Communities v. United Kingdom of Great Britain and Northern Ireland, C-30/90, ECLI:EU:C:1992:74, para. 4, 14.

8. Judgment of February 18, 1992, Commission of the European Commu-

nities v. United Kingdom of Great Britain and Northern Ireland, C-30/90, ECLI:EU:C:1992:74, para. 15.

9. Judgment of February 18, 1992, Commission of the European Communities v. United Kingdom of Great Britain and Northern Ireland, C-30/90, ECLI:EU:C:1992:74, para. 15.

10. Judgment of February 18, 1992, Commission of the European Communities v. United Kingdom of Great Britain and Northern Ireland, C-30/90, ECLI:EU:C:1992:74, para. 26.

11. They were ordered to amend their Patent Act of 1977, section 48 to 50.

12. Judgment of the Court of October 27, 1992, Generics (UK) Ltd and Harris Pharmaceuticals; Ltd v. Smith Kline & French Laboratories Ltd, C-191/90, ECLI:EU:C:1992:407.

13. 527 Parl. Deb. H.L. (5th ser.) (1991) cols. 1318–1334.

14. European Commission, *Thirteenth Annual Report on Monitoring the Application of Community Law*, 1995, 96/C 303/01.

15. *Official Journal of the European Community*, 1998, No. C354, 181; 586 Parl. Deb. H.L. (5th ser.) (1998).

16. Judgment of the Court (Grand Chamber) of 23 October 2007, Commission of the European Communities v. Federal Republic of Germany, C-112/05, ECLI:EU:C:2007:623

17. The Commission's first attempt to remove the 1960 Volkswagen law dates back to 2001; the infringement proceeding was initiated in March 2003.

18. Paul Meller, "Europe Set to Challenge German Law Guarding VW," *New York Times*, October 13, 2004, https://nyti.ms/2z23xoI/.

19. Mark Landler, "Court Strikes Down 'Volkswagen Law,'" *New York Times*, October 23, 2007, https://nyti.ms/2GQkdXY/.

20. Elitsa Vucheva, "EU Court Rules against Germany's 'Volkswagen' Law," *EU Observer*, October 23, 2007, https://euobserver.com/justice/25025/.

21. "Merkel Affirms Support for Volkswagen Veto," *Deutsche Welle*, September 23, 2009, https://p.dw.com/p/FNZW/.

22. "Vorauseilender Gehorsam? Abgelehnt!" (Anticipatory Obedience? Refused!), *Sueddeutsche Zeitung*, May 17, 2010, https://www.sueddeutsche.de/wirtschaft/vw-gesetz-im-bundesrat-vorauseilender-693075/.

23. Judgment of the Court (Grand Chamber), October 22, 2013, European Commission v. Federal Republic of Germany, C-95/12, ECLI:EU:C:2013:676.

24. Judgment of the Court (Grand Chamber), October 22, 2013, European Commission v. Federal Republic of Germany, C-95/12, ECLI:EU:C:2013:676. Also see: "VW takeover law ruling may lead to big EU fine on Germany" *Automotive News Europe*, March 12, 2013, https://europe.autonews.com/article/20130312/ANE/130319971/vw-takeover-law-ruling-may-lead-to-big-eu-fine-on-germany/.

25. That decision required the Hellenic Republic to provide the Com-

mission with information pursuant to art. 10 of Council Regulation (EC) No. 659/1999 of March 22, 1999, laying down detailed rules for the application of Article 88 of the EC Treaty (*Official Journal of the European Communities*, 1999, No. L83, 1).

26. Judgment of the Court (Second Chamber) of May 12, 2005, Commission of the European Communities v. Hellenic Republic, C-415/03, ECLI: EU:C:2005:287, para. 6.

27. Judgment of the Court (Grand Chamber) of July 7, 2009, Commission of the European Communities v. Hellenic Republic, C-369/07, ECLI: EU:C:2009:428

28. This quotation is from page 10 of a 2005 draft of Featherstone and Papadimitriou (2007). Note that the authors wrote this draft in April 2005 in anticipation of the ECJ's final adverse ruling. Their analysis proved prescient.

29. Judgment of the Court (Grand Chamber) of July 7, 2009, Commission of the European Communities v. Hellenic Republic, C-369/07, ECLI: EU:C:2009:428, para. 151.

30. See Commission Decision of July 23, 2014, on State Aid, SA 24639 (C 61/07), granted by Greece to Olympic Airways Services/Olympic Airlines.

31. Commission of the European Communities, *Fourth Annual Report to the European Parliament on Commission Monitoring of the Application of Community Law*, 1986, 87 C/338/01.

32. Judgment of the Court of December 9, 1997, European Commission v. French Republic, C-265/95, ECLI:EU:C:1997:595

33. See Tillotson and Foster (2003, 276).

34. Judgment of the Court of December 9, 1997, Commission of the European Communities v. French Republic, C-265/95, ECLI:EU:C:1997:595, para. 11.

35. Judgment of the Court of December 9, 1997, Commission of the European Communities v. French Republic, C-265/95, ECLI:EU:C:1997:595, para. 12.

36. "Nostalgie de la boue," *The Economist*, May 27, 2004; "Europe's Farm Follies," *The Economist*, December 8, 2005.

37. Judgment of the Court of December 9, 1997, Commission of the European Communities v. French Republic, C-265/95, ECLI:EU:C:1997:595, para. 23. Also see "French Farmers Rebuked," *Journal of Commerce*, December 17, 1997.

38. Commission of the European Communities, *Seventh Annual Report to the European Parliament on Commission Monitoring of the Application of Community Law*, 1989, 90/C 232/01.

39. Judgment of the Court of February 27, 1980, Commission of the European Communities v. Kingdom of Denmark, C-171/78, ECLI:EU:C:1980:54

40. See the Commission's lawsuits against Austria regarding trans-Alpine transport, C-320/03 and C-28/09.

41. For a representative sample of cases in the Börzel and Knoll (2012) data-

base, I independently coded and cross-checked to ensure consistency between my data and the prior data. Coding rules are detailed in the appendix for this chapter.

42. Note that Gabel et al. (2012) only find a trade impact for preliminary reference rulings; they find no effect for infringement rulings, the focus of my analysis.

43. In chapter 4, I evaluated two veto points variables. In this analysis, neither yields significant results. This chapter only report null results for Veto Points$_{\text{II}}$, the version accounting for the judicial branch.

44. Examples of countries with low veto points that are at least partly democratic include Mexico and the Dominican Republic.

45. Estimates are based on setting fractionalization = 0.61, varying the number of adverse rulings from 0 to 1, including economic controls, and using Portugal's intercept. The estimated effect is approximately 0.047% GDP.

46. See EEC No. 922/72, EEC No. 234/79, EC No. 1037/2001, EC No. 1234/2007, and EU No. 1308/2013.

47. An example of one such transition point includes include the 1992 switch from market (price) support to producer support, featuring direct payments to farmers. This had the effect of concentrating direct subsidies in the hands of farmers rather than spreading that support across other steps in the value chain—for example, packaging, shipping, etc.

48. Some disputes show even more extreme delays. In a particularly extended dispute, France was condemned in a 2004 ruling by the ECJ for failing to implement a directive on the management of wastewater. But by 2008, the government still had not taken action. One news source reported that "although France told the Commission in May last year of plans to install wastewater treatment, the facilities will not be completed until 2011, seven years after the court ruling and 12 years after the directive's deadline. The Commission said the delay was deplorable." "WaterFrance Faces Court Fine over Waste Delays," *Utility Week*, February 8, 2008.

49. A lagged dependent variable is not recommended for weakly dynamic data such as these (Keele and Kelly 2006).

Chapter 7

1. Ana Swanson, "Once the WTO's Biggest Supporter, US Is Its Biggest Skeptic," *New York Times*, December 10, 2017.

2. Frank Langfitt, "U.S. Blocks Appointments of New Judges to World Trade Organization," *National Public Radio*, October 2, 2018, https://www.npr.org/2018/10/02/653570018/u-s-blocks-appointments-of-new-judges-to-world-trade-organization/.

3. Yuki Hayashi, "Biden to Nominate Maria Pagan as US Envoy to WTO," *Wall Street Journal,* August 10, 2021.

4. See "Lesser UK Courts Will be Able to Overturn ECJ rulings after Brexit: PM's Spokesman," *Reuters*, December 18, 2019.

5. For example, when US steel and aluminum tariffs raised the costs of inputs for domestic auto manufacturers, some firms shifted their production abroad. Relocating manufacturing back to the US, once the tariffs are lowered, may prove infeasible.

6. It is beyond the scope of my book to recommend bargaining strategies to achieve these reforms. See McKibben (2015).

7. Article 22.3 of the WTO Dispute Settlement Understanding.

8. Article 260.2 of the Treaty on the Functioning of the European Union.

9. Article 22 of the WTO Dispute Settlement Understanding.

A3

1. Previous literature used data for the six core EU members 1970 to 1993. I implement the suggestion by Gabel et al. (2012, 1135) in expanding the analysis to cover newer members of the EU and more recent years.

2. The measure assumes that there are many imported goods that are substitutes, such that domestic demand can be met by either intra- or extra-EU products. For example, consumers in the Netherlands could purchase French wine or Argentinian wine; their choice depends partly on prices, which in turn depend on trade policy.

3. Some controls are only available for recent years. Because I focus on cross-country differences, bias resulting from the truncated time series does not significantly affect my substantive conclusions.

4. This enters my analysis as a control variable because it does not capture the main obstacles to policy implementation. Bicameralism is included in the *Checks* variable.

5. Carrubba and Gabel (2015) evaluate preliminary references involving the EU member states for the years 1960 to 1992, identifying subject matter, which party prevailed, etc. An extensive data collection effort would be required to identify trade-related preliminary reference cases with pro-liberalizing verdicts across the fifteen member states and twenty-five years, which would make for an excellent follow-up study.

References

Abadie, Alberto, Alexis Diamond, and Jens Hainmueller. 2010. "Synthetic Control Methods for Comparative Case Studies: Estimating the Effect of California's Tobacco Control Program." *Journal of the American Statistical Association* 105(490): 493–505.

Abadie, Alberto, Alexis Diamond, and Jens Hainmueller. 2011. "Synth: An R Package for Synthetic Control Methods in Comparative Case Studies." *Journal of Statistical Software* 42(13): 1–17.

Abadie, Alberto, Alexis Diamond, and Jens Hainmueller. 2015. "Comparative Politics and the Synthetic Control Method." *American Journal of Political Science* 59(2): 495–510.

Abadie, Alberto, and Javier Gardeazabal. 2003. "The Economic Costs of Conflict: A Case Study of the Basque Country." *American Economic Review* 93(1): 113–32.

Abadie, Alberto, and Guido W. Imbens. 2008. "On the Failure of the Bootstrap for Matching Estimators." *Econometrica* 76(6): 1537–57.

Abbott, Kenneth W., and Duncan Snidal. 1998. "Why States Act through Formal International Organizations." *Journal of Conflict Resolution* 42(1): 3–32.

Abbott, Kenneth W., and Duncan Snidal. 2000. "Hard and Soft Law in International Governance." *International Organization* 54(3): 421–56.

Abbott, Kenneth W., Robert O. Keohane, Andrew Moravcsik, Anne-Marie Slaughter, and Duncan Snidal. 2000. "The Concept of Legalization." *International Organization* 54(3): 401–19.

Allee, Todd L., and Paul K. Huth. 2006. "Legitimizing Dispute Settlement: International Legal Rulings as Domestic Political Cover." *American Political Science Review* 100(2): 219–34.

Alter, Karen J. 1998. "Who Are the 'Masters of the Treaty'?: European Governments and the European Court of Justice." *International Organization* 52(1): 121–47.

Alter, Karen J. 2001. *Establishing the Supremacy of European Law: The Making of an International Rule of Law in Europe.* Oxford: Oxford University Press.

Alter, Karen J. 2003. "Do International Courts Enhance Compliance with International Law?" *Review of Asian and Pacific Studies* 25: 51–78.

Alter, Karen J. 2008. "Agents or Trustees? International Courts in Their Political Context." *European Journal of International Relations* 14(1): 33–63.

Alter, Karen J. 2014. *The New Terrain of International Law: Courts, Politics, Rights.* Princeton: Princeton University Press.

Alter, Karen J., and Laurence R. Helfer. 2010. "Nature or Nurture? Judicial Lawmaking in the European Court of Justice and the Andean Tribunal of Justice." *International Organization* 64(4): 563–92.

Alter, Karen J., Laurence R. Helfer, and Osvaldo Saldias. 2012. "Transplanting the European Court of Justice: The Experience of the Andean Tribunal of Justice." *American Journal of Comparative Law* 60(3): 629–64.

Amnesty International. 2004. *United States of America—Human Dignity Denied: Torture and Accountability in the "War on Terror."* https://www.amnesty.org/en/documents/amr51/145/2004/en/.

Andersen, Stine. 2012. *The Enforcement of EU Law: The Role of the European Commission.* Oxford: Oxford University Press.

Anderson, Kym, and Rod Tyers. 1995. "Implications of EU Expansion for European Agricultural Policies, Trade and Welfare." In *Expanding Membership of the European Union,* edited by Richard E. Baldwin, Pertti Haaparanta, and Jaakko Kiander, 209–37. Cambridge, UK: Cambridge University Press.

Art, Robert J., and Robert Jervis. 1985. *International Politics: Anarchy, Force, Political Economy, and Decision-Making.* Boston: Little, Brown.

Axelrod, Robert. 1984. *The Evolution of Cooperation.* New York: Basic.

Axelrod, Robert, and Robert O. Keohane. 1985. "Achieving Cooperation Under Anarchy: Strategies and Institutions." *World Politics* 38(1): 226–54.

Bagwell, Kyle, and Robert W. Staiger. 1993. "Multilateral Tarriff Cooperation during the Formation of Regional Free Trade Areas." Working paper, no. 4364, National Bureau of Economic Research.

Bagwell, Kyle, and Robert W. Staiger. 1999. "An Economic Theory of GATT." *American Economic Review* 89(1): 215–48.

Bagwell, Kyle, and Robert W. Staiger. 2001. "Domestic Policies, National Sovereignty, and International Economic Institutions." *The Quarterly Journal of Economics* 116(2): 519–62.

Bagwell, Kyle, and Robert W. Staiger. 2005. "Enforcement, Private Political Pressure, and the General Agreement on Tariffs and Trade/World Trade Organization Escape Clause." *The Journal of Legal Studies* 34(2): 471–513.

Bailey, Michael A. 2001. "Quiet Influence: The Representation of Diffuse Interests on Trade Policy, 1983–94." *Legislative Studies Quarterly* 26(1): 45–80.

Bailey, Michael A., Judith Goldstein, and Barry R. Weingast. 1997. "The Institutional Roots of American Trade Policy: Politics, Coalitions, and International Trade." *World Politics* 49(3): 309–38.

Bailey, Michael A., Anton Strezhnev, and Erik Voeten. 2017. "Estimating Dynamic State Preferences from United Nations Voting Data." *Journal of Conflict Resolution* 61 (2): 430–56.

Ballet, Lucas. 2011. "Losing Flavor: Indonesia's WTO Complaint against the U.S. Ban on Clove Cigarettes." *American University International Law Review* 26(2): 515–41.

Barnett, Michael N., and Martha Finnemore. 1999. "The Politics, Power and Pathologies of International Organizations." *International Organization* 53(4): 699–732.

Barrett, Scott. 1997. "Toward a Theory of International Environmental Cooperation." In *New Directions in the Economic Theory of the Environment*, edited by Carlo Carraro and Domenico Siniscalco, 239–77. Cambridge, UK: Cambridge University Press.

Batory, Agnes. 2016. "Defying the Commission: Creative Compliance and Respect for the Rule of Law in the EU." *Public Administration* 94(3): 685–99.

Bechtel, Michael M., and Thomas Sattler. 2015. "What Is Litigation in the World Trade Organization Worth?" *International Organization* 69(2): 375–403.

Beck, Thorsten, George Clarke, Alberto Groff, Phillip Keefer, and Patrick Walsh. 2001. "New Tools in Comparative Political Economy: The Database of Political Institutions." *World Bank Economic Review* 15(1): 165–76.

Bednar, Jenna, John Ferejohn, and Geoff Farrett. 1996. "The Politics of European Federalism." *International Review of Law and Economics* 16(3): 279–95.

Benson, Todd. 2004. "International Business; Brazil Resolves Complaint on Florida Juice-Import Tax." *New York Times*, May 29, 2004.

Benz, Arthur. 2004. "Path-Dependent Institutions and Strategic Veto Players: National Parliaments in the European Union." *West European Politics* 27(5): 875–900.

Bergman, Torbjörn. 2000. "The European Union as the Next Step of Delegation and Accountability." *European Journal of Political Research* 37(3): 415–29.

Berry, Steven, James Levinsohn, and Ariel Pakes. 1999. "Voluntary Export Restraints on Automobiles: Evaluating a Trade Policy." *American Economic Review* 89(3): 400–430.

Betz, Timm. 2017. "Trading Interests: Domestic Institutions, International Negotiations, and the Politics of Trade." *The Journal of Politics* 79(4): 1237–52.

Betz, Timm, and Amy Pond. 2019. "The Absence of Consumer Interests in Trade Policy." *The Journal of Politics* 81(2): 585–600.

Blauberger, Michael. 2014. "National Responses to European Court Jurisprudence." *West European Politics* 37(3): 457–74.

Bobick, Talya, and Alastair Smith. 2016. "The Impact of Leader Turnover on the

Onset and Resolution of WTO Disputes." *Review of International Organizations* 8(4): 423–45.

Börzel, Tanja A. 2001. "Non-compliance in the European Union: Pathology or Statistical Artefact?" *Journal of European Public Policy* 8(5): 803–24.

Börzel, Tanja A. 2003. "Guarding the Treaty: The Compliance Strategies of the European Commission." In *The State of the European Union, 6: Law, Politics, and Society*, edited by Tanja A. Börzel and Rachel A. Cichowski, 197–220. Oxford: Oxford University Press.

Börzel, Tanja A., and Moritz Knoll. 2012. "Quantifying Non-compliance in the EU: A Database on EU Infringement Proceedings." Working paper, Berlin Working Paper on European Integration, no. 15, Freie Universitat Berlin. https://www.polsoz.fu-berlin.de/polwiss/forschung/international/europa/partner-und-online-ressourcen/arbeitspapiere/2012-15_BoerzelKnoll_Non-Compliance.pdf

Börzel, Tanja A., Tobias Hofmann, and Diana Panke. 2012. "Caving in or Sitting It Out? Longitudinal Patterns of Non-compliance in the European Union." *Journal of European Public Policy* 19(4): 37–41.

Börzel, Tanja A., Tobias Hofmann, Diana Panke, and Carina Sprungk. 2010. "Obstinate and Inefficient: Why Member States Do Not Comply with European Law." *Comparative Political Studies* 43(11): 1363–90.

Bowen, Renee. 2013. "Forbearance in Optimal Multilateral Trade Agreements." Stanford University Graduate School of Business Research Paper No. 2085.

Bowen, Renee. 2015. "Legislated Protection and the World Trade Organization." *International Economic Review* 56(4): 1349–84.

Bown, Chad P. 2002. "The Economics of Trade Disputes, the GATT's Article XXIII, and the WTO's Dispute Settlement Understanding." *Economics & Politics* 14(3): 283–323.

Bown, Chad P. 2004a. "Developing Countries as Plaintiffs and Defendants in GATT/WTO Trade Disputes." *The World Economy* 27(1): 59–80.

Bown, Chad P. 2004b. "On the Economic Success of GATT/WTO Dispute Settlement." *Review of Economics and Statistics* 86(3): 811–23.

Bown, Chad P. 2004c. "Trade Disputes and the Implementation of Protection Under the GATT: An Empirical Assessment." *Journal of International Economics* 62(2): 263–94.

Bown, Chad P. 2005a. "Participation in WTO Dispute Settlement: Complainants, Interested Parties, and Free Riders." *The World Bank Economic Review* 19(2): 287–310.

Bown, Chad P. 2005b. "Trade Remedies and World Trade Organization Dispute Settlement: Why Are So Few Challenged?" *Journal of Legal Studies* 34(2): 515–55.

Bown, Chad P. 2010. *Self-Enforcing Trade: Developing Countries and WTO Dispute Settlement*. Washington, DC: Brookings Institution Press.

Bown, Chad P., and Bernard M. Hoekman. 2005. "WTO Dispute Settlement and the Missing Developing Country Cases: Engaging the Private Sector." *Journal of International Economic Law* 8(4): 861–90.

Bown, Chad P., and Kara M. Reynolds. 2015. "Trade Flows and Trade Disputes." *Review of International Organizations* 10(2): 145–77.

Bown, Chad P., and Rachel Brewster. 2017. "US-COOL Retaliation: The WTO's Article 22.6 Arbitration." *World Trade Review* 16(2): 371–94.

Bräuninger, Thomas, and Thomas König. 2005. *Indices of Power*. V 2.0. MS-DOS 5.0 or later. http://www.tbraeuninger.de/download/.

Brewster, Rachel. 2011. "The Remedy Gap: Institutional Design, Retaliation, and Trade Law Enforcement." *George Washington Law Review* 80(1): 102–58.

Brewster, Rachel, and Adam Chilton. 2014. "Supplying Compliance: Why and When the United States Complies with WTO Rulings." *Yale Journal of International Law* 39(2): 201–46.

Brutger, Ryan. 2017. "Litigation for Sale: Private Firms and WTO Dispute Escalation." Working paper, University of Pennsylvania.

Brutger, Ryan, and Julia C. Morse. 2015. "Balancing Law and Politics: Judicial Incentives in WTO Dispute Settlement." *Review of International Organizations* 10(2): 179–205.

Bueno de Mesquita, Bruce, Alastair Smith, Randolph M. Siverson, and James D. Morrow. 2003. *The Logic of Political Survival*. Cambridge, MA: MIT Press.

Burley, Anne-Marie, and Walter Mattli. 1993. "Europe Before the Court: A Political Theory of Legal Integration." *International Organization* 47(1): 41–76.

Busch, Marc L. 2000. "Democracy, Consultation and the Paneling of Disputes under GATT." *Journal of Conflict Resolution* 44(4): 425–46.

Busch, Marc L., and Krzysztof J. Pelc. 2010. "The Politics of Judicial Economy at the World Trade Organization." *International Organization* 64(2): 257–79.

Busch, Marc L., and Krzysztof J. Pelc. 2016. "Words Matter: How WTO Rulings Handle Controversy." Working paper, McGill University.

Busch, Marc L, and Eric Reinhardt. 2000a. "Bargaining in the Shadow of the Law: Early Settlement in GATT/WTO Disputes." *Fordham International Law Journal* 24(1): 158–72.

Busch, Marc L., and Eric Reinhardt. 2000b. "Geography, International Trade, and Political Mobilization in US Industries." *American Journal of Political Science* 44: 703–19.

Busch, Marc L, and Eric Reinhardt. 2003. "The Evolution of GATT/WTO Dispute Settlement." In *Trade Policy Research*, edited by John M. Curtis and Dan Ciuriak, 143–83. Ottawa: Department of Foreign Affairs and International Trade.

Busch, Marc L., and Eric Reinhardt. 2006. "Three's a Crowd: Third Parties and WTO Dispute Settlement." *World Politics* 58(3): 446–77.

Bybee, Jay S. 2002. "Re: Standards of Conduct for Interrogation Under 18 U.S.C. §§ 2340–2340A." Memorandum to Alberto R. Gonzales, August 1, 2002. U.S. Department of Justice, Office of Legal Counsel.

Caldeira, Gregory A., and James L. Gibson. 1995. "The Legitimacy of the Court of Justice in the European Union: Models of Institutional Support." *American Political Science Review* 89(2): 356–76.

Carbone, Maurizio. 2010. *National Politics and European Integration: From the Constitution to the Lisbon Treaty.* Cheltenham, UK: Edward Elgar Publishing.

Carey, John M., and Matthew Soberg Shugart. 1995. "Incentives to Cultivate a Personal Vote: A Rank Ordering of Electoral Formulas." *Electoral Studies* 14(4): 417–39.

Carrubba, Clifford J. 2005. "Courts and Compliance in International Regulatory Regimes." *Journal of Politics* 67(3): 669–89.

Carrubba, Clifford J., and Matthew Gabel. 2015. *International Courts and the Performance of International Agreements.* Cambridge, UK: Cambridge University Press.

Carrubba, Clifford J., Matthew Gabel, and Charles Hankla. 2008. "Judicial Behavior Under Political Constraints: Evidence from the European Court of Justice." *American Political Science Review* 102(11): 435–52.

Carrubba, Clifford J., Matthew Gabel, and Charles Hankla. 2012. "Understanding the Role of the European Court of Justice in European Integration." *American Political Science Review* 106(1): 214–23.

Carrubba, Clifford J., and Lacey Murrah. 2005. "Legal Integration and Use of the Preliminary Ruling Process in the European Union." *International Organization* 59(2): 399–418.

Chalmers, Damian, Gareth Davies, and Giorgio Monti. 2014. *European Union Law: Text and Materials.* 3rd ed. Cambridge, UK: Cambridge University Press.

Chase, Spencer. 2014. "Farmers Union, Others Urge Appeal of WTO COOL Ruling." *Agri-Pulse,* October 23, 2014.

Chaudoin, Stephen. 2014. "Audience Features and the Strategic Timing of Trade Disputes." *International Organization* 68(4): 877–911.

Chaudoin, Stephen, Jeffrey Kucik, and Krzysztof J. Pelc. 2016. "Do WTO Disputes Actually Increase Trade?" *International Studies Quarterly* 60(2): 294–306.

Chayes, Abram, and Antonia Handler Chayes. 1993. "On Compliance." *International Organization* 47(2): 175–205.

Cochrane, Emily, and Alan Rappeport. 2021. "Democrats to Unveil Up to $3600 Child Tax Credit as Part of Stimulus Bill." *New York Times,* February 7, 2021.

Colantone, Italo, and Piero Stanig. 2018. "Global Competition and Brexit." *American Political Science Review* 112(2): 201–18.

Cole, David. 2009. *The Torture Memos: Rationalizing the Unthinkable.* New York: New Press.

Congressional Research Service. 2021. *The World Trade Organization's Appellate Body: Key Disputes and Controversies,* by Nina M. Hart and Brandon J. Murrill. R46852.

Conrad, Courtenay R., and Emily Hencken Ritter. 2019. *Contentious Compliance: Dissent and Repression Under International Human Rights Law.* Oxford: Oxford University Press.

Conybeare, John A. C. 1984. "Public Goods, Prisoner's Dilemmas and the International Political Economy." *International Studies Quarterly* 28(5): 5–22.

Copeland, Brian R. 1990. "Strategic Interaction Among Nations: Negotiable and Non-Negotiable Trade Barriers." *Canadian Journal of Economics* 23(1): 84–108.

Cox, David Roxbee, and E. Joyce Snell. 1989. *Analysis of Binary Data.* 2nd ed. Vol. 32, *Monographs on Statistics and Applied Probability.* New York: Chapman & Hall/CRC Press.

Creamer, Cosette D. 2017. "Between the Letter of the Law and the Demands of Politics: The Judicial Balancing of Trade Authority within the WTO." Working paper, University of Minnesota.

Crutsinger, Martin. 2006. "Mexico, U.S. Solidify Cement Accord." *The Houston Chronicle,* March 4, 2006.

Dai, Xinyuan. 2005. "Why Comply? The Domestic Constituency Mechanism." *International Organization* 59(2): 363–98.

Dai, Xinyuan. 2006. "The Conditional Nature of Democratic Compliance." *Journal of Conflict Resolution* 50(5): 690–713.

Dai, Xinyuan. 2007. *International Institutions and National Policies.* Cambridge, UK: Cambridge University Press.

Davey, William J. 2005. "The WTO Dispute Settlement System: The First Ten Years." *Journal of International Economic Law* 8(1): 17–50.

Davey, William J. 2009. "Compliance Problems in WTO Dispute Settlement." *Cornell International Law Journal* 42(1): 119–28.

Davis, Christina L. 2012. *Why Adjudicate? Enforcing Trade Rules in the WTO.* Princeton: Princeton University Press.

Davis, Christina L., and Sarah Blodgett Bermeo. 2009. "Who Files? Developing Country Participation in GATT/WTO Adjudication." *The Journal of Politics* 71(3): 1033–49.

Davis, Christina L., and Yuki Shirato. 2007. "Firms, Governments, and WTO Adjudication: Japan's Selection of WTO Disputes." *World Politics* 59(2): 274–313.

Davis, Donald R., and Prachi Mishra. 2007. "Stolper-Samuelson Is Dead: And Other Crimes of Both Theory and Data." In *Globalization and Poverty,* edited by Ann E. Harrison, 87–108. Chicago: University of Chicago Press

Destler, I. M. 2005. *American Trade Politics*. 4th ed. Washington, DC: Institute for International Economics.

Downs, George W., and David M. Rocke. 1995. *Optimal Imperfection? Domestic Uncertainty and Institutions in International Relations*. Princeton: Princeton University Press.

Downs, George W., David M. Rocke, and Peter N. Barsoom. 1996. "Is the Good News about Compliance Good News about Cooperation?" *International Organization* 50(3): 379–406.

Dubin, Jeffrey A., and Douglas Rivers. 1989. "Selection Bias in Linear Regression, Logit and Probit Models" *Sociological Methods and Research* 18(2): 360-390.

Durling, James P. 2000. *Anatomy of a Trade Dispute: A Documentary History of the Kodak-Fujifilm Dispute*. London: Cameron May.

Ehrlich, Sean D. 2009. "Constituency Size and Support for Trade Liberalization: An Analysis of Foreign Economic Policy Preferences in Congress." *Foreign Policy Analysis* 5(6): 215–32.

Ehrlich, Sean D. 2011. *Access Points: An Institutional Theory of Policy Bias and Policy Complexity*. Oxford: Oxford University Press.

Esteban, Joan, and Gerald Schneider. 2008. "Polarization and Conflict: Theoretical and Empirical Issues." *Journal of Peace Research* 45(2): 131–41.

European Commission. 1983. *First Annual Report to the European Parliament on Commission Monitoring of the Application of Community Law*. Brussels: European Commission.

European Commission. 2004. *Twenty-Second Annual Commission Report on Monitoring the Application of Community Law*. Annex V, "Judgments of the Court of Justice Not Yet Implemented." Brussels: European Commission.

European Commission. 2016. Eurobarometer: Public Opinion in the European Union (website). https://europa.eu/eurobarometer/screen/home/.

European Commission. 2017. "The EU in Brief." About the EU. http://europa.eu/european-union/about-eu/eu-in-brief_en/.

European Commission. 2018. *Monitoring the Application of European Union Law: 2018 Annual Report*. Brussels: European Commission.

European Commission. 2019. *Monitoring the Application of European Union Law: 2019 Annual Report*, Part I. "General Statistical Overview." Brussels: European Commission.

European Commission. 2019. *"Eurostat Database."* https://ec.europa.eu/eurostat/web/main/data/database

European Union. 2021. "Summaries of EU Legislation." *EUR-Lex: Access to European Law*. https://eur-lex.europa.eu/browse/summaries.html/.

Falkner, Gerda. 2018. "A Causal Loop? The Commission's New Enforcement Approach in the Context of Noncompliance with EU law Even after CJEU judgments." *Journal of European Integration* 40(6): 769–84.

Falkner, Gerda, Miriam Hartlapp, Simone Leiber, and Oliver Treib. 2007. "Non-compliance with EU Directives in the Member States: Opposition through the Backdoor?" *West European Politics* 27(3): 452–73.

Falkner, Gerda, Miriam Hartlapp, and Oliver Treib. 2007. "Worlds of Compliance: Why Leading Approaches to European Union Implementation are Only 'Sometimes-True Theories.'" *European Journal of Political Research* 46(3): 395–416.

Falkner, Gerda, Oliver Treib, Miriam Hartlapp, and Simone Leiber. 2005. *Complying with Europe: Harmonisation and Soft Law in the Member States.* Cambridge, UK: Cambridge University Press.

Fearon, James D. 1998. "Bargaining, Enforcement, and International Cooperation." *International Organization* 52(2): 269–305.

Featherstone, Kevin, and Dimitris Papadimitriou. 2007. "Manipulating Rules, Contesting Solutions: Europeanisation and the Politics of Restructuring Olympic Airways." *Government and Opposition* 42(1): 46–72.

Feenstra, Robert C. 2015. *Advanced International Trade: Theory and Evidence.* Princeton: Princeton University Press.

Finger, Joseph Michael. 2010. "Administered Protection in the GATT/WTO System." *https://ssrn.com/abstract=1769230.*

Finnemore, Martha. 1993. "International Organizations as Teachers of Norms: The United Nations Educational, Scientific, and Cultural Organization and Science Policy." *International Organization* 47(4): 565–97.

Finnemore, Martha, and Kathryn Sikkink. 1998. "International Norm Dynamics and Political Change." *International Organization* 52(4): 887–917.

Fiorina, Morris P. 1991. "Coalition Governments, Divided Governments, and Electoral Theory." *Governance* 4(3): 236–49.

Fisher, Roger. 1981. *Improving Compliance with International Law.* Charlottesville: University Press of Virginia.

Gabel, Matthew J., Clifford J. Carrubba, Caitlin Ainsley, and Donald M. Beaudette. 2012. "Of Courts and Commerce." *The Journal of Politics* 74: 1125–37.

Garrett, Geoffrey. 1992. "International Cooperation and Institutional Choice: The European Community's Internal Market." *International Organization* 46(2): 533–60.

Garrett, Geoffrey, R. Daniel Kelemen, and Heiner Schulz. 1998. "The European Court of Justice, National Governments, and Legal Integration in the European Union." *International Organization* 52(1): 149–76.

Garrett, Geoffrey, and Barry Weingast. 1993. "Ideas, Interests, and Institutions: Constructing the European Community's Internal Market." In *Ideas and Foreign Policy*, edited by Judith Goldstein and Robert Keohane, 173–204. Ithaca, NY: Cornell University Press.

Garten, Jeffrey E. 1995. "Is America Abandoning Multilateral Trade?" *Foreign Affairs* 74 (November/December): 50–62.

Gascoine, Digby. 2000. "WTO Dispute Settlement: Lessons Learned from the Salmon Case." Paper presented at the Conference on International Trade Education and Research: Managing Globalisation for Prosperity, Melbourne, Australia, October 2000.

Gilligan, Michael J. 1997. *Empowering Exporters: Reciprocity, Delegation, and Collective Action in American Trade Policy*. Ann Arbor: University of Michigan Press.

Gilligan, Michael J. 2006. "Is Enforcement Necessary for Effectiveness? A Model of the International Criminal Regime." *International Organization* 60(4): 935–67.

Gilligan, Michael J., Leslie Johns, and B. Peter Rosendorff. 2010. "Strengthening International Courts and the Early Settlement of Disputes." *Journal of Conflict Resolution* 54(1): 5–38.

Gilpin, Robert. 1981. *War and Change in the International System*. Princeton: Princeton University Press.

Gipe, Paul. 2013. "Two Steps Forward, One Back: Ontario Cancels Feed-in Tariffs for Large Projects." *Renewable Energy World*, June 10, 2013.

Goldsmith, Jack L. 2007. *The Terror Presidency: Law and Judgment inside the Bush Administration*. New York: W. W. Norton.

Goldsmith, Jack L., and Eric A. Posner. 2005. *The Limits of International Law*. Oxford: Oxford University Press.

Goldstein, Judith, and Lisa L. Martin. 2000. "Legalization, Trade Liberalization, and Domestic Politics: A Cautionary Note." *International Organization* 54(3): 603–32.

Goldstein, Judith, and Richard Steinberg. 2008. "Negotiate or Litigate? Effects of WTO Judicial Delegation on US Trade Politics." *Law and Contemporary Problems* 71(1): pp. 257–82.

Goodman, Peter S. 2018. "Trump Just Pushed the World Trade Organization Toward Irrelevance." *New York Times*, May 23, 2018.

Gowa, Joanne, and Soo Yeon Kim. 2005. "An Exclusive Country Club: The Effects of the GATT on Trade, 1950–94." *World Politics* 57(4): 453–78.

Gowa, Joanne, and Edward D. Mansfield. 1993. "Power Politics and International Trade." *American Political Science Review* 87(2): 408–20.

Gray, Julia. 2014. "Domestic Capacity and the Implementation Gap in Regional Trade Agreements." *Comparative Political Studies* 47(1): 55–84.

Gray, Julia. 2018. "Life, Death, or Zombie? The Vitality of International Organizations." *International Studies Quarterly* 62(1): 1–13.

Gray, Julia, and Jeffrey Kucik. 2017. "Leadership Turnover and the Durability of International Trade Commitments." *Comparative Political Studies* 50(14): 1941–72.

Grieco, Joseph M., Christopher F. Gelpi, and T. Camber Warren. 2009. "When Preferences and Commitments Collide: The Effect of Relative Partisan

Shifts on International Treaty Compliance." *International Organization* 63(2): 341–55.

Grossman, Gene M., and Elhanan Helpman. 1992. "Protection for Sale." *American Economic Review* 84(4): 833–50.

Grossman, Gene M., and Elhanan Helpman. 2001. *Special Interest Politics.* Cambridge, MA: MIT Press.

Grossman, Gene M., and Elhanan Helpman. 2005. "A Protectionist Bias in Majoritarian Politics." *The Quarterly Journal of Economics* 120(4): 1239–82.

Guisinger, Alexandra. 2017. *American Opinion on Trade: Preferences without Politics.* Oxford: Oxford University Press.

Guzman, Andrew T. 2002. "A Compliance-Based Theory of International Law." *California Law Review* 90(6): 1823–87.

Guzman, Andrew T., and Beth A. Simmons. 2004. "Power Plays and Capacity Constraints: The Selection of Defendants in World Trade Organization Disputes." *Journal of Legal Studies* 34(2): 557–98.

Haas, Peter. 1998. "Compliance with EU Directives: Insights from International Relations and Comparative Politics." *Journal of European Public Policy* 5(1): 17–37.

Hahn, Robert W., and Kenneth R. Richards. 1989. "The Internationalization of Environmental Regulation." *Harvard International Law Journal* 30(2): 421–46.

Hainmueller, Jens, Jonathan Mummolo, and Yiqing Xu. 2019. "How Much Should We Trust Estimates from Multiplicative Interaction Models? Simple Tools to Improve Empirical Practice." *Political Analysis* 27(2): 1–30.

Hall, Peter, and John Keeler. 2001. "Interest Representation and the Politics of Protest." In *Developments in French Politics*, 2nd ed., edited by Howard Machin, Alain Guyomarch, Peter A. Hall, and Jack Hayward, 50–67. Houndsmills: Palgrave.

Hardin, Garrett, and John Baden. 1977. *Managing the Commons.* New York: Freeman Press.

Hartlapp, Miriam, and Gerda Falkner. 2009. "Problems of Operationalization and Data in EU Compliance Research." *European Union Politics* 10(2): 281–304.

Hausman, Jerry. 1978. "Specification Tests in Econometrics." *Econometrica: Journal of the Econometric Society* pp. 1251–71.

Haverland, Markus. 2000. "National Adaptation to European Integration: The Importance of Institutional Veto Points." *Journal of Public Policy* 20(1): 83–103.

Heckman, James. 1979. "Sample Selection Bias as a Specification Error." *Econometrica* 47(1): 153–61.

Heckman, James. 1990. "Varieties of Selection Bias." *The American Economic Review* 80(2): 313–18.

Henisz, Witold J. 2000. "The Institutional Environment for Economic Growth." *Economics & Politics* 12(1): 1–31.

Henisz, Witold J. 2002. "The Political Constraint Index (POLCON) Dataset." The Wharton School, University of Pennsylvania. http://www-management .wharton.upenn.edu/henisz/.

Henisz, Witold J., and Edward D. Mansfield. 2006. "Votes and Vetoes: The Political Determinants of Commercial Openness." *International Studies Quarterly* 50(1): 189–212.

Henkin, Louis. 1979. *How Nations Behave: Law and Foreign Policy.* 2nd ed. New York: Columbia University Press.

Hershey, Robert D., Jr. 1995. "U.S. to Assess Kodak's Case Against Fuji." *New York Times,* July 4, 1995.

Hiscox, Michael J. 2002. *International Trade and Political Conflict: Commerce, Coalitions, and Mobility.* Princeton: Princeton University Press.

Hiscox, Michael J. 2006. "Through a Glass and Darkly: Attitudes Toward International Trade and the Curious Effects of Issue Framing." *International Organization* 60(7): 755–80.

Hofmann, Andreas. 2018a. "Is the Commission Leveling the Playing Field? Rights Enforcement in the European Union." *Journal of European Integration* 40(6): 737–51.

Hofmann, Andreas. 2018b. "Resistance against the Court of Justice of the European Union." *International Journal of Law in Context* 14(2): 258–74.

Hofmann, Tobias. 2013. "Noncompliance and the Power of Special Interests." *University of Utah Working Paper.*

Hofmann, Tobias. 2018. "How Long to Compliance? Escalating Infringement Proceedings and the Diminishing Power of Special Interests." *Journal of European Integration* 40(6): 785–801.

Hofmann, Tobias, and Soo Yeon Kim. 2017. "Does Trade Comply? The Economic Effectiveness of WTO Disputes." In *Assessing the World Trade Organization Fit for Purpose? World Trade Forum 2015,* edited by Manfred Elsig, Bernard Hoekman, and Joost Pauwelyn. Cambridge, UK: Cambridge University Press.

Holmberg, Sören, and Bo Rothstein. 2012. *Good Government: The Relevance of Political Science.* Cheltenham, UK: Edward Elgar Publishing.

Horan, Blair. 2016. *Brexit and the Free Movement of People.* Dublin, Ireland: The Institute of International and European Affairs.

Horn, Henrik, Giovanni Maggi, and Robert W. Staiger. 2010. "Trade Agreements as Endogenously Incomplete Contracts." *American Economic Review* 100(1): 394–419.

Horn, Henrik, and Petros C. Mavroidis. 2008. "The WTO Dispute Settlement Data Set 1995–2006." The World Bank. https://datacatalog.worldbank.org/ search/dataset/0037789.

Howse, Robert, and Philip I. Levy. 2013. "The TBT Panels: US–Cloves, US–Tuna, US–COOL." *World Trade Review* 12(2): 327–75.

Hudec, Robert E. 1999. "The New WTO Dispute Settlement Procedure: An Overview of the First Three Years." *Minnesota Journal of Global Trade* 8(1): 1–53.

Huelshoff, Michael, James Sperling, and Michael Hess. 2005. "Is Germany a 'Good European'? German Compliance with EU Law." *German Politics* 14(3): 354–70.

Huth, Paul K., Sarah E. Croco, and Benjamin J. Appel. 2011. "Does International Law Promote the Peaceful Settlement of International Disputes? Evidence from the Study of Territorial Conflicts Since 1945." *American Political Science Review* 105(2): 415–36.

Hutton, Susan M., and Eric H. Bremermann. 2013. "Canada Loses WTO Appeal Regarding Ontario's FIT Program." Stikeman Elliott (website). May 7, 2013. https://www.stikeman.com/en-ca/kh/canadian-energy-law/canada-loses-wto-appeal-regarding-ontario-feed-in-tariff-fit-program.

Imai, Kosuke, and Marc Ratkovic. 2014. "Covariate Balancing Propensity Score." *Journal of the Royal Statistical Society* 76(1): 243–63.

Jackson, John H. 2006. *Sovereignty, the WTO, and Changing Fundamentals of International Law.* Cambridge, UK: Cambridge University Press.

Jervis, Robert. 1976. *Perception and Misperception in International Politics.* Princeton: Princeton University Press.

Johns, Leslie. 2012. "Courts as Coordinators: Endogenous Enforcement and Jurisdiction in International Adjudication." *Journal of Conflict Resolution* 56(2): 257–89.

Johns, Leslie. 2014. "Depth versus Rigidity in the Design of International Trade Agreements." *Journal of Theoretical Politics* 26(3): 468–95.

Johns, Leslie. 2015. *Strengthening International Courts: The Hidden Costs of Legalization.* Ann Arbor: University of Michigan Press.

Johns, Leslie, and Krzysztof J. Pelc. 2014. "Who Gets to Be in the Room? Manipulating Participation in WTO Disputes." *International Organization* 68(3): 663–99.

Johns, Leslie, and Krzysztof J. Pelc. 2018. "Free Riding on Enforcement in the World Trade Organization." *The Journal of Politics* 80(3): 873–89.

Johns, Leslie, and Lauren Peritz. 2015. "The Design of Trade Agreements." In *The Oxford Handbook of the Political Economy of International Trade*, edited by Lisa L. Martin, 337–359. Oxford: Oxford University Press.

Johns, Leslie, and B. Peter Rosendorff. 2009. "Dispute Settlement, Compliance, and Domestic Politics." In *Frontiers of Economics and Globalization*, edited by James Hartigan, 139–163. Bingley, UK: Emerald Group.

Johnson, Boris. 2020. "Prime Minister's Statement on EU Negotiations, 24 December 2020." Prime Minister's Office of the United Kingdom.

Johnson, Harry G. 1953. "Optimum Tariffs and Retaliation." *The Review of Economic Studies* 21(2): 142–53.

Kahneman, Daniel, and Amos Tversky. 1979. "Prospect Theory: An Analysis of Decision under Risk." *Econometrica* 47(2): 263–91.

Kam, Cynthia D., and Robert J. Franzese, Jr. 2007. *Modeling and Interpreting Interactive Hypotheses in Regression Analysis*. Ann Arbor: University of Michigan Press.

Karol, David. 2007. "Does Constituency Size Affect Elected Officials' Trade Policy Preferences?" *Journal of Politics* 69(2): 483–94.

Kaufmann, Daniel, and Aart Kraay. 2015. "Worldwide Governance Indicators." http://www.govindicators.org/.

Kaufmann, Daniel, Aart Kraay, and Massimo Mastruzzi. 2010. "The Worldwide Governance Indicators: Methodology and Analytical Issues." *Draft Policy Research Working Paper*. http://info.worldbank.org/governance/wgi/pdf/wgi .pdf/.

Keefer, Philip, and David Stasavage. 2003. "The Limits of Delegation: Veto Players, Central Bank Independence, and the Credibility of Monetary Policy." *American Political Science Review* 97(3): 407–23.

Keele, Luke, and Nathan J. Kelly. 2006. "Dynamic Models for Dynamic Theories: The Ins and Outs of Lagged Dependent Variables." *Political Analysis* 14(2): 186–205.

Kelsen, Hans. 1941. "Recognition in International Law." *American Journal of International Law* 35(4): 605–17.

Keohane, Robert O. 1982. "The Demand for International Regimes." *International Organization* 36(2): 325–55.

Keohane, Robert O. 1984. *After Hegemony*. Princeton: Princeton University Press.

Keohane, Robert O. 1986. "Reciprocity in International Relations." *International Organization* 40(1): 1–27.

Keohane, Robert O., and Helen V. Milner. 1996. *Internationalization and Domestic Politics*. Cambridge, UK: Cambridge University Press.

Kim, In Song. 2017. "Political Cleavages within Industry: Firm-Level Lobbying for Trade Liberalization." *American Political Science Review* 111(1): 1–20.

Kim, Sunhyuk. 2000. "The Politics of Reform in South Korea: The First Year of the Kim Dae Jung Government 1998–1999." *Asian Perspective* 24(1): 163–85.

König, Thomas, and Brooke Luetgert. 2009. "Troubles with Transposition? Explaining Trends in Member-State Notification and the Delayed Transposition of EU Directives." *British Journal of Political Science* 39(1): 163–94.

König, Thomas, and Lars Mäder. 2013. "Non-Conformable, Partial and Conformable Transposition: A Competing Risk Analysis of the Transposition Process of Directives in the EU 15." *European Union Politics* 14(1): 46–69.

König, Thomas, and Lars Mäder. 2014. "The Strategic Nature of Compliance: An Empirical Evaluation of Law Implementation in the Central Monitoring System of the European Union." *American Journal of Political Science* 58(1): 246–63.

Kono, Daniel Y. 2006. "Optimal Obfuscation: Democracy and Trade Policy Transparency." *American Political Science Review* 100(3): 369–84.

Kono, Daniel Y. 2007. "Making Anarchy Work: International Legal Institutions and Trade Cooperation." *Journal of Politics* 69(3): 746–59.

Kono, Daniel Y. 2009. "Market Structure, Electoral Institutions, and Trade Policy." *International Studies Quarterly* 53(4): 885–906.

Koremenos, Barbara. 2005. "Contracting Around International Uncertainty." *American Political Science Review* 99(4): 549–65.

Koremenos, Barbara. 2016. *The Continent of International Law: Explaining Agreement Design*. Cambridge, UK: Cambridge University Press.

Koremenos, Barbara, Charles Lipson, and Duncan Snidal. 2001. "The Rational Design of International Institutions." *International Organization* 55(4): 761–99.

Krasner, Stephen D. 1999. *Sovereignty: Organized Hypocrisy*. Princeton: Princeton University Press.

Krugman, Paul. 1991. "The Move Toward Free Trade Zones." *Economic Review*, November/ December 1991, 5–25.

Kucik, Jeffrey. 2012. "The Domestic Politics of Institutional Design: Producer Preferences over Trade Agreement Rules." *Economics & Politics* 24(2): 95–118.

Kucik, Jeffrey. 2019. "How Do Prior Rulings Affect Future Disputes?" *International Studies Quarterly* 63(4): 1122–32.

Kucik, Jeffrey, and Krzysztof J. Pelc. 2016. "Measuring the Cost of Privacy: A Look at the Distributional Effects of Private Bargaining." *British Journal of Political Science* 46(4): 861–89.

Kucik, Jeffrey, and Lauren Peritz. 2021. "How Do Third Parties Affect Compliance in the Trade Regime?" *Journal of Politics* 83(3): 1184–89.

Kucik, Jeffrey, Lauren Peritz, and Sergio Puig. Forthcoming. "Legalization and Compliance: How Judicial Activity Undercuts the Global Trade Regime." *British Journal of Political Science*.

Kucik, Jeffrey, and Sergio Puig. 2021. "Extending Trade Law Precedent." *Vanderbilt Journal of Transnational Law* 54(3): 539–86.

Kucik, Jeffrey, and Eric Reinhardt. 2008. "Does Flexibility Promote Cooperation? An Application to the Global Trade Regime." *International Organization* 62(3): 477–505.

Laakso, Markku, and Rein Taagepera. 1979. "The 'Effective' Number of Parties: A Measure with Application to West Europe." *Comparative Political Studies* 12(1): 3–27.

Lake, David A., and Robert Powell. 1999. *Strategic Choice and International Relations*. Princeton: Princeton University Press.

Larsson, Olof, and Daniel Naurin. 2016. "Judicial Independence and Political Uncertainty: How the Risk of Override Affects the Court of Justice of the European Union." *International Organization* 70(2): 377–408.

Lauterpacht, Hersch. 1982. *The Development of International Law by the International Court*. Cambridge, UK: Cambridge University Press.

Laver, Michael, and Kenneth A. Shepsle. 1991. "Divided Government: America Is Not 'Exceptional.'" *Governance* 4(3): 250–269.

Leeds, Brett Ashley. 1999. "Domestic Political Institutions, Credible Commitments, and International Cooperation." *American Journal of Political Science* 43(4): 979–1002.

Linos, Katerina. 2007. "How Can International Organizations Shape National Welfare States? Evidence from Compliance with European Union Directives." *Comparative Political Studies* 40(5): 547–70.

Lipson, Charles. 1984. "International Cooperation in Economic and Security Affairs." *World Politics* 37(1): 1–23.

Lohmann, Susanne, and Sharyn O'Halloran. 1994. "Divided Government and US Trade Policy: Theory and Evidence." *International Organization* 48(4): 595–632.

Maggi, Giovanni. 1999. "The Role of Multilateral Institutions in International Trade Cooperation." *American Economic Review* 89(1): 190–214.

Malkin, Elisabeth. 2006. "U.S. Cuts Duty on Cement from Mexico." *New York Times*, January 20, 2006.

Mansfield, Edward D., and Marc L. Busch. 1995. "The Political Economy of Nontariff Barriers: A Cross-National Analysis." *International Organization* 49(4): 723–49.

Mansfield, Edward D., and Helen V. Milner. 2012. *Votes, Vetoes, and the Political Economy of International Trade Agreements*. Princeton: Princeton University Press.

Mansfield, Edward D., Helen V. Milner, and Jon C. Pevehouse. 2007. "Vetoing Co-operation: The Impact of Veto Players on Preferential Trading Arrangements." *British Journal of Political Science* 37(3): 403–32.

Mansfield, Edward D., Helen V. Milner, and B. Peter Rosendorff. 2000. "Free to Trade: Democracies, Autocracies, and International Trade." *American Political Science Review* 94(2): 305–21.

Mansfield, Edward D., Helen V. Milner, and B. Peter Rosendorff. 2002. "Why Democracies Cooperate More: Electoral Control and International Trade Agreements." *International Organization* 56(3): 477–513.

Marshall, Monty G., and Keith Jaggers. 2012. "Polity IV Project: Political Regime Characteristics and Transitions, 1800–2012." Center for Systemic Peace. https://www.systemicpeace.org/polity/polity4.htm.

Martin, Lisa L. 1992. "Interests, Power, and Multilateralism." *International Organization* 46(4): 765–92.

Martin, Lisa L. 1999. "The Political Economy of International Cooperation." In *Global Public Goods: International Cooperation in the 21st Century*, edited by Inge Kaul, Isabelle Grunberg, and Marc A. Stern, 63-76 Oxford: Oxford University Press.

Martin, Lisa L. 2000. *Democratic Commitments: Legislatures and International Cooperation*. Princeton: Princeton University Press.

Martin, Lisa L. 2013. "Against Compliance." In *Interdisciplinary Perspectives on International Law and International Relations: The State of the Art*, edited by Jeffrey L. Dunoff and Mark A. Pollack, 591–610. Cambridge, UK: Cambridge University Press

Martinsen, Dorte Sindbjerg. 2015a. *An Ever More Powerful Court? The Political Constraints of Legal Integration in the European Union*. Oxford: Oxford University Press.

Martinsen, Dorte Sindbjerg. 2015b. "Judicial Influence on Policy Outputs? The Political Constraints of Legal Integration in the European Union." *Comparative Political Studies* 48(12): 1622–60.

Mattli, Walter, and Anne Marie Slaughter. 1998. "Revisiting the European Court of Justice." *International Organization* 52(1): 177–209.

Mbaye, Heather. 2001. "Why National States Comply with Supranational Law Explaining Implementation Infringements in the European Union, 1972–1993." *European Union Politics* 2(3): 259–81.

McCubbins, Matthew D., and Thomas Schwartz. 1984. "Congressional Oversight Overlooked: Police Patrols versus Fire Alarm." *American Journal of Political Science* 28(1): 165–79.

McKibben, Heather Elko. 2015. *State Strategies in International Bargaining: Play by the Rules or Change Them?* Cambridge, UK: Cambridge University Press.

Mearsheimer, John J. 1994. "The False Promise of International Institutions." *International Security* 19(3): 5–49.

Meunier, Sophie, and Kathleen McNamara. 2007. *Making History: European Integration and Institutional Change at Fifty*. Oxford: Oxford University Press.

Milgrom, Paul R., Douglass C. North, and Barry R. Weingast. 1990. "The Role of Institutions in the Revival of Trade: The Law Merchant, Private Judges, and the Champagne Fairs." *Economics & Politics* 2(1): 1–23.

Milner, Helen V. 1991. "The Assumption of Anarchy in International Relations Theory: A Critique." *Review of International Studies* 17(1): 67–85.

Milner, Helen V. 1997. *Interests, Institutions, and Information: Domestic Politics and International Relations*. Princeton: Princeton University Press.

Milner, Helen V. 1999. "The Political Economy of International Trade." *Annual Review of Political Science* 2(1): 91–114.

Milner, Helen V., and Keiko Kubota. 2005. "Why the Move to Free Trade? Democracy and Trade Policy in the Developing Countries." *International Organization* 59(1): 107–43.

Milner, Helen V., and B. Peter Rosendorff. 1996. "Trade Negotiations, Information and Domestic Politics: The Role of Domestic Groups." *Economics & Politics* 8(2): 145–89.

Milner, Helen V., and B. Peter Rosendorff. 1997. "Democratic Politics and International Trade Negotiations Elections and Divided Government as Constraints on Trade Liberalization." *Journal of Conflict Resolution* 41(1): 117–46.

Morrow, James D. 1994. "Modeling the Forms of International Cooperation: Distribution versus Information." *International Organization* 48(3): 387–423.

Neto, Octavio Amorim, and Gary W. Cox. 1997. "Electoral Institutions, Cleavage Structures, and the Number of Parties." *American Journal of Political Science* 41(1): 149–74.

Olson, Mancur. 1965. *The Logic of Collective Action: Public Goods and the Theory of Groups.* Cambridge, MA: Harvard University Press.

Ontario Ministry of Energy. 2011. "Ontario's Solar Energy Industry Creating Jobs." *Technical Report on Northern Development and Mines.*

Osgood, Iain. 2016. "Differentiated Products, Divided Industries: Firm Preferences over Trade Liberalization." *Economics & Politics* 28(2): 161–80.

Osgood, Iain. 2017. "The Breakdown of Industrial Opposition to Trade: Firms, Product Variety, and Reciprocal Liberalization." *World Politics* 69: 184–231.

Oye, Kenneth A. 1985. "Explaining Cooperation under Anarchy: Hypotheses and Strategies." *World Politics* 38(1): 1–24.

Pahre, Robert. 1997. "Endogenous Domestic Institutions in Two-Level Games and Parliamentary Oversight of the European Union." *Journal of Conflict Resolution* 41(1): 147–74.

Panke, Diana. 2007. "The European Court of Justice as an Agent of Europeanization? Restoring Compliance with EU Law." *Journal of European Public Policy* 14(6): 847–866.

Payandeh, Mehrdad. 2014. *Precedents and Case-Based Reasoning in the European Court of Justice.* Oxford: Oxford University Press.

Pelc, Krzysztof J. 2009. "Seeking Escape: The Use of Escape Clauses in International Trade Agreements." *International Studies Quarterly* 53(2): 349–68.

Pelc, Krzysztof J. 2011. "How States Ration Flexibility: Tariffs, Remedies, and Exchange Rates as Policy Substitutes." *World Politics* 63(4): 618–46.

Pelc, Krzysztof J. 2013. "The Cost of Wiggle-Room: Looking at the Welfare Effects of Flexibility in Tariff Rates at the WTO." *International Studies Quarterly* 57(1): 91–102.

Pelc, Krzysztof J. 2014. "The Politics of Precedent in International Law: A Social Network Application." *American Political Science Review* 108(3): 547–64.

Pelc, Krzysztof J. 2016. *Making and Bending International Rules: The Design of Exceptions and Escape Clauses in Trade Law*. Cambridge, UK: Cambridge University Press.

Pelc, Krzysztof J., and Johannes Urpelainen. 2015. "When Do International Economic Agreements Allow Countries to Pay to Breach?" *Review of International Organizations* 10(2): 231–264.

Pempel, T. J. 1997. "Regime Shift: Japanese Politics in a Changing World Economy." *The Journal of Japanese Studies* 23(2): 333–61.

Pempel, T. J. 1998. *Regime Shift: Comparative Dynamics of the Japanese Political Economy*. Ithaca, NY: Cornell University Press.

Peritz, Lauren. 2018. "Obstructing Integration: Domestic Politics and the European Court of Justice." *European Union Politics* 19(3): 427–57.

Peritz, Lauren. 2020. "When are International Institutions Effective? The Impact of Domestic Veto Players on Compliance with WTO Rulings." *International Studies Quarterly* 64(1): 220–34.

Perkins, Richard, and Eric Neumayer. 2007. "Do Membership Benefits Buy Regulatory Compliance? An Empirical Analysis of EU Directives 1978–99." *European Union Politics* 8(2): 180–206.

Persson, Torsten, and Guido Enrico Tabellini. 2005. *The Economic Effects of Constitutions*. Cambridge, MA: MIT Press.

Phelan, William. 2015. *In Place of Inter-state Retaliation: The European Union's Rejection of WTO-Style Trade Sanctions and Trade Remedies*. Cambridge, UK: Cambridge University Press.

Poletti, Arlo, and Dirk DeBievre. 2014. "Political Mobilization, Veto Players, and WTO Litigation: Explaining European Union Responses in Trade Disputes." *Journal of European Public Policy* 21(8): 1181–98.

Przeworski, Adam, and James Raymond Vreeland. 2000. "The Effect of IMF Programs on Economic Growth." *Journal of Development Economics* 62(2): 385–421.

Putnam, Robert D. 1988. "Diplomacy and Domestic Politics: The Logic of Two-Level Games." *International Organization* 42(3): 427–60.

Rasmussen, Hjalte. 1986. *On Law and Policy in the European Court of Justice: A Comparative Study in Judicial Policymaking*. Leiden, Netherlands: Brill Press.

Raustiala, Kal. 2000. "Compliance and Effectiveness in International Regulatory Cooperation." *Case Western Reserve Journal of International Law* 32(3): 387–440.

Reinhardt, Eric. 2001. "Adjudication Without Enforcement in GATT Disputes." *Journal of Conflict Resolution* 45(2): 174–95.

Reus-smit, Christian. 2004. "The Politics of International Law." In *The Politics of International Law*, edited by Christian, Reus-smit, 14–44. Cambridge Studies in International Relations, vol. 96. Cambridge, UK: Cambridge University Press.

Rickard, Stephanie J. 2010. "Democratic Differences: Electoral Institutions and Compliance with GATT/WTO Agreements." *European Journal of International Relations* 16(4): 711–29.

Rickard, Stephanie J. 2012. "A Non-Tariff Protectionist Bias in Majoritarian Politics: Government Subsidies and Electoral Institutions." *International Studies Quarterly* 56(4): 777–85.

Rickard, Stephanie J. 2018. *Spending to Win: Political Institutions, Economic Geography, and Government Subsidies.* Cambridge, UK: Cambridge University Press.

Rodrik, Dani. 2008. "Stolper-Samuelson for the Real World." *Dani Rodrik's Weblog: Unconventional Thoughts on Economic Development and Globalization.* June 16, 2008. *https://rodrik.typepad.com/dani_rodriks_weblog/2008/06/stolper-samuelson-for-the-real-world.html/.*

Rodrik, Dani. 2011. *The Globalization Paradox: Democracy and the Future of the World Economy.* New York: W. W. Norton.

Rogowski, Ronald. 1987. "Trade and the Variety of Democratic Institutions." *International Organization* 41(2): 203–23.

Rogowski, Ronald. 1989. *Commerce and Coalitions: How Trade Affects Domestic Political Arrangements.* Princeton: Princeton University Press.

Rogowski, Ronald, and Mark Andreas Kayser. 2002. "Majoritarian Electoral Systems and Consumer Power: Price-Level Evidence from the OECD Countries." *American Journal of Political Science* 46(3): 526–39.

Romano, Cesare P. R. 1998. "Project on International Courts and Tribunals." Supplement to the *NYU Journal of International Law and Politics* 31(4). http://pict-pcti.org/.

Romano, Cesare P. R. 1999. "The Proliferation of International Judicial Bodies: The Pieces of the Puzzle." *Journal of International Law and Politics* 31(4): 709–51.

Rose, Andrew. 2004. "Do We Really Know That the WTO Increases Trade?" *American Economic Review* 94(1): 98–114.

Rosendorff, B. Peter. 2005. "Stability and Rigidity: Politics and Design of the WTO's Dispute Settlement Procedure." *American Political Science Review* 99(3): 389–400.

Rosendorff, B. Peter, and Helen V. Milner. 2001. "The Optimal Design of International Trade Institutions: Uncertainty and Escape." *International Organization* 55(4): 829–57.

Rubin, Donald B. 2005. "Causal Inference Using Potential Outcomes." *Journal of the American Statistical Association* 100(469): 322–31.

Ruggie, John Gerard. 1982. "International Regimes, Transactions, and Change: Embedded Liberalism in the Postwar Economic Order." *International Organization* 36(2): 379–415.

Ryu, Jeheung, and Randall W. Stone. 2018. "Plaintiffs by Proxy: A Firm-Level

Approach to WTO Dispute Resolution." *Review of International Organizations* 13: 273–308.

Sattler, Thomas, and Thomas Bernauer. 2014. "Does WTO Dispute Settlement Enforce or Inform?" *British Journal of Political Science* 44(4): 877–902.

Schneider, Christina J. 2011. "Weak States and Institutionalized Bargaining Power in International Organizations." *International Studies Quarterly* 55(2): 331–55.

Schneider, Christina J. 2014. "Domestic Politics and the Widening-Deepening Trade-Off in the European Union." *Journal of European Public Policy* 21(5): 699–712.

Schultz, Kenneth A. 2014. "What's in a Claim? De Jure versus De Facto Borders in Interstate Territorial Disputes." *Journal of Conflict Resolution* 58(6): 1059–84.

Schweitzer, Frank J. 1996. "Flash of the Titans: A Picture of Section 301 in the Dispute between Kodak and Fuji and a View Toward Dismantling Anticompetitive Practices in the Japanese Distribution System." *American University International Law Review* 11(5): 847–75.

Seikel, Daniel. 2015. "Class Struggle in the Shadow of Luxembourg. The Domestic Impact of the European Court of Justice's Case Law on the Regulation of Working Conditions." *Journal of European Public Policy* 22(8): 1166–85.

Shaffer, Gregory C. 2003. *Defending Interests: Public-Private Partnerships in WTO Litigation*. Washington, DC: Brookings Institution Press.

Shahabuddeen, Mohammed. 2007. *Precedent in the World Court*. Cambridge, UK: Cambridge University Press.

Shany, Yuval. 2012. "Assessing the Effectiveness of International Courts: A Goal-Based Approach." *American Journal of International Law* 106(2): 225–70.

Shapley, Lloyd S., and Martin Shubik. 1954. "A Method for Evaluating the Distribution of Power in a Committee System." *American Political Science Review* 48(3): 787–92.

Shugart, Matthew Soberg, and John M. Carey. 1992. *Presidents and Assemblies: Constitutional Design and Electoral Dynamics*. Cambridge, UK: Cambridge University Press.

Siegel, Scott N. 2011. *The Political Economy of Noncompliance: Adjusting to the Single European Market*. New York: Routledge.

Simmons, Beth A. 1998. "Compliance with International Agreements." *Annual Review of Political Science* 1(1): 75–93.

Simmons, Beth A. 2000. "International Law and State Behavior: Commitment and Compliance in International Monetary Affairs." *American Political Science Review* 94(4): 819–35

Simmons, Beth A. 2009. *Mobilizing for Human Rights: International Law in Domestic Politics*. Cambridge, UK: Cambridge University Press.

Slaughter, Anne Marie, Alec Stone Sweet, and Joseph Weiler. 1998. *The European Court and National Courts: Doctrine & Jurisprudence: Legal Change in Its Social Context*. New York: Bloomsbury.

Smith, James. 2004. "Inequality in International Trade? Developing Countries and Institutional Change in WTO Dispute Settlement." *Review of International Political Economy* 11(3): 542–573.

Smith, Jeffrey. 2004. "Slim Legal Grounds for Torture Memos." *The Washington Post*, July 4, 2004.

Smith, Jeffrey, and Petra Todd. 2005. "Does Matching Overcome LaLonde's Critique of Nonexperimental Estimators?" *Journal of Econometrics* 125(1): 305–53.

Snidal, Duncan. 1985. "Coordination versus Prisoners' Dilemma: Implications for International Cooperation and Regimes." *American Political Science Review* 79(4): 923–942.

Soroos, Marvin S. 1994. "Global Change, Environmental Security, and the Prisoner's Dilemma." *Journal of Peace Research* 31(3): 317–32.

Staiger, Robert W. 1995. "International Rules and Institutions for Trade Policy." In *Handbook of International Economics*, vol. 2, edited by Gene Grossman and Kenneth Rogoff. New York: North Holland.

Staiger, Robert W., and Guido Tabellini. 1987. "Discretionary Trade Policy and Excessive Protection." *American Economic Review* 77(5): 823–37.

Stein, Arthur A. 1982. "Coordination and Collaboration: Regimes in an Anarchic World." *International Organization* 36(2): 299–324.

Stein, Arthur A. 1990. *Why Nations Cooperate: Circumstance and Choice in International Relations*. Ithaca, NY: Cornell University Press.

Steinberg, Richard H. 2004. "Judicial Lawmaking at the WTO: Discursive, Constitutional, and Political Constraints." *American Journal of International Law* 98(2): 247–75.

Stewart, John. 2010. "Magazines, Ministers and 'Monoculture': The Canada–United States Dispute over 'Split Run Magazines' in the 1990s." *Canadian Foreign Policy Journal* 16(1): 35–48.

Stolper, Wolfgang F., and Paul A. Samuelson. 1941. "Protection and Real Wages." *Review of Economic Studies* 9(1): 58–73.

Stone Sweet, Alec, and Thomas Brunell. 1998a. "Constructing a Supranational Constitution: Dispute Resolution and Governance in the European Community." *American Political Science Review* 92(1): 63–81.

Stone Sweet, Alec, and Thomas Brunell. 1998b. "The European Court and the National Courts: A Statistical Analysis of Preliminary References, 1961–95." *Journal of European Public Policy* 5(1): 66–97.

Stone Sweet, Alec, and Thomas Brunell. 2012. "The European Court of Justice, State Noncompliance, and the Politics of Override." *American Political Science Review* 106(1): 204–13.

Stone Sweet, Alec, and James A. Caporaso. 1998. "From Free Trade to Supranational Polity: The European Court and Integration." In *European Integration and Supranational Governance, edited by Wayne Sandholtz and Alec Stone Sweet*, 92–133. Oxford: Oxford University Press.

Subramanian, Arvind, and Shang-Jin Wei. 2007. "The WTO Promotes Trade, Strongly but Unevenly." *Journal of International Economics* 72(1): 151–75.

Sverdrup, Ulf. 2004. "Compliance and Conflict Management in the European Union: Nordic Exceptionalism." *Scandinavian Political Studies* 27(1): 23–43.

Taborowski, Maciej. 2012. "Infringement Proceedings and Non-compliant National Courts." *Common Market Law Review* 49(6): 1881–914.

Tallberg, Jonas. 2000. "Supranational Influence in EU Enforcement: The ECJ and the Principle of State Liability." *Journal of European Public Policy* 7(1): 104–21.

Tallberg, Jonas. 2002a. "Delegation to Supranational Institutions: Why, How, and with What Consequences?" *West European Politics* 25(1): 23–46.

Tallberg, Jonas. 2002b. "Paths to Compliance: Enforcement, Management, and the European Union." *International Organization* 56(3): 609–643.

Taylor, Matthew D. 2000. "The WTO Panel Decision on Australia's Salmon Import Guidelines: Evidence that the SPS Agreement Can Effectively Protect Human Health Interests." *Pacific Rim Law & Policy Journal* 9(2): 473–506.

Thompson, Alexander. 2009. "The Rational Enforcement of International Law: Solving the Sanctioners' Dilemma." *International Theory* 1(2): 307–21.

Thomson, Robert. 2009. "Same Effects in Different Worlds: The Transposition of EU Directives." *Journal of European Public Policy* 16(1): 1–18.

Tillotson, John, and Nigel G. Foster. 2003. *Text, Cases and Materials on European Union Law*. 4th ed. London: Cavendish.

Tomz, Michael, Joshua A. Tucker, and Jason Wittenberg. 2002. "An Easy and Accurate Regression Model for Multiparty Electoral Data." *Political Analysis* 10(1): 66–83.

Trebilcock, Michael J., and Robert Howse. 1999. *The Regulation of International Trade*. 2nd ed. New York: Routledge.

Tsebelis, George. 1995. "Decision Making in Political Systems: Veto Players in Presidentialism, Parliamentarism, Multicameralism and Multipartyism." *British Journal of Political Science* 25(3): 289–325.

Tsebelis, George. 2000. "Veto Players and Institutional Analysis." *Governance* 13(4): 441–74.

Tsebelis, George. 2002. *Veto Players: How Political Institutions Work*. Princeton: Princeton University Press.

Tudor, Jarrod. 2012. "Compulsory Licensing in the European Union." *George Mason Journal of International and Comparative Law* 4(2): 222–58.

United Nations. 2013. "Commodity Trade Statistics Database (Comtrade)." http://comtrade.un.org.

United Nations General Assembly. 1998. "Rome Statute of the International Criminal Court, 17 July 1998."

United Nations Committee Against Torture. 2013. "Consideration of Reports Submitted by States Parties under Article 19 of the Convention Pursuant to the Optional Reporting Procedure: Third to Fifth Periodic Reports of States Parties Due in 2011, United States of America." CAT/C/USA/3-5 December 4, 2013. https://tbinternet.ohchr.org/_layouts/15/treatybodyexternal/Download.aspx?symbolno=CAT/C/USA/3-5&Lang=en/.

Verdier, Pierre-Hugues, and Erik Voeten. 2014. "Precedent, Compliance, and Change in Customary International Law: An Explanatory Theory." *American Journal of International Law* 108(3): 389–434.

Vilán, Andrea. 2018. "The Domestic Incorporation of Human Rights Treaties." PhD diss., University of California, Los Angeles.

Voeten, Erik. 2007. "The Politics of International Judicial Appointments: Evidence from the European Court of Human Rights." *International Organization* 61(4): 669–701.

von Stein, Jana. 2005. "Do Treaties Constrain or Screen? Selection Bias and Treaty Compliance." *American Political Science Review* 99(4): 611–22.

Walter, Stefanie. 2021. "The Backlash against Globalization." *Annual Review of Political Science* 24(1): 421–42.

Waltz, Kenneth N. 1979. *Theory of International Politics.* Long Grove, IL: Waveland Press.

Warren, Manning Gilbert, III. 1994. "The European Union's Investment Services Directive." *University of Pennsylvania Journal of International Business Law* 15(2): 181–220.

Watson, K. William. 2014. "As Expected, WTO Clove Cigarette Case Goes Nowhere." *Cato at Liberty* (blog), Cato Institute. October 8, 2014. https://www.cato.org/blog/expected-wto-clove-cigarette-case-goes-nowhere/.

Weingast, Barry R., Kenneth A. Shepsle, and Christopher Johnsen. 1981. "The Political Economy of Benefits and Costs: A Neoclassical Approach to Distributive Politics." *Journal of Political Economy* 89(4): 642–64.

Wilson, Bruce. 2007. "Compliance by WTO Members with Adverse WTO Dispute Settlement Rulings: The Record to Date." *Journal of International Economic Law* 10(2): 397–403.

Wilson, Frank L. 1987. *Interest Group Politics in France.* Cambridge, UK: Cambridge University Press.

Wood, Peter John. 2011. "Climate Change and Game Theory." *Annals of the New York Academy of Sciences,* 1219(1): 153–70.

World Bank. 2013. "World Development Indicators." http://data.worldbank.org/indicator.

World Trade Organization. 2021a. "Developing Countries in WTO Dispute Settlement." Dispute Settlement System Training Module, Chapter 11. https://

www.wto.org/english/tratop_e/dispu_e/disp_settlement_cbt_e/c11s1p1_e .htm.

World Trade Organization. 2021b. "Functions, Objectives and Key Features of the Dispute Settlement System." Dispute Settlement System Training Module, Chapter 1.3. https://www.wto.org/english/tratop_e/dispu_e/disp _settlement_cbt_e/c1s3p1_e.htm.

Xu, Yiqing. 2017. "Generalized Synthetic Control Method for Causal Inference with Time-Series Cross-Sectional Data." *Political Analysis* 25(1): 57–76.

Yildirim, Aydin B. 2018. "Domestic Political Implications of Global Value Chains: Explaining EU Responses to Litigation at the World Trade Organization." *Comparative European Politics* 16(4): 549–80.

Yildirim, Aydin B., J. Tyson Chatagnier, Arlo Poletti, and Dirk De Bievre. 2017. "The Internationalization of Production and the Politics of Compliance in WTO Disputes." *Review of International Organizations* 13(1): 49–75.

Yoo, John C. 2002. Letter to the Honorable Alberto R. Gonzales, August 1, 2002. U.S. Department of Justice, Office of Legal Counsel.

Index

Figures and tables are indicated by *f* and *t* following the page numbers.